Educational Evaluation: Theory and Practice

The Charles A. Jones Publishing Company
International Series in Education

Educational Evaluation: Theory and Practice

Blaine R. Worthen

University of Colorado

James R. Sanders

Indiana University

Charles A. Jones Publishing Company

Worthington, Ohio

3 4 5 6 7 8 9 10 / 77 76 75

Library of Congress Catalog Card Number: 72–93896
International Standard Book Number: 0–8396–0031–3 casebound
0–8396–0055–0 paper

Printed in the United States of America

To our wives, Barbara and Susan,
for their patience and support.

Preface

Educational Evaluation: Theory and Practice is a synthesis of the thinking of many leading evaluation practitioners and theoreticians. In preparing this book, we had two major purposes in mind: (1) to pull together in one volume the best of the emerging literature on educational evaluation, much of which could be found only in fugitive documents, and (2) to identify serious gaps in the literature and provide content to fill those gaps. The result is a book which includes both the most promising conceptual frameworks proposed for educational evaluations and practical considerations in conducting such evaluations.

This book can be used in a variety of ways. It is designed as a basic text for courses on educational evaluation, as well as a basic or supplemental book for teacher education, curriculum, or administration courses where efforts are made to teach practitioners how to assess the effectiveness of their educational programs. It should also serve well as a reference for professional educators, graduate students, and advanced undergraduates engaged in evaluation of educational practices at any level as they encounter some of the difficult problems for which the book provides solutions.

The material in this book is readily understandable to the theoretician, the practitioner, and the layman alike and is intended to help persons in all these categories plan better educational evaluations. For most evaluation problems, evaluators must supplement the conceptual strategies and tactics presented in this book with skills in a variety of technical areas — e.g., statistics, psychometrics, and experimental design. Technical areas are not the focus of this book and the person in need of assistance in these areas is referred to the many excellent texts available.

We wish to express our appreciation to the authors and publishers of the articles and papers included in this volume for their permission to reprint them, especially to Michael Scriven, who modified and updated his article specifically for inclusion herein, and to Malcolm Provus who reviewed the manuscript. The influence that Gene V Glass has had upon the thinking of both of us is gratefully acknowledged, as is his permission to allow portions of papers co-authored by him and one of the present authors to be used in this text. And, finally, to Linda Geiger, Margaret Puls, and Lynne Rienner appreciation is extended for their excellent technical assistance in producing this manuscript.

B.R.W.
J.R.S.

Contents

1

Evaluation:
State of the Art

Evaluation is one of the most widely discussed but little used processes in today's educational systems. This statement may seem strange in the present social context where attempts to make educational systems accountable to their publics are proliferating at a rapid pace. The past decade has seen legislative bodies at both national and state levels authorizing funds to be used expressly for evaluating educational programs to determine their effectiveness. Phrases such as "performance contracting" and "using evaluation to support decision making" appear more and more frequently in schoolmen's writings and conversations, and new evaluation units are being established in many public schools, state departments of education, and institutions of higher education. Yet, despite these trends toward accountability, only a tiny fraction of the educational programs operating at any level have been evaluated in any but the most cursory fashion, if indeed at all. Verbal statements about evaluation and accountability? An abundance. Genuine evaluation of educational programs? Unfortunately rare.

Given the social demand for evaluation, how can one account for the relatively little genuine evaluation that is going on at present? To answer this question fully, it is necessary to look at evaluation's antecedents in order to determine how we arrived at where we are today.

Evaluation is not a new concept. One dictionary definition of evaluation is, "To determine the worth of; to appraise." Given such a broad focus for the term, it can be argued that evaluation has been with us always and that everyone is, in his own way, an evaluator. When Hannibal elected to march elephants across the Pyrenees, he did so because he had determined their worth to him not only as beasts of burden but also as instruments of war calculated to terrorize the Romans—that is, he "evaluated" the elephants' worth for his purposes. The fifth-grade teacher who decides to continue using traditional arithmetic workbooks in her class rather than the "modern mathematics" text adopted by the school district has based her decision upon her informal appraisal of the worth of the two alternative books to her instructional program. Even shortsighted legislators who vote to establish graduate programs to train professional personnel and then, without collecting any data about the programs, vote to terminate them before the first graduating classes have taken jobs are also engaged in "evaluation" of a sort. Although the information on which their decision is based is private, very impressionistic, and very possibly inaccurate, the legislators have somehow "appraised" the program and decided that it is not worth the continued expenditure of public funds.

These examples of "evaluation" might be better labeled as "choosing," in which persons make choices among alternatives, based on their *perceptions* of which alternative is best. To the extent that these choices are based on *systematic* efforts to define criteria and obtain *accurate* information about the alternatives, thus enabling the real worth of the alternatives to be determined, evaluation has taken place in a true sense. It is this more formal type of evaluation that is the focus of this book.

The history of formal evaluation is much longer than is generally recognized. The concept of evaluating individuals and programs was evident as early as 2000 B.C. when Chinese officials were conducting civil service examinations (DuBois, 1970). Greek teachers, such as Socrates, used verbally mediated evaluations as part of the learning process. In the United States, the first evidence of program evaluation is recorded in Joseph Rice's 1897-1898 comparative study of the spelling performance of 33,000 students in a large city school system. In the early 1900s Robert Thorndike, called the father of the educational testing movement, was instrumental in convincing educators of the value of measuring human change. The measurement technology for determining human abilities flourished during the first two decades of this century in the United States.[1]

---

1. Historically, formal evaluation has been very closely associated with the measurement tradition in psychology and education. In fact, even today one finds that many writers see little discrimination between the processes of

The development of standardized achievement tests for use in large-scale testing programs was a natural outgrowth of the measurement movement. Also, teacher-made achievement tests flourished and formed a basis for most school grading systems. Techniques of personality and interest testing were also developed during this period. The military and industry began to use these new tools to evaluate applicants or recruits as a part of personnel selection and classification.

During the 1930s, two developments occurred which have had a continuing impact on evaluation practices since that time. First, Tyler and Smith designed and implemented an evaluation of the Eight Year Study. The Eight Year Study made use of a wide variety of tests, scales, inventories, questionnaires, check lists, pupil logs, and other measures in each of thirty high schools to gather information about the achievement of curricular objectives. Tyler's evaluation approach (Smith and Tyler, 1942) had a great influence on the planning of evaluation studies for the next thirty years. Even today, the approach used by Tyler is still influencing planning efforts (witness the Tylerian tradition apparent in the National Assessment Project, a census-like national survey designed to sample cognitive, affective, and psychomotor behaviors at four age levels in ten different subject areas). Second, the accreditation movement, which began in the late 1800s, became stronger during this same period and began for the first time to gain a solid foothold in educational practice. With the establishment of formal accrediting agencies for schools and colleges came the institutionalization of at least a quasi-evaluation process in American education.

More recent significant developments in the history of evaluation include the establishment of the Educational Testing Service (ETS) by a merger in 1947 of the College Entrance Examination Board (CEEB), the American Council on Education (ACE), and the Carnegie Corporation. ETS has become an influential force in evaluation, conducting large-scale evaluation projects with increasing frequency (for example, the recent evaluation of *Sesame Street*). A few years later, Bloom, et al. (1956), completed the first in a proposed series of taxonomies of educational objectives. The first was in the cognitive domain of human behavior. The second (Krathwohl, et al., 1964), which appeared eight years later, was in the affective domain. (A third, planned for the psychomo-

---

measurement and evaluation (e.g., Thorndike and Hagen, 1969). This heritage is also evident in the abundance of psychological measurement tools which are used by the evaluation specialist. Anthropologic, philosophic, econometric, and sociometric techniques are now only beginning to be used by educational evaluators. The reader who is interested in a detailed treatment of the history of measurement per se is referred to DuBois (1970).

tor domain, has not yet appeared, although major works such as that by Simpson (1965-1966) have appeared. These two publications (discussed by Krathwohl later in this book) have had considerable impact on the design of educational evaluation studies.

Three large-scale descriptive studies conducted during the late 1950s and the 1960s provided methodological grounds for future large-scale evaluation studies. The first, most popularly known as the Coleman Study after its principal investigator, James Coleman (1966), was a cross-sectional study of opportunities open to minority persons. The second, a longitudinal study, Project TALENT, was conducted by the American Institutes for Research under the direction of Dr. John Flanagan. This study focused on the careers of some 440,000 students and the abilities associated with success and failure in these careers (Flanagan, 1964). Design of the third large-scale effort, the National Assessment Program, was begun in 1964 under the chairmanship of Ralph Tyler. This program was initiated in 1969 and has provided a wealth of information on the utility of various procedures for any evaluation study. Furthermore, it will provide normative data for judging achievement in specific educational programs.

The late 1950s and early 1960s (the post-Sputnik years) were also years which echoed with cries for curriculum reform. Several major new curriculum projects were initiated across the country; with these innovations came the need for new evaluation procedures. Initially, many curriculum developers attempted to use the familiar controlled experimental design paradigm to evaluate their products; however, this approach proved satisfactory for only some of the evaluation needs, and would-be curriculum evaluators were forced to seek elsewhere for additional methodologies.

The Impact on
Evaluation of the ESEA

The historical unfolding of concern over evaluation provided impetus to conduct evaluations of educational programs, and thus educationists gained important experience in applying evaluation concepts and techniques. However, only a tiny proportion of education programs and products were affected by these embryonic efforts. In the early 1960s there were still only a relative handful of educationists or others who were paid to evaluate the effectiveness of educational practices and processes. Information about educational outcomes was scarce, and schoolmen were hard pressed to defend their practices against critics' attacks on the efficacy of the schools.[2] In short, evaluation seemed to be having little impact on educational practices.

It was in this context that the United States Congress began its deliberations on the proposed Elementary and Secondary Education Act of 1965 (ESEA)—by far the most comprehensive and ambitious educational legislation ever envisioned by the federal government. As the bill was drafted and debated in both houses, those involved increasingly realized that, if passed, it would result in tens of thousands of federal grants to local education agencies and universities. Concerns began to be expressed, especially in the debates on the Senate floor, that there was absolutely no assurance that the large amounts of money authorized for these grants would result in any real improvements in the educational system. It was noted that education did not have an impressive record of providing evidence that prior federal monies had resulted in any meaningful differences in schooling; indeed, some congressmen seemed to feel that federal funds allocated to education in the past had sunk like stones into the morass of education programs with scarcely an observable ripple to mark their passage.

Robert F. Kennedy was among the senators who forcefully insisted that the ESEA carry a proviso requiring educators to be accountable for the federal monies they received and to file an evaluation report for each grant showing what effects had resulted from the expenditure of the federal funds. Although only partially successful (the final version of the bill required evaluation reports under only two of the five titles), these efforts led to the first major evaluation mandate issued by those providing funds for educational programs. Specifically, it was required that *each* project under Titles I and III of the ESEA be evaluated and the report of that evaluation be submitted to the federal government. Translated into operational terms, this meant that thousands of educators were for the first time *required* to spend their time evaluating their own efforts.

It should not be surprising that educators were unprepared to implement the new mandate effectively. Relatively few educators had any expertise in evaluation techniques. In many school districts the best classroom teachers were released from classroom duties and pressed into service as evaluators on Title I and Title III projects. The only recommendation most of these teachers had was their teaching ability—hardly relevant credentials for positions requiring at least a modicum of technical training. Even the

---

2. Few of the critics had any real information on which to base their judgments, either, but this did not seem to inhibit their sound chastisement of the educational system for failure to produce whatever effects the critics viewed as important.

supply of expert consultants was soon exhausted, and many persons who were called into service as consultants were little better prepared in relevant areas than the local evaluators they attempted to assist.

That many of the resulting "evaluations" would be inadequate was inevitable. Egon Guba analyzed the evaluation plans outlined in a sample of Title III proposals and concluded that "It is very dubious whether the results of these evaluations will be of much use to anyone. . . . None of these product evaluations will give the Federal Government the data it needs to review the general Title III program and to decide how the program might be reshaped to be more effective" (Guba, 1967, p. 312).

Lack of trained personnel was not the only reason the response to the ESEA evaluation mandate was poor. In translating the legislation into operational terms, the United States Office of Education (USOE) did not provide adequate guidelines for the local evaluator on the matter of how to conduct an evaluation—or even what should be included in it. Quoting again from Guba, "The present guidelines are markedly inadequate; they do little more than to encourage sloppily conceived product evaluations" (Guba, 1967, p. 313). In the absence of adequate guidelines, evaluation designs for each project had to be newly created by inexperienced personnel.

It seems likely that the inadequate guidelines resulted more from lack of knowledge about what a good evaluation should include than from lack of effort on the part of USOE personnel. Few scholars had turned their attention to the development of generalizable evaluation plans which could be adopted or adapted by local evaluators. Theoretical work in evaluation was almost nonexistent. However, scholars—like nature—abhor a vacuum, and it was not long before several evaluation theoreticians began to develop and test their notions about how one should conduct educational evaluations. These efforts resulted in several new evaluation models, strategies, and plans which could be put into use by educationists. Although the models failed to solve all of the problems of local evaluators, they did help them to design evaluations that avoided several of the more glaring deficiencies that had permeated the first wave of ESEA Title I and Title III evaluation reports. (The best of these generalizable evaluation strategies are presented in Chapter 3 of this book.)

During this period when the ESEA gave such a profound impetus to educational evaluation,[3] other trends were developing

3. A direct (and huge) quantitative increase in evaluation resulted from ESEA, and an indirect qualitative improvement came from the efforts of

which required increasing emphasis on evaluative processes. The growth of teacher militancy, union demands, and demands for civil rights reforms in educational systems all required increased capabilities in evaluation. The public cry for accountability in education continued to increase until several state departments of education began to design state assessment systems and several state legislatures began to require reports from all schools on student achievement in subjects such as reading and mathematics. Professional associations began to encourage their memberships to give more serious consideration to assessing educational practices. The American Educational Research Association (AERA) attempted to disseminate the current thinking in evaluation by initiating a monograph series in curriculum evaluation (see Tyler, et al., 1967; Grobman, 1968; Popham, et al., 1969; DuBois and Mayo, 1970). The Association for Supervision and Curriculum Development (ASCD) encouraged curriculum developers to employ better evaluation techniques in assessing the worth of their products. The ASCD Executive Committee stated:

> Accurate assessment of educational outcomes is essential for sound planning and effective stimulation of growth in our educational structure. Assessment has always been an integral aspect of curriculum development and is a major responsibility of curriculum workers. This responsibility is especially critical in a time of awakened public concern, massive federal commitment and widespread professional reappraisal of our educational endeavors. It is, therefore, necessary that curriculum workers everywhere develop new procedures for assessment far beyond present levels to meet properly the changing needs of our times [Combs, 1967, p. v].

By the end of the 1960s, the various trends, forces, and problems described above had coalesced into an anomalous situation. Evaluation had become a catchword in education which could be heard issuing from the lips of almost every leader in the field. The need for evaluation was widely acknowledged and relatively few educators publicly debated its necessity. The feeling that "Big Brother"—the public and funding agencies—was watching permeated education at all levels. Yet, most educational programs and practices continued unabated without the benefit of genuine evaluation. Despite the newly developed evaluation strategies, the development of the cognitive and affective taxonomies, and the accumulated measurement theory and instruments, the methodology of evaluation remained fuzzy in the minds of most evaluators.

---

scholars to develop generalizable evaluative plans which led to somewhat improved evaluations.

Perhaps the major reason was that the useful information on evaluation plans and techniques (which was scarce at best) was badly fragmented and appeared in a variety of sources, some of which were fugitive materials. As a result, the early 1970s saw evaluation problems and needs still far outstripping the solutions which had been developed and disseminated. Such a situation led the Phi Delta Kappa (PDK) Commission on Evaluation to conclude that "Evaluation is, to choose a metaphor, seized with a great illness" (Stufflebeam, et al., 1971, p. 2). The Commission went on to list several symptoms of the illness, among them the "lack of certain crucial elements without which the science or art of evaluation cannot be expected to make significant forward strides" (Stufflebeam, et al., 1971, p. 8). Five such lacks are listed as (a) lack of adequate evaluation theory, (b) lack of specification of the types of evaluative information which are most needed, (c) lack of appropriate instruments and designs, (d) lack of good systems for organizing, processing, and reporting evaluative information, and (e) lack of sufficient numbers of well-trained evaluation personnel.

This book is, in part, a response to these inadequacies. If evaluation's illness is to be cured, several important steps will be necessary. Evaluators must make more effective (and appropriate) use of extant measurement theory and instruments.[4] Other disciplines must be investigated more vigorously for relevant methodologies that might be applicable in educational evaluation. Most important, evaluators must be provided with useful frameworks and guidelines.

Specifically, the remainder of this volume consists of four parts, as follows:

Chapter 2:　A discussion of evaluation as disciplined inquiry, including a discussion of how (and why) evaluation is distinguished from research.

Chapter 3:　Presentation of eight important frameworks which have been proposed for planning evaluation studies, the application of each to an evaluation problem in education, and a discussion of their relative strengths and weaknesses.

Chapter 4:　Discussion of several important considerations in planning evaluation studies, including: (a) criteria for judging evaluation studies, (b) design of evaluation studies, (c) measurement problems and techniques in evaluation, (d) the relationship of the evaluator to his client, (e) behavioral

---

4. The reader is referred to Stake (1970), Sjogren (1970), and Metfessel and Michael (1967) for reviews of measurement techniques which can be applied in evaluation.

objectives and specifications, and (f) writing evaluation reports.

Chapter 5: A discussion of the future of evaluation and an outline of several additional steps which must be taken if evaluation is to reach its full potential.

Chapters 2 and 3 are addressed directly to the first lack identified by the PDK Commission, lack of adequate evaluation theory. Thorough delineation of phenomena of concern is essential to theory building; such delineation is the focus of chapter 2. Each of the evaluation frameworks presented in chapter 3 either represents evaluation theory of a sort or contains concepts relevant to developing such theory. The considerations discussed in chapter 4 provide information bearing on the third lack identified by the PDK Commission, lack of appropriate instruments and designs. Chapter 5 contains, among other topics, a proposal for satisfying the fifth lack by new strategies for training evaluation personnel.

This volume does not purport to eliminate the inadequacies in the field of evaluation discussed above. By collecting and presenting information necessary to the solution of three of them, however, it should prove most helpful to the evaluator or the student of evaluation.

2 Evaluation as Disciplined Inquiry

Educational leaders and the public both rightly expect the scientific method to play a key role in reshaping and revitalizing educational programs and practices. Cronbach and Suppes phrased this expectation well in their discussion of disciplined inquiry for education.

There has been agreement, both within and without the ranks of educators, that systematic investigation has much to offer. Indeed, there is agreement that *massive, lasting changes in education cannot safely be made except on the basis of deep objective inquiry* [Cronbach and Suppes, 1969, p. 12].

Such systematic investigation, termed by Cronbach and Suppes as "disciplined inquiry," can be of many types (for example, a laboratory experiment or a mail survey); however, there is a quality that is common to each. As Cronbach and Suppes put it:

Disciplined inquiry has a quality that distinguishes it from other sources of opinion and belief. The disciplined inquiry is conducted and reported in such a way that the argument can be painstakingly examined. The report does not depend for its appeal on the eloquence of the writer or on any surface plausibility. The argument is not justified by anecdotes or casually assembled fragments of evidence. Scholars in each field have developed traditional questions that serve as touch-

---

Some portions of this chapter draw heavily on two earlier papers: Glass and Worthen (1971) and Glass and Worthen (1972).

stones to separate sound argument from incomplete or questionable argument. Among other things, the mathematician asks about axioms, the historian about the authenticity of documents, the experimental scientist about verifiability of observations. Whatever the character of a study, if it is disciplined the investigator has anticipated the traditional questions that are pertinent. He institutes controls at each step of information collection and reasoning to avoid the sources of error to which these questions refer. If the errors cannot be eliminated, he takes them into account by discussing the margin for error in his conclusions. Thus the report of a disciplined inquiry has a texture that displays the raw materials entering the argument and the logical processes by which they were compressed and rearranged to make the conclusion credible. . . .

Disciplined inquiry does not necessarily follow well-established formal procedures. Some of the most excellent inquiry is free-ranging and speculative in its initial stages, trying what might seem to be bizarre combinations of ideas and procedures, or restlessly casting about for ideas. . . . But. . . fundamental to disciplined inquiry is its central attitude, which places a premium on objectivity and evidential test [Cronbach and Suppes, 1969, pp. 15-16, 18].

Inquiry, thus defined, encompasses several common activities in education, among them educational evaluation. Research, evaluation, development, and diffusion collectively represent the spectrum of inquiry and inquiry-related activities in education.[1] Distinguishing correctly among these activities has important implications for the behavior of the evaluator, as will be noted later in this chapter. One way to differentiate among evaluation and other inquiry activities is to position each within the broader class of activities subsumed under the rubric of "disciplined inquiry."

The remainder of this chapter is divided into six major sections: (a) a discussion of types of disciplined inquiry; (b) a verbal and graphic attempt to show how evaluation and other inquiry activities draw differentially on the different types of disciplined inquiry; (c) an attempt to define evaluation and discuss quasi-evaluation or "evaluation attendant" activities often confused with evaluation itself; (d) a consideration of evaluation as an

---

1. The term "inquiry-related" is used here to refer only to diffusion and development—activities which either depend in part on inquiry or are essential if inquiry activities are to have an impact on educational practice. Many other activities (e.g., teaching) are related to inquiry in that they may use results of inquiry; however, such activities are not included in our use of the term "inquiry-related" herein.

adjunct to educational development and diffusion; (e) a discussion
of twelve characteristics on which research and evaluation can be
differentiated; and (f) a discussion of the breadth with which the
term "evaluation" will be used in the remaining chapters of the
book.

Types of Disciplined Inquiry

Disciplined inquiry, as defined earlier, includes at least three
somewhat different types of inquiry: empirical inquiry, historical
inquiry, and philosophical inquiry. Interrelationships showing
commonalities and differences among these types of inquiry and
their components might fruitfully be portrayed graphically. Figure
1 is an attempt to depict these interrelationships in the domain of

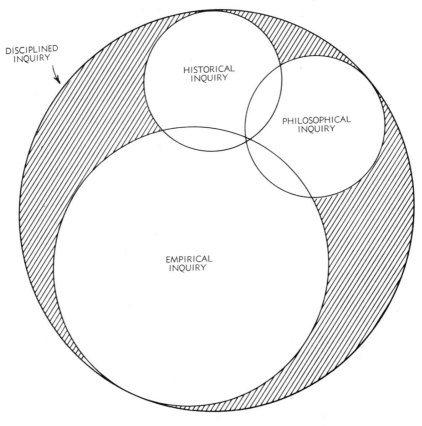

Figure 1

The Inquiry Domain

educational research and research-related activities.[2] The field upon which the diagram in figure 1 is imposed represents the nomenclature used by scholars to identify various forms of inquiry. An element in the field is an instance of an inquiry activity being named by scholars either "empirical inquiry," "historical inquiry," or "philosophical inquiry." The sizes of the circles are approximately indicative of the authors' estimates of the relative frequency of occurrence of the associated terms in informed discourse about educational inquiry.

The interrelationships shown in figure 1 are obvious. The shaded portion is a recognition of other unspecified types of inquiry not included under the rubrics "empirical," "historical," or "philosophical."

Empirical inquiry can be thought of as a composite of all areas of inquiry where observations or experiments are used for purposes such as describing existing conditions or verifying or disproving claims, statements, or hypotheses about relationships among variables. Historical inquiry, in general, is the study of the development of organizations of people (for example, into cultures or nations) and the study of particular lives, movements, or sequences of events. Philosophical inquiry is closely akin to rational analysis, loosely based on formal logic and semantics. In addition, linguistic analysis and the study of morals and ethics are appropriately subsumed under this general rubric.

In empirical inquiry, the data are generally observations or indirect measures of behavior, perceptions, aspirations, and the like. Historical inquiry deals more with narrative examination of available evidence (often the prose of other men) that relates to the historic phenomenon that is of interest. Philosophical inquiry is somewhat like mathematics in that axioms, formal propositions, and rules of logic are often the "data" of concern.

In figure 1, the areas of overlap portray activities which draw from more than one type of inquiry. For example, the overlap between empirical and historical inquiry would include historiography, where empirical techniques such as surveys and interviews might be used to prepare a contemporary history (such as the history of the IBM Corporation or Dow Chemical Company).

The overlap between empirical and philosophical inquiry might contain a variety of activities, such as the use of empirical techniques to study various meanings ascribed to key words by persons with differing philosophic orientation. The use of empirical

---

2. As with any attempt to portray complex phenomena graphically, the figures contained in this section are suggestive and imperfect; the authors do not contend that reality is so easily reduced to line drawings.

methods to collect data on the values of specified groups to enable
one to check logical intra-value consistency would be another
combination of these two types of inquiry, as would be the collection of empirical information to determine the feasibility of using
alternative goals (which themselves are value-based) in establishing
educational priorities and objectives. Still another type of inquiry
that fits here is represented by studies of morals or ethics—
studies aimed at determining what is right or good. For example,
one can espouse the philosophical view that all men have the
prima facie right to live, yet be faced with a dilemma in operational translation of that view when confronted with a greater number
of patients who need heart transplants than the number of such
organs available for transplants. Empirical evidence of other
physical corollaries of probable success of the operation would be
necessary, and one might even argue that each candidate's probable benefit to society should be a criterion.

The overlap between historical and philosophical inquiry might
well include inquiry into the probable impact of the nonaggressive
philosophy of Eskimos on the historical decline of their culture as
contact increased with more aggressive cultures. An examination of
sixteenth-century persecution of religious minorities by church-
influenced sectarian governments as an adjunct to inquiring into
the appropriateness of maintaining church and state as separate
institutions might also illustrate a blend of these types of inquiry.

Evaluation, Research,
Development, and Diffusion
as Inquiry Activities

Evaluation and research are clearly inquiry activities. Both use
systematic inquiry techniques, although for somewhat different
purposes—research to produce new knowledge and evaluation to
judge worth or social utility. In figure 2, the place of educational
research and evaluation in the inquiry domain is depicted. The
field on which they are imposed is the same as in figure 1—
nomenclature used by scholars. An element in the field is an
instance of an inquiry activity being referred to by educationists as
either "research" or "evaluation." The overlap between research
and evaluation shows commonalities between the two which make
it difficult to classify some activities unequivocally as being in
either category alone.

If the field on which figure 2 is imposed is changed, the relative
position of research and evaluation changes also. For example, if
the field on which they are imposed consists of techniques and

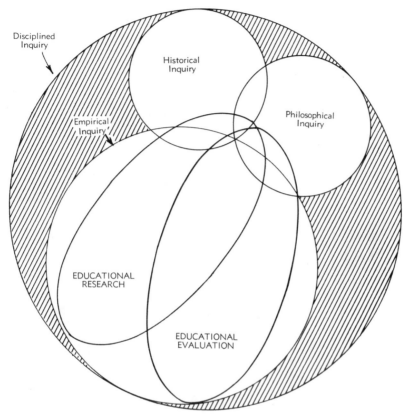

Figure 2

The Inquiry Domain: Educational Research and Evaluation

methods, there would be considerably more overlap between these activities than is shown in figure 2, since both research and evaluation are primarily dependent upon empirical techniques and methods. However, the two ellipses would not be coincident, for research and evaluation draw on nonempirical types of inquiry in somewhat different proportions. Educational research draws somewhat on both historical and philosophical inquiry. Evaluation, with emphasis upon immediate value questions and little interest in generalizing across time, draws heavily on philosophical inquiry but little upon historical inquiry.

If the purpose for which the activity is conducted becomes the field for figure 2, there would be little overlap between research and evaluation since the object of the search is quite different in these activities (as will be argued later in this chapter).

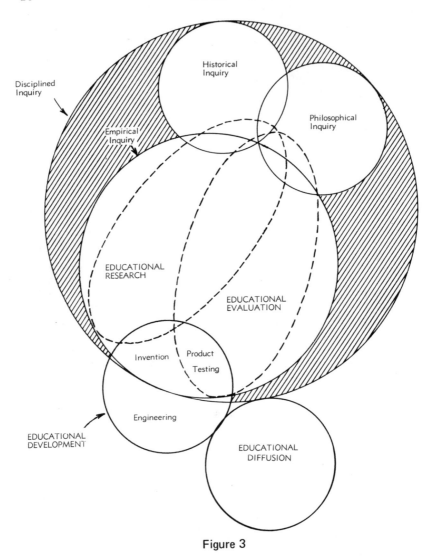

Figure 3

The Inquiry Domain: Educational Research, Evaluation,
Development, and Diffusion

In the case of educational development and diffusion, the relationship to disciplined inquiry is not quite so clearcut. They might
both be more accurately categorized as inquiry-related activities,
since only a portion of the activities associated with either are
inquiry activities per se. For example, educational development
can be viewed as consisting of three basic processes: inventing the
idea or designing the prototype of the product, engineering and
producing the item, and testing the product in settings like that in

which it would be used. Two of these processes seem to be related to inquiry. The invention stage may be heuristically related to research in that research findings may stimulate ideas for developmental efforts. More directly, the testing state is obviously evaluation by another name.

Diffusion of research knowledge or developed products includes at least three stages: dissemination, demonstration, and facilitation of adoption.[3] Although all of these stages are necessary if research and development are to influence educational practices, none of them is an inquiry activity in and of itself.[4] But diffusion is considered as inquiry-related, in that it is essential for the implementation of the products of research-and-development activities.

The relationships of development and diffusion to the inquiry domain are depicted in figure 3.

In the next section, we make further attempts to elaborate the concepts of research, evaluation, development, and diffusion. An argument is presented in support of the proposition that it is especially crucial for the evaluator to distinguish evaluation from research. Definitions are offered and types of research and evaluation are discussed.

Evaluation: An Attempt at Definition

Evaluation is complex. It is not a simple matter of stating behavioral objectives, building a test, or analyzing some data, though it may include these. A thorough evaluation will contain elements of a dozen or more distinct activities. The mixture of activities in which a particular evaluator will be engaged will, of course, be influenced by resources of time, money, expertise, goodwill of schoolmen, or many other factors. But equally important (and more readily influenced) is the image that the evaluator holds of his speciality: its responsibilities, duties, uniquenesses, and similarities to related endeavors.

Some readers may think that entirely too much fuss is being made over defining "evaluation." We cannot help being concerned with the meanings of words and, more importantly, with how they influence action. We frequently meet persons responsible for

---

3. One of the earliest and best descriptions of these processes was provided by Clark and Guba (1965).

4. This is not to say that inquiry relating to diffusion should not be conducted; indeed, activities such as evaluation of alternative diffusion techniques and research on the relationship between various diffusion methods and rate of consumption are most important in improving the diffusion process.

evaluation whose sincere efforts are negated by the particular semantic problem addressed in this chapter. By happenstance, habit, or methodological bias, they may label the trial and investigation of a new curriculum with the epithet "research" or "experiment" instead of "evaluation." The inquiry they conduct will then be different for their having chosen to call it a "research project" or an "experiment" than it would be had they called it an "evaluation." Their choice influences the literature they read (it will deal with research or experimental design), the consultants they call in (only acknowledged experts in designing and analyzing experiments), and how they report the results (always in the best tradition of the *American Educational Research Journal* or the *Journal of Experimental Psychology*). These are not the paths to relevant data or rational decision-making about curricula. Evaluation is an undertaking separate from research. Not every educational researcher can evaluate a new curriculum, any more than every psychologist can perform a tonsilectomy.

Educational research and evaluation have a great deal in common. However, during a time when each is frequently mistaken for the other, we need to emphasize their differences more than their similarities. The best efforts of the investigator whose responsibility is evaluation but whose conceptual perspective is research eventually prove to be worthless as either research or evaluation.

We will not dignify the content of this chapter by terming it theory development, but it does represent an attempt to solve one problem that must be resolved before much conceptual work on evaluation can proceed effectively. That problem is simply how to distinguish the more familiar educational research from the newer, less familiar activity of educational evaluation. Definitions of evaluation and other inquiry activities are offered below as an initial attempt to distinguish evaluation from other activities with which it may be confused.

Definitions: One Point of View

Simple, verbal definitions of research, evaluation, development, and diffusion are never fully satisfactory. Many recent attempts to define these activities treat them as Platonic ideals which would permit simple Aristotelian definitions if the definer were only perceptive enough. These inquiry and inquiry-related activities are far too complex to be defined adequately in the way that a classicist might have given an acceptable one-line definition of a tree. Research, development, diffusion, and evaluation are complicated endeavors. To be pedantic, they are ultimately no more than hypothetical constructs for a disposition of persons to respond with a certain word in the presence of certain instances of the production or utilization of knowledge. The meaning of the words can be seen by examining characteristics of the phenomena which elicit from scholars the terms research, evaluation, development, and diffusion in their writing, their conversation, and their private thoughts.

This is not to argue that no attempt should be made to differentiate these activities at an abstract, verbal level. Indeed, it has been argued elsewhere that attempting to define and distinguish research and evaluation is not mere idleness and that a confusion of them accounts for much wasted motion in educational scholarship (Glass, 1967). Similarly, failure to recognize differences among them complicates the already difficult job of the would-be trainer of inquiry and inquiry-related personnel in education.

In spite of the shortcomings of simple, verbal definitions, such definitions can serve as a point of departure. The simple definitions that follow serve as necessary precursors for later discussions in this chapter.

1. *Research* is the activity aimed at obtaining generalizable knowledge by contriving and testing claims about relationships among variables or describing generalizable phenomena.[5] This knowledge, which may result in theoretical models, functional relationships, or descriptions, may be obtained by empirical or other systematic methods and may or may not have immediate application.

2. *Evaluation* is the determination of the worth of a thing. It includes obtaining information for use in judging the worth of a program, product, procedure, or objective, or the potential utility of alternative approaches designed to attain specified objectives.

3. *Development* (in education) is the production and testing of curriculum materials (such as books, films, computer-assisted instruction programs), organizational or staffing plans (such as team teaching, differentiated staffing, modular scheduling), and other applied media or instruments of schooling.

4. *Diffusion* encompasses planning, designing, and conducting activities leading to the application of the knowledge and products of research and development. This may be done by various means, including (a) the use of communication techniques

---

5. Apologies to mathematics, history, philosophy, etc., for the obvious empirical social-science bias in our definition and our thinking.

to disseminate information about the knowledge or product, (b) the conduct of demonstrations to establish the utility and applicability of the product or knowledge, and (c) procedures which facilitate adoption or application of the product or knowledge.

Definitions:
An Alternative Point of View

We have not defined research very differently from the ways in which it is generally defined (for example, see the definition given by Kerlinger, 1964). However, definitions of evaluation are much more varied. In education, at least three different schools of thought about how evaluation should be defined have co-existed for at least thirty years.[6] With the ascendancy of the measurement movement, evaluation came to be defined as roughly synonymous with educational measurement. This definition of evaluation is evident today in the writing of such measurement specialists as Thorndike and Hagen (1969) and Ebel (1965). Concurrently, formulization of school and university accreditation procedures led to a definition of evaluation as synonymous with professional judgment. This view has continued and is evidenced in many current evaluation practices where judgments are based on opinions of experts, whether or not the data and criteria used in reaching those judgments are clear. A third definition of evaluation emerged during Ralph Tyler's work on the Eight Year Study of the 1930s. In his work, evaluation came to be defined as the process of comparing performance data with clearly specified objectives. This view has continued and is reflected in several current approaches to evaluation which are discussed in the next chapter.

During the last decade, new definitions of evaluation have emerged (see, for example, the definitions of evaluation implicit or explicit in the writing of Stake, 1967; Provus, 1969; and Stufflebeam, et al., 1971). Of these, perhaps the most popular definitions are those in which evaluation is viewed as a process of identifying and collecting information to assist decision-makers in choosing among available decision alternatives.

Although all of these definitions have many adherents and are relevant to evaluation in that they describe or define parts of the total evaluation process or activities attendant to evaluation, they seem to address only obliquely what is for us the touchstone of evaluation, the determination of merit or worth. Of all the definitions of evaluation above, only the professional judgment

---

6. See Stufflebeam, et al. (1971) for an excellent discussion of these three ways of defining evaluation.

definition strikes directly at this issue. However, in practice, this view of evaluation (seen most commonly in accreditation site visits, doctoral oral examinations, proposal review procedures used by funding agencies, etc.) is generally unsystematic and a mild embarrassment to evaluation specialists. The definition we have provided, which is much influenced by Scriven's (1967) work, is intended to focus directly on systematic collection and analysis of information to determine the worth of a thing.

An example of the differing approaches to evaluating a curriculum that would result from these various ways of defining evaluation might be instructive. If one defined evaluation as essentially synonymous with professional judgment, the worth of curriculum X would be assessed by experts (in the view of the evaluation client) observing the curriculum in action, examining the curriculum materials or, in some other way, gleaning sufficient information to record their considered judgments about the curriculum. If evaluation is equated with measurement, the curriculum might well be judged on the basis of student scores on standardized tests in relevant subjects. If evaluation is viewed as a comparison between performance indicators and objectives, behaviorally stated objectives would be established for the curriculum and relevant student behaviors would be measured against this yardstick, using either standardized or evaluator-constructed instruments. (Note that in this process there is no assessment of the worth of the objectives themselves.) Using a decision-oriented definition of evaluation, the evaluator, working closely with the decision-maker, would collect sufficient information about the relative advantages and disadvantages of each decision alternative to warrant a judgment about which is best in terms of specified criteria. However, the decision-maker would judge the worth of each alternative, and evaluation thus would be a shared function.

If one accepted our earlier definition of evaluation, the curriculum evaluator would first identify the curriculum goals and, using input from appropriate reference groups, determine whether or not the goals were good for the students, parents, and community served by the curriculum. Then he would collect evaluative information relevant to those goals as well as to identifiable side effects that resulted from the curriculum. When the data were analyzed and interpreted, the evaluator would judge the worth of the curriculum and, in most cases, communicate this judgment in the form of a recommendation to the individual or group responsible for making ultimate decisions about the curriculum.

Obviously, the way in which one defines evaluation has direct impact on the type of evaluation activities conducted.

Types of Evaluation and Research

So far, we have only attempted to differentiate between broad conceptions of research and evaluation. Distinguishing between such activities is at best extremely difficult and is made no simpler by the fact that each can in turn be subdivided into several distinct activities. Many researchers have proposed their favored schemes for classifying types of research activity (for example, Kerlinger, 1964; Hillway, 1964; Galfo and Miller, 1970), and some have discussed the merits of several alternative classification schemes (for example, Guba and Clark, n.d.). Similarly, several contemporary evaluation theorists (for example, Scriven, 1967; Stake, 1967a; Stufflebeam, 1968; Provus, 1969) have proposed varying types of evaluation. Although there are discernible and perhaps important differences among these more molecular types of research and evaluation, there is a common ingredient in each; in every case the specified research or evaluation activity produces knowledge, however general or specific, not previously available. With this commonality in mind, we will now turn our attention to the more important differences among these phenomena.

The distinction between basic and applied research seems to be well entrenched in educational parlance. Although these constructs might more properly be thought of as the ends of a continuum than as a dichotomy, they do have utility for differentiating between broad classes of activities.[7] The distinction between the two also helps in subsequent consideration of the relationship of research to evaluation. The National Science Foundation adopted the following definitions of basic and applied research:

> *Basic research* is directed toward increase of knowledge; it is research where the primary aim of the investigator is a fuller understanding of the subject under study rather than a practical application thereof. *Applied research* is directed toward practical applications of knowledge. [National Science Foundation, 1960, p. 5].

Applied research, when successful, results in plans, blueprints, or directives for development in ways that basic research does not. In applied research, the knowledge produced must have almost

---

7. Guba and Clark (n.d.) argued that the basic-applied distinction is dysfunctional and that the two kinds of activity do not rightfully belong on the same continuum. The authors admit to problems with this, as with any, classification scheme. However, attempts to replace such accepted distinctions with yet another classification system seem destined to little more success than one would have in discarding the descriptors "Democrat" and "Republican" because of recognition of wide variance within the political parties thus identified.

immediate utility, whereas no such constraint is imposed on basic research. Basic research results in deeper understanding of phenomena within systems of related phenomena, and practical utility of the knowledge need not be foreseen.

Two activities that might be considered variants of applied research are "institutional research" and "operations research," activities aimed at supplying institutions or social systems with data relevant to their operations. To the extent that the conclusions of inquiries of this type are generalizable, at least across time, these activities may appropriately be subsumed under the research rubric. However, where the object of the search becomes nongeneralizable information on performance characteristics of a specific program or process, the label "evaluation" might more appropriately be applied.

Evaluation has sometimes been considered merely a form of applied research which focuses only on one curriculum, one program, or one lesson. This view ignores an obvious difference between the two—the level of generality of the knowledge produced. Applied research (as opposed to basic research) is mission-oriented and aimed at producing knowledge relevant to providing a solution (generalizable) to a *general* problem. Evaluation is focused on collecting *specific* information relevant to a specific problem, program, or product.

It was mentioned earlier that many types of evaluation have been proposed in writings on the subject. Although we are uncomfortable with the artificiality of some of the proposed classification schemes, it is tempting to include as evaluation activities several widely discussed inquiry-related processes, if only for the purpose of enriching the abstract construct by proliferating instances of the class. For example, the process of needs analysis (identifying and comparing intended outcomes of a system with actual outcomes on specified variables) might well qualify as an evaluation activity if, as Scriven (1967) and Stake (1970) suggested, the intended outcomes are themselves thoroughly evaluated. The assessment of alternative plans for attaining specified objectives might also be considered a unique evaluation function (see the discussion of "input" evaluation by Stufflebeam, 1968), although it seems to the authors that it might be considered a variant form of outcome evaluation that occurs earlier in the temporal sequence and is an attempt to establish the worth of alternative plans for meeting desired goals. Other proposed evaluation activities such as "program monitoring" (Worthen and Gagné, 1969) or "process evaluation" (Stufflebeam, 1968) seem in retrospect to belong less to evaluation than to operations management or some other function in which information is collected but no valuation occurs.

The difficulty in deciding whether or not activities of the types described above should be considered as "evaluation" relates closely to the question of whether "valuing" or "judging" was an inherent part of the process. Of course, values are revealed through decisions and choices, but valuing and choosing should be distinguished, if for no other reason than to prevent educational evaluators from turning away from answering difficult value questions and moving toward less threatening activities (such as needs assessment, context description, or process monitoring) that are not intrinsically evaluative. These activities may be *attendant to* a legitimate formative or summative evaluation, but they are means of accomplishing a comprehensive evaluation and not evaluation in and of themselves. We object to the description of context being labelled "context *evaluation*" or the monitoring of the conduct of a program being called "process *evaluation*." Typically neither contexts nor processes have been evaluated when these terms are used; they have simply been observed and described. The practitioner may be led by such reckless language into the error of thinking he has discharged a responsibility to evaluate his program (when in fact he has merely planned it, tried it out, or described it).

Our concern with whether or not essentially nonevaluative activities of the types discussed above should be termed evaluation stems from the conflict between the roles and the goals of evaluation mentioned by Scriven (1967). Evaluation can contribute to the construction of a curriculum, the prediction of academic success, the improvement of an existing course, or the analysis of a school district's need for compensatory education. But these are *roles* it can play and not its *goals*. The goal of evaluation must be to answer questions of selection, adoption, support, and worth of educational materials and activities. It must be directed toward answering questions like "Are the benefits of this curriculum worth its cost?" or "Is this textbook superior to its competitors?" The typical evaluator is trained to play more roles than that of simply evaluating. However, all of his activities (such as test construction, needs assessment, or context description) do not become evaluation by merit of the fact that they are done by an "evaluator." (Evaluators brush their teeth, but teeth brushing is not therefore evaluation.)

There is an inherent danger in attempts to develop evaluation models that are basically models of the collection of data for decision making. Decision-centered evaluation methodologists argue that values are included in their thinking and their models because a decision is always the revelation of a value: if the decision-maker chooses A over B, he values A more than B. They believe that values are implicit in decisions. For example, Guba and Stufflebeam (1968, p. 28) contended that:

> The process described as evaluation here comes much closer to the root meaning of the term, to evaluate, than does the process which currently masquerades under the name; . . . if a name were to be changed it ought to be that of present practice. Values come most meaningfully into play when there are choices to be made, and the making of choices is the essential act of decision-making. What we are proposing here is that the entire act of evaluation should center on the criteria to be invoked in making decisions. . . . it is through the exposing of such criteria that we obtain guidance about the kinds of information that should be collected, how it should be analyzed, and how it should be reported. The term *evaluation* seems to be particularly suited to the process as described here, since that process makes such distinctive use of value concepts.

For a value-centered evaluator, however, decisions are implicit in evaluation, that is, in the process of measurement against value scales, integration of measures into value statements and the justification of the measurement and the means of integrating the measurements. The alternative that scores highest on a weighted combination of value scales would be the preferable alternative. However, a decision-centered evaluation model can be applied without concentrating attention on the process by which a decision-maker integrates information into an overall judgment.

Equating *values* with *preferences* has precedent in economics. To the economist—historically at least—the value of a product is revealed by preferences for it: if the consumer will pay $5.00 for A, then the value of A is $5.00. Such a simplistic definition of "value" treats wise and foolish evaluation equally; any $5.00 product is as valuable as any other $5.00 product. Consumers regularly pay $5.00 per ounce (*market value*) for a beauty cream or hair restorative, although the constituents—materials and labor—of either product cost only 25c (the *true value* of the product). That the cream or potion can be marketed for $5.00 is testimony to the consumers' irrational belief that expensive products must also be high-quality products. The difference between decision-centered evaluation theorists and values-centered theorists is the difference between fixing the value of the product at $5.00 because consumers will pay that price for it and fixing its value at 25c because the total investment is a quarter. The analogy to educational evaluation is distressingly apt. Administrators have been known to choose teaching method A instead of method B, despite evaluative data to the contrary, or no data at all, because A is expensive. The logic runs like this: "Surely all that expensive gadgetry and those priceless materials would not have been produced unless they are an improvement over old methods."

It would be satisfactory to disregard the direct assessment of value and merely provide data to decision-makers if decision-makers' preferences were always logical, rational, intelligent revelations of value. In truth, most decision-makers are perplexed by the decision-making process, and many of them rightly feel guilty and insecure about their inability to justify their decisions. Hence, it seems unwise to view evaluation as the presentation of data to decision-makers who must then make of the data what they will.

Evaluation can play many *roles* in an educational program: it can aid the developers by providing mastery test data, and it can provide data to facilitate administration of the program, to name only two. However, the *goal* of evaluation must always be to provide the answer to an all-important question: Does the phenomenon under observation have greater value than its competitors or sufficient value of itself that it should be maintained?

Characteristics of Inquiry Which Distinguish Evaluation from Research

The various types of evaluation and research discussed above tend to result in some types of research beginning to resemble some types of evaluation and vice versa. However, these gradients on the scale should not be allowed to obscure fundamental differences which exist between most types of research and most types of evaluation. Fundamental differences between the "purest" form of each activity—basic research and outcome evaluation—are discussed below.[8] Contrasting such pure forms of evaluation and research admittedly results in oversimplifications, but it should clarify the major points we wish to make—points that may have been obscured in the preceding discussion.

---

8. It is not our position that, for any one study, the characteristics must be all evaluation attributes to be an evaluation study, or all research characteristics to be a research study. Inquiry takes on many forms and few studies have all evaluation or all research characteristics. However, it does seem useful to make distinctions as sharp as possible to help the would-be evaluator recognize differences in research and evaluation.

Research and evaluation have many defining characteristics. Each is only imperfectly correlated with the tendency of informed men to call activity A "research" and activity B "evaluation" (just as a clinical psychologist uses "anxiety" as a construct to differentiate instances of behavior in a way that is not perfectly reproduced by any single measure or defining characteristic). The conceptualization of research and evaluation is enriched by the identification of any characteristic of inquiry which has a nonzero correlation with the tendency of intelligent men to speak of "research" or "evaluation" when discussing a particular inquiry activity.[9]

Twelve characteristics of inquiry which distinguish basic research from outcome evaluation are discussed below.

1. *Motivation of the inquirer.* Research and evaluation appear generally to be undertaken for different reasons. Research is pursued largely to satisfy curiosity; evaluation is intended to contribute to the solution of a particular kind of practical problem. The researcher is intrigued; the evaluator (or, at least, his client) is concerned.

Although the researcher may believe that his work has great long-range payoff, he is no less motivated by curiosity when performing his unique function. One must be nimble to avoid becoming bogged down in the seeming paradox that the *policy* decision to support basic inquiry because of its ultimate practical payoff does *not* imply that researchers are pursuing practical ends in their daily work.

2. *Objective of the search.* Research and evaluation seek different ends. Research seeks *conclusions;* evaluation leads to *decisions* (see Tukey, 1960). Cronbach and Suppes (1969, pp. 20-21) distinguished between decision-oriented and conclusion-oriented inquiry.

In a decision-oriented study the investigator is asked to provide information wanted by a decision-maker; a school administrator, a government policy-maker, the manager of a project to develop a new biology textbook, or the like. The decision-oriented study is a commissioned study. The decision-maker believes that he needs information to guide his actions and he poses the question to the investigator. The conclusion-oriented study, on the other hand, takes its direction from the investigator's commitments and hunches. The educational decision-maker can, at most, arouse the

---

9. Scriven (1958, p. 175) referred to such terms as "cluster concepts" or "correlational concepts." Such concepts, e.g., "schizophrenia," are known by their indicators, all of which are imperfectly related to them.

investigator's interest in a problem. The latter formulates his own question, usually a general one rather than a question about a particular institution. The aim is to conceptualize and understand the chosen phenomenon; a particular finding is only a means to that end. Therefore, he concentrates on persons and settings that he expects to be enlightening.

Conclusion-oriented inquiry is here referred to as research; decision-oriented inquiry typifies evaluation as well as any three words can.

3. *Laws vs. descriptions.* Closely related to the distinction between conclusion-orientation and decision-orientation are the familiar concepts of *nomothetic* (law giving) and *idiographic* (descriptive of the particular) activities. Research is the quest for laws, that is, statements of relationship among two or more variables or phenomena. Evaluation merely seeks to describe a particular thing with respect to one or more scales of value.

4. *Role of explanation.* The nomothetic and idiographic converge in the act of explanation, namely the conjoining of general laws with descriptions of particular circumstances as in "If you like three-minute eggs back home in Portland you'd better ask for a five-minute egg in the Brown Palace in Denver *because* the boiling point of water is directly proportional to the absolute pressure (the law) and at 5,280 feet, the air pressure is so low in Denver that water boils at 195° F (the circumstances)." Scientific explanations require scientific laws, and the disciplines related to education appear to be far from discovery of the general laws on which explanations of incidents of schooling will be based.

There is considerable confusion among investigators in education about the extent to which evaluators should explain ("understand") the phenomena they evaluate. We do not view explanations as the primary purpose of evaluation. A fully proper and useful evaluation can be conducted without producing an explanation of *why* the product or program being evaluated is good or bad or *how* it operates to produce its effects. It is fortunate that this is so, since evaluation in education is so needed and credible explanations of educational phenomena are so rare.

5. *Autonomy of the inquiry.* Science as an independent and autonomous enterprise is a principle of great importance. At the beginning of his classic, *The Conduct of Inquiry*, Kaplan (1964, pp. 3-6) wrote:

It is one of the themes of this book that the various sciences, taken together, are not colonies subject to the governance of logic, methodology, philosophy of science, or any other discipline whatever, but are, and of right ought to be, free and independent. Following John Dewey, I shall refer to this declaration of scientific independence as the principle of *autonomy of inquiry*. It is the principle that the pursuit of truth is accountable to nothing and to no one not a part of that pursuit itself.

Not surprisingly, autonomy of inquiry proves to be an important characteristic for typifying research and evaluation. As was seen incidentally in the quote from Cronbach and Suppes, evaluation is undertaken at the behest of a client, but the researcher sets his own problems. As will be seen later, the autonomy which the researcher and the evaluator enjoy to differing degrees has implications for how they should be trained and how their respective inquiries are pursued.

6. *Properties of the phenomena which are assessed.* Educational evaluation is an attempt to assess the *worth* of a thing and educational research is an attempt to assess scientific truth. Except that truth is highly valued and thus worthwhile, this distinction serves fairly well to discriminate research and evaluation. The distinction can be given added meaning if "worth" is taken as synonymous with "social utility" (which is presumed[10] to increase with improved health, happiness, life expectancy, etc., and to decrease with increases in privation, sickness, ignorance, etc.) and if "scientific truth" is identified with two of its properties: (a) empirical verifiability, and (b) logical consistency.

Evaluation seeks directly to assess social utility. Research may yield evidence of social utility, but only indirectly, insofar as empirical verifiability of general phenomena and logical consistency may eventually be socially useful. A touchstone for discriminating between an evaluator and a researcher is to ask whether the inquiry he is conducting would be regarded as a failure if it produced no information on whether the phenomenon studied was useful or useless. A researcher answering strictly as a researcher will probably say "no."

In the above view, inquiry is seen as directed toward the assessment of three properties of a particular statement concerning a phenomenon: (a) its empirical verifiability by accepted methods (b) its logical consistency with other accepted or known facts and

10. That evaluators must "presume" that certain conditions are worthwhile and to be sought after leads to what Scriven called the "point-of-entry problem in evaluation" (personal communication). Every act of evaluation must enter a chain of justification of valued states at some point short of the philosopher's rationalization of such elusive concepts as "the good life." Educational evaluation cannot solve the problems of philosophy. Perhaps the best advice for the evaluator is to enter at one stage above his client, seeking justification for the client's definition of "worth" but not for his own.

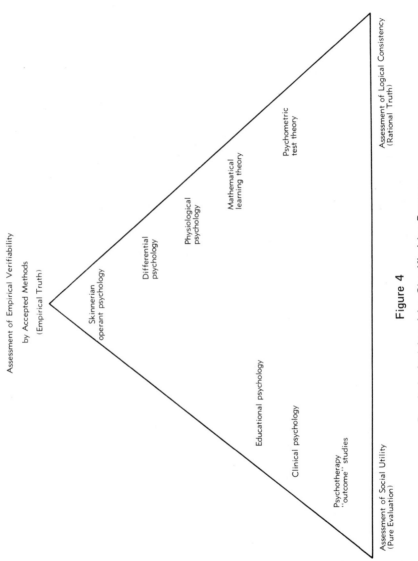

Figure 4

Psychological Inquiries Classified by Purpose

(c) its social utility. Most disciplined inquiry aims to assess each property in varying degrees. In figure 4, for example, several areas of inquiry within psychology are classified with respect to the degree to which they seek to assess each of the above three properties. The distance of a point in the triangle from each of the vertices is inversely related to the extent to which the property represented by the vertex is sought by the particular inquiry.[11]

7. *Generalizability of the phenomena studied.* Perhaps the highest correlate of the research–evaluation distinction is the generalizability of the phenomena being studied. Researchers work with constructs having a currency and scope of application which make the objects one evaluates seem parochial by comparison. An educational psychologist experiments with "reinforcement" or "need achievement" which he regards as neither specific to geography nor to one point in time. The effects of positive reinforcement following upon a response are assumed to be phenomena shared by most men in most times; moreover the number of specific instances of human behavior which are examples of the working of positive reinforcement is great. Not so with the phenomena studied in evaluation. A particular textbook, an organizational plan, or a filmstrip may have a short life expectancy and may not be widely shared. However, whenever their cost or potential pay-off rises above negligible level, they are of interest to the evaluator.

Three aspects of the generalizability of a phenomenon can be identified: (a) generality across time (Will the phenomenon—perhaps a textbook or a self-concept—be of interest fifty years hence?), (b) generality across geography (Is the phenomenon of any interest to people in the next town, the next state, across the ocean?), and (c) applicability to a number of specific instances of the general phenomenon (Are there many specific examples of the phenomenon being studied or is this the only one?). These three qualities of the object of an educational inquiry can be used to classify different inquiry types, as in figure 5.

Three types of inquiry are respresented in figure 5: (a) program evaluation—the evaluation of a complex of people, materials, and organization which make up a particular educational program; (b)

---

11. Since this conceptualization of inquiry was first presented (Glass, 1969), the authors have found some interesting corroboration of an authoritative sort. The definition of "theory" in *Webster's Third New International Dictionary* (definition 3.a[2]) is tripartite: "The coherent set of hypothetical, conceptual and pragmatic principles forming the general frame of reference for a field of inquiry (as for deducing principles, formulating hypotheses for testing, undertaking actions)." The three inquiry activities in Webster's definition correspond closely to the three inquiry properties in figure 4.

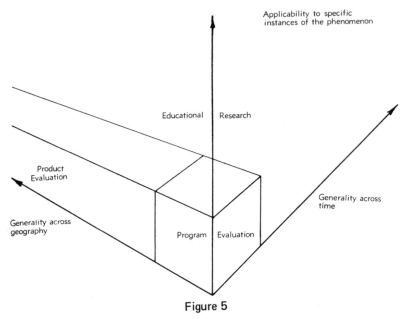

Figure 5

Three Inquiry Types Classified by the Generalizability of
the Phenomenon Investigated.[a]

[a]The property represented by each axis is absent where the three axes meet and increases
as one moves out along each axis.

product evaluation—the evaluation of a medium of schooling such
as a book, a film, or a recorded tape; and (c) educational research.

Program evaluation is concerned with a phenomenon (an
educational program) which has limited generalizability across
time and geography; the innovative "ecology curriculum" (including instructional materials, staff, students, and other courses in the
school) in the Middletown Public Schools will probably not
survive the decade, is of little interest to the schools in Norfolk
which have a different set of environmental problems and instructional resources, and has little relationship to other curricula with
other objectives. Product evaluation is concerned with assessing
the worth of something like a new ecology textbook or an over-
head projector which can be widely disseminated geographically,
but which similarly will not be of interest ten years hence, nor
does the study of its properties produce any reliable knowledge
about the educational process in general. The concepts upon
which educational research is carried out are supposed to be relatively permanent, applicable to schooling nearly everywhere, and
subsuming a large number of instances of teaching and learning.

8. *Salience of the value question.* According to theory, a value
can be placed on the outcome of an inquiry, and all inquiry is

directed toward the discovery of something worthwhile and useful. In what we are calling evaluation, it is usually quite clear that some question of value is being addressed. Indeed, value questions are the *sine qua non* in evaluation and usually determine what information is sought, whereas they are not the direct object of research. This is not to say, however, that value questions are not germane in research. The goals may be the same for both research and evaluation—placing value on alternative explanations or hypotheses—but the roles, the ways in which information is utilized, may be quite different. For example, the acquisition of knowledge and improvement of self-concept are clearly value ladden. The value question in the derivation of a new oblique transformation technique in factor analysis is not so obvious, but it is there nonetheless. In assessing the value of things, the difference between research and evaluation is one of degree, not of kind.

9. *Investigative techniques.* A substantial amount of opinion has recently been expressed to the effect that research and evaluation should employ different techniques for gathering and processing data. It has been proposed that, with respect to techniques of empirical inquiry, evaluation is a thing apart, and that the methods appropriate to research—such as comparative experimental design—are not appropriate to evaluation (Cronbach, 1963; Carroll, 1965; Stufflebeam, 1968; Guba and Stufflebeam, 1968). These views are discussed (and to a large degree refuted) in chapter 4. It suffices to say here that while there may be legitimate differences between research and evaluation methods, we see far more similarities than differences with regard to the techniques by which empirical evidence is collected and judged to be sound. As Stake and Denny (1969, p. 374) indicated: "The distinction between research and evaluation can be overstated as well as understated. . . . Researchers and evaluators work within the same inquiry paradigm . . . [and training programs for] both must include skill development in general educational research methodology."

Hemphill (1969, p. 220) expressed the same opinion when he wrote, "The consequence of the differences between the proper function of evaluation studies and research studies is not to be found . . . in the methods of inquiry of the researcher and of the evaluator." We shall return in a later section to the question of how research and evaluation differ in the techniques of investigation they employ.

The notion that evaluation is really only sloppy research has a low incidence in writing but a high incidence in conversation— usually among researchers but also among some evaluators. This bit of slander arises partly from a misconstruing of the concept of "experimental control."

One form of experimental control is achieved by the randomization of extraneous influences in a comparative experiment so that the effect of an intervention (or treatment) on a dependent variable can be observed. Such control can be achieved either in the laboratory or the field; achieving it is a simple matter of designing an internally valid plan for assigning experimental units to treatment conditions. Basic research has no proprietary rights to such experimental control; it can be attained in the comparative study of two reinforcement schedules as well as in the comparative study of two curricula.

A second form of control concerns the ability of the experimenter to probe the complex of conditions he creates when he intervenes to set up an independent variable and to determine which critical element in a swarm of elements is fundamental in the causal relationship between independent and dependent variables. Control of this type occupies the greater part of the efforts of the researcher to gain understanding, but it is properly of little concern to the evaluator. It is enough for the evaluator to know that *something* attendant ·upon the installation of curriculum A (and not an extraneous, uncontrolled influence not related to the curriculum) is responsible for the valued outcome; to give a more definite answer about what that something is would carry evaluation into analytic research. Analytic research on the nongeneralizable phenomena of evaluation is seldom worth the expense. In this sense only is evaluation (in the abstract) "sloppy."

10. *Criteria for judging the activity.* The two most important criteria for judging the adequacy of research are internal validity (to what extent are the results of the study unequivocal and not confounded with extraneous or systematic error variance) and external validity (to what extent can the results be generalized to other units—for example, Ss or classrooms—with characteristics similar to those used in the study). If one were forced to choose the two most important from among the several criteria which might be used for judging the adequacy of evaluation, the two would probably be isomorphism (the extent to which the information obtained is isomorphic with the reality-based information desired) and credibility (the extent to which the information is viewed as believable by clients who need to use the information).

11. *Disciplinary base.* The suggestion to make educational research multi-disciplinary is good advice for the research community as a whole, but it is doubtful that the individual researcher is well advised to attack his particular area of interest simultaneously from several different disciplinary bases. Some few men can fruitfully work in the cracks between disciplines, but

most will find it challenge enough to deal with the problems of education from the perspective of one discipline at a time. The specialization required to master even a small corner of a discipline works against the wish to make Leonardos of all educational researchers.

That the educational researcher can afford to pursue inquiry within one paradigm and the evaluator cannot is one of many consequences of the autonomy of inquiry. When one is free to define his own problems for solution (as the researcher is), he seldom asks a question that takes him outside of the discipline in which he was trained. Psychologists pose questions that can be solved by the methods of psychology, and so do sociologists, economists, and other scientists—each to his own. The seeds of the answer to a research question are planted along with the question. The curriculum evaluator enjoys less freedom in the definition of the questions he must answer. Hence, the answers are not as likely to be found by use of a stereotyped methodology. Typically, then, the evaluator finds it necessary to employ a wider range of inquiry perspectives and techniques in order to deal with questions that do not have predestined answers[12] (see Hastings, 1969).

12. *Training.* The distinction just considered, relating to disciplinary bases, has implications for the training of researchers that are quite different from those for the training of evaluators. Research aimed at producing understanding of such phenomena as school learning, the social organization of schools, and human growth and development can best be accomplished from the perspectives afforded by the traditional social sciences. Consequently, the best training for many educational researchers is likely to be a thorough mastery of a relatively traditional social science discipline. We regard as mistaken the notion of a unique science of education constructed out of unique educational constructs with methods of inquiry which are not already a part of the traditional social sciences.[13] Psychology, sociology, and the

---

12. The discussion has taken on a utopian tone. In reality much evaluation is becoming as stereotyped as most research. Evaluators often take part in asking the questions they will ultimately answer, and they are all too prone to generate questions out of a particular "evaluation model" (e.g., the Stake model, the CIPP model) rather than out of a "discipline." Stereotyping of method threatens evaluation as it threatens research (Glass, 1969).

13. This does *not* mean that it is inappropriate to continue to train research methodologists *within* the field of education. "Educational research methodology" is an aggregate of techniques borrowed from agronomy, psychology, mathematics, etc., with some refinements by educationists. Persons trained in this area play critical roles in (a) developing and refining statistical techniques and (b) advising other educational researchers (whose strengths lie more in their discipline backgrounds than in their knowledge of methodology) in matters such as design and statistics.

others are not so lacking in conceptual richness that they cannot accommodate most of the phenomena of education. The fact that relatively few researchers trained in these disciplines exhibit interest in working on problems with apparent applicability in education does not negate the argument. Rather, it merely suggests that existing reward structures lead most researchers to conduct inquiry within their home discipline. One proposal for training would be to recruit vigorously among bachelors' and masters' degree holders in these behavioral and social sciences to attract them into our educational research programs. Then their training could consist of continued preparation in their disciplines coupled with application of the tools of those disciplines to educational problems. We would anticipate that persons trained in this manner would do much to improve educational research by bringing the perspectives of their particular disciplines to bear.

This does not argue that any one researcher should receive training in more than one discipline. A research training program that attempts to train the same student in social psychology, physiological psychology, and micro-economic theory is doomed; the result will be a researcher so superficially trained in several areas that he can contribute in none.

By contrast, to the extent that the training of evaluators touches on the traditional disciplines at all, it is best that several disciplines be sampled. The trainee should appreciate the view of education afforded by each of the socially relevant disciplines. In this way, the evaluator can become sensitive to the wide range of phenomena to which he must attend if he is to properly assess the worth of an educational program. That superficial exposure to the many social sciences does not train him to build a science of education is simply irrelevant.

In relation to methodology, some additional differences may be seen. The evaluator's role is largely that of a methodological expert applying inquiry techniques to the solution of a particular type of practical problem. Consequently, emphasis in training must be given to such topics as statistical analysis, measurement and psychometrics, survey research methods, and experimental design. The techniques that a single evaluator might use are little different from the body of techniques used by the empirical social scientist. [14]

---

14. We confess no sympathy with the argument that such techniques as inferential statistics and comparative experimental design are not useful in evaluation, even though we agree that they are often misapplied. Guba and Stufflebeam (1968) argued that comparative experimental design is inappropriate to the purposes of educational evaluation; an attempt to rebut the argument appears in Glass (1969).

The training program for the educational researcher need not be as broad in techniques of inquiry as that for the evaluator. Most sociologists' work is none the worse for their ignorance of confounding relations in fractional factorial designs, and who would argue that an experimental psychologist suffers from his ignorance of scalogram analysis? The training of researchers must be more concerned with substantive matters (such as Keynesian economics, Skinnerian operant conditioning, or the cognitive dissonance theory) than with methods and techniques.

Some provisions in training both researchers and evaluators must be made for the acquisition of practical experience to complement course work. Doubtless there is no better practical experience for the research trainee than apprenticeship to a competent, practicing researcher. Worthen and Roaden (1968) found that there is a significant relationship between genuine research assistantship experiences and subsequent productivity as an educational researcher. Moreover, it was found in a later study (Worthen and Roaden, 1970) that apprenticeship to one researcher over an extended period of time spent working on a variety of projects was positively correlated with subsequent productivity whereas an assignment to work on a single, isolated research project was not.

Internship experiences in public schools, state education departments, and similar "front-line" institutions are probably unproductive in the training of researchers. A researcher's capacity to produce good research has rarely been enhanced by his first-hand knowledge that school administrators are subjected to political pressures, that junior-high teachers seldom have planning periods, or that students are too preoccupied to learn during the last two months of their senior year.

The internship experience "in the field" is an entirely different matter in the curriculum of the evaluation trainee. A protracted apprenticeship to a single researcher would be inappropriate in the training of the evaluator. Breadth of experience in a variety of settings is important. The researcher can afford to ignore—indeed, *must* ignore—the countless practical constraints of contemporary schools in constructing his elegant idealizations, but evaluation that ignores practicalities is just bad evaluation.

Considering how little genuine change takes place in students even in intensive graduate-level training programs, the selection of trainees is as important as the experiences that comprise the programs. Logical criteria for trainee selection which are consistent with our conceptions of research and evaluation can be identified, even though empirical validations of the logical criteria are lacking.

Both evaluators and researchers should be selected from among the most intelligent products of undergraduate education. The notion that researchers should be more intelligent (in the Graduate Record Examination sense, for example) than evaluators is an entirely unjustifiable and repugnant value judgment. Maturity and teaching experience (or comparable educational experience) are not irrelevant in the selection of evaluation trainees, though neither should be overstressed. The irrational imposition of these criteria in the selection of educational researchers works against securing the best candidates. The patterns of interests and values most conducive to success as an evaluator may occur at a slightly greater rate among the graduates of professional colleges (such as those of engineering or education) than among the graduates of liberal arts curricula. Conversely, there may be some coincidence between an undergraduate liberal arts major and an attraction to the life of uninterrupted scholarship so essential to the researcher in any field — and so rare.

Expanding a Definition

In this chapter, we have argued that evaluation must include judgments about the worth of the program, product, or process being evaluated. The term has purposely been defined here so as to exclude activities such as describing programs, collecting and reporting information, or monitoring ongoing programs. These are all activities which might appropriately be conducted by an evaluator and, in many instances, are critical to conducting a complete evaluation. However, for the reasons discussed earlier, we prefer to view them as evaluation-attendant activities rather than evaluation per se.

Many contemporary writers on evaluation use the term more loosely to include the very activities we have opted to exclude from our definition. However much we disagree with others on whether or not activities such as context description or program monitoring are evaluative, we do agree that they are important activities. In the next chapter, several papers are included where the term "evaluation" is used to refer not only to evaluation as we define it, but also to a variety of important, related activities such as those discussed above. For consistency and to avoid the redundancy of constant references to "evaluation-attendant activities" throughout the remainder of this volume, we have chosen to broaden our use of the term evaluation from this point on to also include evaluation-attendant activities. This does not represent abdication of the position we have taken here; we trust that we have made our point, and it seems unnecessary to hinder the reader simply to keep that point continually in the forefront of his attention.

3 Frameworks for Planning Evaluation Studies

Introduction

Three persons — one, a school administrator who has just signed a contract with a commercial firm to install a new remedial reading program in his elementary schools; another, a secondary English teacher who would like to try a new method for teaching spelling; and the third, a national director for social welfare programs — all have something in common. They all need to evaluate their programs to determine the worth of their efforts. How can they go about evaluating such programs? Should they follow the same procedures? Are there any guidelines to help them in planning or designing their evaluation studies? Such questions frequently arise when the need for program evaluation becomes apparent. Obviously, formal evaluation studies can be very complex and can easily get out of hand. Thus, it is essential that starting and finishing points be identified. If possible, a stepwise procedure for program evaluation should be planned in advance.

Planning is essential in systematic evaluation studies. Without rigorous outlines, evaluation studies can easily proceed without direction, and hence, without any end point. Program evaluation is analogous to a Sunday afternoon drive — if you don't know how to proceed or where you're going, how do you know when you get there?

An example of a poorly planned evaluation study appeared in a recent education journal. A performance contract was signed by a school administrator without the knowledge or consent of any of the local school personnel or the community involved. The entire evaluation design was a plan to administer the Metropolitan Achievement Test at the beginning and the end of the school year. Many problems were caused by such inadequate planning. For example, the performance contract was in violation of the state school board regulations and federal regulations, but no one noticed this until midway through the school year — at which time both national and state authorities demanded the discontinuation of the program. The local school board reacted negatively to the apparent "power grab" by the administrator. The teachers reacted negatively to the sudden emphasis on reading and mathematics to the exclusion of instruction in other school subjects. The children disliked the program, and as a consequence, apparently tried to make the project fail by intentionally performing poorly. Parents were upset by the radical change in curriculum. Finally, no statistically significant differences were found between the experimental students and a nonequivalent control group on the Metropolitan Achievement Test. At the end of the year school officials asked, "Did we succeed with our program?" "Was it worthwhile?" "Did the standardized test give us the information we need to judge the program?" and many other relevant questions. Unfortunately, they had no rational, informed basis for finding the answers.

The question of what evaluation strategies might be used is highly important as becomes evident after witnessing a few of the problems caused by lack of planning. There are no systematic taxonomies of evaluation designs analogous to those of Campbell and Stanley (1966) or Lindquist (1953) for experimental designs. However, there are some very valuable general guidelines which have been suggested by several persons working on evaluation problems. In this chapter we have included several papers which represent the best thinking to date on how one goes about planning evaluation studies. The suggested plans are by no means cookbook recipes for evaluation. Rather, these papers contain useful organizational frameworks within which the details of evaluation planning may be placed and, consequently, they should be useful to persons setting out to conduct an evaluation study. Each writer has made a valuable (and often unique) contribution to current thinking in evaluation. We therefore suggest that the would-be evaluator be eclectic, whenever possible, in selecting useful concepts from each of the following papers and combining them into an evaluation plan that is better for having incorporated the best features of several approaches.

The papers and paper summaries included in this chapter are grouped according to similarities and differences in the evaluation strategies proposed. The first section includes material by Cronbach, Scriven, and Stake. These three papers contain strategies that in greater or lesser degree require the evaluator to play a judgmental role. The papers are presented in chronological order, since Scriven reacted to Cronbach's ideas and expanded upon them from the point of view of a philosopher, and Stake was then apparently influenced by both Cronbach and Scriven (though Stake developed his strategy with much more of a measurement orientation).

The second grouping includes two plans proposed by Stufflebeam and Alkin. These plans might best be labeled as decision-management approaches to evaluation. The four evaluation approaches in the third section, proposed by Tyler, Metfessel and Michael, Hammond, and Provus, could be categorized as decision-objectives plans. At the end of the chapter, a comparative description of each of the nine proposed evaluation strategies, based on several important characteristics, is presented.

In order to emphasize major points made in the materials contained in this section, a brief evaluation problem has been created and used throughout as a context within which we discuss major contributions. That problem is summarized below.

An Evaluation Problem

Mrs. Allen is a tenth-grade English teacher. She has recently moved into a new school district and is unfamiliar with the students she will be teaching. She has decided that this is an opportune time to try out a new instructional strategy. Since she will be teaching two sections of tenth-grade English, she has decided to teach one section in a traditional way (using the lecture method she has always used in teaching sophomore English) and to teach the other section her new way, using no lectures. In her tryout, she has decided to use diagnostic tests, programmed materials, and mastery tests to allow students to go through the course at their own pace. However, in approaching the principal with this proposal, she is told that it will be approved on a tentative basis only if she agrees to conduct a formal evaluation of her new self-paced instructional program.

Some ideas relating to Mrs. Allen's problem can be drawn from each of the papers which follow. After each presentation, we will return to Mrs. Allen's evaluation problem as a way to underscore important points from our perspective.

Judgmental Strategies

The following three papers may be considered as judgment-oriented strategies. Actually, only the Scriven and Stake papers contain evaluation strategies which explicitly emphasize judgment as a critical procedure in evaluation studies. Cronbach, however, has apparently so influenced the writing of Scriven and Stake that his paper has been grouped with the latter two papers as a necessary precursor to them.

Course Improvement Through Evaluation

Lee J. Cronbach

Stanford University

The national interest in improving education has generated several highly important projects attempting to improve curricula, particularly at the secondary-school level. In conferences of directors of "course content improvement" programs sponsored by the National Science Foundation, questions about evaluation are frequently raised.[1] Those who inquire about evaluation have various motives, ranging from sheer scientific curiosity about classroom events to a desire to assure a sponsor that money has been well spent. While the curriculum developers sincerely wish to use the skills of evaluation specialists, I am not certain that they have a clear picture of what evaluation can do and should try to do. And, on the other hand, I am becoming convinced that some techniques and habits of thought of the evaluation specialist are ill-suited to current curriculum studies. To serve these studies, what philosophy and methods of evaluation are required? And particularly, how must we depart from the familiar doctrines and rituals of the testing game?

From *Teachers College Record*, 1963, *64*, 672-683. Copyright 1963 by Teachers College, Columbia University. Reprinted with permission of the author and publisher, using editing of the version in R.W. Heath, *New Curricula*, Harper & Row, 1964, at author's request.

1. My comments on these questions and on certain more significant questions that *should* have been raised, have been greatly clarified by the reactions of several of these directors and colleagues in evaluation to a draft of this paper. J. Thomas Hastings and Robert Heath have been especially helpful. What I voice, however, are my personal views, deliberately more provocative than "authoritative."

Decisions Served by Evaluation

To draw attention to its full range of functions, we may define "evaluation" broadly as the *collection and use of information to make decisions about an educational program*. This program may be a set of instructional materials distributed nationally, the instructional activities of a single school, or the educational experiences of a single pupil. Many types of decision are to be made, and many varieties of information are useful. It becomes immediately apparent that evaluation is a diversified activity and that no one set of principles will suffice for all situations. But measurements specialists have so concentrated upon one process — the preparation of pencil-and-paper achievement tests for assigning scores to individual pupils — that the principles pertinent to that process have somehow become enshrined as *the* principles of evaluation. "Tests," we are told, "should fit the content of the curriculum." Also, "only those evaluation procedures should be used that yield reliable scores." These and other hallowed principles are not entirely appropriate to evaluation for course improvement. Before proceeding to support this contention, I wish to distinguish among purposes of evaluation and relate them to historical developments in testing and curriculum making.

We may separate three types of decisions for which evaluation is used:

1. Course improvement: deciding what instructional materials and methods are satisfactory and where change is needed.
2. Decisions about individuals: identifying the needs of the pupil for the sake of planning his instruction, judging pupil merit for purposes of selection and grouping, acquainting the pupil with his own progress and deficiencies.
3. Administrative regulation: judging how good the school system is, how good individual teachers are, etc.

Course improvement is set apart by its broad temporal and geographical reference; it involves the modification of recurrently used materials and methods. Developing a standard exercise to overcome a misunderstanding would be course improvement, but deciding whether a certain pupil should work through that exercise would be an individual decision. Administrative regulation likewise is local in effect, whereas an improvement in a course is likely to be pertinent wherever the course is offered.

It was for the sake of course improvement that systematic evaluation was first introduced. When that famous muckraker Joseph Rice gave the same spelling test in a number of American schools, and so gave the first impetus to the educational testing movement, he was interested in evaluating a curriculum. Crusading against the extended spelling drills that then loomed large in the school schedule — "the spelling grind" — Rice collected evidence of their worthlessness so as to provoke curriculum revision. As the testing movement developed, however, it took on a different function.

The greatest expansion of systematic achievement testing occurred in the 1920s. At that time, the content of any course was taken pretty much as established and beyond criticism save for small shifts of topical emphasis. At the administrator's direction, standard tests covering this curriculum were given to assess the efficiency of the teacher or the school system. Such administrative testing fell into disfavor when used injudiciously and heavy-handedly in the 1920s and 1930s. Administrators and accrediting agencies fell back upon descriptive features of the school program in judging adequacy. Instead of collecting direct evidence of educational impact, they judged schools in terms of size of budget, student-staff ratio, square feet of laboratory space, and the number of advanced credits accumulated by the teacher. This tide, it appears, is about to turn. On many university campuses, administrators wanting to know more about their product are installing "operations research offices." Testing directed toward quality control seems likely to increase in the lower schools as well as is most forcefully indicated by the statewide testing just ordered by the California legislature.

After 1930 or thereabouts, tests were given almost exclusively for judgments about individuals: to select students for advanced training, to assign marks within a class, and to diagnose individual competences and deficencies. For any such decisions, one wants precise and valid comparisons of one individual with other individuals or with a standard. Much of test theory and test technology has been concerned with making measurements precise. Important though precision is for most decisions about individuals, I shall argue that in evaluating courses we need not struggle to obtain precise scores for individuals.

While measurers have been well content with the devices used to make scores precise, they have been less complacent about validity. Prior to 1935 the pupil was examined mostly on factual knowledge and mastery of fundamental skills. Tyler's research and writings of that period developed awareness that higher mental processes are not evoked by simple factual tests, and that instruction that promotes factual knowledge may not promote — indeed, may interfere with — other more important educational outcomes. Tyler, Lindquist, and their students demonstrated that tests can be designed to measure general educational outcomes such as ability to comprehend scientific method. Whereas a student can prepare for a factual test only through a course of study that includes the facts tested, many different courses of study may promote the same *general* understandings and attitudes. In evaluating today's new curricula, it will clearly be important to appraise the student's general educational growth, which curriculum developers say is more important than mastery of the specific lessons presented. Note, for example, that the Biological Sciences Curriculum Study offers three courses with substantially different "subject matter" as alternative routes to much the same educational ends.

Although some instruments capable of measuring general outcomes were prepared during the 1930s, they were never very widely employed. The prevailing philosophy of the curriculum, particularly among "progressives," called for developing a program to fit local requirements, capitalizing on the capacities and experiences of local pupils. The faith of the 1920s in a "standard" curriculum was replaced by a faith that the best learning experience would result from teacher-pupil planning in each classroom. Since each teacher or each class could choose different content and even different objectives, this philosophy left little place for standard testing.

Many evaluation specialists came to see test development as a strategy for training the teacher in service, so that the process of test making came to be valued more than the test — or the test data — that resulted. The following remarks by Bloom (1961) are representative of a whole school of thought: [2]

> The criterion for determining the quality of a school and its educational functions would be the extent to which it achieves the objectives it has set for itself. . . . (Our experiences suggest that unless the school has translated the objectives into specific and operational definitions, little is likely to be done about the objectives. They remain pious hopes and platitudes.). . . Participation of the teaching staff in selecting as well as constructing evaluation instruments has resulted in improved instruments on one hand and on the other hand it has resulted in clarifying the objectives of instruction and in making them real and meaningful to teachers. . . . When teachers have actively participated in defining objectives and in selecting or constructing evaluation instru-

---

2. Elsewhere, Bloom's paper discusses evaluation for the new curricula. Attention may also be drawn to Tyler's highly pertinent paper (1951).

ments they return to the learning problems with great vigor and remarkable creativity. ... Teachers who have become committed to a set of educational objectives which they thoroughly understand respond by developing a variety of learning experiences which are as diverse and as complex as the situation requires.

Thus "evaluation" becomes a local, and beneficial, teacher-training activity. The benefit is attributed to thinking about the data to collect. Little is said about the actual use of test results; one has the impression that when test-making ends, the test itself is forgotten. Certainly there is little enthusiasm for refining tests so that they can be used in other schools, for to do so would be to rob those teachers of the benefits of working out their own objectives and instruments.

Bloom and Tyler describe both curriculum making and evaluation as integral parts of classroom instruction, which is necessarily decentralized. This outlook is far from that of "course improvement." The current national curriculum studies assume that curriculum making can be centralized. They prepare materials to be used in much the same way by teachers everywhere. It is assumed that having experts draft materials, and revising these after tryout, produces better instructional activities than the local teacher would be likely to devise. In this context it seems wholly appropriate to have most tests prepared by a central staff, and to have results returned to that staff to guide further course improvement.

When evaluation is carried out in the service of course improvement, the chief aim is to ascertain what effects the course has—that is, what changes it produces in pupils. This is not to inquire merely whether the course is effective or ineffective. Outcomes of instruction are multidimensional, and a satisfactory investigation will map out the effects of the course along these dimensions separately. To agglomerate many types of post-course performance into a single score is a mistake, since failure to achieve one objective is masked by success in another direction. Moreover, since a composite score embodies (and usually conceals) judgments about the importance of the various outcomes, only a report that treats the outcomes separately can be useful to educators who have different value hierarchies.

The greatest service evaluation can perform is to identify aspects of the course where revision is desirable. Those responsible for developing a course would like to present evidence that their course is effective. They are intrigued by the idea of having an "independent testing agency" render a judgment on their product.

But to call in the evaluator only upon the completion of course development, to confirm what has been done, is to offer him a menial role and make meager use of his services. To be influential in course improvement, evidence must become available midway in curriculum development, not in the home stretch when the developer is naturally reluctant to tear open a supposedly finished body of materials and techniques. Evaluation, used to improve the course while it is still fluid, contributes more to improvement of education than evaluation used to appraise a product already placed on the market.

Insofar as possible, evaluation should be used to understand how the course produces its effects and what parameters influence its effectiveness. It is important to learn, for example, that the outcome of programed instruction depends very much upon the attitude of the teacher; indeed, this may be more important than to learn that on the average such instruction produces slightly better or worse results than conventional instruction.

Hopefully, evaluation studies will go beyond reporting on this or that course, and help us to understand educational learning. Such insight will in the end contribute to the development of all courses rather than just of the course under test. In certain of the new curricula, there are data to suggest that aptitude measures correlate much less with end-of-course achievement than they do with achievement on early units (Ferris, 1962). This finding is not well confirmed, but is highly significant if true. If it is true for the new curricula and only for them it has one implication; if the same effect appears in traditional courses, it means something else. Either way, it provides food for thought for teachers, counselors, and theorists. Evaluation studies should generate knowledge about the nature of the abilities that constitute educational goals. Twenty years after the Eight-Year Study of the Progressive Education Association, its testing techniques are in good repute, but we still know very little about what these instruments measure. Consider "Applications of Principles in Science." Is this in any sense a unitary ability? Or has the able student only mastered certain principles one by one? Is the ability demonstrated on a test of this sort more prognostic of any later achievement than is factual knowledge? Such questions ought to receive substantial attention, though to the makers of any one course they are of only peripheral interest.

The aim to compare one course with another should not dominate plans for evaluation. To be sure, decision makers have to choose between courses, and any evaluation report will be interpreted in part comparatively. But formally designed experiments pitting one course against another are rarely definitive enough to justify their cost. Differences between average test scores resulting from different courses are usually small, relative to the wide differences among and within classes taking the same course. At best, an experiment never does more than compare the present version of one course with the present version of another. A major effort to bring the losing contender nearer to perfection would be very likely to reverse the verdict of the experiment.

Any failure to equate the classes taking the competing courses will jeopardize the interpretation of an experiment and such failures are almost inevitable. In testing a drug, we know that valid results cannot be obtained without a double-blind control in which the doses for half the subjects are inert placebos; the placebo and the drug look alike, so that neither doctor nor patient knows who is receiving medication. Without this control the results are useless even when the state of the patient is checked by completely objective indices. In an educational experiment it is difficult to keep pupils unaware that they are an experimental group. And it is quite impossible to neutralize the biases of the teacher as those of the doctor are neutralized in the double-blind design. It is thus never certain whether any observed advantage is attributable to the educational innovation as such, or to the greater energy that teachers and students put forth when a method is fresh and "experimental." Some have contended that any course, even the most excellent, loses much of its potency as soon as success enthrones it as "the traditional method."[3]

Since group comparisons give equivocal results, I believe that a formal study should be designed primarily to determine the post-course performance of a well-described group, with respect to many important objectives and side effects. Ours is a problem like that of the engineer examining a new automobile. He can set himself the task of defining its performance characteristics and its dependability. It would be merely distracting to put his question in the form: "Is this car better or worse than the competing brand?" Moreover, in an experiment where the treatments compared differ in a dozen respects, no understanding is gained from the fact that the experiment shows a numerical advantage in favor of the new course. No one knows which of the ingredients is responsible for the advantage. More analytic experiments are much more useful than field trials applying markedly dissimilar treatments to different groups. Small-scale, well-controlled studies can profitably be used to compare alternative versions of the same course; in such a study the differences between treatments are few

3. The interested reader can find further striking parallels between curriculum studies and drug research (see Modell, 1963).

enough and well-enough defined that the results have explanatory value.

The three purposes—course improvement, decisions about individuals, and administrative regulation—call for measurement procedures having somewhat different qualities. When a test will be used to make an administrative judgment on the individual teacher, it is necessary to measure thoroughly and with conspicuous fairness; such testing, if it is to cover more than one outcome, becomes extremely time-consuming. In judging a course, however, one can make satisfactory interpretations from data collected on a sampling basis, with no pretense of measuring thoroughly the accomplishments of any one class. A similar point is to be made about testing for decisions about individuals. A test of individuals must be conspicuously fair, and extensive enough to provide a dependable score for each person. But if the performance will not influence the fate of the individual, we can ask him to perform tasks for which the course has not directly prepared him, and we can use techniques that would be prohibitively expensive if applied in a manner thorough enough to measure each person reliably.

Methods of Evaluation

Range of Methods

Evaluation is too often visualized as the administration of a formal test, an hour or so in duration, at the close of a course. But there are many other methods for examining pupil performance, and pupil attainment is not the only basis for appraising a course.

It is quite appropriate to ask scholars whether the statements made in the course are consistent with the best contemporary knowledge. This is a sound, even a necessary, procedure. One might go on to evaluate the pedagogy of the new course by soliciting opinions, but here there is considerable hazard. If the opinions are based on some preconception about teaching method, the findings will be controversial and very probably misleading. There are no theories of pedagogy so well established that one can say, without tryout, what will prove educative.

One can accept the need for a pragmatic test of the curriculum and still employ opinions as a source of evidence. During the tryout stages of curriculum making, one relies heavily on the teachers' reports of pupil accomplishment—"Here they had trouble"; "This they found dull"; "Here they needed only half as many exercises as were provided"; etc. This is behavior observation even though unsystematic, and it is of great value. The reason for shifting to systematic observation is that this is more impartial, more public, and sometimes more penetrating. While I bow to the historian or mathematician as a judge of the technical soundness of course content, I do not agree that the experienced history or mathematics teacher who tries out a course gives the best possible judgment on its effectiveness. Scholars have too often deluded themselves about their effectiveness as teachers—particularly, have too often accepted parroting of words as evidence of insight—for their unaided judgment to be trusted. Systematic observation is costly, and introduces some delay between the moment of teaching and the feedback of results. Hence systematic observation will never be the curriculum developer's sole source of evidence. Systematic data collection becomes profitable in the intermediate stages of curriculum development, after the more obvious bugs in early drafts have been dealt with.

The approaches to evaluation include process studies, proficiency measures, attitude measures, and follow-up studies. A process study is concerned with events taking place in the classroom, proficiency and attitude measures with changes observed in pupils, and follow-up studies with the later careers of those who participated in the course.

The follow-up study comes closest to observing ultimate educational contributions, but the completion of such a study is so far removed in time from the initial instruction that it is of minor value in improving the course or explaining its effects. The follow-up study differs strikingly from the other types of evaluation study in one respect. I have already expressed the view that evaluation should be primarily concerned with the effects of the course under study rather than with comparisons of courses. That is to say, I would emphasize departures of attained results from the ideal, differences in apparent effectiveness of different parts of the course, and differences from item to item; all these suggest places where the course could be strengthened. But this view cannot be applied to the follow-up study, which appraises effects of the course as a whole and which has very little meaning unless outcomes can be compared with some sort of base rate. Suppose we find that 65 per cent of the boys graduating from an experimental curriculum enroll in scientific and technical majors in college. We cannot judge whether this is a high or low figure save by comparing it with the rate among boys who have not had this course. In a follow-up study, it is necessary to obtain data on a control group equated at least crudely to the experimental cases on the obvious demographic variables.

Despite the fact that such groups are hard to equate and that follow-up data do not tell much about how to improve the course, such studies should have a place in research on the new curricula, whose national samples provide unusual opportunity for follow-up that can shed light on important questions. One obvious type of follow-up study traces the student's success in a college course founded upon the high-school course. One may examine the student's grades or ask him what topics in the college course he found himself poorly prepared for. It is hoped that some of the new science and mathematics courses will arouse greater interest than usual among girls; whether this hope is well founded can be checked by finding out what majors and what electives these ex-students pursue in college. Career choices likewise merit attention. Some proponents of the new curricula would like to see a greater flow of talent into basic science as distinct from technology while others would regard this as potentially disastrous; but no one would regard facts about this flow as lacking significance.

Attitudes are prominent among the outcomes course developers are concerned with. Attitudes are meanings or beliefs, not mere expressions of approval or disapproval. One's attitude toward science includes ideas about the matters on which a scientist can be an authority, about the benefits to be obtained from moon shots and studies of monkey mothers, and about depletion of natural resources. Equally important is the match between self-concept and concept of the field: what roles does science offer a person like me? would I want to marry a scientist? and so on. Each learning activity also contributes to attitudes that reach far beyond any one subject, such as the pupil's sense of his own competence and desire to learn.

Attitudes can be measured in many ways; the choices revealed in follow-up studies, for example, are pertinent evidence. But measurement usually takes the form of direct or indirect questioning. Interviews, questionnaires, and the like are quite valuable when not trusted blindly. Certainly, we should take seriously any *un*desirable opinion expressed by a substantial proportion of graduates of a course (e.g., the belief that the scientist speaks with peculiar authority on political and ethical questions, or the belief that mathematics is a finished subject rather than a field for current investigation).

Attitude questionnaires have been much criticized because they are subject to distortion, especially where the student hopes to gain by being less than frank. Particularly if the questions are asked in a context far removed from the experimental course, the returns are likely to be trustworthy. Thus a general questionnaire administered through homerooms (or required English courses) may include questions about liking for various subjects and activities; these same questions administered by the mathematics teacher would give much less trustworthy data on attitude toward mathematics. While students may give reports more favorable than their true beliefs, this distortion is not likely to be greater one year than another, or greater among students who take an experimental course than among those who do not. In group averages, many distortions balance out. But questionnaires insufficiently valid for individual testing can be used in evaluating curricula, both because the student has little motive to distort and because the evaluator is comparing averages rather than individuals.

For measuring proficiency, techniques are likewise varied. Standardized tests are useful. But for course evaluation it makes sense to assign *different* questions to different students. Giving each student in a population of 500 the same test of 50 questions will provide far less information to the course developer than drawing for each student 50 questions from a pool of, say, 700. The latter plan determines the mean success of about 75 representative students on every one of the 700 items; the former reports on only 50 items (See Lord, 1962). Essay tests and open-ended questions, generally too expensive to use for routine evaluation, can profitably be employed to appraise certain abilities. One can go further and observe individuals or groups as they attack a research problem in the laboratory or work through some other complex problem. Since it is necessary to test only a representative sample of pupils, costs are not as serious a consideration as in routine testing. Additional aspects of proficiency testing will be considered below.

Process measures have especial value in showing how a course can be improved because they examine what happens during instruction. In the development of programed instructional materials, for example, records are collected showing how many pupils miss each item presented; any piling up of errors implies a need for better explanation or a more gradual approach to a difficult topic. Immediately after showing a teaching film, one can interview students, perhaps asking them to describe a still photograph taken from the film. Misleading presentations, ideas given insufficient emphasis, and matters left unclear will be identified by such methods. Similar interviews can disclose what pupils take away from a laboratory activity or a discussion. A process study might turn attention to what the teacher does in the classroom. In those curricula that allow choice of topics, for example, it is worthwhile to find out which topics are chosen and how much time is allotted to each. A log of class activities (preferably recorded by a pupil rather than the teacher) will show which of the techniques suggested in a summer institute are actually adopted, and which form "part of the new course" only in the developer's fantasies.

Measurement of Proficiency

I have indicated that I consider item data to be more important than test scores. The total score may give confidence in a curriculum or give rise to discouragement, but it tells very little about how to produce further improvement. And, as Ferris (1962) has noted, such scores are quite likely to be mis- or overinterpreted. The score on a single item, or on a problem that demands several responses in succession, is more likely than the test score to suggest how to alter the presentation. When we accept item scores as useful, we need no longer think of evaluation as a one-shot, end-of-year operation. Proficiency can be measured at any moment, with particular interest attaching to those items most related to the recent lessons. Other items calling for general abilities can profitably be administered repeatedly during the course (perhaps to different random samples of pupils) so that we can begin to learn when and from what experiences change in these abilities comes.

In course evaluation, we need not be much concerned about making measuring instruments fit the curriculum. However startling this declaration may seem, and however contrary to the principles of evaluation for other purposes, this must be our position if we want to know what changes a course produces in the pupil. An ideal evaluation would include measures of all the types of proficiency that might reasonably be desired in the area in question, not just the selected outcomes to which this curriculum directs substantial attention. If you wish only to know how well a curriculum is achieving *its* objectives you fit the test to the curriculum; but if you wish to know how well the curriculum is serving the national interest, you measure all outcomes that might be worth striving for. One of the new mathematics courses might disavow any attempt to teach numerical trigonometry, and indeed, might discard nearly all computational work. It is still perfectly reasonable to ask how well graduates of the course can compute and can solve right triangles. Even if the course developers went so far as to contend that computational skill is no proper objective of secondary instruction, they will encounter educators and laymen who do not share their view. If it can be shown that students who come through the new course are fairly proficient in computation despite the lack of direct teaching, the doubters will be reassured. If not, the evidence makes clear how much is being sacrificed. Similarly, when the biologists offer alternative courses emphasizing microbiology and ecology, it is fair to ask how well the graduate of one course can understand issues treated in the other. Ideal evaluation in mathematics will collect evidence on all the abilities toward which a mathematics course might reasonably aim; likewise in biology, English, or any other subject.

Ferris states that the ACS Chemistry Test, however well constructed, is inadequate for evaluating the new CBA and CHEM programs because it does not cover their objectives. One can agree with this without regarding the ACS test as inappropriate to use with these courses. It is important that this test not stand *alone*, as the sole evaluation device. It will tell us something worth knowing, namely, just how much "conventional" knowledge the new curriculum does or does not provide. The curriculum developers deliberately planned to sacrifice some of the conventional attainments and have nothing to fear from this measurement, competently interpreted (particularly if data are examined item by item).

The demand that tests be closely matched to the aims of a course reflects awareness that examinations of the usual sort "determine what is taught." If questions are known in advance, students give more attention to learning their answers than to learning other aspects of the course. This is not necessarily detrimental. Wherever it is critically important to master certain content, the knowledge that it will be tested produces a desirable concentration of effort. On the other hand, learning the answer to a set question is by no means the same as acquiring understanding of whatever topic that question represents. There is therefore a possible advantage in using "secure" tests for course evaluation. Security is achieved only at a price: One must prepare new tests each year, and cannot make before-and-after comparisons with the same items. One would hope that the use of different items with different students, and the fact that there is less incentive to coach when no judgment is to be passed on the pupils and the teachers, would make security a less critical problem.

The distinction between factual tests and tests of higher mental processes, as elaborated for example in the *Taxonomy of Educational Objectives*, is of some value in planning tests, although classifying items as measures of knowledge, application, original problem solving, etc., is difficult and often impossible. Whether a given response represents rote recall or reasoning depends upon how the pupil has been taught, not solely upon the question asked. One might, for example, describe a biological environment and ask for predictions regarding the effect of a certain intervention. Students who had never dealt with ecological data would succeed or fail according to their general ability to reason about complex events; those who had studied ecological biology would be more likely to succeed, reasoning from specific principles; and those who had lived in such an ecology or read about it might answer successfully on the basis of memory. We rarely, therefore, will want to test whether a student "knows" or "does not know" certain material. Knowledge is a matter of degree. Two persons may be acquainted with the same facts or principles, but one will be more expert in his understanding, better able to cope with inconsistent data, irrelevant sources of confusion, and apparent exceptions to the principle. To measure intellectual competence is to measure depth, connectedness, and applicability of knowledge.

Too often, test questions are course-specific, stated in such a way that only the person who has been specifically taught to understand what is being asked for can answer the question. Such questions can usually be identified by their use of conventions. Some conventions are commonplace, and we can assume that all the pupils we test will know them. But a biology test that describes a metabolic process with the aid of the symbol presents difficulties for students who can think through the scientific question about equilibrium but are unfamiliar with the symbol. A trigonometry problem that requires use of a trigonometric table is unreasonable, unless we want to test familiarity with the conventional names of functions. The same problem in numerical trigonometry can be cast in a form clear to the average pupil *entering* high school; if necessary, the tables of functions can be presented along with a comprehensible explanation. So stated, the problem becomes course-independent. It is fair to ask whether graduates of the experimental course can solve such problems, not previously encountered, whereas it is pointless to ask whether they can answer questions whose language is strange to them. To be sure, knowledge of a certain terminology is a significant objective of instruction, but for course evaluation testing of terminology should very likely be separated from testing of other understandings. To appraise understanding of processes and relations, the fair question is one comprehensible to a pupil who has not taken the course. This is not to say that he should know the answer or the procedure to follow in attaining the answer, but he should understand what he is being asked. Such course-independent questions can be used as standard instruments to investigate any instructional program.

Pupils who have not studied a topic will usually be less facile than those who have studied it. Graduates of my hypothetical mathematics course will take longer to solve trigonometry problems than will those who have studied trig. But speed and power should not be confused; in intellectual studies, power is almost always of greatest importance. If the course equips the pupil to deal correctly even though haltingly with a topic not studied, we can expect him to develop facility later when that topic comes before him frequently.

The chief objective in many of the new curricula seems to be to develop aptitude for mastering new materials in the field. A biology course cannot cover all valuable biological content, but it may reasonably aspire to equip the pupil to understand descriptions of unfamiliar organisms, to comprehend a new theory and the reasoning behind it, and to plan an experiment to test a new hypothesis. This is transfer of learning. It has been insufficiently recognized that there are two types of transfer. The two types shade into one another, being arranged on a continuum of immediacy of effect; we can label the more immediate pole applicational transfer, and speak of slower-acting effects as gains in aptitude (cf. Ferguson, 1954).

Nearly all educational research on transfer has tested immediate performance on a partly-new task. We teach pupils to solve equations in x, and include in the test equations stated in a or z. We teach the principles of ecological balance by referring to forests, and as a transfer test ask what effect pollution will have on the population of a lake. We describe an experiment not presented in the text, and ask the student to discuss possible interpretations and needed controls. Any of these tests can be administered in a short time. But the more significant type of transfer may be the increased ability to learn in a particular field. There is very likely a considerable difference between the ability to draw conclusions from a neatly finished experiment, and the ability to tease insight out of the disordered and inconsistent observations that come with continuous laboratory work on a problem. The student who masters a good biology course may become better able to comprehend certain types of theory and data, so that he gains more from a subsequent year of study in ethnology; we do not measure this gain by testing his understanding of short passages in ethnology. There has rarely been an appraisal of ability to work through a problem situation or a complex body of knowledge over a period of days or months. Despite the practical difficulties that attend an attempt to measure the effect of a course on a person's subsequent learning, such "learning to learn" is so important that a serious effort should be made to detect such effects and to understand how they may be fostered.

The technique of programed instruction may be adopted to appraise learning ability. One might, for example, test the student's rate of mastery of a self-contained, programed unit on heat, or some other topic not studied. If the program is truly self-contained every student can master it, but the one with greater scientific comprehension will hopefully make fewer errors and progress faster. The program might be prepared in several logically complete versions, ranging from one with very small "steps" to one with minimal internal redundancy, on the hypothesis that the better educated student could cope with the less redundant program. Moreover, he might prefer its greater elegance.

Conclusion

Old habits of thought and long-established techniques are poor guides to the evaluation required for course improvement. Traditionally, educational measurement has been chiefly concerned with producing fair and precise scores for comparing individuals. Educational experimentation has been concerned with comparing score averages of competing courses. But course evaluation calls for description of outcomes. This description should be made on the broadest possible scale, even at the sacrifice of superficial fairness and precision.

Course evaluation should ascertain what changes a course produces and should identify aspects of the course that need revision. The outcomes observed should include general outcomes ranging far beyond the content of the curriculum itself: attitudes, career choices, general understandings and intellectual powers, and aptitude for further learning in the field. Analysis of performance on single items or types of problems is more informative than analysis of composite scores. It is not necessary or desirable to give the same test to all pupils; rather, as many questions as possible should be given, each to a different moderate-sized sample of pupils. Costly techniques such as interviews and essay tests can profitably be applied to samples of pupils, whereas testing everyone would be out of the question.

Asking the right questions about educational outcomes can do much to improve educational effectiveness. Even if the right data are collected, evaluation will have contributed too little if it only places a seal of approval on certain courses and casts others into disfavor. Evaluation is a fundamental part of curriculum development, not an appendage. Its job is to collect facts the course developer can and will use to do a better job, and facts from which a deeper understanding of the educational process will emerge.

Cronbach's Paper: An Application

Although Cronbach's was one of the comparatively early papers on evaluation, it contains several major points which have implications for evaluation planning today. These points deserve special consideration. First, evaluation is very closely tied to decision making. Formal evaluation procedures are now recognized as a vital part of rational decision making. Second, there are several different roles evaluation can play in education. The improvement of courses, the making of decisions about individuals, and the making of judgments about administrative operations are three roles identified by Cronbach. Third, pupil performance should definitely not be the only criterion for course or program evaluation. There are many relevant factors which must be considered in an evaluation study. Furthermore, follow-up or longitudinal studies are extremely important in appraising lasting effects of educational programs. Fourth, just as there are a great number of factors to consider in program evaluation, there are also a great number of measurement techniques that the evaluator has available to him. Item sampling, subject sampling, and a variety of instrumentation techniques ought to be considered by the evaluator. Thus, Cronbach has greatly broadened the traditional measurement approach to evaluation.

If Mrs. Allen were to draw on the ideas contained in Cronbach's paper when preparing her evaluation design, she would have some definite guidelines to follow. First, she would concentrate on collecting only the evaluative information she needs for making important decisions about her course improvement. This is especially true since she has limited resources (time, money, expertise, and assistance) with which to conduct the evaluation study. Second, she would not bother with comparing her new course with her old course since Cronbach has argued that such gross comparisons would give her very little information relevant to her needs. Instead she would concentrate on collecting information about all facets of her new program, considering pupil performance, and many other criteria as well. She would consider using the many measurement devices currently available to develop a course description that is as comprehensive as is humanly possible. Her goal would be to identify those aspects of the new course where revision is most desirable and to ascertain what changes the course produces. Drawing on the expertise of measurement technology would be the best way to achieve this goal. She would then be in a position to use the knowledge produced during the evaluation study to improve the course.

The Methodology of Evaluation

Michael Scriven

University of California at Berkeley

Introduction

Current conceptions of the evaluation of educational instruments (e.g., new curricula, programmed texts, inductive methods, individual teachers) are still inadequate both philosophically and practically. This paper attempts to exhibit and reduce some of the deficiencies. Intellectual progress is possible only because newcomers can stand on the shoulders of giants. This feat is often confused with treading on their toes, particularly but not only by the newcomer. I confess a special obligation to Professor Cronbach's (1963) work,[4] and to valuable discussions with the personnel of CIRCE at the University of Illinois, as well as thoughtful correspondence from several others, especially James Shaver and Ray Barglow.

1. Outline

The main focus of this paper is on curricular evaluation but almost all the points made transfer immediately to other kinds of evaluation. Section headings are reasonably self-explanatory and occur in the following order:

1. Outline.
2. Goals of Evaluation versus Roles of Evaluation; Formative and Summative Roles.
3. Professional versus Amateur Evaluation.
4. Evaluation Studies versus Process Studies.
5. Evaluation versus Estimation of Goal Achievement.

An earlier version of this paper was written and circulated during the author's tenure as director of the Evaluation Project of the Social Science Education Consortium, supported by a developmental grant from the U.S. Office of Education, and later by the Kettering Foundation. The present text is a revised version (9-71) of the paper as it appeared in *Perspectives of Curriculum Evaluation* (AERA Monograph 1) by Ralph Tyler, Robert Gagné, and Michael Scriven, ©1967 by Rand McNally and Company, Chicago, pp. 39-83. Reprinted with permission of the author and publisher.

4. In the form of personal comments and correspondence, as well as his well-known article, "Evaluation for Course Improvement," *Teachers College Record, 64,* No. 8, May, 1963, reprinted in *New Curricula* (R. Heath, Ed., New York: Harper & Row, 1964, pp. 231-248). References in this paper are to the latter version.

6. Intrinsic Evaluation versus Pay-off Evaluation.
7. Practical Procedures for Hybrid Evaluations.
8. The Possibility of Pure Pay-off Evaluation.
9. Comparative versus Noncomparative Evaluation.
10. Practical Procedures for Control-Group Evaluation.
11. Criteria of Educational Achievement for Evaluation Studies.
12. Values and Costs.
13. A Marginal Kind of Evaluation—"Explanatory Evaluation."
14. Conclusions.

The discussion in the earlier sections is relatively elementary and etiological, progressing to an occasionally more difficult and generally more practical level in later sections.

2. Goals of Evaluation Versus Roles of Evaluation; Formative and Summative Roles

The function of evaluation may be thought of in two ways. At the methodological level, we may talk of the *goals* of evaluation; in a particular sociological or pedagogical context we may further distinguish several possible *roles* of evaluation.

In terms of goals, we may say that evaluation attempts to answer certain *types of question* about certain *entities*. The entities are the various educational instruments (processes, personnel, procedures, programs, etc.). The types of question include questions of the form: *How well* does this instrument perform (with respect to such-and-such criteria)? Does it perform *better* than this other instrument; *What* merits, or drawbacks does this instrument have (i.e., what variables from the group in which we are interested are significantly affected by its application)? Is the use of this instrument *worth* what it's costing? Evaluation is itself an activity which is methodologically similar whether we are trying to evaluate coffee machines or teaching machines, plans for a house or plans for a curriculum. The activity consists simply in the gathering and combining of performance data with a weighted set of criterial scales to yield either comparative or numerical ratings, and in the justification of (a) the data-gathering instruments, (b) the weightings, and (c) the selection of criteria.

But the *roles* which evaluation has in a particular educational context may be enormously various; it may form part of a teacher training activity, of the process of curriculum development, of a field experiment connected with the improvement of learning theory, of an investigation preliminary to a decision about pur-

chase or rejection of materials; it may be a data-gathering activity
for supporting a request for tax increases or research support, or a
preliminary to the reward or punishment of people as in an
executive training program, a prison, or a classroom. Failure to
make this rather obvious distinction between the roles and goals of
evaluation is one of the factors that has led to the dilution of what
is called evaluation to the point where it can no longer answer the
questions which are its principal goal, questions about real merit
or work. One can be against evaluation only if one can show that
it is improper to seek an answer to questions about the merit of
educational instruments, which would involve showing that there
are *no* legitimate activities (roles) in which these questions can be
raised, an extraordinary claim. Obviously the fact that evaluation
is sometimes given an inappropriate role hardly justifies the
conclusion that we *never* need to know the answers to the goal
questions. Anxiety about "evaluation," especially among teachers
or students, is all too frequently an illicitly generalized response
originating in legitimate objections to a situation in which an
evaluation was given a role quite beyond its reliability or comprehensiveness.

One role that has often and sensibly been assigned to evaluation
is as an important part of the process of curriculum *development*
(another is teacher self-improvement). Obviously such a role does
not preclude evaluation of the *final* product of this process.
Evaluation can and usually should play several roles. But it is clear
from the treatment of evaluation in some of the recent literature
and in a number of recent research proposals involving several
million dollars that the assumption is being made that one's obliga-
tions in the direction of evaluation are fully discharged by having
it appear *somewhere* in a project. Not only can it have several roles
with respect to one educational enterprise, but with respect to
each of these it may have several specific goals. Thus, it may have
a role in the on-going improvement of the curriculum, and with
respect to this role several types of questions (goals) may be raised,
such as: Is the curriculum at this point really getting across the
distinction between prejudice and commitment?, Is it taking too
large a proportion of the available time to make this point?, etc.
We might call this the *formative* role. The evaluation feedback
loop stays *within* the developmental agency (its consultants), and
serves to improve the product.

In another role, the evaluation process may serve to enable
administrators to decide whether the entire finished curriculum,
refined by use of the evaluation process in its first role, represents
a sufficiently significant advance on the available alternatives to

justify the expense of adoption by a school system. We might call this the *summative* role. The evaluation information here goes *outside* the production agency and serves to improve *utilization or recognition* of the product (producer, etc.). A hybrid case of importance is *monitoring;* the loop goes outside, but from an intermediate stage, and the decision serviced usually concerns *intervention or support.*

One of the reasons for the tolerance or indeed encouragement of the confusion between roles and goals is the well-meaning attempt to allay the anxiety on the part of teachers that the word "evaluation" precipitates. By stressing the constructive part evaluation may play in nonthreatening activities (roles) we slur over the fact that its goals always include the estimation of merit, worth, value, etc., which all too clearly contributes in another role to decisions about promotion and rejection of personnel and courses. But we cannot afford to tackle anxiety about evaluation by ignoring its importance and confusing its presentation; the cost to education is too great. Business firms presumably should not keep executives or factories when they know they are not doing good work, and a society shouldn't have to retain textbooks, courses, teachers, and superintendents that do a poor job when a good performance is possible. The appropriate way to handle anxiety of this kind is by finding tasks for which a better prognosis is possible for the individuals whose positions or prestige are threatened. Failure to evaluate pupils' performance leads to the gross inefficiencies of the age-grouped lecture classroom or the "ungraded" reports on pupils, and failure to evaluate teachers' performances leads to the correlative inefficiency of incompetent instruction and the substitution of personality or politics for performance. A little toughening of the moral fiber may be required if we are not to shirk the social responsibilities of the educational branch of our culture. Thus, it may even be true that "the greatest service evaluation can perform is to identify aspects of the course where revision is desirable" (Cronbach, p. 236), though it is not clear how one would establish this, but it is certainly also true that there are other extremely important evaluation services which must be done for almost any given curriculum project or other educational innovation. And there are many contexts in which calling in an evaluator to perform a final evaluation of the project or person is an act of proper recognition of responsibility to the person, product, or taxpayers. It therefore seems a little excessive to refer to this as simply "a menial role," as Cronbach does. It is obviously a great service if this kind of terminal, overall, or "outcome" evaluation can demonstrate that a very expensive textbook (etc.) is not significantly better than the competition, or that it is enormously better than any competitor. In more general terms it may be possible to demonstrate that a certain type of approach to (for example) mathematics is not yielding significantly better pupil performance on any dimension that mathematicians or vocational users are prepared to regard as important. This would certainly save a great deal of expenditure of time and money and constitute a valuable contribution to educational development, as would the converse, favorable, result. Thus there seems to be a number of qualifications that would have to be made before one could accept a statement asserting the greater importance of formative evaluation by comparison with summative. ("Evaluation, used to improve the course while it is still fluid, contributes more to improvement of education than evaluation used to appraise a product already placed on the market."— Cronbach, p. 236). The most obvious counter-example concerns the entrenched, successful, but highly racist history texts of the late 1950s. The only way to widespread adoption of defensible replacements lay through a thorough, negative, summative evaluation (such as Mark Krug's). But fortunately we do not have to make a choice. Educational projects, particularly curricular ones, clearly must attempt to make best use of evaluation in both these roles.

Any curriculum builder is almost automatically engaged in formative evaluation, except on a very strict interpretation of "evaluation." He is presumably doing what he is doing because he judges that the material being presented in the existing curriculum is unsatisfactory, a preliminary summative evaluation. As he proceeds to construct the new material, he is constantly evaluating his own material as better than that which is already current. Unless entirely ignorant of one's shortcomings as a judge of one's own work, he is also presumably engaged in field-testing the work while it is being developed, and in so doing he gets feedback on the basis of which he again produces revisions; this is of course formative evaluation. If the field-testing is elaborate, it may amount to summative evaluation of *the early forms* of the new curriculum. He is usually involved with colleagues, e.g., the classroom teacher or peers, who comment on the material as they see it — again, this is evaluation, and it produces changes which are allegedly for the better.

If a recommendation for formative evaluation has any content at all, it presumably amounts to the suggestion that a *professional* evaluator should be added to the curriculum construction project. There certainly can be advantages in this, though it is equally clear from practical experience that there can be disadvantages. But this question is clearly not the same as the question whether to have summative evaluation. We devote part of the next section to a discussion of these two questions.

3. Professional Versus Amateur Evaluation

The basic fact is that the evaluator, while a professional in his own field, is usually not a professional in the field relevant to the curriculum being reformed or, if he is, he is not committed to the particular development being undertaken. This leads to clashes and countercharges of a kind which are all too familiar to project directors today.

From these "failures of communication" between evaluators and teachers or curriculum makers there have sprung some unfortunate overreactions. The hard-nosed anti-evaluation line is all too frequently a rationalization of the anxiety provoked by the presence of an external judge who is not identified with or committed to (or perhaps does not even understand) the ideals of the project. The equally indefensible opposite extreme is represented by the self-perceived tough-minded operationalist evaluator, all too likely to say "If you can't tell me what variables you claim to be affecting, in operational terms, we can't construct a test for their variation, and as long as they haven't been tested you haven't any reason for thinking you are making a contribution."

In order to develop a fair treatment of these views let us consider the difference between a contemporary educational project involving the development of a new curriculum or teaching method, and the co-authoring of a new ninth-grade algebra text by two or three teachers in the late 1930s. In the first place, the present projects are often supported from government funds on a very large scale. The justification of this expenditure calls for some kind of objective evidence that the product is valuable. Moreover *future* support for work in this area or by these same workers requires some objective evidence as to their merit at this kind of job. Since there are not sufficient funds to support all applicants, judgments of comparative merit are necessary; and objective bases for this are obviously superior to mere person-endorsements by peers, etc. Finally, the enormous costs involved in the *adoption* of such products by school systems commit another great slice of taxpayers' money, and this kind of commitment should presumably be made only on the basis of rather substantial evidence for its justification. In this context, summative evaluation is an inescapable obligation on the project director, an obvious requirement by the sponsoring agency, and a desideratum as far as the schools are concerned. And since formative evaluation is a necessary part of any rational approach to producing good results on the summative evaluation, it can hardly be wholly eschewed; indeed, as we have shown, its occurrence is to some degree guaranteed by the nature of the case. But the separate question of whether and how professional evaluators should be employed depends very much upon the extent to which they do more harm than good — and there are a number of ways in which they can do harm.

Professional evaluators may simply exude a kind of skeptical spirit that dampens the creative fires of a productive group. They may be sympathetic but impose such crushing demands on operational formulation of goals by the group as to divert too much time to an essentially secondary activity. The major compromise that must be effected is to have the evaluator recognize it as partly *his* responsibility to uncover and formulate a testable set of criteria for the course. He may be substantially helped by the fact that the project has explicitly espoused certain goals, or rejected others, and he will certainly be aided by the writing team's criticism of his formulations. However, the exchange has to be a two-way one; curriculum writers are by no means infallible, and often are extremely prejudiced or grandiose in describing their operations. And they are not skilled at noticing negative (or other) side-effects. Evaluators, on the other hand, besides importing their own prejudices, are handicapped so long as they are less than fully familiar with the subject matter being restructured, and less than fully sympathetic with the aims of the creative group. Yet once they become identified with those aims, emotionally as well as economically, they lose something of great importance to an objective evaluation — their independence. For this reason the formative evaluators should, if at all possible, be sharply distinguished from the summative evaluators, with whom they may certainly work in developing an acceptable summative evaluation design. If this distinction between formative and summative evaluation personnel is made, it becomes possible to retain the advantages of eventual objective professional evaluation without so much risk of disrupting the team spirit during development.

There are other problems about the intrusion of evaluation into education, and the intrusion of an evaluator into the curriculum-making process. Several of these have been admirably expressed by J. Myron Atkin (1963). Some of them are taken up elsewhere in this paper, but some mention of two of them should be made here. The first suggestion is that testing for the extent of learning of certain rather delicate and pervasive concepts (or attitudes, etc.) may be itself destructive, in that it makes the student too self-conscious about the role of a concept at too early a stage, thereby preventing its natural and proper development. The problem is that with respect to some of these concepts, e.g., symmetry, equilibrium, and randomness, it might be the case that very little accretion occurs in the understanding of a child during any particular course or indeed any particular year of his education, but that tiny accretion may be of very great importance in the long-run development of good scientific understanding. It would not show up on tests, indeed it might be stultified by the intrusion of tests, in any given year, but it has to be in the curriculum in order to produce the finished product that we desire. In this case, evaluation seems to be both incompetent and possibly destructive (cf. also attitudes such as the scientific, political, and moral).

Such a possibility should serve as an interesting challenge to the creative curriculum-maker. While not dismissing it, he would normally respond by attempting to treat it more explicitly, perhaps at a somewhat later stage in the curriculum than it is normally first mentioned, and see whether some significant and satisfactory accretion of comprehension cannot be produced by this direct attack. Only if this failed would he turn to the evaluator and demand a considerably more sensitive instrument. Again, it would also be possible to deliberately avoid testing for this during all the early years of its peripheral introduction, and test only in the senior year in high school, for example, or only at a long-term follow-up. We can acknowledge the *possibility* that concerns Atkin and allow some extra material in the curriculum to handle it even without any justification in the early feedback from tests. Errors of excess are much less significant than errors of commission or omission in curriculum-making.

It is well known that there are dangers from having a curriculum-making group discuss its work with teachers of the present curriculum—although there are obviously possible advantages from this—so there are dangers and advantages in bringing the evaluator in early. In such situations, some ingenuity on the part of the project director will often make the best of both worlds possible; for example, the evaluator may be simply introduced to the materials produced, but not to the people producing them, and his comments studied by the director with an eye to feeding back any fundamental and serious criticisms, withholding the others until some later stage in the curriculum development activities where, for example, an extensive process of revision is about to begin. But these are practical considerations; there remain two more fundamental kinds of objection that should be mentioned briefly, of which the first is central to Atkin's misgivings.

No one who has been involved in the field-testing of a new curriculum has failed to notice the enormous variability in its appeal to students, often unpredictable from their previous academic performance. The child already interested in bird-watching may find one approach to biology far more attractive than another. Similarly, for some children the relevance of the material to problems with which they are familiar will make an enormous difference to their interest, whereas for others the properties of those curious entities the hexaflexagons and the Moebius strips are immediately fascinating. More fundamentally, the structuring of the classroom stituation may wholly alter the motivation for different students in different ways; the nondirective style of treatment currently regarded as desirable, partly for its supposed connection with the inductive approach, is totally unstimulating for some children, although an aggressive, competitive, critical interaction will get them up and running. In the face of this kind of variation, we are often committed to the use of the very blunt evaluation instrument of the performance, on tests, of the class as a whole. Even if we break this down into improvements in individual performances, we still have not fully exploited the potentialities of the material, which would be manifested only if we were to select the right material *and* the right instructional technique for a child with a particular background, attitudes, interests, and abilities. Perhaps, the antievaluation skeptic suggests, it is more appropriate to place one's faith in the creative and academically impeccable curriculum-maker, using the field tests simply to make sure that it is *possible* to excite and teach students with the material, under appropriate circumstances. That is, our criterion should be markedly improved performance by *some*, even by a *substantial* number, rather than by the class as a whole. To this the evaluator must reply by asking whether one is to disregard possibilities such as serious lack of comprehensibility to many students at this age-level, a marked relative deterioration of performance in some of the students more than offsetting the gains in others, the possibility that it is the pedagogical skill or enthusiasm of the teacher that is responsible for the success in the field tests and not the materials. The material is to go out to other teachers; it must be determined whether it will be of any use to them. To answer these questions—and indeed for the field tests themselves—a professional job in evaluation is necessary. To suppose that *no* answer is possible is a desperate position indeed, for it denies the possibility of progress by design. Too often, such criticisms of criticism are used as support for stagnation, though logically they just as well support ceaseless and chaotic change.

We can learn something important from this criticism, however. We must certainly weigh seriously the opinions of the subject matter expert (and sometimes the social critic) as to the flavor and quality of the curriculum content. Sometimes it will be almost all we have to go on, and sometimes it will even be enough for some decisions. It should in any event be seriously considered and sometimes heavily weighted in the evaluation process, for the *absence* of supporting professional consensus of this kind is often adequate grounds for complete rejection of the material.

Finally, there is the objection that hovers in the background of many of these discussions, the uneasy feeling that evaluation necessitates making value judgments and that value judgments are essentially subjective and not scientific. This is about as intelligent a view as the view that statements about oneself are essentially subjective and hence incapable of rational substantiation. Some value judgments are simply assertions about fundamental personal preferences ("matters of taste") and as such are factual claims which can be established or refuted by ordinary (though sometimes not easy) procedures of psychological investigation. The process of establishing this kind of claim does not show that it is right or wrong for everyone to hold these values; it only shows that it is true that somebody does or does not hold them. Another kind of value judgment is the assessment of the merit or comparative merit of some entity in a clearly defined context where this amounts to a claim that its performance is as good as or better than another's on clearly identifiable and clearly weighted criterion variables. With respect to value judgments of this kind, it is not only possible to find out whether or not they are believed by the individuals who assert them, but it is also possible to determine whether it is right or wrong for anyone to believe them. They are simply complex conflations of various performance ratings and the weightings of the various performances; it is in this sense that we can correctly assert that the Palek Quartz is the best wrist chronometer currently available or that a particular desk dictionary is the best one for somebody with extensive scientific interests. Finally, there are value judgments in which the criteria themselves are debatable, a type of value judgment whose debatability merely reflects the fact that important issues are not always easy ones. Examples of this would be the assertion that the most important role of evaluation is in the process of curriculum writing, or that the IQ test is an unfortunate archaism, or that the Copenhagen interpretation of quantum physics is superior to any known alternative. In each of these cases, the disputes turn out to be mainly disputes about what should count as good, rather than to be arguments about the straightforward "facts of the situation." It is immature to react to this kind of judgment as if it is contaminated with some disgusting disease; the only proper reaction is to examine the reasons that are put forward for one and see if and how the matter may be rationally discussed. The history of the greatest developments in science is the history of the rational triumph of such value judgments, of new conceptions of "good explanation," "good theory," "good model" ("paradigm"), not just of one theory over another in a contest where the rules are agreed, nor just (*pace* Kuhn) of one prejudice over another.

It is sometimes thought that in dealing with people, as we must in the field of education, we are necessarily involved in the field of *moral* value judgments, and that at least *these* really are essentially subjective. But in the first place value judgments about people are by no means necessarily moral, since they may refer to their health, intelligence, and achievements; secondly, even if they are moral, we are all presumably committed to one moral principle (the principle of the equality of the rights of men) and by far the greater part of public moral discourse depends only on the framework built on this assumption with complicated empirical judgments about the consequences of alternatives.[5] So, unless one is willing to challenge this axiom, and the arguments for it, and to provide rational support for an alternative, even moral value judgments are within the realm of rational debate. But whatever the outcome of such a discussion, the facts that some evaluation is moral evaluation and that some moral evaluation is controversial do not conjointly imply any support for the conclusion that curricular evaluation is less than a fully appropriate task for applied science, unless engineering and medicine are to resign from that category.

4. Evaluation Studies Versus Process Studies

In the course of clarifying the concept of evaluation it is important not to simplify it. Although the *typical* goals of evaluation require judgments of merit and worth, when somebody is asked to evaluate *a situation*, or *the impact* of certain kinds of materials on the market, then what is being called for is an analytical description of the process, usually with respect to certain possible causal connections, indeed an *interpretation* (see Section 13 below). In this sense it is not inappropriate to regard some

---

5. Discussed in more detail in Scriven (1966).

kinds of process investigation as evaluation. But the range of process research only overlaps with and is neither subsumed by nor equivalent to that of evaluation. We may conveniently distinguish three types of process research, as the term is used by Cronbach and others.

1. The noninferential study of what actually goes on in the classroom. Perhaps this has the most direct claim to being called a study of the process of teaching (learning, etc.). We might for example be interested in the proportion of the class period during which the teacher talks, the amount of time that the students spend in homework for a class, the proportion of the dialogue devoted to explaining, defining, opining, etc. (Meux and Smith, 1961). The great problem about work like this is to show that it is worth doing, in *any* sense. *Some* pure research is idle research, some is not. The Meux and Smith work mentioned is clearly original and offers promise in a large number of directions. Skinner's attack on controlled studies and his emphasis on process research are more than offset by his social-welfare orientation which ensures that the process work is aimed at valuable improvements in control of learning. It is difficult to avoid the conclusion, however, that most process research of this kind in education, as in psychotherapy (though apparently not in medicine), is fruitful at neither the theoretical nor the applied level.

2. The second kind of process research involves the investigation of causal claims ("dynamic hypotheses") about the process. Here we are interested in such questions as whether an increase of time spent on class discussions of the goals of a curriculum, at the expense of time spent on training drills, leads to improved comprehension in (a) algebra, (b) geography, etc. This kind of investigation is essentially a miniature "new instrument" project. Another sub-species looks for the answer to such questions as: Is the formation of subgroup allegiance and identification with the teacher facilitated by strong emphasis on pupil-teacher dialogue? The feature of this subset of process hypotheses that distinguishes them from evaluation hypotheses is that the dependent variables either are ones which would not figure among the set of criteria we would use in a summative evaluation study (though we might think of them as important because of their relevance to improved teaching techniques) or they are only a subgroup of such summative criteria; and in either case no attempt is made to justify any correlative assignments of merit.

Process hypotheses of this second kind are in general about as difficult to substantiate as any "outcome" hypothesis, i.e., summative evaluation. Indeed they are sometimes harder to substantiate because they may require identifying the effects of only one of several independent variables that are present, and it is extremely hard—though usually not impossible—to apply ordinary matching techniques to take care of the others. The advantage of some summative evaluation investigation is that it is concerned with evaluating the effects of a whole teacher-curriculum package and has no need to identify the specific agent responsible for the overall improvement or deterioration. That advantage lapses when we are concerned to identify the variance due to the curriculum as opposed to the teacher.

3. Formative Evaluation. This kind of research is often called process research, but it is of course simply outcome evaluation of an intermediate stage in the development of the teaching instrument. The distinction between this and the first kind of dynamic hypothesis mentioned above is twofold. There is a distinction of role; the role of formative evaluation is to discover deficiencies and successes in the intermediate versions of a new curriculum; the role of dynamic hypothesis investigation is *sui generis:* it is to provide the answer to a question about the mechanism of teaching. And there is a distinction in the extent to which it matters whether the criteria used are an adequate analysis of the proper goals of a curriculum. The dynamic hypothesis study has no obligation to this; the formative evaluation does. But the two types of study are not always sharply distinct. They both play an important role in good curriculum research.

Now of course it is true that anybody who does an experiment of any kind at all should at some stage evaluate *his results.* It is even true that the experiment itself will usually be designed in such a way as to incorporate procedures for evaluation of the results—e.g., by using an "objectively validated" test, which has a certain kind of built-in comparative evaluation in the scoring key. None of this shows that most research is evaluation research. In particular, even process research is not all evaluation research. That interpretation of data can be described as evaluation of results does not show that the interpretations (and the explanations) are about the *merit* of a teaching instrument. They may, for example, be about the temporal duration of various elements of the instrument, etc. Such points are obvious enough, but a good deal of the comment pro and con evaluation research betokens considerable lack of clarity about its boundaries. The "value of a variable" is not its merit but its magnitude. "Evaluation" is just as ambiguous; but in the sense of paramount concern to education, it is clear enough.

5. Evaluation Versus
Estimation of Goal Achievement

One of the reactions to the threat of evaluation, or perhaps to the use of over-crude evaluative procedures, was the extreme relativization of evaluation research. The slogan became: How well does the course achieve its goals? instead of: How good is the course? But it is obvious that if the goals aren't worth achieving then it is uninteresting how well they are achieved. The success of this kind of relativism in the evaluation field rests entirely upon the question whether goals are open to rational criticism. An American History curriculum, K-14, which consisted of the memorization of names and dates would surely be absurd—it could not possibly be said to be a good curriculum, no matter how well it attained its goals. Nor could one which led to absolutely no recall of names or chronology. A "Modern Math" curriculum for general use which produced high school graduates largely incapable of reliable addition and multiplication would be (and possibly is) simply a disgrace, no matter what else it conveyed. This kind of value judgment about goals is not beyond debate in principle, but *good* arguments to the contrary have not been forthcoming so far. These are value judgments with excellent backing; namely, every plausible account of the nature and justification of education. Nor is their defensibility due to their lack of specificity. Much more precise ones can be given just as excellent backing; a physics curriculum which does not discuss the kinetic theory at any stage would be deficient, no matter how well it achieved whatever goals it espoused. And so on.

Thus evaluation proper must include, as an equal partner with the measuring of performance against intended goals, procedures for the evaluation of the goals. That is, if it is to have any reference to such goals at all. In the next two sections we will discuss procedures of evaluation that involve reference to intended goals, and procedures which attempt to short-circuit such reference. First it should be pointed out that it is one thing to maintain that judgment of goals is part of evaluation, i.e., that we cannot just accept anyone's goals, and quite another to maintain that these goals should be the same for every school, for every school district, for every teacher, for every level, etc. It is entirely appropriate that a school with primarily vocational responsibilities should have somewhat different goals from those of a school producing 95 per cent college-bound graduates. It just does not follow from this that the people who give the course or run the school or design the curriculum can be regarded as in any way immune from criticism in setting up their goals. A great deal of the energy behind the current attempts to reform the school curriculum springs straight out of the belief that the goals have been fundamentally wrong, e.g., that life-adjustment has been grossly overweighted. To swing in the opposite direction is all too easy, and in no way preferable.

The process of relativization, however, has not only led to over-tolerance for over-restrictive goals, but has also led to incompetent evaluation of the extent to which these are achieved. Whatever one's views about evaluation, it is easy enough to demonstrate that there are not enough professionally competent evaluators in the country today. The very idea that every school system, or every teacher, can today be regarded as capable of meaningful evaluation of his own performance is as absurd as the view that every psychotherapist today is capable of evaluating his work with his own patients. Certainly they can learn something very important from carefully studying their own work; indeed they can identify some good and bad features about it. But if they or someone else needs to know the answers to the important questions, whether process or outcome, they need skills and resources which are conspicuous by their rarity even at the national level.

6. Intrinsic Evaluation
Versus Pay-Off Evaluation

Two basically different approaches to the evaluation of a teaching instrument appear possible, and are sometimes contrasted in the literature. If you want to evaluate a tool, say an axe, you might study the design of the bit, the weight distribution, the steel alloy used, the grade of hickory in the handle, etc., or you might just study the kind and speed of the cuts it makes in the hands of a good axeman. In either case, the evaluation may be either summative or formative, for these are roles of evaluation, not procedures for doing evaluation. And in either case, the criteria may be, or may not be, operationally or behaviorally specified.

The first approach involves an appraisal of the instrument itself; in the analog this would involve evaluation of the content, goals, grading procedures, teacher attitude, etc. We shall call this kind of approach secondary evaluation, or *intrinsic* evaluation. The criteria are usually not operationally formulated, and they refer directly to the instrument itself but only indirectly to its educational effectiveness or results. The other approach proceeds via an examination of the effects of the teaching instrument on the pupil, and these alone, and it more usually specifies these rather operationally. (Effects on teachers, parents, etc. may also be relevant.) It may involve an appraisal of the differences between pre- and post-tests, between experimental group tests and control group tests, etc., on a number of criterial parameters. We can call this pay-off evaluation. Defenders of the second procedure would support their approach by arguing that all that really counts are the effects of the course on the pupils, appeal to the features of goals, method, and content being defensible only insofar as evaluations of these really correlate with pay-off evaluations. Since these correlations are largely *a priori* in our present state of knowledge, they argue, the intrinsic approach is too much an armchair affair. The intrinsic evaluator is likely to counter by talking about important values that do not show up in the outcome study to which the pay-off man restricts himself, due to the deficiencies of present test instruments and scoring procedures and the time required for follow-ups: he is likely to exemplify this claim by reference to qualities of a curriculum such as elegance, modernity, structure, integrity, readiness considerations, etc., which can best be judged by looking at the materials directly. (Or he may mention process barometers like amount of student participation, happy atmosphere, inquiry approach, etc.)

It was maintained in the preceding section that evaluation in terms of goal achievement is typically a very poor substitute for good summative evaluation, since it merely relativizes the problem. If we are going to evaluate in a way that brings in goals at all, then we shall typically have some obligation to evaluate the goals. The trouble with intrinsic evaluation is the same; it brings in secondary criteria, and hence automatically raises the question of the value of these criteria, presumably by reference to the pay-off or primary criteria. One of the charms of the pay-off type of evaluation is this duplex character of a thorough intrinsic evaluation.

The possibility obviously emerges that an evaluation involving some weighting of intrinsic criteria and some of pay-off criteria might be a worthwhile compromise. There are many kinds of evaluation situations where this will be so, and before any assessment of the correct relative weighting we shall look a little further into practical procedures.

7. Practical Suggestions for Hybrid Evaluations

Any curriculum project has some kind of general objectives at the very beginning. Even if these are only put in terms of producing a more interesting or more up-to-date treatment, there must be some kind of grounds for dissatisfaction with the present curriculum if the project is to be a worthwhile activity. Usually something rather more specific emerges in the course of planning discussions. For example, the idea of a three-track approach, aimed at various kinds of teacher or student interest, may emerge out of a rather explicit discussion of the aims (i.e., primary criteria) of a project, when it becomes clear that three equally defensible aims can be formulated which will lead to incompatible requirements for the curriculum. Or, we may decide that the same aim—in a very general sense—can be served in three equally defensible ways. These "ways" often then become secondary criteria for the curriculum. The mere fact that these aims (or these means) can be seen as incompatible makes clear that they must have fairly substantial content.

Another typical secondary criterion refers to coverage; it is recognized from the beginning that at least certain topics should be covered, or if they are not then there must be some compensatory coverage of other topics. Typically, a project involves several of these abstractly formulated criteria, both for primary and secondary qualities (i.e., goals for student achievement and intrinsic qualities of the instrument). The natural approach to evaluation in such a case would be what we can call hybrid evaluation—checking on success with respect to both kinds of criteria.

At this early stage of discussing the curriculum a member or members of the project team should be appointed to the task of goal-formulation. Many of the objections to this kind of activity stem from reactions to over-rigid requirements on the way in which goals can be formulated at this stage. Any kind of goal on which the group agrees, however abstractly or specifically formulated, even goals which it thinks should just be considered as a possibility in the developing stage, should be listed at this point. None of them should be regarded as absolute commitments in any way—simply as reminders. It is not possible to overlook the unfortunate examples of projects in which the creative urge has outdistanced reality restraints; it has to be faced from the beginning that too gross a divergence from a certain minimum coverage is going to make the problem of adoption insuperable. If adoption is a goal, it should be listed along with the motivational and cognitive ones. Having market-type goals such as substantial adoption on the list is in no way inappropriate: one can hardly reform education with curricula that never reach the classroom. But one may think it desirable at an early stage (if it is possible) to translate such goals into constraints on content, e.g., on coverage, vocabulary, and attitudes towards society's sacred cows, etc. Or one may handle adoption by a separate plan for dissemination.

As the project develops, three types of activities centering around the formulation of goals should be distinguished and encouraged. In the first place the goals as so far formulated should be regularly reexamined and modified in the light of divergences from them that have arisen during the developmental activities, where it is felt that these changes have led to other, more valuable goals. Even if no modification seems appropriate, the reexamination serves the useful purpose of reminding the writers of the overall goals of the project.

Secondly, work should be begun on the construction of a test-question pool. Progress tests will be given, and the items in these can be thrown into this pool. The construction of this pool (plus the scoring key for it) is the construction of the operational version of the goals. It should therefore be scrutinized at the same time as reexamination of the more abstractly formulated goals occurs. Even though the project is only at the stage of finishing the first unit of a projected ten-unit curriculum, it is entirely appropriate to be formulating questions of the kind that it is proposed to include in the final examination on the final unit or, for that matter, in a follow-up quiz a year later. It is a commonplace that in the light of formulating such questions, the conception of the goals of the course will be altered. It is undesirable to devote a large proportion of the time to this activity, but it is typically not "undue influence" to encourage thinking about course goals in terms of "What kind of question would tap this learning achievement or motivation change in the final examination or in a follow-up test?" At times the answer to this will rightly be "None at all!" because not all values in a course manifest themselves in the final or later examinations. But where they do *not* thereby manifest themselves, some indication should be given of the time and manner in which they might be expected to be detectable: as in career choices, adult attitudes, classroom behavior, teaching learning, etc.

The third activity that should commence at an intermediate stage in curriculum development is that of getting some external judgments as to the cohesiveness of the alleged goals, the actual content, and the test question pool. Without this, the validity of the tests and/or the utility of the curriculum will suffer, possibly fatally. There is no need at all for the individual judge at this task to be a professional evaluator; indeed professional evaluators are all too frequently not good at this. A good logician, an historian of science, a professional in the subject-matter field, an educational psychologist, or a curriculum expert are possible resource categories. The necessary skill, a very striking one when located, is not co-extensive with any standard professional requirement; we might call it "consistency analysis," or "congruence perception." This is an area where appointments should not be made without trial periods. It is worth considering whether the activities of this individual, at least in a trial period, may be best conducted without face-to-face confrontation with the project team. A brief written report may be adequate to indicate the extent of possible useful information from this source at this stage. But at some stage, and the earlier the better, this kind of activity is essential if gross divergences between (a) espoused, (b) implicit, and (c) tested-for goals are to be avoided. Not only can a good consistency analyst prevent sidetracking of the project by runaway creative fervor, misconceptions of its actual achievement, etc., but he can provide a valuable stimulus to new lines of development. He must be alert for deficiencies in the item-pool as well as irrelevancies. Ultimately, the justification of psychotherapy does not lie in the fact that the therapist *felt* he was doing the patient some good, but in the fact that he was; and the same applies to curricular research.

At about this point, a more sophisticated though similar skill needs to be brought to bear, namely the identification of mismatch between the course materials/goals/tests and an *ideal* set for such a course. Presumably the producers believe these sets to be congruent, so mismatch detection requires an external evaluator. If skilled and knowledgeable, he will anticipate side-effects and detect omissions that are serious for the funding source or eventual user. The proof that he is not just bringing his prejudices to bear will be his reasons—and there is a long history of these being entirely persuasive to the *producers* (who are not the only judges of such reasons).

If the above procedure is followed throughout the development of a curriculum, we will end up with an oversize test pool of which one should be prepared to say that any significant desired outcome of the course will show up on these tests, administered at the appropriate time, and that what does show up will (normally) only come from the course. Possession of this pool has various important advantages. In the first and second place, as an operational encapsulation of the goals of the course (if the various cross-checks on its construction have been adequate) it can be used (i) to give the students an idea of what is expected of them, (ii) to provide a pool from which the final examinations can be constructed. In the third place it can be used by the curriculum-developer to get an extremely detailed picture of his own success (and the success of the cross-checks on pool construction) by administering a different random sample of questions from this pool to each student in a formative evaluation study, instead of administering a given random sample to every student as justice perhaps requires in a final examination (see Cronbach, p. 242).

What has been described is the bare bones of an adequate mediated evaluation. We have made some reference to content characteristics as one of the types of goal, because curriculum groups frequently argue that one of the merits of their output is its superiority as a representation of contemporary advanced thinking about the subject. The natural way to test this is to have the course read through by some highly qualified experts in the field. It is obvious that special difficulties arise over this procedure. For the most that we can learn from it is that the course does not contain any gross distortions of the best contemporary views, or gross deficiencies with respect to them. There remains the question, as the pay-off evaluator would be the first to point out, of the extent to which the material is being communicated. Even a course with gross oversimplifications, professionally repugnant though it may be to the academic expert, may be getting across a better idea of the truth about its subject than a highbrow competitor. The real advantage of the preceding methodology is to provide a means for jumping the gap between intrinsic and pay-off evaluation, between mere measures of goal-achievement and complete evaluation.

A number of further refinements on the above outline are extremely desirable, and necessary in any serious study. They center around the role of the consistency analysis, and they are crucial for formative evaluation studies, rather than summative, since they help diagnose the cause of poor results. Ideals apart, we need to know about the success of three connected matching problems; first, the match between goals and course content; second, the match between goals and examination content; third, the match between course content and examination content. Technically we only need to determine two of these in order to be able to evaluate the third; but in fact there are great advantages in attempting to get an estimate of each independently, in order to reduce the error range. We have talked as if one person or group might make each of these matching estimates. It is clearly most desirable that they should all be done independently, and in fact duplicated by independent workers. Only in this way are we likely to be able to track down the real source of disappointing results.

Even the P.S.S.C. study, which has been as well tested as most recent curriculum projects, has nowhere approached the desirable level of analysis indicated here. And if we bring in the necessary step of judging the goals, too, (e.g., by matching with an ideal), the process of evaluation will cost all that the ten percent rule-of-thumb suggests. If one doubts that it is a bargain at the price, one has only to look at the wasted millions spent on projects whose materials are, and always were, destined for disuse. Dedication is no substitute for direction. And direction in the development process depends entirely on formative evaluation.

In general, of course, the most difficult problem in tests and measurement theory is the problem of construct validity, and the present problem is essentially an exercise in construct validity. The problem can be ignored only by someone who is prepared to accept immediately the consequences that their supposed goals cannot be regarded as met by the course, or that their examinations do not test what the course teaches, or that the examinations do not test the values/materials that are supposed to be imparted by the course. There are, in practice, many ways in which one can implement the need for the comparisons here described; the use of Q-sorts and R-sorts, matching and projective tests for the analysis, etc. In one way or another the job has to be done, if we are going to do a mediated evaluation at all, i.e., if we are going to bring in goals described in any way except by simply giving the answers to be expected on the final examination, follow-ups, etc.

8. The Possibility
of Pure Pay-Off Evaluation

The pay-off evaluator watches the developing intricacies of the above kind of experimental design with scorn, for he believes that the whole idea of bringing in content-assessment or any other secondary indicator is not only an irrelevant but also an extremely unreliable procedure for doing the job of course evaluation. In his view it isn't very important to examine what a teacher says he is doing, or what the students say he is doing (or say they are learning), or even what the teacher says in class and the students read in the texts; the only important datum is what the student says (does, believes, etc.) at the end of the course that he wouldn't have said at the beginning (or, to be more precise, would not have said at the end if he had not taken this course). In short, says the hard-headed one, let's just see what the course does, and let's not bother with the question of whether it had good intentions.

But the would-be operationalist has difficulties of his own. He cannot avoid the construct validity issue entirely, that is, he cannot avoid the enormous difficulties involved in correctly describing *at a useful level of generality* what the student has learned. It is easy enough to give the exact results of the testing in terms of the percentage of the students who gave certain answers to each specific question; but what we need to know is whether we can say, in the light of their answers, that they have a *better understanding* of the *elements of astronomy* (or the chemical-bond approach to chemistry, or the ecological approach to biology). And it is a long way from data about answers to specific questions, to that kind of conclusion. It is not necessary for the route to lie through a discussion of goals—the operationalist is quite right about this. But *if* it does not lie through a discussion of goals, then we shall not have available the data that we need to distinguish between importantly different explanations of success or failure. For example, if we attempt a pure pay-off approach to evaluating a curriculum, and discover that the material retained and/or regurgitated by the student is regarded as grossly inadequate by the subject-matter specialists, we have no idea whether this is due to an inadequacy in the intentions of the curriculum-makers, or to imperfections in their curriculum with respect to these goals, or to deficiencies in their examinations with respect to either of the preceding.

To illustrate again. Suppose that we try a pure pay-off approach and have the students' performance at the end of the course, and only this, rated by an external judge. Who do we pick for a judge? What do we ask the judge to tell us? The answer to that question appears to depend on our interest in goals which we might as well acknowledge explicitly. The evaluator will have to relate the students' performance to *some* abstract criterion, whether it is his conception of an adequate *professional* comprehension of the *whole* subject, or what he thinks it is reasonable to expect a tenth-grader to understand, or what somebody should understand who will not continue to college, etc. The operationalist is right in saying that we can dispense with any discussion of goals and still discover exactly what students have learned, and right to believe that the latter is the most important variable; but he is mistaken if he supposes that we can in general give the kind of description of what is learned that is valuable for our purposes, or give a justification for the curriculum without any reference to goals. So the purity of pay-off evaluation is somewhat superficial. At this stage of the debate between the supporter of pure pay-off and that of mediated evaluation, the latter would seem to be having the best of it.

But the issue is not so one-sided; the pay-off evaluator is performing an invaluable service in reminding us of the potential irresponsibility of producing "elegant," "up-to-date," "rigorous," "progressive" curricula if these qualities are not coming through to the students. We can take them on faith insofar as they are recognized as being the frosting on the cake, but we can't take the food-value of the cake on faith. The only real alternative to which the pay-off position leads is the use of an academic evaluator who is asked to look, not at the curriculum materials nor the test-item pool, but at the exact performance of the class on each question, and from this directly assess the adequacy of the course to the subject, for that age-level, aspiration, and background, as he sees it. Of course, we still suffer with respect to diagnosing the cause of deficiencies and hence this is poor formative methodology; but we can simplify summative evaluation by this device.

Thus the need to include in our comprehensive design a thorough analysis of the *results* of the students' tests, and not only of the course and examination content. It is not usually adequate to go to great trouble setting up and cross-analyzing the goals, tests, and content of a curriculum and then attempt to use a mere percentage-of-possible-maximum-points figure as the indication of goal achievement (unless the figure happens to be pretty close to 100 per cent or zero per cent). The performance of the students on the final tests, as upon the tests at intermediate stages, must be analyzed in order to determine the exact locations of short-comings of comprehension, shortages of essential facts, lack of practice in basic skills, etc. Percentages are not very important. It is the *nature* of the mistakes that is important in evaluating the curriculum, and in rewriting it. For both formative and summative purposes we need perspicuous descriptions of any clusters of errors or strengths. The technique of the large test pool provides us with an extremely refined instrument for locating deficiencies in the curriculum. But this device can only be exploited fully if evaluation of the results is itself handled in a refined way, with the same use of independent judges, hypothesis formation and testing about the nature of the mistakes, longitudinal analysis of same-student variations, etc. It should be clear that the task of proper evaluation of curriculum materials is an enormous one. The use of essay type questions, the development and use of novel tests, the use of reports by laboratory-work supervisors, the colligation of all this material into specially developed rating schemata, all of this is expensive and time-consuming. It is not more time-consuming than good R & D work in engineering, however. In a later section some comment will be made on the consequences of this conception of the scale of evaluation activities. At this point, however, it becomes necessary to look into a further and final divergence of approaches.

9. Comparative Versus Noncomparative Evaluation

The result of attempts to evaluate recent new curricula has been remarkably uniform; comparing students taking the old curriculum with students taking the new one, it usually appears that students using the new curriculum do rather better on the examinations designed for that curriculum and rather worse on those designed for the old curriculum, while students using the old curriculum perform in the opposite way. Certainly, there is a remarkable absence of striking improvements on the same criteria (with some exceptions). Initially, one's tendency is to feel that the mountain has labored and brought forth a mouse — and that it is a positive mouse and not a negative one entirely depends upon the evaluation of the criteria, i.e., (mainly) the tests used. A legitimate reaction is to look very seriously into the question of whether one should not weight the judged merit of content and goals by subject-matter experts a great deal more heavily than small differences in level of performance on unassessed criteria. If we do this, then relatively minor improvements in performance, on the right goals, become very valuable, and in these terms the new curriculum looks considerably better. Whether this alteration of weights can really be justified is a matter that needs very serious investigation; it requires a rather careful analysis of the real importance to the understanding and use of contemporary physics, as it is seen by, e.g., physicists, of the elements missing from the old curriculum. It is all too tempting to feel that the reweighting must be correct because one is so thoroughly convinced that the new course is better.

Another legitimate reaction is to wonder whether the examinations are really doing a good job testing the depth of understanding of the people trained on the new curriculum. Here the use of the oversize question pool becomes extremely important. Cronbach speaks of a 700-item pool (without flinching!) and this is surely the order of magnitude that makes sense in terms of a serious evaluation of a one- or two-year curriculum. Again, it is going to be tempting to put items into the pool that reflect mere differences of terminology in the new course, for example. Of course if the pool consists mainly of questions of that kind, the new-curriculum students will do much better. But their superiority will be almost entirely illusory. Cronbach warns us against this risk of course-dependent terminology, although he goes too far in segregating understanding from terminology (this point is taken up below). So here, too, we must be certain to use external evaluators in the construction or assessment of the question pool.

Illegitimate reactions run from the charming suggestion that such results simply demonstrate the weaknesses of evaluation techniques, to a more interesting suggestion implicit in Cronbach's paper. He says:

> Since group comparisons give equivocal results, I believe that a formal study should be designed primarily to determine the post-course performance of a well-described group, with respect to many important objectives and side-effects (Cronbach, p. 238).

Cronbach is apparently about to suggest a way in which we can avoid comparison, not with goals or objectives, but with another group, supposedly matched on relevant variables. What is this noncomparative alternative procedure for evaluation? He continues:

> Ours is a problem like that of the engineer examining a new automobile. He can set himself the task of defining its performance characteristics and its dependability. It would be merely distracting to put his question in the form: 'Is this car better or worse than the competing brand?' (Cronbach, p. 238).

It is perfectly true that the automobile engineer *might* only just be interested in the question of the performance and dependability of the new automobile. But no automobile engineer ever has had this pure interest, and no automobile engineer ever will have it. Objectives do not become "important" except in a context of practical choice. Unrealistic objectives, for example, are not important. The very measures of the performance and dependability of an automobile and our interest in them spring *entirely* from knowledge of what has and has not so far proved possible, or possible within a certain price-class, or possible with certain interior space, or with a certain overall weight, etc. The use of calibrated instruments is not an alternative to, but only an indirect way of, doing comparative studies. What we measure is indeed an absolute property; but why we measure it is because we have found it to be a critical comparative variable, or part of a set that provides a basis for comparison. If we are certain that every car has property P, then we skip measuring it, however important it is. But usually P is a variable with merit attached to greater or less values (mpg or seconds to sixty) and we measure it because it *will* provide a basis for comparison.

The same applies in the field of curriculum development. We already have curricula aimed at almost every subject known to man, and there isn't any real interest in producing curricula for curricula's sake; to the extent that there is, there isn't any interest in evaluating them. We are interested in curricula because they may prove to be better than what we now have, in some important way. We may assign someone the task of rating a curriculum on certain variables, without asking them simultaneously to look up the performance of other curricula on these variables. But when we come to *evaluate* the curriculum, as opposed to merely describing its performance, then we inevitably confront the question of its superiority or inferiority to the competition. To say it's a "valuable contribution," a "desirable" or "useful" course, even to assay—in the usual context—that it's very good, is to imply relative merit. Indeed the very scales we use to measure its performance are often percentile scales or others with a built-in comparison. And the moment *cost* is considered, we can and should compare.

There are even important reasons for putting the question in its comparative form immediately. Comparative evaluations are often very much easier than noncomparative evaluations, because we can often use tests which yield differences instead of having to use an absolute scale and then eventually compare the absolute scores. If we are discussing chess-teaching courses, for example, we might match two groups for background variables, and then let them play each other off in a round-robin tournament. Attempting to devise a measure of skill of an absolute kind would be a nightmare, but we might easily get consistent and significant differences from this kind of comparative evaluation. Cronbach is not making the "pure pay-off" mistake of thinking that one can avoid all reference to general objectives; but he is proposing an approach which underestimates the implicit comparative element in any field of social engineering including automobile assessment and curriculum evaluation, just as the pay-off approach underestimates the implicit appeal to abstract criteria.

Cronbach continues in this paragraph with a line of thought about which there can be no disagreement at all; he points out that in any cases of comparisons between importantly different teaching instruments, no real understanding of the reason for a difference in performance is gained from the discovery that one of them *is* notably superior to the other: "No one knows which of the ingredients is responsible for the advantages." But understanding is not our *only* goal in evaluation. We are also interested in questions of support, encouragement, adoption, reward, refinement, etc. And these extremely important questions can be given a useful, though in some cases not a complete, answer by the mere discovery of superiority. It will be recalled that in an earlier section we argued that the pure pay-off position suffers by comparison with the supporter of mediated evaluation (i.e., evaluation that brings in reference to goals) in that his results will not include the data we need in order to locate sources of difficulty, etc. Here Cronbach is arguing that his noncomparative approach will be more likely to give us the data we need for future improvement. But this is not in any way an advantage of the noncomparative method as such. It is simply an advantage of methods in which more variables are examined in more detail. If we want to pin down the exact reasons for differences between programs, it is quite true that "small-scale, well-controlled studies can profitably be used to compare alternative versions of the same course" whereas the large-scale overall comparison will not be so valuable. But that in no way eliminates the need for comparative studies at some point in our evaluation procedures. In short, his argument is simply that in order to get *explanations,* one needs more control groups, and possibly more short-run studies, than one needs for summative *evaluation.* This is incontestible; but it does not show that for the purposes of overall evaluation we can or should avoid overall comparison.

One might put the point in terms of the following analogy: in the history of automobile engine design there have been a number of occasions when a designer has turned out an engine that was quite inexplicably superior to the competition — the Kettering GM V8, the Coventry Climax and the Weslake Ford conversions are well-known examples. Perhaps thirty variables are significantly changed in the design of any new engine and for a long time after these had been in production nobody, including the designer, knew which of them had been mainly responsible for the improvement. But the decision to go into production, the decision to put the further research into the engine that led to finding out what made it great, indeed the beginning of a new era in engine design, required *only the comparative evaluation.* You set a great team to work and you hope they are going to strike gold; but then you assay the ore before you start the big capital expenditure involved in finding out the configuration of the lode and in mining it. This is the way we have to work in any field where there are too many variables and too little time.

10. Practical Procedures for Control-Group Evaluation

It is a major theme of Cronbach's that control group comparisons in the curriculum game are not really very suitable. We have just seen how his attempt to provide a positive alternative does not develop into a realistic answer in the context of typical evaluation enquiries. It is therefore appropriate for us to attempt to meet some of the objections that he raises to the control group methods since we are recommending that this be regarded as the method of choice.

The suggestion that gross comparisons yield only small differences must first be met, as indicated above (and as Cronbach recommends elsewhere), by increasing the power of the microscope — that is, by increasing the type and number of items that are being tested, increasing the size of the group in order to get more reliability into differences that do appear, and developing new and more appropriate tests where the present ones seem to be the weakness. And where we pin down a beneficial factor, we then attempt to rewrite with more emphasis on it, to magnify the gain. But once all this has been said, the fact remains that we shall often have to proceed in terms of rather small differences; that producing large differences will usually require a multiple-push approach, one that attacks not only the curriculum but the student-grouping procedures, the teacher presentation, the classroom time allocation, seeking above all to develop the global long-term effects that improvements in every subject in the school curriculum will eventually produce for us — a general increase in the level of interest and preparedness. This is not too depressing a prospect, and it is exactly paralleled in that other field in which we attempt to change human behavior by altering the subjects' environment for a few hours a week over a period of one or several years — the field of psychotherapy. We are perhaps too used to the discovery of miracle drugs or technolological breakthroughs in the aerospace field to recognize the atypicality of such (apparently) "instant progress." Even in the automobile engineering field, to stay with Cronbach's example, it is a well-known theorem that developing a good established design yields better results than introducing a promising but radically new design in about five times as many cases as engineers under forty are willing to believe. What one may reasonably expect as the reward for work is *not* great leaps and bounds, but slow and steady improvement. And of course we shall sometimes go down dead ends. Cronbach says that "formally designed experiments pitting one course against another are rarely definitive enough to justify their cost" but he does not allow sufficiently for the fact that the lack of definite results is often just the kind of knowledge that we need. If we have really satisfied ourselves that we are using good tests of the main criterion variable (and we surely can manage that, with care) then to discover parity of performance *is* to have discovered something extremely informative. "No difference" is not "no knowledge." And the vast expense of new curricular adoptions, which is saved by a null result, surely far offsets the cost of the study.

Of course, we cannot conclude from a null result that all the techniques involved in a new curriculum are worthless improvements. We must go on to make the micro-studies that will enable us to see whether any one of them is worthwhile. But we have discovered something very significant. Doing the gross comparative study is going to cost the same whatever kind of results we get, and we have to do it sooner or later. Of course it is absurd to stop after discovering an insignificant difference; we must continue in the direction of further analytical research, of the kind Cronbach enthusiastically recommends. The impact of his article is to suggest the unimportance of the control group study, whereas the case can only be made for its inadequacy as a *total* approach to *the whole* of curriculum research.[6] We shall here try to provide some practical suggestions for experimental designs that will yield more than a gross comparative evaluation.

A significant part of the reason for Cronbach's despair over comparative studies lies in his belief that we are unable to arrange for double-blind conditions. "In an educational experiment it is difficult to keep people unaware that they are an experimental group. And it is quite impossible to neutralize the biases of the teacher as those of the doctor are neutralized in the double-blind design. It is thus never certain whether any observed advantage is attributable to the educational innovation as such, or to the greater energy that teachers and students put forth when a method is fresh and 'experimental.' " (p. 237). But Cronbach despairs too quickly. The analogy in the medical field is not with drug studies, where we are fortunate enough to be able to achieve double-blind conditions, but with psychotherapy studies where the therapist is obviously endowed with enthusiasm for his treatment, and the patient cannot be kept in ignorance of whether he is getting some kind of treatment. If Cronbach's reasoning is correct, it would not be possible to design an adequate psychotherapy outcome study. But it *is* possible to design such a study, and the way to do it — as far as this point goes[7] — is to use more than one comparison group. If we use only one control group, we cannot tell whether it's the enthusiasm or the experimental technique that explains a difference. But if we use several experimental groups, we can estimate the size of the enthusiasm effect. We made comparisons

---

6. Yet he does agree with the necessity for making the practical decisions, e.g., between textbooks (p. 232), for which nothing less than a valid comparative study is adequate.

7. Other difficulties are discussed in more detail in Hook (1959).

between a number of therapy groups, in each of which the therapist is enthusiastic, but in each of which the method of therapy is radically different. As far as possible, one should employ forms of therapy in which directly incompatible procedures are adopted, and as far as possible match the patients allocated to each type (close matching is not important). There are a number of therapies on the market which meet the first condition in several dimensions, and it is easy enough to develop pseudo-therapies which would be promising enough to be enthusiasm-generating for some practitioners (e.g., newly graduated internists inducted into the experimental program for a short period). The method of differences plus the method of concomitant variations (analysis of covariance) will then assist us in drawing conclusions about whether enthusiasm is the (or a) major factor in therapeutic success, even though double-blind conditions are unobtainable. Nor is this the only kind of design which can do this; other approaches are available (one more is discussed below), and ingenious experimenters will doubtless think of still more, to enable us to handle this kind of research problem. There is nothing indispensable about the double-blind study.

It is true that the curriculum field is slightly more difficult than the psychotherapy field, because it is harder to meet the condition of excluding common elements from the several comparison groups. Although the average intelligent patient will accept almost any nonsense as a form of therapy, thanks to the witchdoctor tradition, need to be healed, etc., it is not equally easy to convince students and teachers that they are receiving and giving instruction in geometry unless what is going on really is a kind of geometry that makes some sense. And if it is, then interpretation of one of the possible outcomes is ambiguous, i.e., if several groups do about as well, it may be *either* because enthusiasm does the trick, or because the common context is efficacious. However, comparative evaluation is still well worthwhile, because if we find a very marked *difference* between the groups, when enthusiasm on the part of the teachers and students occurs in both cases, we may be reasonably sure that the difference is due to the curriculum content. And it is surely possible to vary presentation sequence, methods, difficulty, example, etc., enough so that indistinguishable results are improbable.

Now it is not particularly difficult to arrange for the enthusiasm matching. Corresponding to the cut-rate "new therapy" comparison groups, where the therapy procedures are brainstormed up in a day or two of wild free-associating by the experimenters assisted by much beer and some guilt-ridden eclectic therapists, we set up some cut-rate "new curricula" in the following way. First, we get two advanced graduate students or instructors in (let us suppose) economics, give them a vocabulary list for the tenth grade and pay them $500 a chapter for a translation of Samuelson's text into tenth grade language, encouraging them to use their originality in introducing the ideas. They could probably handle the whole text in a summer and thus for a few thousand dollars, including costs of reproducing pilot materials, we have something we could set up against one of the fancier new economics curricula, based on a great deal of high-priced help and laborious field-testing. Then we find a couple of really bright college juniors, majoring in economics, from different colleges, who have not used Samuelson, and give *them* a summer to turn their recent experience at the receiving end of introductory economics courses, and their current direct acquaintance with the problems of concept grasping in the field, into a curriculum outline (filled in as much as possible) of a brief introduction to economics for the tenth grade, not centered around any particular text. And for a third comparison group we locate some enthusiasts for one of the *current* secondary school texts in "economics" and have them work on a revision of it with the author(s) and in the light of some sampling of their colleagues' reactions to the text in class use.

Preferably using the curriculum-makers as teachers (*pace* State Departments of Education) we then turn them loose on loosely matched comparison groups, in school systems geographically well removed from the ones where we are running the tests on the high-priced spread. We might toss in a little incentive payment in the way of a preannounced bonus for these groups if they don't get significantly outscored by the supercurriculum. Now then, if we *still* get a big difference in favor of the supercurriculum, we have good reason for thinking that we have taken care of the enthusiasm variable. Moreover we don't have to pull this stunt with every kind of subject matter, since enthusiasm is presumably reasonably (though definitely not entirely) constant in its effects across subject matter. At any rate, a modest sampling should suffice to check this.

One of the nice things about this kind of comparative study is that even if we get the slightly ambiguous negligible-difference result, which will leave us in doubt as to whether a common enthusiasm is responsible for the result, or whether a roughly comparable job in teaching economics is being done by all the curricula, we get a big economic bonus. If we can whomp up new curricula on a shoestring which are going to produce pretty good results, so much the better; we can do it often and thereby keep up the supply of enthusiasm-stoked project directors, and increase the chances of hitting on some really new big-jackpot approach from a Newton of curriculum reform.

Moreover, still on a shoestring, we can settle the question of enthusiasm fairly quickly even in the event of a tie between the various curricula, by dumping them into the lap of some *antagonistic* and some *neutral* teachers to use during the next school year or two, while on the other hand arranging for the original curriculum-makers to lovingly train a small group of highly selected and innovation-inclined teachers to do the same job. Comparisons between the performance of these three new groups and that of the old ones should enable us to pin down the role of enthusiasm rather precisely, and in addition the doubtless variable immunity of the various curricula to lack of enthusiasm.

A few obvious elaborations of the above procedures, including an opportunity for the novice curriculum-makers to spend a couple of afternoons on field-testing early sections of their new curriculum to give them some "feel" for the speed at which students at this level can grasp new concepts, the use of some care in selecting teachers for their conservatism, allergy, or lethargy, using self-ratings plus peer-ratings plus attitude inventories or projective tests, would of course be incorporated in an actual study.

The enthusiasm "difficulty" here is simply an example of experimentation effects (or coupled variable phenomena), of which the placebo effect in medicine and the Hawthorne effect in industrial and social psychology are well-known instances. In each case we are interested in finding out the effects of a certain factor, but we cannot introduce the factor into the experimental situation without producing a disturbance which may itself be responsible for the observed changes. In the drug field, the disturbance consists in the *act* of giving the patient something which he considers to be a drug, an event which is significant to him, and which consequently may produce effects of its own, quite apart from the "intrinsic" effects of the drug. In the Hawthorne effect, the disturbance is changing, e.g., the conditions of work, which may suggest to the worker that he is the subject of special study and interest, and *this* may lead to improved output, rather than the physical changes in the environment which are the intended control variables under study. [In each case, ingenuity can often bypass the problem, e.g., administering the drug in food (if tasteless) or while unconscious (with permission granted for in advance); or using new workers.]

The cases so far mentioned are all ones where the beliefs of the subjects are the mediating factor between the disturbance and the ambiguous effects. This is characteristic in the field of psychology, but the situation is not essentially different from that occurring in technological research where we face problems such as the absorption of heat by a thermometer which thereby alters the temperature that it is supposedly measuring. That is, some of the effect observed (which is here the eventual length of the mercury column) is due to the fact that in order to get a measurement at all you have to alter what you are trying to measure. The measuring process introduces another physical object into proximity with the measured object, and the instrument itself has a certain heat capacity, a factor in whose influence you are not interested, though in order to find out what you do need to know you eventually have to make an estimate of its magnitude. The ingenious double-blind design is only appropriate in certain circumstances, and is only one of many ways in which we can compensate for these effects. It therefore seems unduly pessimistic of Cronbach to suppose that the impossibility of a double blind in curriculum work is fatal to comparative evaluation. Indeed, when he comes to discuss follow-up studies, he agrees that comparative work is essential (p. 240). The conclusion seems obligatory that comparative evaluation, mediated or not, is the method of choice for evaluation problems.

11. Criteria of Educational Achievement for Evaluation Studies

We may now turn to the problem of specifying in more detail the criteria which should be used in evaluating a teaching instrument. The check-list to follow serves as a useful mnemonic for the goal-formulator and consistency-analyst. We may retain Bloom's (Bloom et al., 1956) convenient trichotomy of cognitive, affective, and motor variables, though we shall often refer to the last two as motivational and physical or nonmental variables respectively, but under the first two of these we shall propose a rather different structure, especially under the knowledge and understanding subdivisions of the cognitive field. We also simplify considerably and add others, such as social effects.

Some preliminary notes follow:

(i) It should be stressed at the beginning that the word "knowledge" can be used to cover understanding (or comprehension) and even affective conditions ("knowing how it feels to be completely rejected by one's peer group"), but that it is here used in the sense in which it can be contrasted with comprehension and experience or valuation, i.e., in the sense in which we think of it as "mere knowledge." Comprehension (or understanding), in terms of this contrast, refers to a psychological state involving knowledge, not of one item, nor of several separate items, but of a field. A field of knowledge is a set of items related in a systematic way, and knowledge of the field involves knowledge not only of the items but of their relations. Understanding particular items in a field, the "facts of the field," requires knowledge of the relation of the item to other items in the field, i.e., some knowledge of the field. A field is often open-ended in the sense of having potential reference or applicability to an indefinite number of future examples. In this latter case, comprehension involves the capacity to apply to these novel cases the appropriate rule, rubric or concept. A field may be a field of abstract or practical knowledge, of thought or of skills: one may understand the field of patent law, or how to retime two-stroke engines.

(ii) With respect to any field of knowledge we can distinguish between a relatively abstract or *conceptual* description of the parameters (which are to occupy the role of dependent variables in our study) and a *manifestation* description, the latter being the next stage towards the specification of the particular tests to be used, which we may call the *operational* description. It is appropriate to describe the criteria at all three levels, although we finally apply only the third, just as it is appropriate to give the steps of a difficult proof in mathematics, because it shows us the conceptual foundations for adopting the particular final step proposed.

(iii) I have followed the usual practice here in listing positive goals (with the possible exception of the example in 5) but a word of caution is in order. Although most negatively desired effects are the absence of positively desired effects, this is not always true, and more generally we often wish to alter the weighting of a criterion variable when it drops below a certain level. For example, we may not be worried if we get *no* change in socialization with a course that is working well in the cognitive domain, and we may give small credit for large *gains* in this dimension. But if it produces a marked rise in sociopathic behavior (i.e., large *losses*) we may regard this as a fatal defect in the course. The same applies to a by-product like forgetting or rejection of material in other subject areas. Another example is discussed below.

(iv) A word about originality or "creativity." This may be manifested in a problem-solving skill, as an artistic skill (which combines motor and perceptual and sometimes verbal skills) and in many other ways. Unless constrained by problem-orientation, it is hard to distinguish from mere idiosyncrasy. If problem-related, it appears to be a virtue only insofar as it indicates (a) deeper understanding, (b) a higher probability of future success in problem-solving, (c) individuality, (d) reduced boredom for the instructor correcting exercises. On the whole it seems as mistaken to make it a wholly separate criterion as to make "cleverness" one.

(v) In general, I have tried to reduce the acknowledged overlap among the factors identified in Bloom's analysis, and am prepared to pay a price for this desideratum, if necessary. There are many reasons for avoiding overlap, of which one of the more important and perhaps less obvious ones is that when the comparative weighting of criteria is undertaken for a given subject, independence greatly simplifies the process, since a straight weighting by individual merit will overweight the hidden loading factors.

(vi) There is still a tendency in the literature to regard factual recall and knowledge of terminology with general disdain. But for many subjects, a very substantial score on that dimension is an absolutely necessary condition for adequate performance. This is not the same as saying that a sufficiently high score on that scale will compensate for lack of understanding, even where we use a single index compounded from the weighted scores: we must taper off the weighting in the upper ranges of the recall scales. There are other subjects, especially mathematics and physics, where knowing how to apply the terminology requires and hence guarantees a very deep understanding and terminology-free tests are just bad tests. (cf. Cronbach, p. 245.)

11.1 Conceptual Description of Educational Objectives

1. Knowledge, of

   a. Items of specific information including rules and definitions of terms in the field.
   b. Sequences or patterns of items of information including sets of rules, procedures or classifications for handling or evaluating items of information (we are here talking about mere knowledge of the rule or classification and not the capacity to apply it).

2. Comprehension or Understanding, of

   a. Internal relationships in the field,[8] i.e., the way in which some of the knowledge claims are consequences of others and imply yet others, the way in which the terminology applies within the field; in short what might be called understanding of the intrafield syntax of the field or subfield (e.g., most of algebra).
   b. Interfield relations, i.e., relations between the knowledge claims in this field and those in other fields; what

---

8. "The field" can be construed more widely or more narrowly than "the subject."

we might call the interfield syntax (e.g., relation of geometry to algebra).

c. Application of the field or the rules, procedures, and concepts of the field to appropriate examples, where the field is one that has such applications; this might be called the semantics and pragmatics of the field (e.g., application of geometry to surveying, psychology to teaching, economics to foreign policy, political theory to the university, etc.).

3. Motivation (Attitude/values/affect)

a. Attitudes toward the course, e.g., acoustics.
b. Attitudes toward the subject, e.g., physics.
c. Attitudes toward the field, e.g., science.
d. Attitudes toward material to which the field is relevant, e.g., increased skepticism about usual advertising claims about "high fidelity" from miniature radios (connection with 2c above).
e. Attitudes toward learning, reading, discussing, enquiring in general, etc.
f. Attitudes toward the school
g. Attitudes toward teaching as a career, teacher status, etc.
h. Attitudes toward (feelings about, etc.) the teacher as a person.
i. Attitude toward classmates, attitude toward society (obvious further subheadings).
j. Attitude toward self, e.g., increase of realistic self-appraisal (which also involves cognitive domain).

4. Nonmental Abilities

a. Perceptual.
b. Psycho-motor.
c. Motor, including, e.g., some sculpting skills.
d. Social skills.

5. Noneducational Variables

There are a number of noneducational goals, usually implicit, which are served by many existing courses and even by new courses, and some of them are even justifiable in special circumstances as, e.g., in a prison. The crudest example is the "keeps 'em out of mischief" view of schooling. Others include the use of the schools to handle unemployment problems, to provide a market for textbook sales, to avoid unhappiness or ill-health (or to increase the happiness) of the students. It is realistic to remember that these criteria may be quite important to parents, teachers, publishers, authors, and legislatures even if not to children.

11.2 Manifestation Dimensions of Criterial Variables

1. Knowledge

In the sense described above, this is evinced by
a. Recital skills.
b. Discrimination skills.
c. Completion skills.
d. Labeling skills.
Note: Where immediate performance changes are not discernible, there may still be some acquisition of latent capacity, manifesting itself in a reduction in relearning time or time for future learning to criterion.

2. Comprehension

This is manifested on some of the above types of performance and also on
a. Analyzing skills, including laboratory analysis skills, other than motor, as well as the verbal analytic skills exhibited in criticism, précis, etc.
b. Synthesizing skills.
c. Evaluation skills, including self-appraisal.
d. Problem-solving skills (speed-dependent and speed-independent).

3. Attitude

Manifestations are usually simultaneous with demonstration of some cognitive acquisition. The kinds of instrument involved are questionnaires, projective tests, Q-sorts, experimental choice situations, and normal lifetime choice situations (choice of college major, career, political party, degree of activism, spouse, friends, etc.). Each of the attitudes mentioned is characteristically identifiable on a passive to active dimension. (This relates to the distinctions expounded on in Bloom, but disregards extent of systematization of value system which can be treated as a (meta-) cognitive skill.)

4. The Nonmental Abilities

All are exhibited in performances of various kinds, which again can be either artifically elicited or extracted from life-history. Typical examples are the capacity to speak in an organized way in front of an audience, to criticize a point of view (immediately upon hearing it) in an effective way, etc. (This again connects with the ability conceptually described under 2c.)

11.3 Follow-up

The time dimension is a crucial element in the analysis of performance and one that deserves an extensive independent investigation. Retention, recall, depth of understanding, extent of imprinting, can all be tested by reapplications of the tests or observations used to determine the instantaneous peak performance, on the dimensions indicated above. However, some follow-up criteria are not repetitions of earlier tests or observations; eventual choice of career, longevity of marriage, extent of adult social service, career success, are relevant and important variables which require case history investigation. But changes of habits and character are often not separate variables, being simply long-term changes on cognitive and affective scales.

11.4 Secondary Effects

A serious deficiency of previous studies of new curricula has been a failure to sample the teacher population adequately. When perfecting a teaching instrument, we cannot justify generalizing from pilot studies unless not only the students but the teachers are fair samples of the intended population. This need to predict/select favorable classroom performance for the new materials also underlines the importance of studies of experimentation effects. Just as generalizing has been based upon inadequate analysis of the teacher sample, so criterion discussions have not paid sufficient attention to teacher benefits. It is quite wrong to evaluate a teaching instrument without any consideration of the effects on the operator as well as on the subjects. In an obvious sense, the operator *is* one of the subjects.

We may distinguish secondary effects (i.e., those on others than the students taking the course) from tertiary effects. Secondary effects are those arising from or because of direct exposure to the material, and it is mainly the teachers and teachers' helpers who are affected in this way. Tertiary effects are those effects on the school or other students brought about by someone who exhibits the primary or secondary effects.

Secondary *effects* are quite different from secondary *indicators* or *criteria*, the use of which characterizes intrinsic evaluation. Typical secondary indicators are: the teacher's opinion of the course, the use of color illustrations in the text, student participation in course design. Secondary *effects* are part of a pay-off evaluation, and the distinction from primary effects is goal-dependent, hence not methodologically fundamental. It just serves as a convenient distinction for weighting purposes.

11.41 Effects on the Teacher

A new curriculum may have very desirable effects on updating a teacher's knowledge or pedagogy, with subsequent pay-off in various ways including the better education of other classes at a later stage (a tertiary effect), whether he/she is there using the old curriculum or the new one. Similarly, it may have very bad effects on the teacher, perhaps through induction of fatigue, or through failing to leave her any feeling of status or significant role in the classroom (as did some programmed texts), etc.

It is easy to itemize a number of such considerations, and we really need a minor study of the taxonomy of these secondary effects under each of their several headings. Interestingly, what I have called the experimentation effects, e.g., those due to enthusiasm, may be of immediate value themselves. Very often the introduction of new curriculum material is tied to teacher in-service training institutes or special in-service training interviews. These of course have effects on the teacher herself with respect to status, self-concept, pay, interests, etc., and indirectly on later students. Many of these effects on the teacher show up in her other activities; at the college level there will normally be some serious reduction of research time resulting from association with an experimental curriculum, and this may have results for promotion expectations in either the positive or the negative direction, depending upon departmental policy. All of these results are effects of the new curriculum at least for a long time, and in certain circumstances they may be sufficiently important to count rather heavily against other advantages. Involvement with curricula of a highly controversial kind may have such strongly damaging secondary effects for the teacher as to raise questions as to whether it is proper to refer to it as a good curriculum for schools in the social context in which these secondary effects are so bad.

11.42 Effects on Teacher's Colleagues

Tertiary effects are the effects on people other than those directly exposed to the curriculum: once again they may be highly significant. Simple examples of tertiary effects involve other members of the staff who may be called upon to teach less attractive courses, or more courses, or whose load may be reduced for reasons of parity, or who may be stimulated by discussions with the experimental group teachers, etc. In many cases, effects of this kind will vary widely from situation to situation, and such effects may then be less appropriately thought of as effects of the curriculum (although even the primary effects of this, i.e., the effects on the students, will vary widely geographically and temporally) but there will sometimes be constancies in these effects which will require recognition as "characteristic effects" of this particular teaching instrument. This will of course be noticeable in the case of controversial experimental courses, but it will also be significant where the course bears on problems of school administration, relation of the subject to other subjects, and so on. Good evaluation requires some attempt to identify effects of this kind.

11.43 Effects on Other Students

Another tertiary effect, already referred to in discussing the effect of the curriculum on the teacher, is the effect on other students. Just as a teacher may be improved by exposure to a new curriculum, and this improvement may show up in benefits for students that she has in other classes, or at a later period using the old curriculum, etc., so there may be an effect of the curriculum on students not in the experimental class through the intermediary of *students* who are. Probably more pronounced in a boarding school or small college, the communication between students is still a powerful enough instrument in ordinary circumstances for this to be a significant influence. The students may of course be influenced in other ways; there may be additions to the library as a result of the funds available for the new course that represent values for the other students, etc. All of these are educationally significant effects of the course adoption.

11.44 Effects on Administrators

The school administrators may be affected by new teaching instruments in various ways: their powers of appointment may be curtailed, if the teaching instrument's efficiency will reduce faculty; they may acquire increased prestige (or nuisance) through the use of the school as an experimental laboratory; they may find this leads to more (or less) trouble with the parents or alumni or legislators; the pay-off through more national scholarships may be a value to them, either intrinsically or incidentally to some other end, etc. Again, it is obvious that in certain special cases this variable will be a very important part of the total set that is affected by the new instrument, and evaluation must include some recognition of this possibility. It is not so much the factors common to the use of novel material, but the course-specific effects that particularly require estimation and almost every new science or social studies course has such effects.

11.45 Effects on Parents

Effects on the parents are of course well known, but they tend to be regarded as mainly nuisance-generating effects. On the contrary, many such effects should be regarded as part of the adult education program in which this country is still highly deficient. In some subjects, e.g., Russian, there is unlikely to be a very significant effect, but in the field of, e.g., problems of democracy, elementary accounting, or literature, this may be a most important effect.

11.46 Effects on the School or College

Many of these are covered above, particularly under the heading of effects on the administrator, but there are of course some effects that are more readily classified under this heading, such as improvement in facilities, support, spirit, applicants, integration, etc.

11.47 Effects on the Taxpayer

These are partly considered in the section on costs below, but certain points are worth mentioning here. We are using the term taxpayer and not ratepayer to stress the support from the total tax structure. The most important kinds of effects here are the possibility of very large-scale curriculum reform, which in toto, including evaluation on the scale envisioned, is likely to add a substantial amount to the overall tax burden. For the unmarried or childless taxpayer, this will be an effect which may with some grounds be considered a social injustice. Insofar as evaluation of a national armament program must be directly tied to questions of the tax loads it imposes (the draft being one of the taxes), the same must be done in any national evaluation of large-scale curriculum reforms.

11.48 Sundry Effects

There are also potential effects on: the authors or production team; the evaluators; scientists studying cognitive processes, etc.; state departments of education; legislators; police; churches; hospitals; and many others. In a particular case, one of these may outweigh all other effects (think of some sex education and drug education courses in recent years). Spotting such special effects is a skill that marks a good evaluator.

12. Values and Costs

12.1 Range of Utility

No evaluation of a teaching instrument can be considered complete without reference to the range of its applicability and the importance of improvement of education in that range. If we are particularly concerned with the underprivileged groups, then it will be a value of considerable importance if our new teaching instrument is especially well adapted for that group. Its utility may not be very highly generalizable, but that may be offset by the special social utility of the effects actually obtained. Similarly, the fact that the instrument is demonstrably usable by teachers with no extra training sharply increases its short-term utility. Indeed it may be so important as to make it one of the explicit criteria of instrument development, for short-run high-yield improvements.

Another special merit comes from providing for everyone some information that is of considerable social importance but hitherto lacking (black studies, woman studies, ecology). Sometimes the intended market, originally, is by no means the most important framework for a new instrument, and a good evaluator should spot the wider significance (Synanon groups, Kinsey reports, etc.).

12.2 Moral Considerations

Considerations of the kind that are normally referred to as moral have a place in the evaluation of new curricula. If the procedures for grading, or for treating students in class (the use of scapegoats, for example, or excessive discipline or even boring presentations), although pedagogically effective, are unjust, then we may have grounds for judging the instrument undesirable which are independent of any directly testable consequences. If one conceives of morality as a system of principles aimed at maximizing long-run social welfare, based on an egalitarian axiom, then moral evaluations will usually show up somewhere else on the criteria given above, as primary or secondary effects. But the time lag before they do so may be so long as to make it appropriate for us to introduce this as an intrinsic criterion or prerequisite, one based on a theory with which there can be little disagreement from theists or humanists. There are a number of other features of teaching instruments to which we react morally; "the dehumanizing influence of teaching machines" is a description often used by critics who are partly affected by moral considerations; whether misguidedly or not is a question that must be faced. Curricula stressing the difference in performance on the standardized intelligence tests of Negro and white children have been attacked as morally undesirable, and the same has been said of textbooks in which the role of the United States in world history has been viewed somewhat critically, and of sex education. But the factual or scientific soundness of the course content will be picked up at

the content-critique level of intrinsic evaluation, and in assessing
the students' learning in pay-off evaluation. The reaction is not
just to the truth or insight provided by the program, but to some
other consequences of providing what may well be truths or
insights, namely consequences involving the welfare of the society
as a whole. And those claims must be faced squarely and discussed
explicitly in evaluation. Often some further factual claim is
involved in the complaint ("sex education encourages experimentation") and the truth of this as well as its immorality if true must
be contrasted with the alternative of ignorance and its moral
effects.

12.3 Costs

The costing of curriculum adoption is a rather poorly
researched affair. Enthusiasts for new curricula tend to overlook a
large number of secondary costs that arise, not only in the experimental situation, but in the event of large-scale adoption.
Evaluation, particularly of items for purchase from public funds,
should have a strong commitment to examination of the cost
situation. Most of the appropriate analysis can be best obtained
from an experienced industrial accountant, but it is perhaps worth
mentioning here that even when the money has been provided for
the salaries of curriculum-makers and field-testers and in-service
training institutes, there are a number of other costs that are not
easily assessed, such as the costs of rearrangements of curriculum,
differential loads on other faculty, diminished availability for
supervisory chores of the experimental staff (and in the long run,
where the instrument requires more of the teacher's time than the
one it replaces, this becomes a permanent cost), the "costs" of
extra demands on *student time* (presumably at the expense of
other courses they might be taking), and of energy drain on the
faculty as they acquire the necessary background and skills in the
new curriculum, and so on through the list of other indirect effects, many of which have cost considerations attached, whether
the cost is in dollars or some other valuable.

13. A Marginal Kind of Evaluation—
"Explanatory Evaluation"

Data relevant to the variables outlined in the preceding section are the basic elements for almost all types of evaluation. But
sometimes, as was indicated in the fourth section, evaluation refers
to *interpretation* or *explanation*. While not considering this to be a
primary or even a fully proper sense, it is clear from the literature
that there is some tendency to extend the term in this direction. It

seems preferable to distinguish between evaluation and the attempt to discover an explanation of certain kinds of result, even when both are—though they should not be—using the same data. Explanation-hunting is sometimes part of process research and sometimes part of other areas in the field of educational research. When we start looking for explanations, data of a quite different variety are called for. We shall, for example, need to have information about specific skills and attitudes of the students who perform in a particular way; we shall call upon the assistance of experts who—or tests which—may be able to demonstrate that the failure of a particular teaching instrument is due to its use of an inappropriately advanced vocabulary, rather than to any weakness of organization. Evaluation of this kind, however, is and should be secondary to evaluation of the kinds discussed previously, for the same reason and in the same sense that therapy is secondary to identification of the need for therapy.

14. Conclusions

The aim of this paper has been to move some steps further in the direction of an adequate methodology of curriculum evaluation. It is clear that taking these steps involves considerable complication of the model of an adequate evaluation study by comparison with what has passed under this heading all too frequently in the past. Further analysis of the problem may reveal even greater difficulties that must be sorted out with an attendant increase in complexity. Complex experiments on the scale we have been discussing are very expensive in both time and effort. But it has been an important part of the argument of this paper that no substitutes will do. If we want to know the answers to the questions that matter about new teaching instruments, we have got to do experiments which will yield those answers. The educational profession is suffering from a completely inappropriate conception of the cost scale for educational research. To develop a new automobile engine or a rocket engine is a very, very expensive business despite the extreme constancy in the properties of physical substances. When we are dealing with a teaching instrument such as a new curriculum or classroom procedure, with its extreme dependence upon highly variable operators and recipients, we must expect considerably more expense. The social pay-off is enormously more important, and this society can, in the long run, afford the expense. At the moment the main deficiency is trained evaluation manpower, so that short-term transition to the appropriate scale of investigation is possible only in rare cases. But the long-term transition must be made. We are dealing with something more important and more difficult to evaluate than an engine design, and we are attempting to get by with something like one per cent of the cost of developing an engine design. The educational profession as a whole has a primary obligation to recognize the difficulty of good curriculum development with its essential concomitant, evaluation, and to begin a unified attack on the problem of financing the kind of improvement that may help us towards the goal of a few million enlightened citizens on the earth's suface, even at the expense of one on the surface of Mars.

Scriven's Paper: An Application

Scriven has built upon the foundation laid by Cronbach to suggest distinctions and procedures which are of great practical value for the evaluation specialist. He has elaborated on the functions of evaluation by noting that, while evaluation can *play many roles* in education (such as in accountability studies, curriculum development, or teacher education programs), the evaluation process has only *one functional goal*—that of determining the *worth or merit* of something. By making this distinction, Scriven has emphasized that no study of any program can be labeled as evaluation unless some judgment is made. In other words, values as standards are a central consideration in evaluation studies. Furthermore, the distinction between *formative* evaluation (evaluation used to improve a program while it is still fluid by providing feedback to the developer) and *summative* evaluation (evaluation of a completed product, aimed at the potential consumer) is a useful distinction. Understanding the difference between these two evaluative roles will help the evaluator to delineate the methods which may be appropriately used in any one evaluation study. It is most appropriate, as Scriven has suggested, to assign the formative evaluation task to a professional evaluator who is a regular part of the program being evaluated—a person internal to the organization, someone who knows the details of the project. On the other hand, it is essential that a disinterested, unbiased professional evaluator from outside the program be brought in as the summative evaluator. The reason for using an external evaluator for summative evaluation studies is that consumers of the evaluation report must be assured that the evaluation was done by an *independent* person and that no "whitewash" or favorably biased report was written. Thus, Scriven suggests credibility as a critical criterion in judging an evaluation report.

A third distinction of Scriven's—that between *intrinsic* evaluation (evaluation of the means used to reach certain ends) and *pay-off* evaluation (evaluation of the ends or effects)—is useful in that both types of evaluation may be parts of a formative or summative evaluation study. Thus, a formative vs. summative distinction *and* an intrinsic vs. pay-off distinction can be made for a particular evaluation study. These distinctions are illustrated in Table 1.

Table 1

Distinctions between Intrinsic and Pay-off Evaluation
and Formative and Summative Evaluation

	INTRINSIC	PAY-OFF
Formative	Judge intellectual integrity of content (e.g., structure sequence of content).	Judge interim effects for feedback to developers.
Summative	Final judgment of materials.	Final judgment of effects.

The authors wish to thank Professor Gene V Glass for originally suggesting these examples.

A theme which runs throughout Scriven's paper is the concern over the *evaluation of objectives* as a prerequisite for program evaluation. The argument is that even though program objectives are all met, the program cannot be judged as valuable if the objectives are not worthwhile. This suggestion by Scriven should be a critical concern in all evaluation studies. Methods for collecting judgmental data about program objectives have been suggested elsewhere by Stake (1970).

Finally, the taxonomy of criteria for evaluation studies suggested by Scriven is a valuable checklist for evaluators to consider. For evaluation studies, this taxonomy has proven to be as useful as or even more useful than the taxonomies which are discussed later in this text in a paper written by David Krathwohl. The Scriven taxonomy should be considered as a heuristic device for generating evaluation plans, rather than as an end in itself.

If Mrs. Allen wished to apply Scriven's suggestions to her evaluation problem, she would first appraise the objectives of her new course to determine their value. If she had trouble writing the course objectives she would consult an evaluation specialist who could help her on that task. Since the evaluation would be considered a formative evaluation study, Mrs. Allen could assume that Scriven would recommend that the study be conducted by an evaluation specialist closely associated with the project. Since Mrs. Allen recognizes that she is by no means an evaluation specialist, she would seek the help of an evaluator who could work closely with her on the course development. If no evaluator were available, then she would proceed on her own since even partial information about the new course would be preferable to abandoning the idea of evaluating it. Within the formative evaluation design, Mrs. Allen may want to consider planning both intrinsic and interim pay-off evaluation activities.

The goal of Mrs. Allen's evaluation study would be to determine the worth of her new course. To reach that goal she would consider many facets of the course and objectively assign weights to each of these facets (that is, describe their relative importance) in arriving at an overall appraisal. The determination of the weights would be accomplished through the objective collection of value data; thus, the values associated with the determination of the worth of the program must be explicated. The facets of the program considered by Mrs. Allen would include student knowledge, comprehension, motivation, social variables, and effects on the teacher, the teacher's colleagues, other students, administrators, parents, taxpayers, and the school itself. Furthermore, the costs and generalization possibilities of the course would be considered. Data on each of these facets then would be weighted by the values data to arrive at an overall appraisal of the course.

It is worth noting that the methods required to reliably arrive at an overall appraisal have by no means been fully specified. Thus the practical applications of Scriven's suggestions, although appealing in the abstract, have not been fully realized at this point in the development of the evaluation process.

The Countenance of Educational Evaluation

Robert E. Stake

University of Illinois

President Johnson, President Conant, Mrs. Hull (Sara's teacher) and Mr. Tykociner (the man next door) are quite alike in the faith they have in education. But they have quite different ideas of what education is. The value they put on education does not reveal their way of evaluating education.

Educators differ among themselves as to both the essence and worth of an educational program. The wide range of evaluation

From *Teachers College Record*, 1967, *68*, 523-540. Copyright 1967 by Teachers College, Columbia University. Reprinted with permission of the author and publisher.

purposes and methods allows each to keep his own perspective. Few see their own programs "in the round," partly because of a parochial approach to evaluation. To understand better his own teaching and to contribute more to the science of teaching, each educator should examine the full countenance of evaluation.

Educational evaluation has its formal and informal sides. Informal evaluation is recognized by its dependence on casual observation, implicit goals, intuitive norms, and subjective judgment. Perhaps because these are also characteristic of day-to-day, personal styles of living, informal evaluation results in perspectives which are seldom questioned. Careful study reveals informal evaluation of education to be of variable quality—sometimes penetrating and insightful, sometimes superficial and distorted.

Formal evaluation of education is recognized by its dependence on check-lists, structured visitation by peers, controlled comparisons, and standardized testing of students. Some of these techniques have long histories of successful use. Unfortunately, when planning an evaluation, few educators consider even these four. The more common notion is to evaluate informally: to ask the opinion of the instructor, to ponder the logic of the program, or to consider the reputation of the advocates. Seldom do we find a search for relevant research reports or for behavioral data pertinent to the ultimate curricular decisions.

Dissatisfaction with the formal approach is not without cause. Few highly-relevant, readable research studies can be found. The professional journals are not disposed to publish evaluation studies. Behavioral data are costly, and often do not provide the answers. Too many accreditation-type visitation teams lack special training or even experience in evaluation. Many checklists are ambiguous; some focus too much attention on the physical attributes of a school. Psychometric tests have been developed primarily to differentiate among students at the same point in training rather than to assess the effect of instruction on acquisition of skill and understanding. Today's educator may rely little on formal evaluation because its answers have seldom been answers to questions *he* is asking.

Potential Contributions of Formal Evaluation

The educator's disdain of formal evaluation is due also to his sensitivity to criticism—and his *is* a critical clientele. It is not uncommon for him to draw before him such curtains as "national norm comparisons," "innovation phase," and "academic freedom" to avoid exposure through evaluation. The "politics" of evaluation is an interesting issue in itself, but it is not the issue here. The issue here is the *potential* contribution to education of formal evaluation. Today, educators fail to perceive what formal evaluation could do for them. They should be imploring measurement specialists to develop a methodology that reflects the fullness, the complexity, and the importance of their programs. They are not.

What one finds when he examines formal evaluation activities in education today is too little effort to spell out antecedent conditions and classroom transactions (a few of which visitation teams do record) and too little effort to couple them with the various outcomes (a few of which are portrayed by conventional test scores). Little attempt has been made to measure the match between what an educator intends to do and what he does do. The traditional concern of educational-measurement specialists for reliability of individual-student scores and predictive validity (thoroughly and competently stated in the American Council on Education's 1950 edition of *Educational Measurement)* is a questionable resource. For evaluation of curricula, attention to individual differences among students should give way to attention to the contingencies among background conditions, classroom activities, and scholastic outcomes.

This paper is not about what should be measured or how to measure. It is background for developing an evaluation plan. What and how are decided later. My orientation here is around educational programs rather than educational products. I presume that the value of a product depends on its program of use. The evaluation of a program includes the evaluation of its materials.

The countenance of educational evaluation appears to be changing. On the pages that follow, I will indicate what the countenance can, and perhaps should, be. My attempt here is to introduce a conceptualization of evaluation oriented to the complex and dynamic nature of education, one which gives proper attention to the diverse purposes and judgments of the practitioner.

Much recent concern about curriculum evaluation is attributable to contemporary large-scale curriculum-innovation activities, but the statements in this paper pertain to traditional and new curricula alike. They pertain, for example, to Title I and Title III projects funded under the Elementary and Secondary Act of 1966. Statements here are relevant to any curriculum, whether oriented to subject-matter content or to student process, and without regard to whether curriculum is general-purpose, remedial, accelerated, compensatory, or special in any other way.

The purposes and procedures of educational evaluation will vary from instance to instance. What is quite appropriate for one school may be less appropriate for another. Standardized achievement tests here but not there. A great concern for expense there but not over there. How do evaluation purposes and procedures vary? What are the basic characteristics of evaluation activities? They are identified in these pages as the evaluation acts, the data sources, the congruence and contingencies, the standards, and the uses of evaluation. The first distinction to be made will be between description and judgment in evaluation.

The countenance of evaluation beheld by the educator is not the same one beheld by the specialist in evaluation. The specialist sees himself as a "describer," one who describes aptitudes and environments and accomplishments. The teacher and school administrator, on the other hand, expect an evaluator to grade something or someone as to merit. Moreover, they expect that he will judge things against external standards, on criteria perhaps little related to the local school's resources and goals.

Neither sees evaluation broadly enough. *Both* description and judgment are essential—in fact, they are the two basic acts of evaluation. Any individual evaluator may attempt to refrain from judging or from collecting the judgments of others. Any individual evaluator may seek only to bring to light the worth of the program. But their evaluations are incomplete. To be fully understood, the educational program must be fully described and fully judged.

Towards Full Description

The specialist in evaluation seems to be increasing his emphasis on fullness of description. For many years he evaluated primarily by measuring student progress toward academic objectives. These objectives usually were identified with the traditional disciplines, e.g. mathematics, English, and social studies. Achievement tests— standardized or "teacher-made"—were found to be useful in describing the degree to which some curricular objectives are attained by individual students in a particular course. To the early evaluators, and to many others, the countenance of evaluation has been nothing more than the administration and normative interpretation of achievement tests.

In recent years a few evaluators have attempted, in addition, to assess progress of individuals toward certain "inter-disciplinary" and "extracurricular" objectives. In their objectives, emphasis has been given to the integration of behavior within an individual; or to the perception of interrelationships among scholastic disciplines; or to the development of habits, skills, and attitudes which permit the individual to be a craftsman or scholar, in or out of school. For the descriptive evaluation of such outcomes, the Eight-Year Study (Smith and Tyler, 1942) has served as one model. The proposed National Assessment Program may be another—this statement appeared in one interim report:

> ... *all committees worked within the following broad definition of 'national assessment:'*
> *1. In order to reflect fairly the aims of education in the U.S., the assessment should consider both traditional and modern curricula, and take into account ALL THE ASPIRATIONS schools have for developing attitudes and motivations as well as knowledge and skills ... [Caps added]* (Educational Testing Service, 1965).

In his paper, "Evaluation for Course Improvement," Lee Cronbach (1963) urged another step: a most generous inclusion of behavioral-science variables in order to examine the possible causes and effects of quality teaching. He proposed that the main objective for evaluation is to uncover durable relationships—those appropriate for guiding future educational programs. To the traditional description of pupil achievement, we add the description of instruction and the description of relationships between them. Like the instructional researcher, the evaluator—as so defined— seeks generalizations about educational practices. Many curriculum project evaluators are adopting this definition of evaluation.

The Role of Judgment

Description is one thing, judgment is another. Most evaluation specialists have chosen not to judge. But in his recent *Methodology of Evaluation* Michael Scriven (1967) has charged evaluators with responsibility for passing upon the merit of an educational practice. (Note that he has urged the evaluator to do what the educator has expected the evaluator to be doing.) Scriven's position is that there is no evaluation until judgment has been passed, and by his reckoning the evaluator is best qualified to judge.

By being well experienced and by becoming well-informed in the case at hand in matters of research and educational practice the evaluator does become at least partially qualified to judge. But is it wise for him to accept this responsibility? Even now when few evaluators expect to judge, educators are reluctant to initiate a formal evaluation. If evaluators were *more* frequently identified with the passing of judgment, with the discrimination among poorer and better programs, and with the awarding of support and censure, their access to data would probably diminish. Evaluators collaborate with other social scientists and behavioral research workers. Those who do not want to judge deplore the acceptance of such responsibility by their associates. They believe that in the eyes of many practitioners, social science and behavioral research will become more suspect than it already is.

Many evaluators feel that they are not capable of perceiving, as they think a judge should, the unidimensional *value* of alternative programs. They anticipate a dilemma such as Curriculum I resulting in three skills and ten understandings and Curriculum II resulting in four skills and eight understandings. They are reluctant to judge that gaining one skill is worth losing two understandings. And, whether through timidity, disinterest, or as a rational choice, the evaluator usually supports "local option," a community's privilege to set its own standards and to be its own judge of the worth of its educational system. He expects that what is good for one community will not necessarily be good for another community, and he does not trust himself to discern what is best for a briefly known community.

Scriven reminds them that there are precious few who can judge complex programs, and fewer still who will. Different decisions must be made—P.S.S.C. or Harvard Physics?—and they should not be made on trivial criteria, e.g. mere precedent, mention in the popular press, salesman personality, administrative convenience, or pedagogical myth. Who should judge? The answer comes easily to Scriven partly because he expects little interaction between treatment and learner, i.e., what works best for one learner will work best for others, at least within broad categories. He also expects that where the local good is at odds with the common good, the local good can be shown to be detrimental to the common good, to the end that the doctrine of local option is invalidated. According to Scriven the evaluator must judge.

Whether or not evaluation specialists will accept Scriven's challenge remains to be seen. In any case, it is likely that judgments will become an increasing part of the evaluation report. Evaluators will seek out and record the opinions of persons of special qualification. These opinions, though subjective, can be very useful and can be gathered objectively, independent of the solicitor's opinions. A responsibility for processing judgments is much more acceptable to the evaluation specialist than one for rendering judgments himself.

Taylor and Maguire (1966) have pointed to five groups having important opinions on education: spokesmen for society at large, subject-matter experts, teachers, parents, and the students themselves. Members of these and other groups are judges who should be heard. Superficial polls, letters to the editor, and other incidental judgments are insufficient. An evaluation of a school program should portray the merit and fault perceived by well-identified groups, systematically gathered and processed. Thus, judgment data and description data are both essential to the evaluation of educational programs.

Data Matrices

In order to evaluate, an educator will gather together certain data. The data are likely to be from several quite different sources, gathered in several quite different ways. Whether the immediate purpose is description or judgment, three bodies of information should be tapped. In the evaluation report it can be helpful to distinguish between *antecedent, transaction,* and *outcome* data.

An antecedent is any condition existing prior to teaching and learning which may relate to outcomes. The status of a student prior to his lesson, e.g. his aptitude, previous experience, interest, and willingness, is a complex antecedent. The programmed-instruction specialist calls some antecedents "entry behaviors." The state accrediting agency emphasizes the investment of community resources. All of these are examples of the antecedents which an evaluator will describe.

Transactions are the countless encounters of students with teacher, student with student, author with reader, parent with counselor—the succession of engagements which comprise the process of education. Examples are the presentation of a film, a class discussion, the working of a homework problem, an explanation on the margin of a term paper, and the administration of a test. Smith and Meux (n.d.) studied such transactions in detail and have provided an 18-category classification system. One very visible emphasis on a particular class of transactions was the National Defense Education Act support of audio-visual media.

Transactions are dynamic whereas antecedents and outcomes are relatively static. The boundaries between them are not clear, e.g. during a transaction we can identify certain outcomes which are feedback antecedents for subsequent learning. These boundaries do not need to be distinct. The categories should be used to stimulate rather than to subdivide our data collection.

Traditionally, most attention in formal evaluation has been given to outcomes—outcomes such as the abilities, achievements, attitudes, and aspirations of students resulting from an educational experience. Outcomes, as a body of information, would include measurements of the impact of instruction on teachers, administrators, counselors, and others. Here too would be data on wear and tear of equipment, effects of the learning environment, cost incurred. Outcomes to be considered in evaluation include not only those that are evident, or even existent, as learning sessions end, but include applications, transfer, and relearning effects which may not be available for measurement until long after. The description of the outcomes of driver training, for example, could well include reports of accident avoidance over a lifetime. In short, outcomes are the consequences of education—immediate and long-range, cognitive and conative, personal and community-wide.

Antecedents, transactions, and outcomes, the elements of evaluation statements, are shown in figure 6 to have a place in both description and judgment. To fill in these matrices the evaluator will collect judgments (e.g. of community prejudice, of problem solving styles, and of teacher personality) as well as descriptions. In figure 6 it is also indicated that judgmental statements are classified either as general standards of quality or as judgments specific to the given program. Descriptive data are classified as intents and observations. The evaluator can organize his data-gathering to conform to the format shown in figure 6.

The evaluator can prepare a record of what educators intend, or what observers perceive, of what patrons generally expect, and of

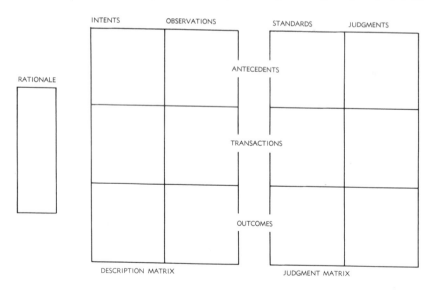

Figure 6

A Layout of Statements and Data to Be Collected by the
Evaluator of an Educational Program.

what judges value the immediate program to be. The record may treat antecedents, transactions, and outcomes separately within the four classes identified as *Intents, Observations, Standards*, and *Judgments*, as in figure 6. The following is an illustration of 12 data, one of which could be recorded in each of the 12 cells, starting with an intended antecedent, and moving down each column until an outcome judgment has been indicated.

Knowing that (1) Chapter XI has been assigned and that he intends (2) to lecture on the topic Wednesday, a professor indicates (3) what the students should be able to do by Friday, partly by writing a quiz on the topic. He observes that (4) some students were absent on Wednesday, that (5) he did not quite complete the lecture because of a lengthy discussion and that (6) on the quiz only about 2/3 of the class seemed to understand a certain major concept. In general, he expects (7) some absences but that the work will be made up by quiztime; he expects (8) his lectures to be clear enough for perhaps 90 percent of a class to follow him without difficulty; and he knows that (9) his colleagues expect only about one student in ten to understand thoroughly each major concept in such lessons as these. By his own judgment (10) the reading assignment was not a sufficient background for his lecture; the students commented that (11) the lecture was provocative; and the graduate assistant who read the quiz papers said that (12) a discouragingly large number of students seemed to confuse one major concept for another.

Evaluators and educators do not expect data to be recorded in such detail, even in the distant future. My purpose here was to give twelve examples of data that could be handled by separate cells in the matrices. Next I would like to consider the description data matrix in detail.

Goals and Intents

For many years instructional technologists, test specialists, and others have pleaded for more explicit statements of educational goals. I consider "goals," "objectives," and "intents" to be synonymous I use the category title *Intents* because many educators now equate "goals" and "objectives" with "intended student outcomes." In this paper Intents includes the planned-for environmental conditions, the planned-for demonstrations, the planned-for coverage of certain subject matter, etc., as well as the planned-for student behavior. To be included in this three-cell column are effects which are desired, those which are hoped for, those which are anticipated, and even those which are feared. This class of data includes goals and plans that others have, especially the students. (It should be noted that it is not the educator's privilege to rule out the study of a variable by saying, "that is not one of our objectives." The evaluator should include both the variable and the negation.) The resulting collection of *Intents* is a priority listing of all that may happen.

The fact that many educators now equate "goals" with "intended student outcomes" is to the credit of the behaviorists, particularly the advocates of programmed instruction. They have brought about a small reform in teaching by emphasizing those specific classroom acts and work exercises which contribute to the refinement of student responses. The A.A.A.S. Science Project, for example, has been successful in developing its curriculum around behavioristic goals (Gagné, 1966). Some curriculum-innovation projects, however, have found the emphasis on behavioral outcomes an obstacle to creative teaching (Atkin, 1963). The educational evaluator should not list goals only in terms of anticipated student behavior. To *evaluate* an educational program, we must examine what teaching, as well as what learning, is intended. (Many antecedent conditions and teaching transactions can be worded behavioristically, if desired). How intentions are worded is not a criterion for inclusion. Intents can be the global goals of the Educational Policies Commission or the detailed goals of the programmer (Mager, 1962). Taxonomic, mechanistic, humanistic, even scriptural—any mixture of goal statements are acceptable as part of the evaluation picture.

Many a contemporary evaluator expects trouble when he sets out to record the educator's objectives. Early in the work he urged the educator to declare his objectives so that outcome-testing devices could be built. He finds the educator either reluctant or unable to verbalize objectives. With diligence, if not with pleasure, the evaluator assists with what he presumes to be the educator's job: writing behavioral goals. His presumption is wrong. As Scriven has said, the responsibility for describing curricular objectives is the responsibility of the evaluator. He is the one who is experienced with the language of behaviors, traits, and habits. Just as it is his responsibility to transform the behaviors of a teacher and the responses of a student into data, it is his responsibility to transform the intentions and expectations of an educator into "data." It is necessary for him to continue to ask the educator for statements of intent. He should augment the replies by asking, "Is this another way of saying it?" or "Is this an instance?" It is not wrong for an evaluator to teach a willing educator about behavioral objectives—they may facilitate the work. It is wrong for him to insist that every educator should use them.

Robert E. Stake

Obtaining authentic statements of intent is a new challenge for the evaluator. The methodology remains to be developed. Let us now shift attention to the second column of the data cells.

Observational Choice

Most of the descriptive data cited early in the previous section are classified as *Observations*. In figure 6 when he described surroundings and events and the subsequent consequences, the evaluator[9] is telling of his Observations. Sometimes the evaluator observes these characteristics in a direct and personal way. Sometimes he uses instruments. His instruments include inventory schedules, biographical data sheets, interview routines, check lists, opinionnaires, and all kinds of psychometric tests. The experienced evaluator gives special attention to the measurement of student outcomes, but he does not fail to observe the other outcomes, nor the antecedent conditions and instructional transactions.

Many educators fear that the outside evaluator will not be attentive to the characteristics that the school staff has deemed most important. This sometimes does happen, but evaluators often pay *too much* attention to what they have been urged to look at, and too little attention to other facets. In the matter of selection of variables for evaluation, the evaluator must make a subjective decision. Obviously, he must limit the elements to be studied. He cannot look at all of them. The ones he rules out will be those that he assumes would not contribute to an understanding of the educational activity. He should give primary attention to the variables specifically indicated by the educator's objectives, but he must designate additional variables to be observed. He must search for unwanted side effects and incidental gains. The selection of measuring techniques is an obvious responsibility, but the choice of characteristics to be observed is an equally important and unique contribution of the evaluator.

An evaluation is not complete without a statement of the rationale of the program. It needs to be considered separately, as indicated in figure 6. Every program has its rationale, though often it is only implicit. The rationale indicates the philosophic background and basic purposes of the program. Its importance to evaluation has been indicated by Berlak (1966). The rationale should provide one basis for evaluating Intents. The evaluator asks himself or other judges whether the plan developed by the educa-

---

9. Here and elsewhere in this paper, for simplicity of presentation, the evaluator and the educator are referred to as two different persons. The educator will often be his own evaluator or a member of the evaluation team.

tor constitutes a logical step in the implementation of the basic purposes. The rationale also is of value in choosing the reference groups, e.g. merchants, mathematicians, and mathematics educators, which later are to pass judgment on various aspects of the program.

A statement of rationale may be difficult to obtain. Many an effective instructor is less than effective at presenting an educational rationale. If pressed, he may only succeed in saying something the listener wanted said. It is important that the rationale be in his language, a language he is the master of. Suggestions by the evaluator may be an obstacle, becoming accepted because they are attractive rather than because they designate the grounds for what the educator is trying to do.

The judgment matrix needs further explanation, but I am postponing that until after a consideration of the bases for processing descriptive data.

Contingency and Congruence

For any one educational program there are two principal ways of processing descriptive evaluation data: finding the contingencies among antecedents, transactions, and outcomes and finding the congruence between Intents and Observations. The processing of judgments follows a different model. The first two main columns of the data matrix in figure 6 contain the descriptive data. The format for processing these data is represented in figure 7.

The data for a curriculum are *congruent* if what was intended actually happens. To be fully congruent the intended antecedents, transactions, and outcomes would have to come to pass. (This seldom happens—and often should not). Within one row of the data matrix the evaluator should be able to compare the cells containing Intents and Observations, to note the discrepancies, and to describe the amount of congruence for that row. (Congruence of outcomes has been emphasized in the evaluation model proposed by Taylor and Maguire.) Congruence does not indicate that outcomes are reliable or valid, but that what was intended did occur.

Just as the Gestaltist found more to the whole than the sum of its parts, the evaluator studying variables from any two of the three cells in a column of the data matrix finds more to describe than the variables themselves. The relationships or *contingencies* among the variables deserve additional attention. In the sense that evaluation is the search for relationships that permit the improvement of education, the evaluator's task is one of identi-

Descriptive data

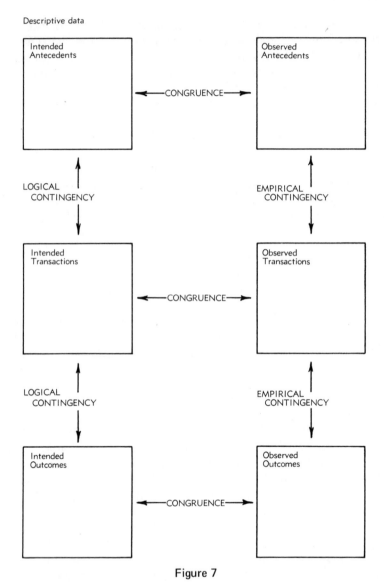

Figure 7

A Representation of the Processing of Descriptive Data

fying outcomes that are contingent upon particular antecedent conditions and instructional transactions.

Lesson planning and curriculum revision through the years have been built upon faith in certain contingencies. Day to day, the master teacher arranges his presentation and selects his input materials to fit his instructional goals. For him the contingencies, in the main, are logical, intuitive, and supported by a history of satisfactions and endorsements. Even the master teacher and certainly less-experienced teachers need to bring their intuitive contingencies under the scrutiny of appropriate juries.

As a first step in evaluation it is important just to record them. A film on floodwaters may be scheduled (intended transaction) to expose students to a background to conservation legislation (intended outcome). Of those who know both subject matter and pedagogy, we ask, "Is there a logical connection between this event and this purpose?" If so, a logical contingency exists between these two Intents. The record should show it.

Whenever Intents are evaluated the contingency criterion is one of logic. To test the logic of an educational contingency the evaluators rely on previous experience, perhaps on research experience, with similar observables. No immediate observation of these variables, however, is necessary to test the strength of the contingencies among Intents.

Evaluation of Observation contingencies depends on empirical evidence. To say, "this arithmetic class progressed rapidly because the teacher was somewhat but not too sophisticated in mathematics" demands empirical data, either from within the evaluation or from the research literature (Bassham, 1962). The usual evaluation of a single program will not alone provide the data necessary for contingency statements. Here too, then, previous experience with similar observables is a basic qualification of the evaluator.

The contingencies and congruences identified by evaluators are subject to judgment by experts and participants just as more unitary descriptive data are. The importance of non-congruence will vary with different viewpoints. The school superintendent and the school counselor may disagree as to the importance of a cancellation of the scheduled lessons on sex hygiene in the health class. As an example of judging contingencies, the degree to which teacher morale is contingent on the length of the school day may be deemed cause enough to abandon an early morning class by one judge and not another. Perceptions of importance of congruence and contingency deserve the evaluator's careful attention.

Standards and Judgments

There is a general agreement that the goal of education is excellence—but how schools and students should excell, and at what sacrifice, will always be debated. Whether goals are local or national, the measurement of excellence requires explicit rather than implicit standards.

Today's educational programs are not subjected to "standard-oriented" evaluation. This is not to say that schools lack in aspiration or accomplishment. It is to say that standards—benchmarks of performance having widespread reference value—are not in common use. Schools across the nation may use the same evaluation checklist[10] but the interpretations of the checklisted data are couched in inexplicit, personal terms. Even in an informal way, no school can evaluate the impact of its program without knowledge of what other schools are doing in pursuit of similar objectives. Unfortunately, many educators are loathe to accumulate that knowledge systematically (Hand, 1965; Tyler, 1965).

There is little knowledge anywhere today of the quality of a student's education. School grades are based on the private criteria and standards of the individual teacher. Most "standardized" tests scores tell where an examinee performing "psychometrically useful" tasks stands with regard to a reference group, rather than the level of competence at which he performs essential scholastic tasks. Although most teachers are competent to teach their subject matter and to spot learning difficulties, few have the ability to *describe* a student's command over his intellectual environment. Neither school grades nor standardized test scores nor the candid opinions of teachers are very informative as to the excellence of students.

Even when measurements are effectively interpreted, evaluation is complicated by a multiplicity of standards. Standards vary from student to student, from instructor to instructor, and from reference group to reference group. This is not wrong. In a healthy society, different parties have different standards. Part of the responsibility of evaluation is to make known which standards are held by whom.

It was implied much earlier that it is reasonable to expect change in an educator's *Intents* over a period of time. This is to say that he will change both his criteria and his standards during instruction. While a curriculum is being developed and disseminated, even the major classes of criteria vary. In their analysis of nationwide assimilation of new educational programs, Clark and Guba (1965) identified eight stages of change through which new programs go. For each stage they identified special criteria (each with its own standards) on which the program should be evaluated

---

10. One contemporary checklist is *Evaluative Criteria* (National Study of Secondary School Evaluation, 1960). It is a commendably thorough list of antecedents and possible transactions, organized mostly by subject-matter offerings. Surely it is valuable as a checklist, identifying neglected areas. Its great value may be as a catalyst, hastening the maturity of a developing curriculum. However, it can be of only limited value in *evaluating,* for it guides neither the measurement nor the interpretation of measurement. By intent, it deals with criteria (what variables to consider) and leaves the matter of standards (what ratings to consider as meritorious) to the conjecture of the individual observer.

before it advances to another stage. Each of their criteria deserves elaboration, but here it is merely noted that there are quite different criteria at each successive curriculum-development stage.

Informal evaluation tends to leave criteria unspecified. Formal evaluation is more specific. But it seems the more careful the evaluation, the fewer the criteria; and the more carefully the criteria are specified, the less the concern given to standards of acceptability. It is a great misfortune that the best trained evaluators have been looking at education with a microscope rather than with a panoramic view finder.

There is no clear picture of what any school or any curriculum project is accomplishing today partly because the methodology of processing judgments is inadequate. What little formal evaluation there is is attentive to too few criteria, overly tolerant of implicit

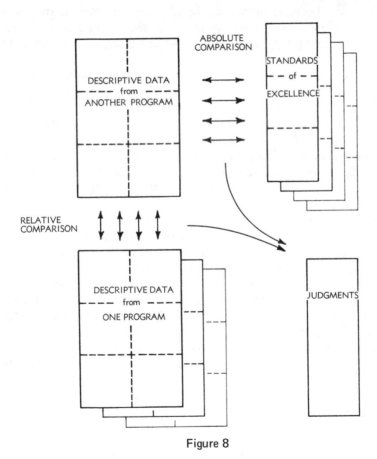

Figure 8

A Representation of the Process of Judging the Merit of an
Educational Program

standards, and ignores the advantage of relative comparisons. More needs to be said about relative and absolute standards.

Comparing and Judging

There are two bases of judging the characteristics of a program, (1) with respect to absolute standards as reflected by personal judgments and (2) with respect to relative standards as reflected by characteristics of alternate programs. One can evaluate SMSG mathematics with respect to opinions of what a mathematics curriculum should be or with regard to what other mathematics curricula are. The evaluator's comparisons and judgments are symbolized in figure 8. The upper left matrix represents the data matrix from figure 7. At the upper right are sets of standards by which a program can be judged in an absolute sense. There are multiple sets because there may be numerous reference groups or points of view. The several matrices at the lower left represent several alternate programs to which the one being evaluated can be compared.

Each set of absolute standards, if formalized, would indicate acceptable and meritorious levels for antecedents, transactions, and outcomes. So far I have been talking about setting standards, not about judging. Before making a judgment the evaluator determines whether or not each standard is met. Unavailable standards must be estimated. The judging act itself is deciding which set of standards to heed. More precisely, judging is assigning a weight, an importance, to each set of standards. Rational judgment in educational evaluation is a decision as to how much to pay attention to the standards of each reference group (point of view) in deciding whether or not to take some administrative action.[11]

Relative comparison is accomplished in similar fashion except that the standards are taken from descriptions of other programs. It is hardly a judgmental matter to determine whether one program betters another with regard to a single characteristic, but there are many characteristics and the characteristics are not equally important. The evaluator selects which characteristics to attend to and which reference programs to compare to.

From relative judgment of a program, as well as from absolute judgment we can obtain an overall or composite rating of merit (perhaps with certain qualifying statements), a rating to be used in making an educational decision. From this final act of judgment a recommendation can be composed.

---

11. Deciding which variables to study and deciding which standards to employ are two essentially subjective commitments in evaluation. Other acts are capable of objective treatment; only these two are beyond the reach of social science methodology.

Absolute and Relative Evaluation

As to which kind of evaluation—aboslute or relative—to encourage, Scriven and Cronbach have disagreed. Cronbach (1963) suggests that generalizations to the local-school situation from curriculum-comparing studies are sufficiently hazardous (even when the studies are massive, well-designed, and properly controlled) to make them poor research investments. Moreover, the difference in purpose of the programs being compared is likely to be sufficiently great to render uninterpretable any outcome other than across-the-board superiority of one of them. Expecting that rarely, Cronbach urges fewer comparisons, more intensive process studies, and more curriculum "case studies" with extensive measurement and thorough description.

Scriven, on the other hand, indicates that what the educator wants to know is whether or not one program is better than another, and that the best way to answer his question is by direct comparison. He points to the difficulty of describing the outcomes of complex learning in explicit terms and with respect to absolute standards, and to the ease of observing relative outcomes from two programs. Whether or not Scriven's prescription is satisfying will probably depend on the client. An educator faced with an adoption decision is more likely to be satisfied, the curriculum innovator and instructional technologist less likely.

One of the major distinctions in evaluation is that which Scriven identifies as *formative* versus *summative* evaluation. His use of the terms relates primarily to the stage of development of curricular material. If material is not yet ready for distribution to classroom teachers, then its evaluation is formative; otherwise it is summative. It is probably more useful to distinguish between evaluation oriented to developer-author-publisher criteria and standards and evaluation oriented to consumer-administrator-teacher criteria and standards. The formative-summative distinction could be so defined, and I will use the terms in that way. The faculty committee facing an adoption choice asks, "Which is best? Which will do the job best?" The course developer, following Cronbach's advice, asks, "How can we teach it better?" (Note that neither are now concerned about the individual student differences.) The evaluator looks at different data and invokes different standards to answer these questions.

The evaluator who assumes responsibility for summative evaluation—rather than formative evaluation—accepts the responsibility of informing consumers as to the merit of the program. The judgments of figure 8 are his target. It is likely that he will attempt to describe the school situations in which the procedures or

materials may be used. He may see his task as one of indicating the
goodness-of-fit of an available curriculum to an existing school
program. He must learn whether or not the intended antecedents,
transactions, and outcomes for the curriculum are consistent with
the resources, standards, and goals of the school. This may require
as much attention to the school as to the new curiculum.

The formative evaluator, on the other hand, is more interested
in the contingencies indicated in figure 7. He will look for
covariations within the evaluation study, and across studies, as a
basis for guiding the development of present or future programs.

For major evaluation activities it is obvious that an individual
evaluator will not have the many competencies required. A team
of social scientists is needed for many assignments. It is reasonable
to suppose that such teams will include specialists in instructional technology, specialists in psychometric testing and scaling,
specialists in research design and analysis, and specialists in
dissemination of information. Curricular innovation is sure to have
deep and widespread effects on our society, and we may include
the social anthropologist on some evaluation teams. The economist
and philosopher have something to offer. Experts will be needed
for the study of values, population surveys, and content-oriented
data-reduction techniques.

The educator who has looked disconsolate when scheduled for
evaluation will look aghast at the prospect of a team of evaluators
invading his school. How can these evaluators observe or describe
the natural state of education when their very presence influences
that state? His concern is justified. Measurement activity—just the
presence of evaluators—does have a reactive effect on education,
sometimes beneficial and sometimes not—but in either case
contributing to the atypicality of the sessions. There are specialists,
however, who anticipate that evaluation will one day be so
skilled that it properly will be considered "unobtrusive measurement". (Webb, et al., 1966)

In conclusion I would remind the reader that one of the largest
investments being made in U.S. education today is in the development of new programs. School officials cannot yet revise a curriculum on rational grounds, and the needed evaluation is not under
way. What is to be gained from the enormous effort of the
innovators of the 1960s if in the 1970s there are no evaluation
records? Both the new innovator and the new teacher need to
know. Folklore is not a sufficient repository. In our data banks we
should document the causes and effects, the congruence of intent
and accomplishment, and the panorama of judgments of those
concerned. Such records should be kept to promote educational

action, not obstruct it. The countenance of evaluation should be one of data gathering that leads to decision-making, not to trouble-making.

Educators should be making their own evaluations more deliberate, more formal. Those who will—whether in their classrooms or on national panels—can hope to clarify their responsibility by answering each of the following questions: (1) Is this evaluation to be primarily descriptive, primarily judgmental, or both descriptive and judgmental? (2) Is this evaluation to emphasize the antecedent conditions, the transactions, or the outcomes alone, or a combination of these, or their functional contingencies? (3) Is this evaluation to indicate the congruence between what is intended and what occurs? (4) Is this evaluation to be undertaken within a single program or as a comparison between two or more curricular programs? (5) Is this evaluation intended more to further the development of curricula or to help choose among available curricula? With these questions answered, the restrictive effects of incomplete guidelines and inappropriate countenances are more easily avoided.

Stake's Model: An Application

Stake has elaborated on the distinctions made by Cronbach and Scriven to formalize evaluation into a systematic procedure. Stake has discriminated between *formal* (objective) and *informal* (subjective) evaluation procedures and has suggested that educators must abandon informal procedures if rational judgments are to be made. Stake suggests that the two major activities of formal evaluation studies are *description* and *judgment* of the program being evaluated. In relation to the measurement aspects of evaluation, Stake has suggested two data matrices in which the evaluator may list the information necessary to rationally judge a program. The Stake model is thus a useful mnemonic device for planning an evaluation study. It is not an evaluation recipe, but it is an organizational framework which emphasizes the two most important components of program evaluation. In addition, operations which should be performed on the data (such as, looking for contingencies and congruencies) are suggested as appropriate methods for analyzing the vast amount of data which are collected in many evaluation studies. Finally, the emphasis on explicating judgmental criteria as a part of formal evaluation studies is important. All too often judgmental statements are made about educational programs without describing the procedures used in arriving at the judgments. To insure the publicness of evaluative statements, standards and procedures for making judgmental statements must be explicated. All evaluation studies are comparative in nature, in the sense that descriptive data are compared to either absolute or relative standards. If these comparisons are not made public, the credibility of evaluative statements can be legitimately questioned. Stake's model is most helpful in this area.

In attempting to apply Stake's thinking to her evaluation problem, Mrs. Allen would probably decide that the principal has acted wisely in requesting a formal evaluation study of the new course. She would likely decide to use description and judgment data matrices to organize antecedent, transaction, and outcome data.[12] The information which Mrs. Allen set out to collect would also be classified as intended (objectives) and observed aspects of the course, and standards for each part of the total description matrix would be listed. These standards may be either relative or absolute criteria. An example of a relative standard might involve comparison of end-of-year achievement test scores in Mrs. Allen's two sophomore English sections. The criterion might be that the average score of the students in the new section should be at least one standard deviation above the average score of students in the traditional section. An absolute standard might be that all students in the new class should score at or above the 80th percentile, based on national norms, on a standardized sophomore English achievement test.

The comparison of descriptive data with standards would lead, then, to a series of recommendations or evaluative statements concerning future action on the new course. It is evident that Mrs. Allen will not have many of the competencies needed to complete the evaluation study and would be well advised to seek the assistance of specialists in areas such as instructional technology, psychometric testing, research design, and statistical analysis, if the evaluation study is to be complete.

Other "Professional Judgment" Approaches to Evaluation

There are additional examples of evaluation approaches which seem to fit under the heading of judgmental strategies, but they are not comprehensive, objective approaches like those suggested by Cronbach, Stake, and Scriven. This general approach to evaluation, which historically has been the most widely used evaluation strategy of educators, is exemplified by the use of experts to produce professional judgments about a phenomenon being

---

12. If Mrs. Allen were fortunate, she might happen across Sjogren's (1970) suggestions of types of information that would logically fall into each of the three categories. These suggestions would probably be quite useful to her (see chapter 4).

observed. Examples of the use of this approach are found routinely in such activities as doctoral oral examinations, review groups empaneled by funding agencies to review proposals, site visits to evaluate federally supported programs, and visits by accrediting agencies to secondary schools and universitites. It is difficult to trace the exact origins of this approach since oral accrediting examinations have been documented as early as 2000 B.C. in early Chinese civil service procedures (DuBois, 1970). However, the accreditation movement among school administrators, which has become the most formalized approach of this type, arose during the 1920s and 1930s in the United States. In accreditation, standards against which schools or universities are measured are generally arrived at through the collective judgments of persons seen as possessing expertise about secondary or higher education. Institutions are asked to undergo an extensive self-study, based on a set of guidelines provided by the accrediting agency. Experts, then, conduct a site visit at regular intervals (the North Central Association, for example, reevaluates school programs once every seven years). Using a set of criteria developed by the accrediting agency, the site visitors observe the operation of the institution, meet with officials of the institution, and talk to various persons affected by that institution's operation. The visiting team deliberates on the quality of the program and writes a final report which is sent to the accrediting agency. The agency then meets, deliberates, and takes any actions which seem advisable. If deficiencies are found in the program, certification is withheld until the substandard conditions are corrected. Membership in the accreditation organization is entirely voluntary on the part of the schools, but schools do feel considerable pressure to join.

The main emphasis of the professional judgment approach to evaluation is that of application of presumed expertise to yield judgments about quality or effectiveness. In accreditation per se, self-study and the maintenance of defined standards are also formalized.

If Mrs. Allen were to rely on the professional judgment approach for evaluating her new course, she would seek direct assistance from persons viewed as experts in instructional processes. She would invite these experts to observe the conduct of her classes, and seek any additional information they wished by verbal questions or application of rating scales, checklists, and so forth. The judgment of the experts (either in written or verbal form) would provide the basis for future decisions about adopting, modifying, or abandoning the new teaching technique.

Decision-Management Strategies

The most important contributions to a decision-management oriented approach to educational evaluation have been presented by Stufflebeam (1968), Guba and Stufflebeam (1968), Alkin (1969), and Stufflebeam, et al. (1971). Although the judgmental component of evaluation has been alluded to in these papers, the primary emphasis has been placed on program description (data collection and storage for use by decision-makers).

Stufflebeam's (CIPP) Model

The Stufflebeam approach to evaluation is most widely recognized as the CIPP (*C*ontext, *I*nput, *P*rocess, *P*roduct) evaluation model. The CIPP approach is described in the paper and excerpt reprinted below. The paper was prepared for the Eleventh Phi Delta Kappa Symposium on Educational Research, for the purpose of introducing the audience to the report of the Phi Delta Kappa Study Committee on Evaluation entitled *Educational Evaluation and Decision-Making*.[13] The paper selectively summarizes major parts of the book, including especially the major concepts of the CIPP Model. These concepts are the definition of evaluation; decision settings and decision types; and evaluation types. The paper is concluded with the presentation of an overall evaluation model which is based on the given definition of evaluation and which interrelates the evaluation and decision-making concepts.

An Introduction to the PDK Book

Educational Evaluation and Decision-Making

Daniel L. Stufflebeam

The Ohio State University

Evaluation Defined

The unifying theme for the PDK book is the following new definition of evaluation.

---

13. D.L. Stufflebeam et al. *Educational Evaluation and Decision-Making.* Itasca, Illinois: F.E. Peacock Publishers, Inc., 1971.

From an address delivered at the Eleventh Annual PDK Symposium on Educational Research, The Ohio State University, June 24, 1970. Reprinted with permission of the author.

EVALUATION IS THE PROCESS OF DELINEATING, OBTAINING, AND PROVIDING USEFUL INFORMATION FOR JUDGING DECISION ALTERNATIVES.

The basis for this definition is found in dictionary definitions of its two key terms. Among other ways, evaluation is defined as the ascertainment of value, and decision, as the act of making up one's mind. When a decision-maker needs to make up his mind he obviously is faced with competing alternatives. To choose one over the other(s) he must in some way ascertain their relative values. In other words he must evaluate the alternatives he is faced with so that he can choose the best one. Hence, it would seem both natural and appropriate for a decision-maker to define evaluation as the process of ascertaining the relative values of competing alternatives. Though less specific, this definition of evaluation is consistent with the one proposed in the PDK book.

Several key points should be kept in mind regarding the new definition.

1. Evaluation is performed in the service of *decision-making*, hence, it should provide information which is useful to decision-makers.

2. Evaluation is a cyclic, continuing *process* and, therefore, must be implemented through a systematic program.

3. The evaluation process includes the three main steps of delineating, obtaining and providing. These steps provide the basis for a methodology of evaluation.

4. The delineating and providing steps in the evaluation process are *interface* activities requiring collaboration

Definition: EVALUATION IS THE (1. PROCESS) OF (2. DELINEATING), (3. OBTAINING), AND (4. PROVIDING) (5. USEFUL) (6. INFORMATION) FOR (7. JUDGING) (8. DECISION ALTERNATIVES).

Terms: 1. Process, A particular, continuing and cyclical activity subsuming many methods and involving a number of steps or operations.

2. Delineating, Focusing information requirements to be served by evaluation through such steps as specifying, defining, and explicating.

3. Obtaining, Making available through such processes as collecting, organizing, and analyzing, and through such formal means as statistics and measurement.

4. Providing, Fitting together into systems or subsystems that best serve the needs or purposes of the evaluation.

5. Useful. Appropriate to predetermined criteria evolved through the interaction of the evaluator and the client.

6. Information, Descriptive or interpretive data about entities (tangible or intangible) and their relationships.

7. Judging, Assigning weights in accordance with a specified value framework, criteria derived therefrom, and information which relates criteria to each entity being judged.

8. Decision Alternatives. A set of optional responses to a specified decision question.

Figure 9

Definition of Evaluation and Its Terms

between evaluator and decision-maker, while the obtaining step is largely a *technical* activity which is executed mainly by the evaluator.

The proposed definition of evaluation together with definitions of its specific terms appear in figure 9. This definition is also discussed in detail in Chapter 2 of the PDK book.

Educational Decision-Making

Given this new definition of evaluation with its emphasis on decision-making, it has been necessary to describe educational decision-making so as to provide a basis for conceptualizing a relevant methodology for evaluation. This has been done particularly from the aspects of the *settings* within which decisions occur, and the *types* of decisions that are made.

Decision Settings

The first decision-making concept to be considered then, concerns desision *settings*. In this connection our formulations are based heavily on the work of Braybrooke and Lindblom in the area of public policy, although we have not conformed exactly to their proposals.[14]

Figure 10 summarizes a conceptualization of four generally different decision settings. These have been differentiated through

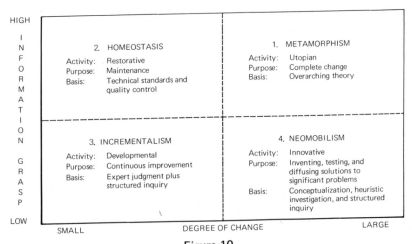

Figure 10

Decision-Making Settings

14. David Braybrooke and Charles E. Lindblom, *A Strategy of Decision*, New York: The Free Press, 1963. This most insightful work is based on the authors' wide experience in the arena of public policy decision-making. A

the intersection of two continua: "small" versus "large" educational change, and "high" versus "low" information grasp to support change.

The utility of these two continua arises directly as a consequence of the definition of evaluation which we have proposed. First, it is clear that the rigor and extensiveness of an evaluation is likely to be determined by the importance of the decision which is to be serviced; this importance in turn is gauged by the significance of the change to be brought about through the execution of the decision. Decisions with unimportant consequences clearly would not demand the expense and thoroughness in an evaluation study that would be required by decisions that will have serious consequences. Second, as an evaluator goes about determining what information he should obtain and provide, he must have in mind the information that is already available and the ability of his client to use it in its present form. Evaluations must be more extensive when there is only little information available (or when the client cannot use available information in its present form).

Combining these two continua—amount of change and degree of information grasp produces the four different decision-making settings of figure 10. These are: (1) decisions to effect large changes supported by a high level of relevant information grasp (the upper right cell of figure 10: Metamorphism); (2) decisions to effect small changes supported by a high level of relevant information grasp (the upper left cell of figure 10: Homeostasis); (3) decisions to effect small changes supported by a low level of relevant information grasp (the lower left cell of figure 10: Incrementalism); and (4) decisions to effect large changes supported by a low level of relevant information grasp (the lower right cell of figure 10: Neomobilism). Let us briefly consider each of these decision settings.

Metamorphic decision-making denotes utopian activity intended to produce complete changes in an educational system, based

---

significant portion of the book is taken up with a discussion of the inadequacies of ordinary formulations of decision-making processes, which treat decision-making as rational. Braybrooke and Lindblom instead espouse a strategy of decision-making which they term "disjointed incrementalism," and which is based on the lower left quadrant of figure 10 (q.v.), called "incrementalism" by us. We believe that the educational situation is sufficiently different from that normally encountered in public policy arenas to make viable certain decision strategies in the upper left and lower right quadrants of figure 10 (homeostasis and neomobilism), which quadrants Braybrooke and Lindblom believe have little utility in guiding policy decision strategies in most cases. It is chiefly in this regard that we differ from their formulations. We acknowledge a great indebtedness to them for the concepts of high vs. low change and high vs. low understanding, which form the basis for the strategies implied in figure 10 and which are further explicated in the text.

upon full knowledge of how to effect the desired changes. The probability favoring this kind of change in any educational institution is indeed slim. Therefore, in the interest of time we will not deal further with this setting here.

Homeostatic decision-making denotes restorative activity aimed at the purpose of maintaining the normal balance in an educational system and guided by technical standards and a routine, cyclical data collection system.

Settings of this type are the most prevalent in education of the four types being considered. Staff assignments, scheduling of students, and establishment of bus routes illustrate this type of decision-making setting. Most schools have adequate quality control evaluation programs to service their homeostatic decision needs. Further, the changes effected by these decisions are small and remedial. All in all, no major breakthroughs in evaluation theory are needed to service such minor adjustments which are already based on adequate supplies of information. We shall therefore not consider this setting in further detail.

Incremental decision-making denotes developmental activity having as its purpose continuous improvement in a program. Such activity usually is supported by expert judgment and structured inquiry into the efficacy of the present program and the recommended changes. Decision-making in this quadrant differs from homeostatic decision-making in two respects. First, incremental decisions are intended to shift the program to a *new* normal balance based upon small, serial improvements, while homeostatic decisions are intended to *correct* the program and change it *back* to its normal balance. Second, while homeostatic decisions are supported by technical standards and a continuing supply of routinely collected information, evaluations for incremental change are usually *ad hoc* and supported by little extant knowledge. Special studies, the employment of expert consultants, and the formation of special committees characterize most efforts to introduce incremental change.

Incremental decision-making is very prevalent in education. Many so-called educational innovations are of the incremental type. They are attempts to make improvements in the present program without risking a major failure or major expense. Though there is little information to support such changes, the adjustments are sufficiently small that corrections can be made as problems are detected. As might be expected, such changes are based on trial and error and are iterative and serial in nature. Also, such changes often require allocations of special resources. Title I of the Elementary and Secondary Education Act has fostered much incremental change.

Neomobilistic[15] decision-making denotes innovative activity for inventing, testing and diffusing new solutions to significant problems. Such change is supported by little theory or extant knowledge; yet, the change is large, often because of great opportunities such as those being produced by the knowledge explosion, or because of critical conditions such as riots in inner cities. Evaluation strategies to support neomobilistic decision-making usually are *ad hoc* types of investigations. Often, these studies are exploratory and heuristic at the beginning of a change effort and then increasingly rigorous as the change progresses.

Neomobilistic decision-making is becoming more prevalent in education. Critics of education who advocate higher rates of change, the explosive conditions in our cities, and the knowledge explosion, are all factors which have served to motivate this kind of change. Title III projects, educational development laboratories, educational policy research centers, and the proposed National Institute for Education are all illustrations of expenditures of risk capital to stimulate educators to create and to try out new solutions to significant problems. Let us now turn to the concept of decision type.

Types of Decisions

Knowledge of the four decision-making settings just discussed is a necessary but not sufficient condition for formulating an evalu-

	INTENDED	ACTUAL
ENDS	PLANNING DECISIONS to determine objectives	RECYCLING DECISIONS to judge and react to attainments
MEANS	STRUCTURING DECISIONS to design procedures	IMPLEMENTING DECISIONS to utilize, control, and refine procedures

Figure 11

Types of Decisions

---

15. A term, contrived by the authors, intended to convey the idea of *change or movement toward the new.*

ation model capable of serving decision-making. Also needed is a typology or taxonomy of decisions whose categories are exhaustive of all possible educational decisions while also being mutually exclusive. Under those circumstances generalizable evaluation designs to fit all decision types within similar categories become feasible.

Figure 11 presents the conceptual base from which a proposed typology of decisions has been generated. According to this chart decisions should be classified as a function of whether they pertain to *ends* or *means;* and whether they pertain to *intentions* or *actualities.* Thus, all educational decisions may be exhaustively and unambiguously classified as pertaining to (1) intended ends

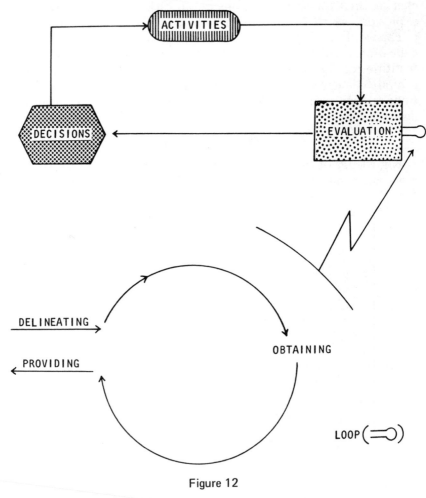

Figure 12

The Relation of Evaluation to Decision-Making

(goals), (2) intended means (procedural designs), (3) actual means (procedures in use), or (4) actual ends (attainments). This schema has allowed the identification of four types of educational decisions: (1) *planning decisions* to determine objectives, (2) *structuring decisions* to design procedures, (3) *implementing decisions* to utilize, control and refine procedures, and (4) *recycling decisions* to judge and react to attainments.

So far we have seen that decison-making has two major features. It can occur in four settings called metamorphic, homeostatic, incremental, and neomobilistic. And, it can relate to four types of decisions called planning, structuring, implementing and recycling. Next, we shall analyze the nature of the evaluation studies that are needed to service decision-making as it has been conceptualized in this paper.

Evaluation

The general logic of the proposed new approach to evaluation is shown in figure 12. Program operations are evaluated to influence decisions which influence program operations which are in turn evaluated, *ad infinitum.* The loop to the right of the evaluation block in figure 12 is included to remind one that the evaluation process includes three steps: *delineation* of the information to be collected, *obtaining* of the information, and *providing* of the information. According to this paradigm any evaluation study involves these three steps.

Corresponding to the four decision types identified in the PDK book are four types of evaluation—context, input, process, and

	INTENDED	ACTUAL
ENDS	PLANNING DECISIONS supported by CONTEXT EVALUATION	RECYCLING DECISIONS supported by PRODUCT EVALUATION
MEANS	STRUCTURING DECISIONS supported by INPUT EVALUATION	IMPLEMENTING DECISIONS supported by PROCESS EVALUATION

Figure 13

Types of Decisions and Evaluation

product. These are portrayed in figure 13 in relation to the four types of decisions. *Context* evaluation serves planning decisions to determine objectives; *input* evaluation serves structuring decisions to determine project designs; *process* evaluation serves implementing decisions to control project operations; and *product* evaluation serves recycling decisions to judge and react to project attainments.

As a means of monitoring a system and, thereby, providing information on needed changes, context evaluation is mainly general and systematic. However, the other three types of evaluation are specific and *ad hoc;* they come into play only after a planning decision has been reached to effect some sort of system change, and specific evaluation designs for each of these three design types vary according to the setting for the change. Generally speaking, the greater the change and the lower the information grasp (decision-maker's knowledge of how to effect the change), the more formal, structured, and comprehensive is the evaluation required.

Context Evaluation

Context evaluation is the most basic kind of evaluation. Its purpose is to provide a rationale for determination of objectives. Specifically, it defines the relevant environment, describes the desired and actual conditions pertaining to that environment, identifies unmet needs and unused opportunities, and diagnoses the problems that prevent needs from being met and opportunities from being used. The diagnosis of problems provides an essential basis for developing objectives whose achievement will result in program improvement.

The method of context evaluation begins with a conceptual analysis to identify and define the limits of the domain to be served as well as its major sub-parts. Next, empirical studies are performed to identify unmet needs and unused opportunities. Finally, context evaluation involves both empirical and conceptual analyses, as well as appeal to theory and authoritative opinion, to aid judgments regarding the basic problems which must be solved.

Decisions served by context evaluation include deciding upon the setting to be served, the general goals to be sought, and the specific objectives to be achieved. Such decisions usually appear in the introductory sections of proposals to funding agencies or in requests for proposals by funding agencies.

Input Evaluation

The purpose of input evaluation is to provide information for determining how to utilize resources to achieve project objectives.

This is accomplished by identifying and assessing (1) relevant capabilities of the responsible agency, (2) strategies for achieving project objectives and (3) designs for implementing a selected strategy. Ultimately, alternative designs are assessed in terms of their resource, time and budget requirements; their potential procedural barriers, the consequences of not overcoming these barriers, the possibilities and costs of overcoming these barriers; relevance of the designs to project objectives; and overall potential of the design to meet project objectives. This information is essential for structuring specific designs to accomplish project objectives.

Methods for input evaluation are lacking in education. The prevalent practices include committee deliberations, appeal to the professional literature, the employment of consultants, and pilot experimental projects. It also is to be noted that the methodology of input evaluation varies greatly, depending upon whether large or small change is involved and whether high or low information grasp is available to support the change. In a homeostatic setting where small change is needed and where much information is available to support it, little formal evaluation is usually required. However, when the change setting is either incremental or neomobilistic (innovative) this situation reverses; then, extensive efforts are required to provide the information which is not now available but needed if the projected projects are to be successful.

Essentially, input evaluation provides information for deciding whether outside assistance should be sought for achieving objectives, what strategy should be employed, e.g., the adoption of available solutions or the development of new ones, and what design or procedural plan should be employed for implementing the selected strategy.

Process Evaluation

Once a designed course of action has been approved and implementation of the design has begun, process evaluation is needed to provide periodic feedback to persons responsible for implementing plans and procedures. Process evaluation has three main objectives—the first is to detect or predict defects in the procedural design or its implementation during the implementation stages, the second is to provide information for programmed decisions, and the third is to maintain a record of the procedure as it occurs.

There are four essential features of process evaluation methodology. These are the provision for a full-time process evaluator, instruments for describing the process, regular feedback meetings between the process evaluator and project personnel, and frequent updating of the process evaluation design. This is especially true in incremental and neomobilistic settings. The project director and his staff simply do not have the needed combination of time, objectivity, and expertise to perform their own process evaluation; and their information requirements evolve throughout the life of their project. However, in homeostatic settings, the project director may be able to carry on his own process evaluation, since he already knows a great deal about how his design will operate in practice, and since his project likely will be a much shorter-range one than one performed in a neomobilistic setting.

In summary, process evaluation provides project decision-makers with information needed for anticipating and overcoming procedural difficulties, for making preprogrammed decisions, and for interpreting project outcomes.

Product Evaluation

The fourth type of evaluation is product evaluation. Its purpose is to measure and interpret attainments not only at the end of a project cycle, but as often as necessary *during* the project term.

The general method of product evaluation includes devising operational definitions of objectives, measuring criteria associated with the objectives of the activity, comparing these measurements with predetermined absolute or relative standards, and making rational interpretations of the outcomes using the recorded context, input, and process information.

In the change process, product evaluation provides information for deciding to continue, terminate, modify or refocus a change activity, and for linking the activity to other phases of the change process. For example, a product evaluation of a program to develop after-school study for students from disadvantaged homes might show that the development objectives have been satisfactorily achieved and that the developed innovation is ready to be diffused to other schools which need such an innovation.

This concludes the description of the four types of evaluation. Figure 14 summarizes their main features, and each one is described in detail in Chapter 7 of the PDK book. Next, let us consider the overall model of evaluation which is also presented in Chapter 7 of the book.

A Total Evaluation Model

Reliance upon *ad hoc* evaluation studies can be an ineffective and inefficient means of providing information for decision-

	CONTEXT EVALUATION	INPUT EVALUATION	PROCESS EVALUATION	PRODUCT EVALUATION
OBJECTIVE	To define the operating context, to identify and assess needs and opportunities in the context, and to diagnose problems underlying the needs and opportunities.	To identify and assess system capabilities, available input strategies, and designs for implementing the strategies.	To identify or predict, in process, defects in the procedural design or its implementation, to provide information for the preprogrammed decisions, and to maintain a record of procedural events and activities.	To relate outcome information to objectives and to context, input, and process information.
METHOD	By describing the context; by comparing actual and intended inputs and outputs; by comparing probable and possible system performance; and by analyzing possible causes of discrepancies between actualities and intentions.	By describing and analyzing available human and material resources, solution strategies, and procedural designs for relevance, feasibility and economy in the course of action to be taken.	By monitoring the activity's potential procedural barriers and remaining alert to unanticipated ones, by obtaining specified information for programmed decisions, and describing the actual process.	By defining operationally and measuring criteria associated with the objectives, by comparing these measurements with predetermined standards or comparative bases, and by interpreting the outcomes in terms of recorded context, input and process information.
RELATION TO DECISION-MAKING IN THE CHANGE PROCESS	For deciding upon the setting to be served, the goals associated with meeting needs or using opportunities, and the objectives associated with solving problems, i.e., for planning needed changes.	For selecting sources of support, solution strategies, and procedural designs, i.e., for structuring change activities.	For implementing and refining the program design and procedure, i.e., for effecting process control.	For deciding to continue, terminate, modify, or refocus a change activity, and for linking the activity to other major phases of the change process, i.e., for recycling change activities.

Figure 14

Four Types of Evaluation

making within a system. Rather, educational systems should have well functioning evaluation programs that provide a dynamic baseline of information about the system. Such an evaluation program should meet the regular, evaluative information requirements of the system, and it should be responsive to emergent needs for idiosyncratic data. Figure 15 is presented as an overall model for the total evaluative program being proposed herein; it provides for systematic context evaluation and *ad hoc* input, process, and product evaluations. This chart retains the basic relationships between activities, evaluation and decisions that were protrayed in figure 12. Further, the small loop (⊃) attached to each evaluation block denotes the general process of delineating, obtaining, and providing information that was projected in figure 12 as being inherent in any evaluation study.

The outer cycle represents a continuous, systematic context evaluation mechanism. This mechanism delineates, obtains, and

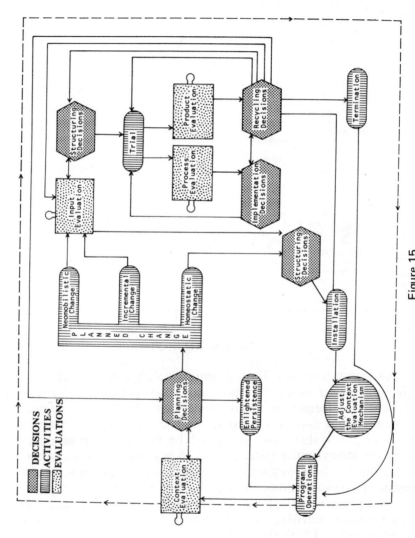

Figure 15

An Evaluation Model

provides information to the planning body of a system to make decisions either to change the system or to continue with present procedures because they are serving important objectives effectively and efficiently. If the context evaluation indicates no discrepancies between the intentions and actualities or between possibilities and probabilities, the planning body might feel confident to continue at the same level.

However, if the context evaluation indicated a deficiency or identified some unused opportunities for improvement, a rational decision-making body would probably decide to bring about changes in accordance. Such changes can be of three types.

1. *Homeostatic change* would be based upon decisions to effect small changes supported by a high level of relevant information grasp on the part of relevant program personnel.
2. *Incremental change* would be based upon decisions to effect a small change supported by an initially low level of relevant information grasp.
3. *Neomobilistic change* would be based upon decisions to effect large change supported by an initially low level of relevant information grasp.

We have excluded the metamorphic setting since we believe that it has only theoretical relevance in education.

Depending upon the type of change to result from planning decisions, vastly different evaluation measures might be called for. In response to homeostatic change, where adequate information to support decision-making is already available from the research literature and/or the context evaluation mechanism, an expensive evaluation study to provide redundant information would be unwise. Therefore, the model in figure 15 shows: (1) that decision-makers would make structuring decisions regarding the means necessary to bring about homeostatic change *without* any intervening formal evaluation support mechanism other than context evaluation, and (2) that these structuring decisions would lead *directly* to installation of change in the program and subsequent adjustment to the context evaluation mechansim to provide for routinely monitoring the new feature in the system by the systematic context evaluation.

If neomobilistic or incremental changes are called for, *ad hoc* evaluation mechanisms to support such change are definitely needed, since both the context evaluation mechanism and the research literature provide inadequate supplies of information to support these types of changes.

First, an input evaluation study must be done to identify and evaluate strategies and procedures to effect desired changes. Such input evaluation information should assist decision-makers to make decisions in designing desired change procedures. As already noted, neomobilistically oriented input evaluations will be much more extensive than incrementally oriented input evaluations. Upon completion, the structuring decisions usually lead to some kind of a trial or pilot phase, because the desired change is still an innovation and has not been adequately tested; therefore, it is not ready for installation in the total system. However, structuring decisions can bypass trial projects and lead to the installation of change procedures in the overall system.

Process and product evaluation are included next to aid in decisions pertaining to the trial phase. Process evaluation would provide information for decisions involved in efficient implementation of the trial, including the modification of previous structuring decisions as necessary. Product evaluation would go on simultaneously throughout the trial in conjunction with process evaluation and would support recycling decisions leading to a reformulation of the change to be brought about, modification either in strategy or procedure, termination of the change effort, or installation of the innovation in the total system. In the case of installation, again, the context evaluation mechanism would be adjusted to allow systematic monitoring of the new element in the total system and, thereby, to assess its generalized impact.

The model depicted in figure 15 is explicated and illustrated in Chapters 7 and 8 of the PDK book.

Conclusion

This paper has tried to combine four evaluation and evaluation-related concepts into a single generalizable model for evaluation. These are the three classes of decision settings (homeostasis, incrementalism, and neomobilism), the four types of decisions (planning, structuring, implementing, and recycling), and three major steps in the evaluation process (delineating, obtaining, and providing), and the four types of evaluation (context, input, process, and product). This proposed model is the conceptual basis for applying the theory of evaluation proposed in the PDK book.

In addition to the concepts presented in the paper reprinted above, Stufflebeam has produced a set of generalizable steps for developing evaluation designs. These steps are reprinted below.

Excerpts from

Evaluation as Enlightenment For Decision-Making

Daniel L. Stufflebeam

The Ohio State University

The Structure of Evaluation Design

Once an evaluator has selected an evaluation strategy, e.g., context, input, process, or product, he must next select or develop a design to implement his evaluation. This is a difficult task since few generalized evaluation designs exist which are adequate to meet emergent needs for evaluation. Thus, educators must typically develop evaluation designs de novo. The remainder of this paper is an attempt to provide a general guide for developing evaluation designs. Specifically, I will attempt to define design in general terms and to explicate the general structure of designs for educational evaluation. Hopefully, this general treatment of evaluation design will be of some help to educators in ordering their minds as they approach problems of designing evaluations. Also, I am hopeful that the following material might stimulate methodologists who are more capable than I to develop generalized designs for context, input, process, and product evaluation.

Design Defined

In general, design is the preparation of a set of decision situations for implementation toward the achievement of specified objectives. This definition says three things. First, one must identify the objectives to be achieved through implementation of the design. In a product evaluation, for example, such an objective might be to make a determination of whether all students in a remedial reading program attained specified levels of specific reading skills. Second, this definition says that one should identify and define the decision situations in the procedure for achieving the evaluation objective. For example, in the remedial reading case

From Beatty, W.H. (Ed.). *Improving Educational Assessment and an Inventory of Measures of Affective Behavior.* Washington, D.C.: Association for Supervision and Curriculum Development, NEA, 1969. This excerpt was taken from an address, "Evaluation as Enlightenment for Decision-Making," delivered at Sarasota, Florida, January 19, 1969. Reprinted with permission of the author and the publisher.

cited above one would want to identify the available measuring devices which might be appropriate for assessing the specified reading skills. Third, for each identified decision situation the evaluator needs to make a choice among the available alternatives. Thus, the completed evaluation design would contain a set of decisions as to how the evaluation is to be conducted and what instruments will be used.

It should be useful to evaluators to have available a list of the decision situations which are common to many evaluation designs. This would enable them to approach problems of evaluation design in a systematic manner. Further, such a list could serve as an outline for the content of evaluation sections in research and development proposals. Funding agencies should also find such a list useful in structuring their general guidelines for evaluations which they provide to potential proposal writers. Also, such a list should be useful to training agencies for defining the role of the evaluation specialist.

The logical structure of evaluation design is the same for all types of evaluation, whether context, input, process or product evaluation. The parts, briefly, are as follows:

A. Focusing the Evaluation
   1. Identify the major level(s) of decision-making to be served, e.g., local, state, or national.
   2. For each level of decision-making, project the decision situations to be served and describe each one in terms of its locus, focus, criticality, timing, and composition of alternatives.
   3. Define criteria for each decision situation by specifying variables for measurement and standards for use in the judgment of alternatives.
   4. Define policies within which the evaluator must operate.

B. Collection of Information
   1. Specify the source of the information to be collected.
   2. Specify the instruments and methods for collecting the needed information.
   3. Specify the sampling procedure to be employed.
   4. Specify the conditions and schedule for information collection.

C. Organization of Information
   1. Provide a format for the information which is to be collected.
   2. Designate a means for performing the analysis.

D. Analysis of Information
   1. Select the analytical procedures to be employed.
   2. Designate a means for performing the analysis.

E. Reporting of Information
   1. Define the audiences for the evaluation reports.
   2. Specify means for providing information to the audiences
   3. Specify the format for evaluation reports and/or reporting sessions.
   4. Schedule the reporting of information.

F. Administration of the Evaluation
   1. Summarize the evaluation schedule.
   2. Define staff and resource requirements and plans for meeting these requirements.
   3. Specify means for meeting policy requirements for conduct of the evaluation.
   4. Evaluate the potential of the evaluation design for providing information which is valid, reliable, credible, timely, and pervasive.
   5. Specify and schedule means for periodic updating of the evaluation design.
   6. Provide a budget for the total evaluation program.

Figure 16

Developing Evaluation Designs

Figure 16 is an attempt to provide such a general list of decision situations for evaluation designs. By presenting this general list I am asserting that the structure of evaluation design is the same for context, input, process, or product evaluation. This structure includes six major parts. These are 1) focusing the evaluation, 2) information collection, 3) information organization, 4) information analysis, 5) information reporting, and 6) the administration of evaluation. Each of these parts will be considered separately.

Focusing the Evaluation

The first part of the structure of evaluation design is that of focusing the evaluation. The purpose of this part is to spell out the ends for the evaluation and to define policies within which the evaluation must be conducted. Specifically, this part of evaluation design includes four steps.

The first step is to identify the major levels of decision-making for which evaluation information must be provided. For example, in the Title III program of the Elementary and Secondary Education Act evaluative information from local schools is needed at ιocal, state and national levels. It is important to take all relevant levels into account in the design of evaluations since different levels may have different information requirements and since the different agencies may need information at different times.

Having identified the major levels of decision-making to be served by evaluation, the next step is to identify and define the decision situations to be served at each level. Given our present low state of knowledge about decison-making in education, this is a very difficult task. However, it is also a very important one and should be done as well as is practicable. First, decision situations should be identified in terms of those responsible for making the decisions, e.g., teachers, principals, the board of education members, state legislators, etc. Next, major types of decision situations should be identified, e.g., appropriational, allocational, approval, or continuation. Then these types of decision situations should be classified by focus, e.g., research, development, diffusion or adoption in the case of instrumental outcomes, or knowledge or understanding in the case of consequential outcomes. (This step is especially helpful toward identifying relevant evaluative criteria.) These identified decision situations should then be analyzed in terms of their relative criticality. In this way relatively less important decisions which would expend evaluation resources needlessly can be eliminated from further consideration. Next, the timing of the decision situation to be served should be estimated so that the evaluation can be geared to provide relevant data prior to the time when decisions must be made. And, finally, an attempt should be made to explicate each important decision situation in terms of the alternatives which may reasonably be considered in reaching the decision.

Once the decision situations to be served have been explicated, the next step is to define relevant information requirements. Specifically, one should define criteria for each decision situation by specifying variables for measurement and standards for use in the judgment of alternatives.

The final step in focusing the evaluation is to define policies within which the evaluator must operate. For example, one should determine whether a "self evaluation" or "outside evaluation" is needed. Also, it is necessary to determine who will receive evaluation reports and who will have access to them. Finally, it is necessary to define the limits of access to data for the evaluation team.

Collection of Information

The second major part of the structure of evaluation design is that of planning the collection of information. This section must obviously be keyed very closely to the criteria which were identified in the Evaluation Focus part of the design.

Using those criteria one should first identify the sources of the information to be collected. These information sources should be defined in two respects: first, the origins for the information, e.g., students, teachers, principals or parents, and second, the present state of the information, i.e., in recorded or non-recorded form.

Next, one should specify instruments and methods for collecting the needed information. Examples include achievement tests, interview schedules and searches through the professional literature. Michael and Metfessel[16] have recently provided a comprehensive list of instruments with potential relevance for data collection in evaluations.

For each instrument that is to be administered, one should next specify the sampling procedure to be employed. Where possible, one should avoid administering too many instruments to the same person. Thus, sampling without replacement across instruments can be a useful technique. Also, where total test scores are not needed for each student, one might profitably use multiple matrix sampling where no student attempts more than a sample of the items in a test.

16. Newton S. Metfessel and William B. Michael. "A Paradigm Involving Multiple Criterion Measures for the Evaluation of the Effectiveness of School Programs," *Educational and Psychological Measurement*, 1967, 27, 931-936.

Finally, one should develop a master schedule for the collection of information. This schedule should detail the interrelations between samples, instruments, and dates for the collection of information.

Organization of Information

A frequent disclaimer in evaluation reports is that resources were inadequate to allow for processing all of the pertinent data. If this problem is not to arise, one should make definite plans regarding the third part of evaluation design: organization of information. Organizing the information that is to be collected includes providing a format for classifying information and designating means for coding, organizing, storing, and retrieving the information.

Analysis of Information

The fourth major part of evaluation design is analysis of information. The purpose of this part is to provide for the descriptive or statistical analyses of the information which is to be reported to decision-makers. This part also includes interpretations and recommendations. As with the organization of information it is important that the evaluation design specify means for performing the analyses. The role should be assigned specifically to a qualified member of the evaluation team or to an agency which specializes in doing data analyses. Also, it is important that those who will be responsible for the analysis of information participate in designing the analysis procedures.

Reporting of Information

The fifth part of evaluation design is the reporting of information. The purpose of this part of a design is to insure that decision-makers will have timely access to the information they need and that they will receive it in a manner and form which facilitates their use of the information. In accordance with the policy for the evaluation, audiences for evaluation reports should be identified and defined. Then means should be defined for providing information to each audience. Subsequently, the format for evaluation reports and reporting sessions should be specified. And, finally, a master schedule of evaluation reporting should be provided. This schedule should define the interrelations between audiences, reports, and dates for reporting information.

Administration of Evaluation

The last part of evaluation design is that of administration of the evaluation. The purpose of this part is to provide an overall plan for executing the evaluation design. The first step is to define the overall evaluation schedule. For this purpose it often would be useful to employ a scheduling technique such as Program Evaluation and Review Technique. The second step is to define staff requirements and plans for meeting these requirements. The third step is to specify means for meeting policy requirements for conduct of the evaluation. The fourth step is to evaluate the potential of the evaluation design for providing information which is valid, reliable, credible, timely, and pervasive. The fifth step is to specify and schedule means for periodic updating of the evaluation design. And, the sixth and final step is to provide a budget for the evaluation.

Finally, I have reached the end of my paper. While I have only scratched the surface regarding educational evaluations, it is clear to me that the design and analysis of educational evaluation is a most complex and difficult undertaking. Surely, all of us who are committed to reshaping the world of educational evaluation must work very, very hard if we are to make any progress. If progress is not made in this area, I am convinced that education will be a casualty for want of adequate information to support vital decisions in and about education.

Stufflebeam's Model: An Application

It is noteworthy that the approach suggested by Stufflebeam is cyclical in that feedback is continuously being provided to the decision-maker and new information may lead to reexamination of earlier decisions. Thus it is possible, for example, that information provided during process evaluation may lead the decision-maker to reconsider a structuring decision which he made earlier and, thus, initiate a new input evaluation or revise the previous one. Such practical considerations are among the major contributions derived from Stufflebeam's approach to evaluation. He clearly states that evaluation studies are closely related to management procedures and decision-making and that the nature of evaluation is such that it does not go on in a vacuum, but, instead, is influenced greatly by many diverse contextual factors. It is essential that the evaluator be fully aware of these factors when evaluating a program.

Stufflebeam has also emphasized the importance of the descriptive aspects of program studies. By highlighting the various stages of program development, he has focused the evaluator's attention on a detailed description of the program being evaluated.

If Mrs. Allen wished to use Stufflebeam's approach to evaluation, she would probably first identify the types of decision for which the evaluation was intended to provide information. Does she need to decide on an appropriate set of objectives, or has she already set her objectives and need now to decide which of several alternative strategies is best for attaining them? In the evaluation problem described for Mrs. Allen, she has already made both of these types of decisions (that is, both planning and structuring decisions), resulting in a set of written instructional objectives and a strategy for attaining them. In this regard, Mrs. Allen has made several important decisions about her evaluation program without explicit use of evaluation data—something she would not have done if she had followed the logic of Stufflebeam's approach. If she wished to use the CIPP evaluation model more fully, she might decide to reexamine the decisions she has reached by means of a formal context evaluation. As part of such an evaluation, she would work collaboratively with the decision-maker to focus the evaluation, describe the existing instructional program, identify any problems or needs that exist in the program, and identify and articulate objectives which, if attained, would solve the problems or satisfy the needs. Once objectives had been established, Mrs. Allen would conduct an input evaluation to assess the potential utility of several alternative strategies for attaining her objectives, to determine which is likely to prove most effective. Use of formal context and input evaluation methods might provide information that would cause Mrs. Allen to adopt a set of instructional objectives or an instructional approach different from her original choice.

However, for the sake of the example, let us assume that Mrs. Allen is convinced of the soundness of her original plans and that she is satisfied with both her objectives and her strategy for achieving them. In this case, she is no longer concerned with planning and structuring decisions and needs now to collect information relevant to the implementing and recycling decisions she has yet to make.[17] Thus her immediate concern would be with process evaluation, and product evaluation would be necessary to help her reach recycling decisions at the end of the school year. In process evaluation, Mrs. Allen would establish a system for providing continual feedback about how well the instructional strategy she has chosen is working. This would enable her to detect unanticipated defects in either her strategy or its implementation.

In designing a product evaluation study, Mrs. Allen would first focus the evaluation study by delineating the program outcomes

---

17. In "real-life" evaluations, this state of affairs is typical. Few educators seem aware of the procedures suggested by Stufflebeam to support planning and structuring decisions. Educators most often seem inclined to set general goals for a program, decide on a strategy for conducting the program, and, with the direction of the program firmly set, begin to think of evaluation as a way to determine whether or not the program achieves its objectives.

she wishes to use as a basis for making judgments about the effectiveness of the program (in other words, for determining whether
the objectives have been attained). She would next specify the
information she needs on each outcome, the sources of this
information, how the information will be collected (the schedule
of data collection). To follow Stufflebeam's suggestions fully, she
must also identify the audiences to which she will address her
report(s); that is, those people who will be influenced by or who
will influence the course she is initiating. Having done this, the
collection, organization, and analysis of the information, and the
reporting of the findings should all logically fall into place.

Again, it is obvious that Mrs. Allen would not have all the
competencies required to conduct the evaluation study. It is
essential that she consult specialists in the areas in which she needs
help as she designs and implements the study.

Alkin's Model

The second decision-management approach to evaluation is one
described by Alkin (1969). Excerpts from that paper are reprinted
below.

Excerpts from

Evaluation Theory Development

Marvin C. Alkin

University of California, Los Angeles

. . . .

Evaluation is the process of ascertaining the decision areas of
concern, selecting appropriate information, and collecting and
analyzing information in order to report summary data useful to
decision-makers in selecting among alternatives.

. . . .

Five areas of evaluation may be identified.

These five areas represent attempts to provide evaluation
information to satisfy unique decision categories. In other words,
there are evaluations necessary in providing information for

From *Evaluation Comment*, 1969, 2, 2-7 (Center for Study of Evaluation,
University of California at Los Angeles). Reprinted with permission of the
author.

decisions about the state of the system. (We call such evaluations *systems assessment.)* There are evaluations necessary in providing information to assist in the selection of particular programs likely to be effective in meeting specific educational needs. (We call this kind of evaluation, which takes place prior to the implementation of the program, *program planning.)* There are evaluations necessary in providing information relative to the extent to which a program has been introduced in the manner in which it was intended and to the group for which it was intended (*program implementation*). There are evaluations necessary in providing information during the course of a program about the manner in which the program is functioning, enroute objectives are being achieved, and what unanticipated outcomes are being produced. Such information can be of value in modifying the program (*program improvement*). Evaluations are necessary in providing information that might be used by decision-makers in making judgments about the worth of the program and its potential generalizability to other related situations (*program certification*).

Systems Assessment

Systems assessment is a means of determining the range and specificity of educational objectives appropriate for a particular situation. The needs may be represented as a gap between the goal and the present state of affairs. The evaluative problem, then, becomes one of assessing the needs of students, of the community, and of society in relation to the existing situation. Assessment, therefore, is a statement of the status of the system as it presently exists in comparison to desired outputs or stated needs of the system.

A systems assessment might be related to evaluation of a specific instructional program and thus the change would be to determine the present status relative only to a specific objective and related objectives. We would refer to this as a "sub-system assessment."

Systems assessment does not refer to specification of process characteristics appropriate for a district, school, or classroom. A statement such as "this district needs a lower pupil-teacher ratio" or "a need of this district is to install team teaching" is not a systems assessment. The systems assessment must be related to the ultimate behavior of clients of one type or another (pupils, parents, community, etc.—all clients of the school). To put it simply, systems assessment must result in a statement of objectives in terms of outputs of the school.

The process in the systems-assessment area of ascertaining the decision area, specifying and collecting information and reporting summary data, requires methodology and techniques different from that which might be employed, for example, in a typical experimental design. The data are concerned with the status of the system. The summary data might be comparative, historical, or other descriptive information.

Program Planning

Program planning, the second need area, is concerned with providing information which will enable the decision-maker to make planning decisions—to select among alternative processes in order to make a judgment as to which of them should be introduced into the system to fill most efficiently the critical needs previously determined. In an instance where we are proceeding through severe need areas in sequential fashion, the following might occur. After the decision-maker receives the systems assessment evaluation, he might make a decision as to the appropriate means of fulfilling that need. Alternatively, he might designate several possibilities and ask the evaluator to provide information on the possible impact of each. Hence, in program planning, the evaluator provides the data for an evaluation of a program prior to its inception. The task of the evaluator is to anticipate the attainment of goals and to assess the potential relative effectiveness of different courses of action.

It is quite obvious that the collection and analysis of data of the type required for this evaluation need area will be quite different from collection and analysis problems for other areas. The techniques may require both internal and external evaluation procedures. (See Lumsdaine, 1965.)

By way of internal evaluation, programs may be examined to determine the extent to which their reproducible segments purport to achieve the objectives of the program being evaluated. Technical features of style or construction, practicality, and cost are other means of providing internal evaluation. To date, the evaluations of products by EPIE [Educational Products Information Exchange] have been primarily based upon internal evaluations.

External evaluations of programs yet to be implemented might take the form of examining research data on the results of implementation in similar or near-similar situations. Or external evaluations might attempt to utilize some of the various educational planning techniques to obtain data. Computer simulations might be developed: Delphi analysis might provide insights into the potential outcomes of a program; gaming and various other systems analytic approaches might also provide external evaluation data.

Program Implementation

After the decision-maker has selected the program to be implemented, an evaluation of program implementation determines the extent to which the implemented program meets the description formulated in the program planning decision. In the case of an existing program where no known changes have been implemented, the evaluation task at this stage is to determine the degree to which planning descriptions of the program coincide with the implemented program and the extent to which assumed descriptions of inputs to the system (students) correspond with observed inputs.

There have been numerous examples in the educational literature of conflicting results relative to the impact of a specific instructional treatment. We would maintain that in large part this is attributable to the lack of specificity of the precise nature of the instructional treatment that was employed. Team teaching is *not* always team teaching. More precisely, team teaching in Santa Rosa might be quite different from team teaching in Boston or from team teaching in Palo Alto, California. The precise definition of the parameters defined as team teaching in a given situation would help to insure an understanding of what is being evaluated and whether what is being evaluated is what the investigator thought the program was.

Program Improvement

The evaluator can play an important role in program improvement, the fourth need area, by providing as much information as possible about the relative success of the parts of the program. In order to perform program improvement evaluation, it is necessary to recognize the basically interventionist role that the evaluator has been asked to take.

The key point in the understanding of the role of the evaluator in performing evaluations in this need area is that he is first and foremost an interventionist attempting to provide data which will lead to the immediate modification and, hopefully, improvement of the program. As the evaluator identifies problems and collects and analyzes related information, data are presented immediately to the decision-maker so that changes may be executed within the system to improve the operation of the program. Information might include data on the extent to which the program appears to be achieving the prescribed objectives, as measured by regular tests; information also might be presented which relates to the impact of the program on other processes or programs.

This need area has often been overlooked or ignored by the traditional evaluator who has attempted to impose the antiseptic sterility of the laboratory on the real world. Such an approach may make for a fine experiment, but it does little to improve a program which is often not in its final form.

Program Certification

In the fifth evaluation need area, program certification, the role of the evaluator is to provide the decision-maker with information that will enable him to make decisions about the program as a whole and its potential generalizability to other situations. The evaluator might attempt to provide information which will enable the decision-maker to determine whether the program should be eliminated, modified, retained, or introduced more widely.

The kind of information collected for program certification decisions is in large part dependent upon who is the intended decision-maker. It is obvious that different information will be required if the potential decision-maker is the teacher, the principal, or a funding agency. Evaluations in this area will be concerned with examining the extent to which the objectives have been achieved, as well as with the impact on the outcomes of other programs.

In program certification evaluations, there is a requirement for valid and reliable data which would generally require that the evaluator attempt to apply as rigid a set of controls as possible. The evaluator might use pre- and post-test designs and employ sophisticated methods for analyzing the data. Intervention should be avoided in evaluations in this need area. Here the traditional evaluator is "at home."

In considering the situations in which evaluation might take place in various need areas, we have found it helpful to differentiate between the evaluation of educational systems and the evaluation of instructional programs. In terms of the conceptual framework that has been presented, one can view the evaluation of educational systems as involving the first two need areas and the evaluation of instructional programs as largely involving the last three.

In evaluating any educational system it is necessary to determine the educational needs in terms of the most appropriate objective for the given system and to devise a procedure for providing regular information on the progress of the system relative to these dimensions. This procedure is the evaluative device for decision-making about the assessment of system needs (Systems Assessment). When decisions have been made about the objectives of the system which are inadequately met, the decision-maker might then be concerned with the selection of programs to meet these objectives. Evaluation information might be sought relative to the possible impact of various courses of action or programs (Program Planning).

. . . .

The evaluation of an instructional program assumes the prior assessment of the program or of a larger system, a decision about objectives to be attended to, and the selection of programs considered to be appropriate for meeting these objectives. That is, the evaluation of an instructional program ordinarily begins after the decisions related to need areas 1 and 2 of the evaluation have been made. In evaluating an instructional program, the objectives to be achieved and the program which it is assumed will be most successful in achieving these objectives are generally considered as "given." Thus, the evaluation of an instructional program focuses primarily on the last three need areas of evaluation.

Where the evaluation task commences with the evaluation of the instructional program, we envisage the necessity for a sub-system assessment dealing with the area of concern of the selected instructional program. Thus, it is seen that the evaluation need areas are not necessarily sequential with the steps easily defined. In some instances, moreover, the data collection, analysis, and reporting appropriate to a decision might be so easy to obtain or so inextricably tied to the making of the decision that the decision-maker and his staff would perform the evaluation themselves. In some instances, the project begins for the evaluator after a number of decisions have already been made. Thus, the evaluator might have to attend to only selected evaluation need areas.

Alkin's Model: An Application

If Mrs. Allen wished if implement Alkin's model, it is evident that the procedures she would use to conduct her evaluation study would be almost identical with those described earlier in applying Stufflebeam's CIPP model, with the exception that she must focus separately on program implementation and program improvement, two subdivisions of what Stufflebeam terms process evaluation. If she chooses to develop a monitoring system like the one discussed earlier in relation to process evaluation, it will provide her with the information she needs to determine whether the proposed teaching strategy is being implemented correctly and, if not, what revisions are necessary.

Decision-Objective Strategies

The most pervasive influence in this evaluation school of thought has been that of Ralph Tyler (1942, 1958). According to Tyler, the major steps in program evaluation are:

(a) to establish broad goals or objectives;
(b) to classify objectives;
(c) to define objectives in behavioral terms;
(d) to find situations in which achievement of objectives can be shown;
(e) to develop or select measurement techniques;
(f) to collect student performance data; and
(g) to compare data with behaviorally stated objectives.

The evaluation process outlined above is essentially "objectives-oriented." If the objectives are achieved, one type of decision will be made. If they are not achieved, or are achieved only to a limited extent, other decisions may be made. Evaluation, as Tyler defined it, is a recurring process: evaluation feedback may be used to reformulate or redefine objectives, and information derived from previous evaluation studies may be used to further develop plans for assessment and interpretation. Modifications of the objectives and of the program being evaluated will result in corresponding revisions of the plan and program of evaluation.

Tyler's approach to evaluation is evident both in the Eight Year Study of the 1930s (Smith and Tyler, 1942) and the more recent National Assessment Project (Womer, 1970). Recent papers by Metfessel and Michael (1967), Hammond (1969), and Provus also follow the Tylerian tradition in that the primary emphasis of the evaluation is on the congruence of behavioral performance with stated objectives.[18] The Metfessel-Michael paper, while containing an evaluation strategy very much like that proposed by Tyler, is more valuable for its appendix of measurement techniques and therefore is presented in a later section. The Hammond and Provus papers are presented here as the best-developed recent decision-objectives approaches to evaluation.

---

18. Provus's paper also contains elements of a decision-management strategy and represents a hybrid of these two general types of evaluation.

Evaluation at the Local Level

Robert L. Hammond

University of Oregon

Introduction

The need for a systematic approach to the evaluation of innovations has become one of educations's most pressing problems. Only by systematic evaluation can education avoid the fads, pressures, pendulum-swingings of educational practice and address itself to the basic question concerning an educational innovation: Is it really effective in achieving its expressed objectives?

At present, there is little or no evidence gathered concerning the effectiveness of educational innovations in meeting their objectives. On what basis, then, are innovations currently adopted or continued in practice? Unfortunately, we often rely on educational ideology or the persuasive claims of advocates or salesmen. Often we claim the merits of an innovation are self-evident. More frequently, we seek the opinions of the consumers, interpreting the enthusiasm of the teachers and students (found in most new programs) as evidence of the complete success of the innovation. Or, conversely, we interpret teacher or student aversion to the new program as evidence of program failure.

Because there are few criteria of educational effectiveness, many suggest that achievement of objectives is difficult, if not impossible, to assess. The procedures, structure, and model described in this paper are proposed as a systematic way to assess the effectiveness of an innovation. Utilizing the basic structure, model, and the consulting, technological and information retrieval services offered by the Center concept, any district can systematically gather valid data needed to decide whether to adopt or continue in practice a given innovation.

Evaluation as a Process

Research has failed to produce adequate guidelines and procedures to be utilized by school districts for the purpose of evaluating both current and innovative programs. The problem is complicated further by the fact that the school districts of the past have not included the process of evaluation as one of the

Reprinted with permission of the author.

major criteria for curriculum improvement. A lack of guidelines and the reluctance on the part of educators to include evaluation as a major function of curriculum development have produced a situation in which little evidence is available as to what should be evaluated, and how evaluation should take place. The guidelines offered in the literature are usually in the form of recommendations for administering achievement and intelligence tests. With these over-simplified approaches to the problem of evaluation, teachers and administrators are left with the problem of drawing conclusions from inadequate data and the general enthusiasm of teachers and pupils.

Recognizing the need for guidelines and the development of evaluation programs, a team of educators representing elementary and secondary curriculum, administration, guidance, educational psychology, and sociology developed an approach to the problem of evaluation through a ten-month planning period. The results of their efforts described in this paper are not proposed as eternal verities, but as a systematic way in which to assess the effectiveness of both current and innovative programs. The structure and model will undoubtedly undergo modification, or even major changes of form as study progresses.

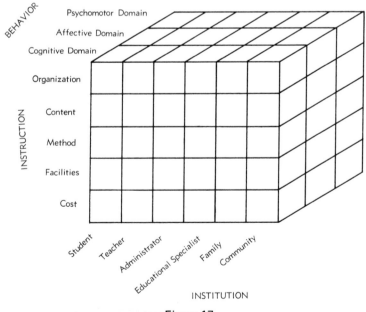

Figure 17

Structure for Evaluation

A Structure for Evaluation

The success or failure of innovations in modern programs of instruction is determined by the interaction of specific forces within the educational environment. The forces affecting innovation are described in terms of specific dimensions and variables operating in a three-dimensional structure (See figure 17). The interaction of variables from each of the three dimensions produces combinations of variables described as factors to be considered in the evaluation of a given program. The importance of any combination of variables is determined by the nature of the instructional program selected for study.

Instructional Dimension

The Instructional Dimension is that dimension of the model which describes the innovation in terms of specific variables. The first of these variables is that of Organization. Organization is defined as the matrix in which teachers and pupils are brought together so that instruction can take place. The organizational matrix may be divided into two components known as time and space.

1. *Time* refers to the duration and sequence of blocks of time devoted to the subjects taught. Duration may be defined as the length of any given period. Sequence may be defined as the order in which subjects are taught. Duration and sequence may be thought of in terms of both daily and weekly scheduling. (Example: Science may be taught only twice a week.)

2. *Space* refers to the vertical and horizontal organization of students. Vertical organization serves to classify students and move them upward from the point of admission to the point of departure. Horizontal organization divides students among teachers. Both grouping processes may be homogeneous, heterogeneous, or a combination of the two.

   a. Vertical Organization: Vertically, schools may be graded or non-graded, or fall somewhere in between.

      (1) Graded: In pure grading, the content of the instruction program and its sequential arrangement are determined by assignment of subject matter to various grade levels, by designation of instructional materials suitable for particular grade levels, and by promotion of pupils upon satisfactory completion of the work specified for each grade.

(2) Non-graded: In pure non-grading, sequence of
content is determined by the inherent difficulties of subject matter in the children's demonstrated ability to cope with it; materials are
selected to match the spread of individual
differences existing within the instructional gap;
and the children will operate according to their
readiness to perceive. Promotion or non-
promotion does not exist as such. An important
goal is to provide continuous progress of each
child.

b. Horizontal Organization: Horizontally, schools may
be organized into any one of many alternative patterns. But all of these horizontal patterns are derived
from essentially four different kinds of considerations—considerations of the child, of the curriculum,
or the teacher's qualifications, and the school's
philosophy.

(1) Self-contained: Self-contained classroom is
defined as a classroom in which a group of
children of similar social maturity, ability, age,
etc., are grouped together under the continued
guidance of a single teacher.

(2) Departmentalization: The characteristic feature
of departmental instruction is that a teacher
who is highly trained in a field of knowledge is
assigned to teach English, which in the elementary school would include reading, writing, spelling, and literature; other teachers assigned to the
Social Studies, including history, geography, and
citizenship; another teacher to Mathematics;
another to Natural Sciences; etc.

(3) Cooperative teaching: Under the general heading
of cooperative teaching may be found dozens of
different patterns of school and staff organization. Some of these are derived from, or associated with, attempts to achieve greater flexibility in pupil grouping. Others are associated
with efforts to eliminate the administrative and
instructional characteristics of rigid, lock-step,
organization structure. One of the most important forms of cooperative teaching is the
organizational pattern known as team teaching.

The second variable is that of Content. Content is defined as
that structure or body of knowledge which is identified with the
subject matter of a discipline and controls its inquiries. Content

may be described in terms of specific topics to be covered at a given grade level.

A third variable is that of Methodology. Methodology is that process designed to facilitate learning. It may be divided into three levels: teaching activities, types of interaction, and learning principles or theories utilized.

1. *Teaching Activities*

   a. Lecture
   b. Discussion
   c. Question-Answer
   d. Committee
   e. Round table
   f. Symposium
   g. Drill
   h. Homework
   i. Review
   j. Individual supervised study
   k. Resource person(s)
   l. Field trips
   m. Inquiry
   n. Debate
   o. Media*

   *Includes: texts, resource books (dictionaries, encyclopedias, library, etc.), workbooks, films, film strips (with and without tapes), tapes/records, television (commercial, educational, closed circuit), laboratories (science, language), programmed teaching machines/texts.

2. *Types of Interaction*

   a. Teacher ←→ Student
   b. Student ←→ Student
   c. Media ←→ Student
   d. Teacher ←→ Teacher**

   **Principally team teaching. (In addition to identifying the interaction participants, there are a number of codes that have been developed to describe the interaction such as: (1) Interaction Analysis—Ned Flanders; (2) Teaching Interaction—Marie Hughes; (3) Classroom Transaction—Stanford University.) (Sample: Devised and revised by many members of staff.)

3. *Learning Theory*

   a. Behavior which represents the achievement or partial achievement of an educational objective should be reinforced.
   b. The introduction of cues which arouse motivation toward the achievement of an educational objective will increase the effectiveness with which that objective is achieved.
   c. Practice in applying a principle to the solution of problems will increase the probability of transfer of training to new problems which require the use of the same principle for their solution.

    d. Since learners differ in their capacity to make the responses to be acquired, learning will be most effective if it is planned so that each learner embarks on a program commensurate with his capacity to acquire new responses.

    e. If a pupil has training in imitation, then he is capable of learning by observing demonstrations of skills to be acquired.

    f. The learner will learn more efficiently if he makes the responses to be learned than if he learns by observing another make the responses or makes some related response.

The fourth and fifth variables are Facilities and Cost. Facilities is defined as that space, special equipment, and expendables needed to support an educational program. Cost is the money required for facilities, maintenance, and personnel to accomplish a given task.

The variables defined in the above represent important categories to be considered in the instuctional program. The innovation to be considered may be contained in any one of the variables (e.g., team teaching—organization). Yet all variables must be considered in the analysis of the total program. If innovations are to be adopted on a wide scale, a complete picture of the program must be studied with its various components carefully analyzed.

Institutional Dimension

The Institutional Dimension is that dimension of the model defined by the variables of Child, Teacher, Administrator, Educational Specialist, Family, and Community. Any given innovation will be influenced by the unique qualities of the individuals involved. For the purposes of evaluation, each of the variables is described in terms of sub-variables that may have a direct influence on the given program. The following examples are a sample of these descriptive sub-variables.

1. *Student*

    a. Age

    b. Grade level

    c. Sex

    d. Familial variables

    e. Socio-economic variables

    f. Physical health

    g. Mental health

    h. Achievement

    i. Ability

    j. Interest

    k. Relationship to innovation

2. *Teacher, Administrator, and Educational Specialist*
   a. Identification Data
   - (1) Age
   - (2) Sex
   - (3) Race, nationality, religion
   - (4) Physical health
   - (5) Personality characteristics
   b. Educational Background and Work Experience
   - (1) Undergraduate major and minor
   - (2) Graduate major
   - (3) Highest degree
   - (4) Educational experience
   - (5) Experience outside education
   c. Environmental Factors
   - (1) Professional salary
   - (2) Professional affiliations
   - (3) Non-professional affiliations
   - (4) Socio-economic status of residence
   - (5) Professional and non-professional reading habits
   - (6) Leisure activities outside professional work time
   d. Degree of Involvement in Program
3. *Family*
   a. Degree of Involvement with Innovation
   - (1) Have children in school; all affected by the innovation.
   - (2) Have children in school; some affected by, some not affected by, the innovation.
   - (3) Have children in school; none affected by the innovation.
   - (4) Have no children in school (these are treated under descriptive items in the Community variable).
   b. General Characteristics
   - (1) Ethnic/national/linguistic
   - (2) Size
     - (a) Total
     - (b) Siblings
     - (c) Other relatives present
   - (3) Age distribution
   - (4) Marital status
   - (5) Pattern
     - (a) Nuclear
     - (b) Extended

(6) Income
   (a) Approximate level
   (b) Number of wage earners
   (c) Source
   (d) Occupation
(7) Residence
   (a) Urban
   (b) Suburban
   (c) Rural
   (d) Cost range
(8) Education
   (a) Approximate formal level
      i. Parents
      ii. Siblings
      iii. Other relatives present
   (b) Informal
      i. Industrial
      ii. Military
      iii. Community service
      iv. Other
(9) Affiliations
   (a) Religious   (d) Professional
   (b) Political   (e) Other
   (c) Social
(10) Mobility
   (a) Parents' place of origin
   (b) Length of time in community
   (c) Frequency of moving
   (d) Extent of traveling
4. Community
  a. Geographical Setting
    (1) Location
    (2) Environment—general
  b. Historical Development
  c. Population Characteristics
    (1) Demographic data
      (a) Population size   (d) Birth and death rates
      (b) Population density   (e) Age distribution
      (c) Marriage and divorce rates
    (2) Ethnic/nationality
    (3) Linguistic

    (4) Change patterns
       (a) Mobility patterns
          i. Immigration
          ii. Emigration
          iii. Migrant-indigenous ratio
       (b) Growth patterns
  d. Economic Characteristics
    (1) Commercial/industrial organization and development
    (2) Occupational range
    (3) Sources/range of individual incomes
    (4) Sources/range of tax base
  e. Social Characteristics
    (1) Institutions and organizations
       (a) Government/political   (f) Commercial/financial
       (b) Educational   (g) Labor
       (c) Religious   (h) Professional
       (d) Service   (i) Recreational
       (e) Social   (j) Protection
    (2) Power structure
    (3) Socio-economic stratification

Assessment programs of the past have focused primarily on the child and his response to content in a given subject area. With the changes taking place in instructional programs, more evidence is needed as to the influence of the teacher, administrator, parent, and community on a given innovation.

Behavioral Dimension

The Behavioral Dimension is defined by the variables of Cognitive, Affective, and Psychomotor Behavior. Evaluation as a process is best approached through objectives stated in behavioral terms. At this point in the development of the structure for evaluation, three variables for classifying these objectives are recognized. The first of these variables is Cognitive Behavior. Cognitive Behavior includes the recall, comprehension, and application of knowledge and the utilization of intellectual skills of analysis, synthesis, and evaluation. The best example of tests in this area are the standardized tests of achievement. In the majority of programs this is the only test utilized to describe the success or failure of both current and innovative programs.

The second variable in this dimension is Affective Behavior. Affective Behavior is defined as the interest, attitudes, values, appreciations, and adjustments of the individual. In recent years

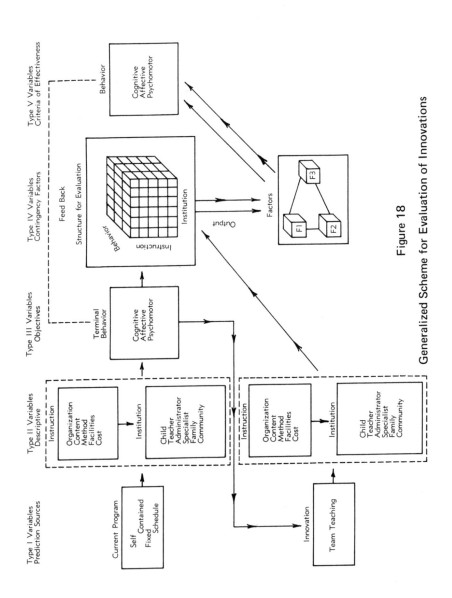

Figure 18

Generalized Scheme for Evaluation of Innovations

we have reached a point in the evaluation process where we are now concerned not only with the knowledge gained, but with the willingness of the student to identify himself with a given subject. Many instructional programs today repel students for reasons other than academic ability. Recognizing this fact, it is important that we look at the reasons for this behavior.

Psychomotor Behavior is the third variable in this domain. It includes those acts which involve neuro-muscular coordination. Handwriting and physical education utilize this variable to draw conclusions about special programs.

A fourth variable, Perceptual Behavior, is now under study at the Center. It is hoped that this area will be adequately defined so that it may be utilized in the evaluation process for the coming year. At this point, it may be classified as experimental.

The structure developed provides a framework to produce factors that have a direct influence on a given innovation. The factors created by the interaction of one variable from each of the dimensions may be studied in any depth desired by a school district. In most cases, the study of a given factor will be determined by time, availability of tests and procedures, and the needs of a given school district.

A Model for
Evaluation as a Process

Once the forces affecting a given innovation have been identified and placed in a structure which permits an analysis of the interaction of these forces, the next step is that of placing the structure in a working model for evaluation (see figure 18).

The application of this model in school evaluation programs must be approached with caution through carefully defined steps. Teachers and administrators have not been adequately trained in the skills necessary to evaluate instructional programs. Once these skills have been developed through the cooperative efforts of the school and Center, the school district personnel should progress to the point that they can operate independently. The training period demands the first step toward adequate evaluation be limited to the capabilities of the personnel in the given school district.

Sound evaluation procedures require that the process begin with the current programs. Before attempts at innovation are made, adequate baseline data is required to make those decisions which determine the direction of the change process.

Beginning with the prediction source, the program must be defined in terms of what is to be evaluated. All too frequently, the school district moves into the evaluation process by attacking the total school program. Due to the limited skills of personnel, the evaluation process is doomed before it starts, or more often returns to the use of standardized achievement tests as the only criteria for evaluation. The first step should be one of beginning with a single subject area of the curriculum, such as mathematics, and even then it would be advisable to limit this problem to begin with, as it is assumed that a given innovation would not be applied across all grade levels until verification of intended objectives had been completed.

The second step is that of defining the descriptive variables in the Instructional and Institutional Dimensions. Before moving to step three, all variables with the exception of Cost and those within the Institutional Dimension should be defined.

The third step in the evaluation process is that of stating objectives in behavioral terms. This represents one of the most crucial steps in the evaluation process. Properly stated objectives will:

1. specify the kind of behavior which will be accepted as evidence that the learner has achieved the objective.
2. state the conditions under which the behavior will be expected to occur.
3. specify the criteria of acceptable performance by describing how well the learner must perform.

In the process of stating objectives, the structure for evaluation (figure 17) will be used to point out a need for objectives in addition to those involving Content, Child, and Cognitive Behavior.

Once the behavioral objectives have been developed, the fourth step in the evaluation process is that of assessing the behavior described in the objectives. The Center will provide information regarding standardized tests, techniques, test research, and the technical help necessary for creating additional instruments and techniques to be used by the classroom teacher. The final phase of step four is the output of factors determined by the current program for the innovation under consideration.

With the factors identified, the fifth step is that of analyzing the results within factors and the relationships between factors, to arrive at conclusions based on actual behavior. Once the outcomes have been defined, there is a feedback process to the terminal behavior defined through objectives to determine the effectiveness of a given program in reaching the desired outcomes.

With the current program evaluated through the process described, the school or district is ready to consider change in the instructional program. Change will take place in the form of innovations. The decisions for innovation will be determined by evidence gathered as to what the change process should involve, and most important of all, it will provide data for the school boards, community, and administration to make those important decisions necessary for providing instructional programs which meet the needs of every child.

Hammond's Paper: An Application

Hammond has suggested that local personnel ought to be trained to carry on the evaluation process. That is, after appropriate training by outside evaluation specialists, personnel in local innovative programs should be able to conduct their own evaluation studies. This is an excellent strategy for involving local personnel in evaluation.

In addition to using Tyler's suggestions of specifying behavioral objectives and using evaluation feedback to revise the objectives of the program development, Hammond has made a unique contribution to strategies of evaluation in the "program description cube" presented in figure 17. The elaboration on instructional and institutional variables which may affect the outcomes of innovative programs provides a useful set of guidelines for the evaluator. Furthermore, a consideration of possible two-or three-dimensional interactions within the cube serves as a reminder of important program factors which are often overlooked in evaluation studies. The structure for evaluation which Hammond has presented may also be used for generating program objectives or in designing needs assessment or "context evaluation" plans (see Hammond, 1969). Of course, the cube is not invariably applicable, and attempts to design each evaluation study around it may result in Kaplan's "law of the instrument" fallacy,[19] or may create a design predestined to consist of mostly empty cells, while excluding many other important variables. However, used properly, Hammond's program-description cube is an extremely useful tool for the evaluator.

If Mrs. Allen decided to implement Hammond's suggestions, she would first consider each of the three dimensions and their interactions in the cube to help her (a) plan her evaluation study, and (b) define the objectives for her new course. She would produce a full description of both the traditional program and the new sophomore English course, using Hammond's cube as a guide.

---

19. Abraham Kaplan (1964, p. 28) formulated what he calls the law of the instrument: "Give a small boy a hammer, and he will find that everything he encounters needs pounding. It comes as no particular surprise to discover that a scientist formulates problems in a way which requires for their solution just those techniques in which he himself is especially skilled."

Objectives, stated in behavioral terms, would then be defined for each of her two classes. Once the objectives have been defined, it will be up to Mrs. Allen to measure the behavior described in the objectives, to analyze the information she has collected, and to report to the principal the effectiveness of each of the two instructional techniques in attaining the stated objectives. It will be up to the principal to determine whether her innovation meets the needs of the students, the school, and the community. Although Mrs. Allen would still need to secure the help of measurement and analysis specialists, she might well follow Hammond's suggestion and seek assistance from someone who would at the same time train her sufficiently to carry out most steps on her own in future evaluation studies.

Evaluation of Ongoing Programs in the Public School System

Malcolm Provus

University of Virginia

Introduction

To the school administrator who needs information about the effectiveness of school programs, the word "evaluation" conjures up some unpleasant memories: a report that took "too long" to prepare and overlooked the obvious while concentrating on the trite, a university consultant who proved unintelligible and eventually hostile, an investigator who got in everyone's way and never seemed able to draw definitive conclusions.

It is entirely possible that most public school evaluations are meaningless because they reflect the confusion of administrators regarding educational programs which are equally meaningless. It is also possible that most evaluators do not know their business. No doubt, the weakness of educational programs, evaluation methodology, and the training provided in institutions that prepare both administrators and evaluators are related.

Recent public school programs are marked by a lack of program control and by measured outcomes that suggest there is greater program variation within programs than between programs (Miles, 1964). A recent unpublished evaluation of team teaching in a large

From the *NSSE 68th Yearbook, Part II*, 1969, 242-283. Copyright 1969 by the National Society for the Study of Education. Reprinted with permission of the author and the Society.

city school system revealed forty different programs in forty different schools, none of which adhered to the essential principles of team teaching as originally conceived by the school system (Kresh, 1963). It is not surprising that students who had been exposed to this kind of "team teaching" for six years showed no greater growth in academic performance than did a control group.

A clause of the 1965 Elementary-Secondary Education Act established evaluation as a necessary building block in the design of American educational reform. The evaluation requirements of that act eventually may prove to have greater impact on education than the program itself. The Congress mandated that billions of dollars be spent in new ways to serve new purposes, yet there is reason to doubt that the administrative capacity exists at each level of government to insure that the money is well spent. Perhaps before we can build effective new programs, we must establish creative new ways to monitor and eventually judge the effectiveness of such programs. This capacity to evaluate programs must ultimately depend upon a management theory that utilizes pertinent, reliable information as the basis for administrative decisions.

Those of us from university research backgrounds who started out in September of 1965 to implement the congressional mandate to evaluate ESEA programs did so with good cheer: "At last," we said, "curriculum evaluation has come into its own." We began our work by oversimplifying the problem—by attempting to determine whether new programs were better than the ones they replaced. We did not then realize that our first problem was to find out what, in fact, constituted a new program. We continued our work by applying the quasi-experimental designs that had served us well in research settings. We soon found that these designs were inapplicable. And finally we settled down to grapple with the formulation of better statements of program objectives and the design of new instruments to measure these objectives— largely ignoring the constrictive influence our activity was having on people responsible for making new programs work.

There is surprisingly little theory on which to base good evaluation practice. The theoretical constructs which appear most relevant to the practitioner are derived from studies by Lippitt, et al. (1958) and Miles (1965) on organizational health and change; Rogers (1955), Lewin (1951), and Corey (1953) on self-realization through group work; the work of Silvern (1965) on functional analysis of curriculum; Wiener (1948) on control and communication systems; and from Tyler's (1950) original work on curriculum-development theory.

This is not to say that there is no new work in evaluation theory going on in the country today. Stufflebeam (1966) and Guba (1965, 1962) have published a number of papers which make substantial contributions to the understanding of institutional change and growth and provide a theoretical frame of reference for the assessment of change. However, despite the title of a new educational periodical, *Theory into Practice*, there appears to be very little linkage between program evaluation going on in public schools today and the kind of theory discussed by university theorists.

The Pittsburgh Evaluation Model

The conclusions and techniques described in this chapter are the result of an attempt to apply evaluation and management theory to the evaluation of programs in a large city school system. As a result of this effort, a model of program evaluation was eventually developed. It serves as the basis for most of the material presented in this chapter.[20]

The purpose of program evaluation is to determine whether to improve, maintain, or terminate a program. Evaluation is the process of (*a*) agreeing upon program standards, (*b*) determining whether a discrepancy exists between some aspect of the program and the standards governing that aspect of the program, and (*c*) using discrepancy information to identify the weaknesses of the program. As a practical matter, it is generally necessary for those concerned with the conduct of education to employ problem-solving techniques once the weaknesses of a program have been identified. These techniques have been widely discussed elsewhere and will be referred to by the author only to indicate their place in the usual sequence of evaluation activity.

Program standards are of two kinds: content and development. These standards are based on the generalizable content and development of educational programs. The content of programs has been classified in a useful way by systems analysts employing the notion that human activity processes inputs to produce outputs (Kershew and McKean, 1959). The development of educational programs has received attention from management engineers, but little has been said in their literature about the relevance of stages of program development to the generalization of program standards for evaluation purposes. It is assumed in this chapter that every educational program undergoes an evolutionary

20. The research described was supported by grants to the author from the Bureau of Research and the Bureau of Elementary and Secondary Education, Office of Education, and the Pennsylvania State Department of Public Instruction.

sequence of development and that evaluation must take these stages into account by applying standards governing the sequence and rate of program development.

It follows that if types of programs having different developmental characteristics exist, the development standards for these program types also will vary. Therefore, it is important that a typology of programs of varying developmental characteristics be attempted. On the basis of the writer's experience, it can be asserted that there are three types of programs exhibiting three different patterns of program development.

The first and most common type of program in public school work is the "instant installation" variety. Most federal programs, especially those funded under Title I of ESEA and often those under Title III as well, are of this variety. They have been quickly formulated without careful planning or design to utilize available resources. Also in the quick-cast category are most of the "new" programs mounted by public school staffs determined to do "something better" on their own initiative. These efforts are rarely planned and defined with sufficient precision to permit adequate evaluations of the new programs.

The second, less common but still widely used, type of program is the "canned" variety. For this kind of program, either a commercial, a public, or a non-profit developer has carefully determined its standards in advance of installation, and guidelines for installation, including staff training, are generally explicit.

The third and least common type of program is that which has been carefully designed by the school system itself. A few school systems have managed to organize the technical skills necessary to do this job successfully. However, in the two instances of such success best known to the author, sizable funds from outside the school system were needed. Of course, the availability of such funds for planning or development purposes, in no way insures that a program's design will be adequate. Vast sums have been wasted as a result of poor design work or of the failure of educators to recognize the necessity for incorporating design activity within the developmental life of a school program in instances in which program specifications were lacking.

For most public school systems, evaluation of school programs consists of efforts to improve programs which were poorly administered. The remainder of this chapter deals with explicit methods for evaluating the first of the three forementioned types. The amount of effort, time, and resources needed for a school system to do the kind of "in-process" program-design work that is described in this chapter fully explains the dependence of school

systems on independent "canned" program-developers such as the
national research and development (R & D) centers. Unfortunately, only a few people in the government and the centers themselves seem to be aware of the kind of program-development work
and supporting program specifications and standards that are
necessary before either regional laboratories, Title III centers, or
public schools can move to install and maintain these programs.

The evaluation of a program already staffed and under way
contains four major developmental stages and involves three major
content categories which in turn can be broken into nineteen
sub-categories. The four development stages can for the time being
be best described as dealing with (*a*) definition, (*b*) installation, (*c*)
process, and (*d*) product. The process of evaluation consists of
moving through stages and content categories in such a way as to
facilitate a comparison of program performance with standards
while at the same time identifying standards to be used for future
comparisons.

This process of comparisons over stages may be clarified by a
flow chart (figure 19).

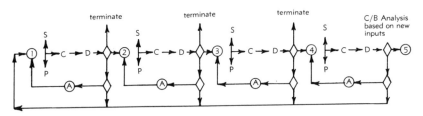

Figure 19

A Flow Chart Designed to Facilitate Comparisons
of Program Performance with Standards

In figure 19, S = standard, P = program performance, C =
compare, D = discrepancy information, and A = change in program
performance or standards. Stage 5 represents a cost-benefit option
available to the evaluator only after the first four stages have been
negotiated. Notice that the use of discrepancy information always
leads to a decision to (*a*) go on to the next stage, (*b*) recycle the
stage after there has been a change in the program's standards or
operations, (*c*) recycle to the first stage, or (*d*) terminate the
project. Discrepancy information permits the program manager to
pinpoint a shortcoming in the program the identification of which
necessarily leads to a change in the operation of the program or to
a change in the specifications under which the program operates.
A superintendent of schools or board of education will be as much

concerned with the movement of a project through its evaluation stages as with discrepancy information at any given stage. The longer it takes to get to stages 2, 3 and 4, the greater the cost if the project fails. The more rapidly a project moves into advanced stages, the less the risk of its failure.

The generalizable content of a program is shown in figure 20. To follow Stake (1967), the transactions that transform input into output are emphasized. Equally important are precise estimates of the amount of time and money needed to locate and use resources.

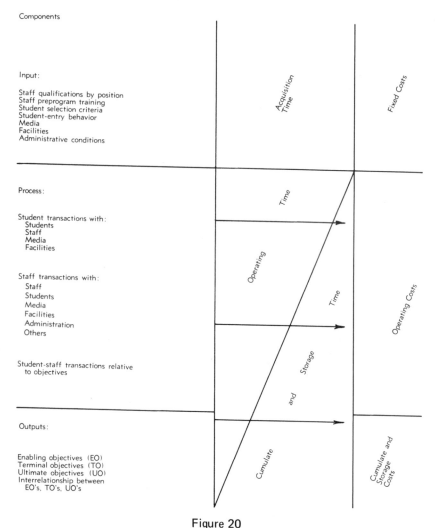

Figure 20

Taxonomy of Program Content

The time and cost columns may be easily understood if one views an educational program as an industrial process. For example, the manufacture of plastic glasses would require raw materials, labor, equipment, and a facility. Time and money would be needed to acquire each of these, and the investments made would be of a fixed amount. Once the actual manufacture of plastic glasses began, both time and money would be required to sustain the operation. As the operation continued, the same time period used to manufacture glasses could be used to assemble and store them for some ultimate purpose (e.g., selling them as they are or making them into some elaborate plastic decorative structure). Hence, although operating costs may be distinguished from cumulate and storage costs, manufacture and storage time overlap (hence the diagonal line in figure 20).

In all stages of the development and evaluation of an educational program, the content specifications remain the same: input, process, and output relative to time and money. Taken in their form in figure 20, they represent a taxonomy. At Stage I the evaluation task is to obtain a definition of the program based on the program-content taxonomy. The definition obtained becomes the program-performance information to be compared with the taxonomy. A discrepancy between any component in the program definition and the same component in the taxonomy represents evaluative information to be used by those responsible for the nature and effectiveness of the program. At stage 2 (figure 19) the standard for comparison is the program definition arrived at in Stage I. Program-performance information consists of observations from the field regarding the installation of the program's components. Discrepancy information is used to redefine the program or to change installation procedures. At stage 3 the standard is that part of the program definition which describes the relationship between program processes and enabling objectives. Discrepancy information is used either to redefine process and relationship of process to interim product or to better control the process being used in the field. At stage 4 the standard is that part of the program definition which refers to terminal objectives. Program-performance information consists of criterion measures used to estimate the terminal effects of the project. At this point, if decision-makers have more than one project with similar outcomes available to them for analysis, they may elect to do a cost-benefit analysis to determine program efficiency.

Methodological Considerations

The manner in which an evaluation based on a content taxonomy and developmental stages can be conducted is perhaps of greater importance to practitioners than the postulation of the existence of evaluation standards. As is usually the case, a discussion of methodology will disclose new theoretical issues to be further considered and resolved. Such a discussion, if based on experience, also constitutes the essential test of sound theory. Therefore an essential purpose of this chapter is to illuminate the distinctions and procedures needed to operationalize the evaluation model described. The major distinction necessary to actualize the model is that between evaluation- and program-staff functions. Assumptions must be posited and further discussion of the evaluation task is necessary if we are to proceed with a clear description of evaluation methodology. Some of the assumptions are as follows:

1. It is necessary to evaluate ongoing school programs in such a way as to make sound decisions as to whether to improve, terminate, or maintain them.
2. There is administrative support for program change initiated by the program staff as opposed to change engineered by authority superordinate to the staff.
3. There is administrative support for making a distinction between program- and evaluation-staff personnel and functions. Program staff is defined as those persons responsible for planning, organizing, and conducting the work of a project.
4. A non-directive, objective evaluation staff can identify and collect information essential to program improvement.
5. Problem-solving activity is required to improve school programs.
6. Problem-solving will be successful only if the program staff is involved in and committed to the change process.
7. A state of tension can be fostered in the program staff which will result in problem-solving activity.
8. Problem-solving success requires pertinent information from the evaluation staff and sound decisions from the program staff.

To distinguish between the functions of the evaluation staff and the program staff, it is necessary to look at the entire web of questions and answers that constitute the problem-solving situation that we call program evaluation. Figure 21 depicts the flow of questions raised in the course of an evaluation and also makes clear how these questions are often nested one within another (see pages 178 to 179 for Figure 21).

The answer to these questions is as much contained in the criterion used to answer them as in the new information used to

STAGE 1.

Step 1. Is The Program Defined?

Standard (Taxonomy) (S)

vs.

Performance (Program Description) (P)

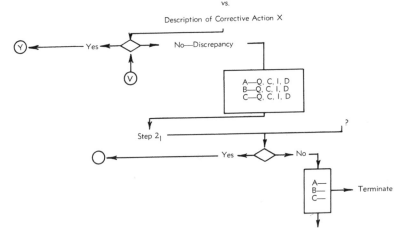

Ⓩ ◄———— Yes ◄ ◇ ———► No—Discrepancy at point X

Ⓦ

A—(Q) Why?
— (C) Process Model for defining point X.
— (I) Actual process used.
— (D) Identify breakdown.
B—(Q) What corrective actions are possible?
— (C) Divergent ideation which may pro-
duce solution sets
— (I) Detailed analysis of problem field
— (D) Selection of ideas which best fit solu-
tion requirements as defined by the
problem field.

C—(Q) Which correction alternative is best?
— (C) Web of administrative predisposition
and value.
— (I) Information which describes hypothetical process alternatives for corrective
alternatives (General R staff)
— (D) Definition of corrective action.

Step 2. Is The Corrective Action X Adequately Defined?
Standard (Process model for defining corrective action
at point X)

vs.

Description of Corrective Action X

Ⓨ ◄———— Yes ◄ ◇ ———► No—Discrepancy

Ⓥ

A—Q, C, I, D
B—Q, C, I, D
C—Q, C, I, D

Step 2₁

◯ ◄———— Yes ◄ ◇ ———► No

A—
B— ———► Terminate
C—

Figure 21

Flow of Questions Raised in Course of an Evaluation

(continued on facing page)

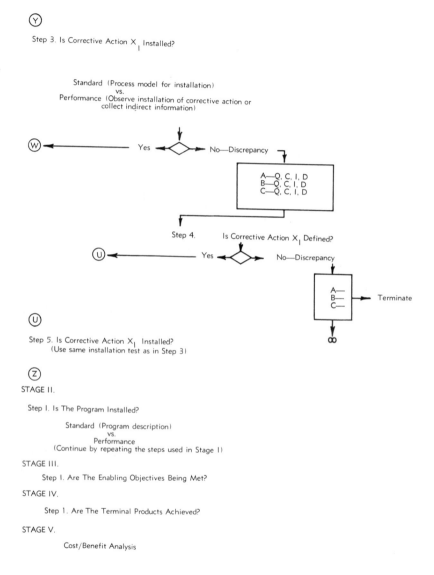

Figure 21

Flow of Questions Raised in Course of an Evaluation

(continued from facing page)

obtain an answer.[21] For our purposes it is only necessary that every question implies a criterion (C), new information (I), and a decision (D), and that different functions are involved in answering a question. It is a tenet of our model that these functions should be carried out by different people with different responsibilities. The formulation of the question is the job of the evaluator; the criterion is the responsibility of the program manager; and the information to be used is a function of both evaluation and program-staff activity. The decision alternatives are outlined by the evaluator while the choice between alternatives belongs to the project director. More about this later.

Figure 21 shows that there are five major steps in Stage I. Each step is defined by a question. These are: Step 1—Is the program defined? Step 2—If not, is a corrective action adequately defined? Step 3—Is the corrective action installed? Step 4—If not, is a corrective action defined for securing installation in Step 3? Step 5—Is the corrective action defined in Step 4 installed?

These five steps represent a sequence of problem-solving efforts that may be needed to define an ongoing program. The same steps are used in Stage II to determine whether the program has been installed as defined. Whenever neither a definition nor an installation is obtained, further definition of some new process for definition or installation becomes necessary. If after considerable problem-solving effort the program still is not defined and installed, the principle of diminishing returns dictates program termination.

Block ⓦ in figure 21 shows the essential problem-solving sequence used to identify a corrective alternative whenever discrepancy information exists as to definition (Stage I), installation (Stage II), process (Stage III), or product (Stage IV). A three-step series of questions is raised: A. Why is there a discrepancy? B. What corrective actions are possible? C. Which corrective action is best? To answer these questions, three elements are necessary: (a) Criteria, based on some ideal type or standard for that which is being investigated, which serve to identify relevant information and to provide a framework for interpreting it; (b) new information about actual performance or practice; (c) a decision to act to change performance based on a comparison of information with criteria and on any resultant discrepancy.

Let us see how Block ⓦ in figure 21 might be applied to the study of one of the program components in the content taxonomy; for example, the "input variable"—student-entry behavior.

---

21. See chapter 5 of *Educational Evaluation and Decision-Making* (Phi Delta Kappa National Study Commission on Evaluation, 1971).

Remember, Block ⓦ is applied only when a discrepancy exists between performance and standard—in this case, the taxonomy and program description. For example, the program description may fail to provide any information about student-entry behavior. Question A in Block ⓦ asks, Why does this discrepancy exist? The criteria for this question describe the ideal way in which a description should have been formulated. For example, the staff might study prior to their enrollment in the program the behavior of students for whom the program is intended. The staff could then isolate performance variables which on their face appear relevant to criterion performance. The staff should find ways to measure at least some of these variables in pretreatment subjects and then describe how such information will be routinely obtained as part of the program. Such a process model for defining any component so that it is congruent with the program taxonomy constitutes the essential criterion for answering question A. The information (I) required to answer question A is a description of the process which was actually used in order to arrive at a definition of student-entry level. Perhaps, upon investigation, it is determined that someone was merely told by someone else to "describe students to be enrolled in the program" and in fact this description took the form of age and grade-level measures. A comparison of the process model with actual practice, (C) with (I), makes likely a clear-cut decision (D) as to the cause of the discrepancy. The "Why" question, A, has been answered. Question B, "What corrective actions are possible?" is now pertinent. Again the answer to this question depends on criteria (C), information (I), and a decision (D) based on a comparison of (C) with (I). Continuing with our example, question B asks, "How many ways are there of obtaining a definition of student-entry behavior?" The criteria for this question consist of a variety of ways of generating this type of information under various situational constraints. For example, given no one with a knowledge of tests and measurements in the school system, consultants may be employed. Given no students in the system who have not already been enrolled in the program, students in other systems may be identified and studied, or the behavior of students now in the program may be extrapolated to their level prior to the program. The need under (I) is for the collection of all information from the system which is capable of satisfying the possible ideal courses of action which have been devised under (C). The identification of those courses of action compatible with the existing conditions and constraints of the school system is permitted by (D).

Step C of Block Ⓦ raises the final question in the problem-solving sequence.: Given a number of alternative courses of action, which is best? The criteria for this question are located in the judgmental web of the decision-maker. These criteria are rarely explicit, though through introspection they can be made so. Such values as system homeostasis, societal norms, professional standards, the importance of interest groups, and personal expectations are all involved. The decision-maker obtains estimates of the value consequences of each possible alternative under (I) and compares these consequences with his criterion of value. He is thereby enabled to make a decision as to which alternative is best (i.e., optimally satisfies the value web).

It should be noted that the use of the problem-solving Block Ⓦ inevitably raises questions demanding further refinement of criteria. The criterion problem consists of unraveling the values implicit in descriptions of standards, processes, or models needed to identify relevant information for problem-solving. Ultimately, some assumption or absolute is discovered as the basis for an operational criterion and, beyond the identification of this microcosmic value, it is generally not safe for the evaluator to transgress.

Further inspection of figure 21 will now show that the problem-solving block can be used to resolve discrepancies which arise under each of the five steps for each stage of evaluation. Discrepancies may occur at any of the points at which a comparison is made between the program taxonomy and the program definition. Since there are 21 such points and two interactive factors—time and cost—a total of 57 possible discrepancies may arise for each step. Further, since at least five distinct steps may have to be negotiated, some 285 questions could conceivably be generated for Stage I. As has already been pointed out, the (Q), (C), (I), (D) sequence needed to answer each question raised, necessitates additional questions as to criteria and relevant information. If only one criterion question and one information question are raised (and there generally are several such questions), a total of 855 possible questions exist for Stage I.

Figure 21 suggests that the same five steps exist for Stages II, III, and IV. That is, to answer such a question as, "Is the program as defined in Stage I installed?", it is necessary to compare actual installation, that is, field performance (P) with the program definition, which becomes the new standard (S). If a discrepancy at any point in the program definition is discovered in any of the stages, problem-solving Block Ⓦ must be used, and in turn, Steps 2, 3, 4, and 5 may have to be employed. Hence, another 720 potential questions exist for each stage, cumulating to a total of 3,420 questions.

It may be helpful to look at examples of questions from Stages II, III and IV.

Stage II Examples

(Q) Step II: Has the program been installed?

(C)   Compare program definition with installation information for congruence

(I)   Information about installation obtained from field observations

(D)   Decide if program is congruent with standards for Stage II

Block (w)

(Q)   If program is not congruent, why has the program not been installed?

(C)   Model of program installation procedure

(I)   Description of actual installation procedure used

(D)   Decide where procedural breakdown exists

(Q)   What should be done to install the program?

(C)   Alternative installation strategies of a general nature

(I)   Information about operational constraints on alternative strategies

(D)   Select possible specific strategies

(Q)   What strategy is best?

(C)   Value priorities of the decision-maker

(I)   Estimates of the actual value consequences of each workable strategy

(D)   Selection of that strategy which optimizes values

Stage III Examples

(Q)   Is the program achieving its enabling objectives?

(C)   Model of relationship of student-teacher interactions to enabling objectives

(I)   Discrepancy information based on actual program performance of students

(D)   Yes, No

(Q)   If not, why not?

(C)   Model of curriculum-analysis procedure

(I)   Actual analysis of learning events and their sequence

(D)   Description of breakdown points

(Q)   What corrective alternatives appear possible under the model?

(C)   Create solution-set alternatives possible within the problem field

(I)   Detailed analysis of actual constraints in the problem field

(D)   Choose from among them the set which meets field requirements

(Q)   What corrective alternative appears best?

(C)   Model of value web

(I)   Information describing value consequences of alternatives

(D)   Choose alternative with best value-configuration fit

(Q)   Is the "corrective action" adequately defined?

(C)   Model of "corrective action," definition-adequacy criteria

(I)   Information descriptive of existing "corrective action" definition

(D)   Determine if corrective action is adequate in terms of the model

(Q)   If not, why not?

(C)   Detailed description or analysis of corrective-action definition-model (also reanalyze previous models)

(I)   Identify definition process actually used

(D)   Describe points at which the definition process has broken down

(Q)   What corrective alternatives appear possible under the model?

(C)   Create solution-set alternatives

(I)   Detailed description-analysis of problem field based on problem-solving model

(D)   Choose from among them that set which satisfies field demands

(Q)   What corrective alternative appears best?

(C)   Model of value web

(I)   Information describing value consequences of corrective alternatives

(D)   Choose alternative with best value-configuration fit.

(Q)   Is the corrective action installed?

(C)   Model of corrective action derived from definition of corrective action

(I)   Information descriptive of actual field conditions

(D)   Determine if congruence exists

(Q)   If discrepancy, why? (If not, why not?)

(C)   Restate and reanalyze all previous models from III 1. C to III 9.c

(I)   Describe actual processes used in the field

(D)   Identify breakdown points (actual vs. model discrepancies)

The similarity of the questions raised in an evaluation at different stages should now be apparent. It is the content of the questions which varies across the components in the program taxonomy and across stages of development. A question which asks why in-service training of teachers has not been installed obviously differs from one which asks why administrative support has not been provided. And although the criterion problem is the same, the criteria will also differ. Similarly a question about in-service training installation at Stage II differs from one about the meaningfulness of the processes of an in-training program at Stage III. However, both questions lead to similar questions about the adequacy of definitions and the actualization of these definitions in the program. Again all these questions pose similar criterion problems but most will be distinct in terms of the specific information needed and the basis on which relevant information is identified.

The use of a computer comes to mind as an aid in charting one's decision-making course through an evaluation composed of such a maze of steps. A computer could be used to control the sequence of questions, to store criteria generated by previous decision-makers who faced similar evaluation questions, to store information descriptive of a particular school system or educational program that might be "called up" by criteria, and finally to identfy for the decision-maker the alternatives available to him. In fact, except for the need of a human solution to the criterion problem, machines would appear capable of carrying out all necessary decision-making activity. It should be remembered, however, that criteria are dependent on value assumptions and, until a single value system is universal, man will not be dispensable.

Implementing the Model

Having described in some detail the steps involved in the evaluation of an ongoing program, let us now turn to a consideration of who takes these steps and how they are implemented.

A few years ago when school systems first tried to decide how they should organize to satisfy the evaluation requirements of ESEA, there was a rather spirited discussion in the literature as to whether evaluation should be the responsibility of an internal unit of the school system or performed by an external organization. The importance of objectivity and credibility was given emphasis at that time. It was said that if a school system subcontracted with a university or a non-profit agency, an evaluation would be free from charges of self-interest and partiality. Now with hindsight it seems safe to say that this strategy has not in fact worked. On the other hand, from somewhat random information coming from throughout the country, it appears that, although the internal evaluation units of school systems are producing highly reliable reports, they are of little real meaning or value to administrators.

Obviously what is needed is a better understanding of how evaluation can serve management as well as the dictates of the canons of research. Whether an evaluation unit be internal or external is perhaps less important than that its functions be clearly defined, its purposes agreed upon by all parties concerned, and its staff adequately selected and trained to do the necessary job. The characteristics that an evaluation takes on when an established institution commits itself to change in the flux of "urban ecology" are critically important. Problems common to big-city-school-system evaluations have been identified, and at least one programatic strategy for their solution has been advanced.

Table 2 makes clear how evaluation serves as the handmaiden of administration in the management of program development through sound decision-making. (See page 188).

The evaluator tells the program-manager what decisions must be made and the manager makes these decisions on the basis of information provided by the evaluator. The choice between available decision alternatives as well as the selection of criteria underlying the generation of alternatives is the responsibility of the administrator.

Evaluation is the watchdog of program management. It insures that standards can be used for assessing program performance. It applies to standards the criteria of clarity, internal consistency, comprehensiveness, and compatibility in order that they can be operationalized at each stage of program performance. When standards are not stated clearly, the evaluation unit restates them on its own initiative and then obtains confirmation of the validity of this restatement from the program staff. Only the program staff, however, may reformulate program standards so as to improve their internal consistency, comprehensiveness, or compatibility. Generally, they will not do so unless specific contradictions or omissions in the standard are pointed out to them by the evaluation staff.

Evaluation is also responsible for insuring that the "standard-vs. performance" comparison is actually made and that any resultant discrepancy information is reported to the program staff. To facilitate this comparison, the evaluation staff stands ready to identify necessary information, collect it, and analyze it for report purposes. Such activity results in "reports of discrepancy" to the program staff.

The problem-solving loop Block ⓦ (figure 21) is in the province of the program staff. The evaluator's job is to track the administrator through the problem-solving process, remind him of his methodological alternatives and choice points, and collect and analyze information as needed—though such activity could be carried out equally well by the R and D unit of the school system if one is available to the program-manager.

Skills unique to the evaluator-member of the team permit him to achieve a close working relationship with the program director and to accomplish productive small-group work with the program staff. Measurement, sampling-report writing, statistical analysis, and other technical functions are generally provided by specialists on the evaluation team.

Evaluation is a team effort, preferably a task-oriented team of the type suggested by Miles (1965). Generally, it will consist of the following team members:

1. Several non-directive evaluation specialists skilled in small-group process work and ethnological techniques, each of whom has responsibility for project-evaluation management but all of whom may team up to facilitate group work

2. One or more psychometrists familiar with a wide range of group cognitive and affective instruments and capable of rapidly designing *ad hoc* instruments.

3. A research-design specialist capable of drawing carefully-defined samples, designing experiments, and directing the statistical analysis of data

4. One or more technical writers familiar with educational "language" and evaluation concepts.

5. A data-processing unit with the capacity for data storage, retrieval, and statistical analysis as directed

6. Subject-specialist consultants

7. A status figure capable of communicating directly with the superintendent of schools and all program directors

Table 2 shows the interrelationship of the evaluation and the program staff's activity.

Table 2

Relation of Activities
of the Evaluation and Program Staffs

EVALUATION-STAFF ACTIVITY	PROGRAM-STAFF ACTIVITY
Identify decision points in the entire evaluation process. Establish and maintain an apparatus whereby staff may formulate standards.	
	Identify standards.
	Find ways in which to work with staff to reformulate standards if necessary.
Insure the adequacy of standards through the application of explicit criteria.	
	Find ways to resolve differences in standards used by the program staff.
Communicate statement of standards to staff.	
Indentify information needed to compare performance with standards.	Identify information available or attainable in order to compare performance with standards.
Design a method of obtaining program-performance information.	
	Provide information descriptive of program performance.
Report standards vs. performance discrepancy.	
	Choose between action alternatives in regard to discrepancy.
Identify decision points in the problem-solving process.	
	Identify kind of information needed to identify cause of program-performance deficiency.
Locate information as to cause of program-performance deficiency.	
Identify decision points in choosing criteria to be used for selecting "possible" and "best" corrective alternatives.	
	Explicate the criteria used to identify cause of discrepancy.
	Identify available corrective alternatives.
	Identify information needed to generate alternatives.
Locate and synthesize information as requested.	
	Identify criteria underlying choice of best alternative.
	Choose "best" alternative for corrective action.

Public school systems are traditionally monolithic, hierarchical, and monopolistic. Any such organization, be it educational, industrial, or religious, is obviously relatively insensitive to change. Further, if change is to come about, it must be due either to explosive external force or to internally directed, gradual force: a delicately balanced movement that produces within the members of the organization, first uncertainty, then an awareness of discrepancy, self-appraisal, a readiness for change, a commitment to change, and ultimately the satisfaction of actualization and self-realization.

If an evaluation is to provide information effecting change, it follows that the relationship between a program unit and an evaluation unit must be clearly defined and agreed upon by all members of an organization who may be affected by the evaluation.

Further, since an evaluation unit like a program unit derives its reason for existence from the parent school district organization, it is obviously subject to the same organizational constraints as the program unit. Even when the evaluation unit is an outside contractor, it exists within the web of expectations and relationships laid down by the school system. Therefore, interdependence between program and evaluation staff and mutual dependence on the parent structure is generally an evaluation fact of life.

If an evaluation staff is to have the support of the program staff that it seeks to evaluate, it must provide visible assistance to that staff in effecting change. Such assistance must be in a form acceptable to the program staff. The only assurance of such acceptability is that program purposes be defined by the program staff and the methods of change be determined by them as well. There must be maximum involvement of the program staff in every step of the evaluation process. Further, it follows that there must be continual rapport between the program staff and the evaluation staff (fostered particularly by the evaluation staff) resulting in a continuous communication of concern as well as acceptable verbalizations. The relationships to which an evaluation unit submits itself are binding and pervasive; however, it does not follow that evaluation therefore operates at the administrative discretion of the program unit. Evaluation is the handmaiden of program development and the quiet counselor to administrators—but in accordance with its own rules of operation and on an authority independent of the program unit.

An organizational paradigm which makes these intricate and demanding relationships understandable is that of an action system which contains a feedback loop. The processing of input is at the discretion of the program unit. The definition of output and the shaping of input is at the discretion of the parent organization. The management of the feedback loop is in the hands of the evaluation staff. The feedback consists of information concerning the discrepancy between performance and the standard. There can be no evaluation without discrepancy information. There can be no discrepancy without a standard; therefore, the first task of any evaluation is to obtain program standards.

A feedback loop of discrepancy information based on standards derived from the program staff will necessarily be of interest to a program staff which has been given responsibility for the success of its program.

Some Basic Concerns
of the Evaluation Staff

What are the specific questions to be raised by an evaluation unit concerned with adequately executing its own functions as they have been defined in the preceding pages? How does it know how to apply criteria governing the adequacy of standards and the conditions that must be established if evaluation units are to be successful?

Only after the program's antecedent conditions, transactions, and purposes have been clearly described in the program definition can the evaluator be reasonably confident of what he is evaluating. His second concern is for the clarity, comprehensiveness, internal consistency, and compatibility of the program definition.

Clarity is judged by an experienced writer or editor. The "comprehensiveness" of a definition is determined by the evaluator and his supervisor after careful reference to the program-content taxonomy. There is a face validity for the exercise of this criterion based on the observation of omissions in the program definition. Internal consistency is often determined by the entire evaluation team including one or more consultants as well as the program-manager. Their task is to study the interrelationship of program components with regard to time and money in order to discover if inconsistencies exist in the definition of these relationships. Compatibility is judged by the program-manager working in concert with the evaluator to determine whether the program as defined conflicts with programs or the support of programs already installed in a school or system.

Inevitably in the course of an evaluation, an evaluator will ask: "Is the organization which has been created to conduct the new program healthy and does it appear capable of executing the purposes of the project?" Pertinent concerns will be (a) staff competence, (b) communication apparatus, (c) flexibility of the program unit, and (d) commitment to a shared vision. The evaluator will ask: "Is there compatibility between the purposes and anticipated procedures of the program unit and the parent school system?" "Is there an adequate political-economic base available to the school system to support the program unit and the attainment of its purposes?"

Such questions will be best answered from an attitude of patient optimism—no matter how harried the evaluator.

Most important to the evaluator are his answers to the questions, "Do both the program unit and the parent organization understand the developmental stages any new program must go through before it can be effective?" and "Does the administration of the school system recognize the responsibility of the evaluation unit to independently monitor program-unit activity in order to provide information relevant to management decisions that must be made at each stage of program development?"

A negative answer to the first question indicates the necessity for general in-service training for the program staff on the initiative of the evaluation staff. The dramatic presentation of causes of past system-program failures and of the value of feedback information may be a useful part of a program-staff workshop. A negative answer to the second question will generally mean that the evaluation unit will fail. If the evaluation unit has not been specifically charged with authority to make its own management decisions independent of program-staff and line-authority, its reports will ultimately fail to be objective and hence, whether positive or negative, they will be suspect.

Given the pressure of school board members and community groups for product evaluations, the time constraints placed on evaluations are generally unrealistic, regardless of the acceptance of these limitations by an evaluator. Evaluations must go through the same progressive stages that characterize the development of a project. Too often, evaluators agree to do product evaluation within a one- or two-year period of time. They employ an experimental design borrowed from research methodology and thereby short-circuit the natural stages of program development which provide the only sound basis on which evaluation work can be done. The result is an evaluation beset by classic design problems: (a) inadequate sampling, (b) faulty instrumentation, (c) faulty design, (d) lack of knowledge of critical independent variables, (e) lack of treatment stability.

The purpose of experimental design is to establish a relationship between treatment and effect. Design represents a method of receiving the experimental and statistical controls necessary to obtain evidence of such a relationship. These controls can be exercised only when a treatment is stable, the conditions of the treatment are under the control of the experimenter, and most of the important factors bearing on the outcomes are known to the experimenter. To apply an experimental design to a situation over which the evaluator has little control and about which he has little knowledge is like trying to practice the art of sailing without wind.

There are conditions prerequisite to the use of experimental design in a school setting, and one of the purposes of the early stages of an evaluation is to secure these conditons—just as in program development the early stages form the base on which later program growth may be realized.

In actual practice, it turns out that movement through the stages of an evaluation requires frequent recycling through those stages which are prior to the stage under negotiation at any point in time. Successive reappraisals of program operations and of the program standards from which program operations are derived are generally consequences of the decisions made by program staff on the basis of discrepancy information reported at Stages II, III, and IV (figure 21). If a decision is made to reformulate standards rather than to revise program performance, there are immediate implications for the renegotiation of all subsequent evaluation stages. Hence, the soundness of judgment of program decision-makers and the support they derive from their organizational milieu are of prime importance to evaluators.

Stage I Work

In the first stage of evaluation, a documentation of the program staff's description of their program provides the best estimate of the conditions of the experiment.

The evaluation unit facilitates this description by working with the program staff in accordance with small-group techniques. The evaluator uses the content taxonomy to coax from the program staff a comprehensive program description:

1. A description of the client population and the criteria employed in their selection as they are reflected in the program staff's understanding of the program
2. A description of the staff, the criteria for their selection, the level of their preprogram competency, and the expected level of their competence following any in-service training
3. The major terminal objectives of the program—that is, the behaviors clients will be expected to demonstrate upon completion of the program
4. The enabling or intervening objectives that must be negotiated before terminal objectives can be realized—that is, the intervening behaviors or tasks students must complete as a necessary basis for terminal behavior
5. The sequence of enabling objectives and the nature and sequence of learning experiences that will lead to the attainment of enabling objectives (This sequence generally takes the form of an ordinal list at this first stage of evaluation)
6. Characteristics and entry behaviors of clients—that is, those characteristics or behaviors students should exhibit upon entry into the program

7. A descriptive list of administrative support requirements, facilities, materials, and equipment
8. A description of staff functions and the number and type of positions
9. Finally, the casting of all program activity in a time frame so as to position events relative to each other over time

The program staff must provide these definitions. It is the responsibility of the evaluation staff to insure that such definitions are, in fact, obtained.

Perhaps the most difficult part of defining a program is deciding how much detail is needed in the formulation of educational objectives. The adequacy of criteria for statements of educational objectives has for many years been a controversial question in the literature of evaluation. For most purposes, it is still considered essential that program objectives be stated in behavioral terms. Such definitions constitute the beginning point of most evaluations. However, the complexity and scope of any new program determine the level of specificity at which its objectives can be initially stated. Most ongoing school projects are so very complex that, in the early stages of evaluation, definitions should be over simplified. There is a relationship between the specificity with which objectives can be stated and the level of understanding of the program staff at various time points in the ongoing program. To define all of the objectives of an educational program with complete specificity at the beginning of a program is recognized as patently impossible by anyone who is engaged in a program of a size and complexity worthy of serious support.

Objectives must be arrived at by a method of successive approximation. In the early life of a new program, only the terminal objectives of a project and the major enabling objectives needed to reach the terminal objectives are usually understood by the staff. As the staff works in the program, it comes to recognize new terminal purposes as well as to discover many intermediate or linking objectives which must be negotiated if ultimate goals are to be realized. Therefore, the definition of program objectives is a continuous and increasingly more detailed effort resulting from program-staff-operations experience.

As goals and program antecedents and processes are gradually better defined, the project moves from a stage of limited and tentative definition to one of comprehensive and reliable definition. This natural evolution of a developing program from adolescent self-discovery to mature self-determination eventually permits Stage III evaluation activity to occur in which the relationship between project outcomes and processes can be systematically studied.

After a comprehensive blueprint of the new program has been obtained by the evaluation staff from the program staff, it becomes possible to submit the design of the program to rigorous analysis. This analysis provides those responsible for the program with new information as to resources required, internal consistency, compatibility with other programs already in existence, and comprehensiveness. Information is presented in the form of a series of judgments which the evaluation staff makes certain have been based on well-defined criteria used by appropriate persons. Judgments may be made by program staff, parents, students, authoritative consultants, or others. All may contribute to a synthesis of judgment, or only those closest to a particular question may provide a judgmental answer.

In any event, the administration is eventually afforded some degree of certainty as to whether or not there is justification for sustaining a program through its next developmental stage. When the human and monetary resources available to a program are obviously below the level required to sustain it, when the program's operating components are inconsistent with one another or with other activity already under way in the school, or when a program after repeated efforts defies comprehensive definition, administrators may terminate a program with some confidence as to the soundness of their decision.

It is important to note that the feedback given to the program staff as to the discrepancy between program definition and standard is necessarily information with negative affect. The program staff is informed of what it has failed to do. Because such reports are always given to all members of the program staff and to all of the superordinates to whom they may report, it is vital that the purpose as well as the tone and intent of the report be understood and accepted. The content of a cover page written to achieve these ends may be of interest to the reader:

Explanation of the
Program Definition

What Is the Program Definition?

The program definition (Duda and McBroom, 1968) is a detailed description of an educational program as it is perceived by the staff of that program. The definition is divided into three essential components: (1) the objectives of the program; (2) the students, staff, media, and facilities that must be present before the objectives of the program can be realized; and (3) the student and staff activities that form the process whereby the objectives are achieved. These components are referred to in the definition as OUTCOMES, ANTECEDENTS, and PROCESS.

How Is the Definition Obtained?

The definition is obtained at a meeting which is attended by all levels of program staff. The participants are divided into discussion groups where they contribute information about the three essential components of the program. The Office of Research compiles the comments into the program definition, which is then mailed to all members of program staff, with a request for further comments. These comments are incorporated into the definition which is continually subject to updating and modification as the program develops.

What Is the Purpose of the Definition?

This definition is used as a standard against which to evaluate the program. After the definition has been obtained, the Office of Research attempts to determine whether the program is operating as the definition specifies. If not, there are two alternatives: (1) either the definition can be modified, or (2) the program can be brought into line with the definition. Only after a definition has been obtained and the adjustment between the definition and the program has been made, can the Office of Research attempt to assess the impact of the program on students.

Have Any Changes Been Made Since the Last Program Definition?

This definition contains a more comprehensive description of the program's objectives for students, teachers, and administrators. The last program definition did not describe any ENABLING OBJECTIVES—i.e., the skills, attitudes, and information which students must acquire during the program to ensure the accomplishment of the major program objectives. These objectives have been specified in this current definition.

Staff functions and duties have been modified and are now stated more precisely. Other minor alterations have been made in the following areas: general description of staff, administrative support, time constraints and communications.

Stage II Work

When an evaluation goes through its *program-installation* stage, it is necessary for the evaluation unit to observe student and teacher activity in order that they may be compared with the appropriate activity program standards.

Evaluation designs in widespread use today call for the comparison of teacher-student activity in a new program situation with such activity in non-program or control schools. The conclusion often drawn is that, if the level or quality of activity is no different in both types of schools, the new program is not effective. Such reasoning assumes that the non-program-school activity is less effective (which may or may not be true) but, more important, it ignores the importance of the only reliable standard against which the program-school activity may be compared—the program specifications themselves. Of course, in instances in which these specifications have never existed and the evaluator has not forced them into existence as prerequisite to his evaluation, other less reliable standards of program activity must be found.

Once the standard for comparison has been determined, the enormous problem of collecting and analyzing reliable and valid information remains. Some standards call for comparisons of non-quantified information such as visual verification of described conditions or behavior. In such cases, the criterion problem is solved simply by referring to the program definition. Other standards require the quantification of comparative data on at least an ordinal scale. In this event, it is possible to encounter psychometric problems which require more time and energy than are available for the entire evaluation. Particularly if one is interested in documenting the nature of student-teacher transactions, instruments relevant to the information needs of the program are less than adequate. Yet this does not mean that estimates cannot be obtained. Reliable judges making repeated observations in carefully defined classroom situations represent perhaps the most effective, expeditious means available to the evaluator to obtain a record of complex human interactions. Such techniques are best used to verify the existence of unexpected variation in teacher activity rather than that differences do not exist, since the latter conclusion assumes an exhaustive classification system.

It is noteworthy that, when the fidelity of teaching associated with a new program has been the topic of careful investigation, the results have almost always shown as much variation within the program as across different programs. It is possible to argue that this finding is due to inadequate and arbitrary schema for classifying teacher behavior. However, the more precise an investigator is in classifying his data and the more discrete his observations of specific types of behavior, the less likely it is that this extreme variation will be due to the artificialities of measurement. That is, the more rigorous the classification constraints imposed on data in order to meet instrumentation standards, the less likely it is that variance within treatment groups will be exaggerated by instrumentation inadequacies.

Instead, we are left with good reason to believe that great variation in teacher behavior exists within many experimental programs and that these behaviors reflect pretreatment sets that are characteristic of teachers not in an experimental program.

When such variation exists, it is a major responsibility of the evaluation unit to document the discrepancy between staff behavior and program specifications. Decisions to be made by the program staff on the basis of this information may direct the retraining of teachers, the redesigning of program specifications, or the termination of the project.

At this point in the life of a project, it is often necessary to build an *ad hoc* staff-training design to compensate for lack of specificity in teacher behavior. When such project activity is initiated, it immediately becomes the responsibility of the evaluation unit to design a training-program evaluation which is predicated on the same stages of program development as those underlying the original program-evaluation strategy.

A study within a study and a program within a program are thus undertaken respectively by the evaluation and program units. Sometimes it is evident that the staff must be expanded to support unexpected training activities. If, as a result of this expansion, available resources should be exhausted, the project's infeasibility is demonstrated.[22]

In Stage II of the evaluation, then, information as to the discrepancy between expected and actual installation is obtained and the program staff is aided in eventually securing effective control over the treatment to which students are exposed.

Stage III Work

In Stage III, the initial effects of the treatment are assessed, further adjustments in treatment based on an analysis of interim product data are made, and greater understanding is achieved as to the relationship between treatment outcomes and the conditions of the experiment. At Stage III, the evaluation staff should collect data describing the extent to which student behavior is changing as predicted. The emphasis should be on validating the enabling objectives rather than the terminal or ultimate objectives. The program staff must be helped to analyze more carefully the behav-

---

22. The importance of teacher training in support of almost any conceivable new program and the readiness of the evaluation staff to determine the effect of that training cannot be overemphasized. In-service-training evaluation is, if anything, more complex than preservice-training evaluation which has been the source of considerable uncertainty among professors in teacher-training institutions. See, for example, Provus (1969).

ior it expects students to exhibit as a function of learning activity. Learning activities are appraised for their effectiveness relative to assumptions about student readiness and rate of learning. Such evaluation depends heavily on the production and use of highly specific instruments that provide empirically determined answers to cause-and-effect questions. As a consequence of this stage of evaluation, the program staff learns whether or not its intermediate-program payloads are being realized on target dates, and if not, why not.

The existence of a data base from which to draw quantifiable, comparable descriptions of students' behavior at various points in time is generally essential at this stage of evaluation. However, rarely is it possible to establish this data base at the initiation of a new program. Instead, the first, second, and third stages of an evaluation must be negotiated before the staff can be reasonably sure of the variables on which data are to be collected.

Hence a data base can be seen as an expandng file which is a function of program description and modification, and of increased staff awareness of related factors. Unfortunately, the data base is often defined prior to treatment, representing data available from student or school records such as standardized achievement results, *ad hoc* instruments for measuring such intangibles as attitude, self concept, and creativity. The validity of these instruments (they often have compelling face validity) is less to be questioned than is their acceptability by the program unit or their interpretation by the evaluation unit in the context of the complex maze of program variants and conditions. It would be difficult, for example, to interpret the meaning of "a positive shift in self-esteem accompanied by a lack of significant change in rate of reading" if one did not have knowledge of what had been done to students, of the characteristics of the group that relate to the change data, or of the relationship of such change data to other program outcomes. The argument here is not for more exhaustive and precise statistical analysis but for more understanding of the relevance of data before it is collected. Unless considerable program-definition work has been done, such understanding is unlikely.

Stage III evaluation work generally requires much greater specificity in that part of the program definition dealing with instructional process than has been possible or necessary in previous stages.

In seeking an answer to the question, "Is the program achieving its enabling objectives?", the evaluator must enlist the aid of the program staff in flow-charting the relationship between learning experiences, enabling objectives, and terminal objectives.

Figure 22 shows one format that can be used for this purpose.

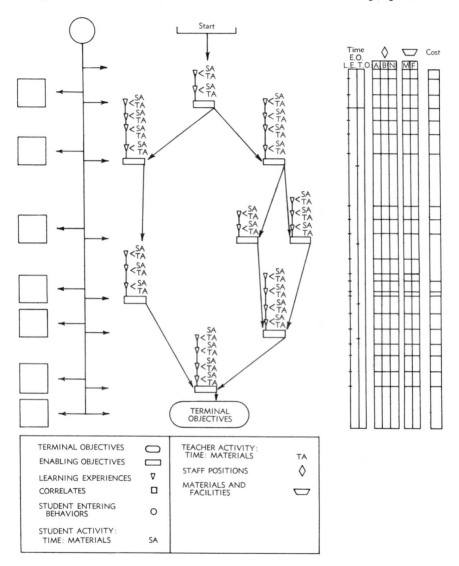

Figure 22

Program Design Analysis

The steps in constructing such a flow chart are as follows:[23]

1. List student and teacher activities associated with each learning experience.
2. Show the sequence of learning experiences leading to each enabling objective.
3. List the sequence of all enabling objectives.
4. Show the structural relationships of all enabling objectives to each terminal objective.
5. Repeat 1 to 4 for all terminal objectives.
6. Estimate the time between each node on the flow chart.
7. Group teacher activities over time into teaching functions. Aggregate functions to define teaching positions.
8. Estimate facilities (includes equipment and media) needed to support teaching activity. List.
9. Cost out facilities and staff requirements relative to nodes on flow chart. (It is possible to prorate fixed staff and facilities cost on a proportional time basis.)
10. Identify entry behaviors of students.
11. Throughout Stage III, correlates of student-entry behavior and inprocess, student and teacher behavior will be gradually obtained. These correlates are listed as they are identified and may serve as independent variables in Stage IV.

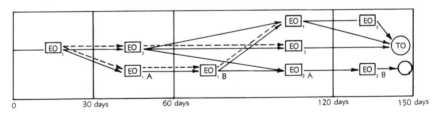

Figure 23

Enabling Objective Attainment and the Interim
Product-Flow Analysis

Figure 23 shows a simplified example of the flow of enabling objectives (solid lines) compared with the actual flow of enabling objectives as determined by evaluation field work (dotted lines).[24] The time line at the bottom permits a comparison of actual attainments with expected attainments at some of the target dates for the attainment of enabling objectives defined in the program

23. A number of flow charts are available. See Cook (1966).

24. The flow chart applies to each group of students identified for similar instruction in a given program.

specifications. Such a chart is an essential aid to Stage-III-evaluation procedure. The activities which make up this procedure are described in figure 24, "Interim product-evaluation-activity sequence." Column A includes a description of who administers what, when, and to whom, and details the activity needed to support administration of both pretest and posttest instruments for an evaluation of the program sequence relative to enabling objective, EO. Column B includes the administration of the pretest and description of the results in terms of levels for each valid subscore. Column C represents performance level on the instrument to be used as program-success criteria. This level is determined as a function of pretest performance estimates of the effectiveness of treatment and estimates of the importance of the enabling objective in the overall structure of objectives contributing to terminal objectives. Column D represents the administration of program treatment in the form of a learning-activity sequence. Column E calls for the administration of the posttest and data descriptions comparable to those of Column B. Column F compares posttest with pretest and performance-level criteria defined under Column C. As a result of this comparison, a determination is made either to move to EO_2 or to re-examine EO_1. On the assumption that student and teacher activity has been monitored through the continuous operations-research design so as to remain consonant with program specifications, it follows that the predicted relationship between treatment and enabling objective has been faulty. An analysis of EO_1 takes the form of the identification of subobjectives (EO_{1a} and EO_{1b}) subsumed in EO_1 for which learning experiences must be devised. This faulty relationship is generally due to inadequate analysis of student behavior relative to task completion. Having just completed an attempt to produce learning experiences conducive to EO_1 and having information as to the pre- and post-performance of students on criterion tasks, the teacher is in the best possible position to intuitively postulate new behaviors which must be learned as requisite to the achievement of EO_1. These new behaviors become a new set of objectives (EO_{1a} and EO_{2b}), shown in Column G, for which new learning experiences must be devised (Column H) and administered (Column I).

Since no instrumentation is available to measure the attainment of objectives of the class $EO_1 a$, evaluation of this second alternative learning sequence must be conducted subjectively by the classroom teacher (Column J). Limited resources and time generally militate against the employment of criterion measures at this level of program development work in a public school setting.

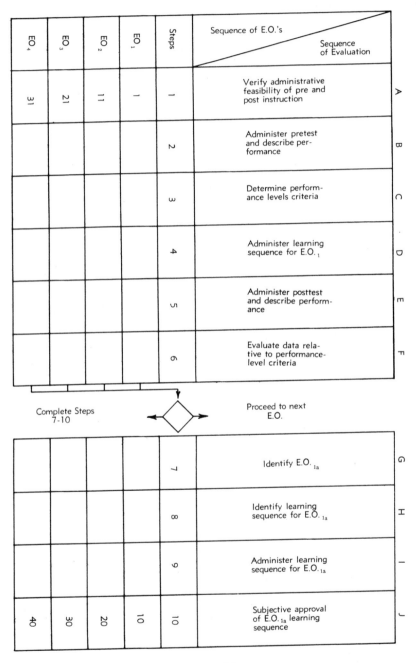

Figure 24

Interim Product-Evaluation-Activity Sequence

The involvement of the program staff in curriculum-development research is crucial to its success. In many school systems, resources will be insufficient to support such work. However, some systems will value such work highly enough to provide the considerable support necessary.

The discovery by the program staff of new objectives subsumed under previously stated enabling objectives will be a consequence of teaching problems that result from unexpected reactions from students, insights gained from introspection and/or task analysis, and insights gained from successful teaching. Such discovery will no doubt have a bearing on the teacher's incentive to engage in curriculum analysis, and a desire to increase staff initiative may be an important consideration in any administrator's determination to support such work.

The staff may be aware of many layers of underlying enabling objectives but, owing to limited time and energy, fail to state them. The failure of teachers to utilize their existing knowledge of curriculum and student interaction prior to teaching, of course, results in enormously inefficient programs.

A delicate balance seems necessary between spending time and effort on curriculum analysis *prior* to the teaching of the sequence and *after* obtaining feedback regarding the success of that learning experience. Cost and staff-satisfaction requirements would seem to dictate that minimum resources be used to achieve standard levels of student performance. Since in most cases this minimum cannot be identified prior to feedback about the success of learning experience, it would appear wise to use the collective judgment of the staff in defining objectives at whatever levels of complexity are possible and in determining appropriate learning sequences. Unfortunately such collective judgment is often not considered a necessary part of in-process program-development work.

The time required to complete a learning sequence, the time expected to complete a learning sequence, and the objectives of a program at various levels of complexity are obviously related.

When enabling and terminal objectives are first defined in Stage I, time estimates for their completion are given. However, as teaching difficulties are encountered in Stage III and new subobjectives are discovered or employed, the time dimension of the project must be adjusted to accommodate these changes.

An important in-process set of administrative decisions therefore deals with setting time limits for the attainment of new subobjectives. Herein lies a dilemma. A program can be lost for failure to reach terminal objectives or it can fail to achieve its terminal objectives (even though it completes its entire planned sequence of activity) because of inattention to the achievement of enabling objectives. The captain who reaches port "come hell or high water" may have lost his cargo while the captain who nurses his cargo along may never reach port.

Again, an administrative decision relative to the use of resources over time is critical to program success. Obviously what is needed is periodic information concerning movement toward terminal objectives as well as feedback on new enabling objectives.

The question as to whether to move forward to the next enabling objective (EO_2) in a flow chart (figure 23) or to a subobjective (EO_1a) is a question of importance. Considerations which bear on this general decision are as follows:

1. The validity of performance data concerning EO_1
2. The time estimated to complete EO_1a
3. The time available to reach terminal objectives
4. The ability of staff to identify more efficient learning experiences to reach EO_1
5. The ability of staff to identify alternatives to EO_1a (such as EO_1b or EO_1c) and to estimate their relative time requirements
6. The ability of staff to identify and locate necessary support requirements such as materials and trained personnel, as well as evaluation requirements such as instruments, and so forth

From the foregoing, it appears that the efficiency of the staff in researching the cause of failure and in devising a solution is the overriding consideration.

The problem-solving effort at this point requires careful teamwork between the evaluation and program staffs (see table 2 and discussion). The criteria required to answer the research and development (R and D) questions posed by the problem consist of models of learning and curriculum structure appropriate to the particular program under study. These models are suggested by such theoreticians as Gagné (1962) and Bloom (1963, 1966).

The value of structural analysis of the type proposed by Gagné and Bloom is now obvious. A serious question remains as to the feasibility of such analytic work by a public school staff. Clearly, a research center or university (in conjunction with a public school system) will be best equipped to do this work. Ultimately, public schools may be the recipients of packaged curriculum programs containing precisely defined relationships between instructional process and pupil performance. Then, school systems will more properly devote their evaluation resources to such installation activity as pupil selection, in-service teacher training, and the conditions of administrative program support.

Stage IV

Finally, at Stage IV the evaluator may cast an experimental design for arriving at an answer to the question: "Has the program achieved its terminal objectives?"

Stage IV calls for the kinds of designs we have long employed in educational research and have more recently employed in evaluation. These designs have been "employed in error," not because the quasi-experimental designs of the type described by Stanley and Campbell (1963) do not belong in an evaluation strategy, but because they have consistently been used in the wrong stage of a program's development.

In Stage IV, many of the relationships between treatment conditions and effects discovered in Stage III, can be properly expressed as independent variables in the experimental design. The administrative control secured over the new program in Stages II and III ensures treatment stability. Problems of sampling and instrumentation are more likely to be solved as a result of increased staff knowledge of factors interacting with treatment.

Stage V Option

A word about cost-benefit analysis may be in order at this point. There is a lot of "econometrics" discussion today about applying cost-benefit analysis to school system outputs as a method of identifying efficient programs. This discussion is meaningful if the following conditions exist or can be established:

1. The programs that produce measurable benefits are sufficiently well defined to be replicable.
2. There is agreement on both the value and measure of benefit.
3. Antecedent conditions can be sufficiently well defined and measured to determine their effect on output.
4. At least two programs are in existence for which inputs have been "costed out," that share common benefits, and for which comparable data exist describing antecedent conditions.

It may be possible to find programs which meet these conditions, but given the present state of the evaluation art, it is extremely unlikely. Moreover, it must be remembered that cost-benefit analysis answers the question: "Which program from among two or more that are available achieves its purpose at the lowest cost?" It does not answer questions pertinent to the operation or success of any single program.

Some Old Wives' Tales

At this point, it would seem desirable to dismiss a few old wives' tales about the evaluation process.

1. *The evaluation unit must participate in the planning of a program if it is to be effective.*
   Since most programs have not been planned, it follows that, if they are to be evaluated, they must employ an evaluation strategy which is not dependent on planning. Such a strategy has been described in this article and can be used to capitalize on planning omissions.

2. *It is necessary to wait three to five years before any evaluative judgment can be passed on a new program.*
   On the contrary, the position of this paper is that a whole series of judgments can be passed on a project at various points of its life relative to the various developmental stages through which it goes.

3. *There is inevitable conflict between the interests of program and evaluation staffs.*
   Surely this need not be so. Both staffs have the same mission: either to continue and improve a program or to reject it as soon as there is reliable evidence that its probability of success is very low. In pursuit of this mission, both staffs share the desire to secure and appraise information pertinent to discrepancies between program operation and program specifications.

4. *Evaluation activity gets in the way of program activity.*
   When evaluation is seen as a necessary part of program development, the activity of the evaluator is seen by the program staff as complementary, and that activity of the program staff which is essential to the installation and maintenance of program treatment is always given precedence over evaluation activity by the evaluation staff.

5. *Good evaluation from its inception depends on a sound experimental design.*
   According to the evaluation strategy advanced in this paper, experimental design is irrelevant to evaluation until a program is in its final stages of development. When an evaluation is properly conceived and conducted, it has the power to sound the death knell of a project long before it reaches stability and maturity. Evidence as to excessive cost, inconsistency, unreliability, or the incompatibility of a project at various stages in its development will provide a sound base from which to estimate its probable success at various points in time.

An evaluation which begins with an experimental design denies the program staff that which it needs most: information that can be used to make judgments about the program while it is in its dynamic stages of growth. Furthermore, the imposition of an experimental design in the formulative stages of a program deprives the staff of their desired opportunity to improve a program on the basis of experience. Sound evaluation practice provides administrators and the program staff with information they need and freedom to act on that information.

Conclusions

There is a need for administrators to better understand that the installation of school programs, whether innovative or not, involves high risk of failure. There is a need for evaluators to better understand the kind of information administrators need if the cost of these risks is to be reduced. Both administrators and researchers must see evaluation as a continuous information-management process which serves program-improvement as well as program-assessment purposes. The complexity and concomitant high cost of effective evaluation must be recognized as a necessary management expense somewhat similar to high insurance premiums. Everyone concerned with public education must be willing to spend much larger sums for evaluation if we are to have an adequate management system for protecting federal investments under the present reform strategy of the Office of Education.

Those involved in public school reform through new program development must recognize:

1. The natural developmental stages of any new program.
2. The evaluation activity that is appropriate to each stage
3. The dependence of administrators on information obtained through evaluation if they are to make sound, defensible decisions

If a new brand of evaluation can be developed and supported in the years ahead, school programs and evaluation reports are going to look very different than they do today. Our national interest will eventually demand nothing less.

Provus's Paper: An Application

Much like Tyler, Provus defined the goal of evaluation as that of determining whether to improve, maintain, or terminate a given program. To reach this goal the evaluator must:

(a) define program standards;

(b) look for a discrepancy (thus, Provus's approach is often called the Discrepancy Model) between observations about the program and the standards or objectives for that program; and

(c) use the discrepancy information as feedback to the program developers.

Like Stufflebeam, Provus has suggested focusing evaluation on four stages of program development. Although Provus's and Stufflebeam's conceptualizations are slightly different, both serve to focus the attention of the evaluator on several different stages in the development of a program. Because Provus is very specific about explicating standards, and because he describes in detail the application of his approach to educational programs, his paper serves as a valuable practical guide to the evaluator. In addition, the emphasis which Provus puts on a "team approach" to program evaluation is noteworthy. The fact that the evaluator has "gotten his hands dirty" with information about the program leaves him in a most advantageous position for knowing exactly what is happening within the program. At the same time, the program director is aware of new forces influencing the operation of the program and has a legal charge for making decisions. The cooperation of these two positions can lead to a more informed evaluation. Provus also suggests that involvement of the program staff in decision making will establish a feeling of rapport with the evaluator and may lead to the collection of relevant information which is not always available to the evaluator. Thus, continuous communication between the program staff and the evaluator is proposed as a necessary component of good evaluation.

To follow Provus's model, Mrs. Allen might form a team of administrators, colleagues, and perhaps even students to work with her on the course development and evaluation. Having moved through the program definition stage of development, Mrs. Allen would concentrate her efforts on the installation and process stages. Since she will act both as the decision-maker in program development and the director of the evaluation activities, she will have to sort out her roles so that the credibility of evaluation findings are preserved. Ideally, another person (perhaps the school's evaluation director, if one exists) would direct the evaluation part of the study.

The tasks involved in the evaluation study include (a) the generation of a list of program standards or objectives on which everyone can agree and which can be modified if necessary, (b) the identification of information needed to compare performance with standards, (c) the design of methods to obtain the information (such as observation of teacher and student activity in the program installation stage or the use of criteria-referenced achievement measures in the program improvement stage to observe the achievement of enabling objectives, (d) the comparison of intended performance with actual performance to identify discrepancies in the new course, (e) the location of the causes of discrepancies (if any), and (f) the operation of corrective actions (modifications of the course, the standards, or both) to eliminate any discrepancies that have occurred. To be effective, the study would be accomplished so that all parties involved (for example, Mrs. Allen, the principal, other team members) agree on the actions taken. The operation of the measurement and data analysis portions of the evaluation study require the assistance of specialists in these areas. Such assistance would be sought at the very beginning of the evaluation study.

A Comparative Description of Evaluation Approaches

In order to highlight the important points presented in the preceding discussions, a descriptive multi-page matrix of the way various authors view different aspects of the evaluation process is presented as Table 3.[25] The twelve considerations represented as rows in the matrix are important components of evaluation that can be profitably compared across evaluation approaches. The list of considerations is not an exhaustive one, but it is representative and pertinent.[26] Each consideration is described briefly below to aid in the interpretation of the matrix.

1. *Definition.* The way in which each author has defined the process of evaluation is presented here.

2. *Purpose.* The author's view of the goal of the evaluation process is shown in this row. How an evaluation specialist defines evaluation will determine the procedures he uses to conduct an evaluation study. The design (content and scope) of the study should be consistent with both the definition and purpose ascribed to the evaluation process.

3. *Key emphasis.* In this row the major distinguishing characteristics of the author's suggested approach to educational evaluation are presented.

4. *Role of the evaluator.* Different duties, authority, and responsibility are assigned to the evaluator by each author. The

---

25. The paper by L. J. Cronbach was not summarized in the table since it does not contain a formal logical framework for evaluation as is contained in the other presentations.

26. The authors wish to thank Professor Helen James, Southern Illinois University, and Mrs. Virginia G. Sturwold for their valuable contributions to this section of the text.

Table 3

Comparisons of Contemporary Evaluation Models on Selected Characteristics
(Table appears on pages 210-215)

	STAKE	SCRIVEN	PROVUS	HAMMOND
DEFINITION	Describing and judging an educational program.	Gathering & combining performance data with weighted set of goal scales.	Comparing performance against standards.	Assessing effectiveness of current & innovative programs at the local level by comparing behavioral data with objectives.
PURPOSE	To describe and judge educational programs based on a formal inquiry process.	To establish & justify merit or worth. Evaluation plays many roles.	To determine whether to improve, maintain, or terminate a program.	To find out whether innovation is effective in achieving expressed objectives.
KEY EMPHASIS	Collection of descriptive & judgmental data from various audiences.	Justification of data gathering instruments, weightings, & selection of goals. Eval. model: combining data on different performance scales into a single rating.	Identifying discrepancies between standards & performance using team approach.	Local program development.
ROLE OF EVALUATOR	Specialist concerned with collecting, processing, & interpreting descriptive & judgmental data.	Responsible for judging the merit of an educational practice for producers (formative) & consumers (summative).	A team member who aids program improvement & counsels administration. He should be independent of the program unit.	Consultant who should provide expertise in data collection. He is also a trainer of local evaluators (program personnel).
RELATIONSHIP TO OBJECTIVES	Examination of goal specifications & priorities. Identification of areas of failures & successes. It is up to the evaluator to assist in writing behavioral objectives.	Look at goals & judge their worth. Determine whether they are being met.	Agreement of evaluation team & program staff on standards. Comparison of performance against standards to see whether a discrepancy exists.	Evaluation focuses on the definition & measurement of behavioral objectives.
RELATIONSHIP TO DECISION-MAKING	Descriptive & judgmental data result in reports (including recommendations) to various audiences. Judgments may be based on either absolute or relative standards.	Evaluation reports (with judgments explicitly stated for producers or consumers) used in decision-making.	Evaluation staff collects information essential to program improvement & notes discrepancies between performance & standards. Every question involves a criterion (C), new information (I), & a decision (D). Eval. provides the new information.	Evaluation is the source on which to base decisions about instructional, institutional, & behavioral dimensions.

Table 3
Comparisons of Contemporary Evaluation Models on Selected Characteristics
(Table appears on pages 210-215)

STUFFLEBEAM	ALKIN	PERSONAL JUDGEMENT (e.g. Accreditation)	TYLER[a]
Defining, obtaining, & using information for decision-making.	The process of ascertaining the decision areas of concern, selecting appropriate information, & collecting & analyzing information.	Focusing attention on processes of education using professional judgment. Development of standards for educational programs.	Comparing student performance with behaviorally stated objectives.
To provide relevant information to decision-makers.	To report summary data useful to decision-makers in selecting among alternatives.	To identify deficiencies in the education of teachers & students relevant to content & procedures; self-improvement.	To determine the extent to which purposes of a learning activity are actually being realized.
Evaluation reports used for decision-making.	Evaluation reports used for decision-making.	Personal judgment used in evaluating processes of education; self-study.	Specification of objectives & measuring learning outcomes of pupils.
Specialist who provides evaluation information to decision-makers.	Specialist who provides evaluation information to decision-makers.	Professional colleagues who make recommendations—a professional judge.	Curriculum specialist who evaluates as part of curriculum development & assessment.
Terminal stage in context eval. is setting objectives; input eval. produces ways to reach objectives; product eval. determines whether objectives are reached.	Range & specificity of program objectives determined in systems assessment; program planning produces ways to reach objectives; program improvement provides data on the extent to which objectives are being achieved; program certification determines whether objectives are reached.	Self-study judgments are based on sets of predetermined criteria.	Evaluation implies attainment of behavioral objectives stated at the beginning of the course.
Evaluation provides information for use in decision-making.	Evaluation provides information for use in decision-making.	When deficiencies are found, program revisions are requested, thus correcting sub-standard conditions; corrective process built in.	Actual pupil performance data will provide information for the decision-maker to use on strengths & weaknesses of a course or curriculum.

Table 3
Comparisons of Contemporary Evaluation Models on Selected Characteristics
(Table appears on pages 210-215)

		STAKE	SCRIVEN	PROVUS	HAMMOND
TYPES OF EVALUATION		(1) Formal vs. informal.	(1) Formative— summative. (2) Comparative— noncomparative (3) Intrinsic—payoff. (4) Mediated.	(1) Design. (2) Installation. (3) Process. (4) Product. (5) Cost.	(1) Instructional dimension. (2) Institutional dimension. (3) Behavioral dimension used for describing programs.
CONSTRUCTS PROPOSED		(1) Data matrices: description (intents & observations) & judgment. (2) Processing descriptive data: contingency among antecedents, transactions, outcomes; congruence between intents & observations. (3) Bases for forming absolute & relative judgments.	(1) Distinction between goals (claims) & roles (functions). (2) Several types of evaluation.	(1) Discrepancy concept. (2) Feedback & revision of objectives and/or program.	(1) The application of evaluation design to existing program. (2) Decisions about adequacy of current program in relationship to the objectives. (3) Feedback from (2) leads to innovation. (4) Application of evaluation to innovation itself. (5) Notion that feedback could continue.
CRITERIA FOR JUDGING EVALUATION		(1) Should be panoramic, not microscopic. (2) Should include descriptive & judgmental data. (3) Should provide immediate relative answers for decision-making. (4) Should be formal (e.g. objective, scientific, reliable.)	(1) Should be predicated on goals. (2) Must indicate worth. (3) Should have construct validity. (4) Should be a wholistic program evaluation.	(1) Team involvement. (2) Assume one-to-one correspondence between design & solution. (3) Compare performance against standards as a tool for improvement & assessment. (4) Periodic feedback.	(1) Related to behavioral objectives. (2) An on-going process. (3) Provides feedback on goal achievement for program modification. (4) Uses local personnel, and is part of local educational program.
IMPLICATIONS FOR DESIGN		Very general structure. Matrices should be included in design.	(1) Look at many factors. (2) Be involved in value judgments. (3) Require use of scientific investigations. (4) Evaluate from within (formative) or from without (summative).	(1) Provide continuous evaluation (feedback loops). (2) Provide relevant & timely information for making decisions. (3) Provide cost-benefit analysis. (4) Involvement of evaluation in program development.	(1) Use of multi-variate structure—focus on interactions of dimensions. (2) Generate empirical research. (3) Necessity for inclusion of local personnel.

Table 3

Comparisons of Contemporary Evaluation Models on Selected Characteristics
(Table appears on pages 210-215)

STUFFLEBEAM	ALKIN	PERSONAL JUDGEMENT (e.g. Accreditation)	TYLER[a]
(1) Context. (2) Input. (3) Process. (4) Product.	(1) Systems assessment. (2) Program planning. (3) Program implementation. (4) Program improvement. (5) Program certification.	(1) Self-study. (2) Visitation. (3) Annual reports. (4) Evaluation panels.	Pre-post measurement of performance.
(1) Context eval. for planning decisions. (2) Input eval. for programming decisions. (3) Process eval. for implementing decisions. (4) Product eval. for recycling decisions.	Evaluation of educational systems vs. evaluation of instructional programs; five areas of evaluation.	Use of content specialists as judges.	(1) Statements of objectives in behavioral terms. (2) Teaching objectives are pupil-oriented. (3) Objectives must consider: pupil's entry behavior, analysis of our culture, school philosophy, learning theories, new developments in teaching, etc.
(1) Internal validity. (2) External validity. (3) Reliability. (4) Objectivity. (5) Relevance. (6) Importance. (7) Scope. (8) Credibility. (9) Timeliness. (10) Pervasiveness. (11) Efficiency.	Information provided to a decision-maker should be effective & not confusing or misleading. Appropriate evaluation procedures should be used for different decisions.	(1) Reflects interests of program administrators. (2) Standard criteria often used.	(1) Behavioral objectives clearly stated. (2) Objectives should contain references not only to course content but also to mental processes applied.
(1) Experimental design not applicable. (2) Use of systems approach for evaluation studies. (3) Directed by administrator.	Evaluation domain determined by the decision-maker; the objects of evaluation vary along a continuum from discrete, definable objects to complex systems.	(1) Involvement of professional community. (2) Quick feedback.	(1) Need to interpret & use results of assessment. (2) Develop designs to assess student progress.

Table 3

Comparisons of Contemporary Evaluation Models on Selected Characteristics
(Table appears on pages 210-215)

	STAKE	SCRIVEN	PROVUS	HAMMOND
CONTRIBUTIONS	(1) Provides a systematic method for arranging descriptive & judgmental data, thus emphasizing inter- & intra-relations between them. (2) Considers both absolute & relative judgment. (3) Requires explicit standards. (4) Generalizability of the model.	(1) Discriminates between formative (on-going) & summative (end) evaluation. (2) Focus on direct assessment of worth, focus on value. (3) Applicable in diverse contexts. (4) Analysis of means & ends. (5) Delineation of types of evaluation. (6) Evaluation of objectives.	(1) Provides continuous communication between program & evaluation staff through feedback loops. (2) Allows for program improvement as well as assessment either at early stages or at end. (3) Acknowledges alternative procedures in adjusting objectives & in changing treatment. (4) Forces explicit statement of standards.	(1) Makes use of local personnel who can carry on evaluation process once initiated. (2) Considers inter-action of several dimensions & variables. (3) Provides feedback on program development & revisions: stresses self-evaluation. (4) Requires specification of behavioral objectives.
LIMITATIONS	(1) Inadequate methodology for obtaining information on key constructs. (2) Some cells of design matrix overlap; some distinctions not clear. (3) Possibility of leading to internal strife within program; value conflicts possible.	(1) Equating performance on different criteria & assigning relative weights to criteria creates methodological problems. (2) No methodology for assessing validity of judgments. (3) Several overlapping concepts.	(1) Demands a lengthy time commitment; may be expensive to carry through. (2) Inadequate methodology for establishing standards. (3) Requires large, expert, well-articulated staff. (4) Designed for complete evaluation; partial evaluation not considered.	(1) Difficulty of quantifying data involving several dimensions & variables. (2) May be complex & time-consuming to set up. (3) Possible fixation of evaluation on the "cube." (4) Neglects judgmental dimension. (5) Motivation problem in local personnel.

Robert E. Stake, "The Countenance of Educational Evaluation," Teachers College Record, 68 (1967), 523-40.

Michael Scriven, "The Methodology of Evaluation," in Perspectives of Curriculum Evaluation, ed. R. W. Tyler (Chicago: Rand McNally, Inc., 1967), 39-83.

Malcolm Provus, "Evaluation of Ongoing Programs in the Public School Systems," The Sixty-eighth Yearbook of the National Society for the Study of Education (Chicago: The University of Chicago Press. 1969), Part II, 242-83.

Robert L. Hammond, "Evaluation at the Local Level," EPIC Evaluation Center, Tucson, Arizona (mimeo, n.d.).

Daniel L. Stufflebeam, "Evaluation as Enlightenment for Decision-Making," Ohio State University Evaluation Center (mimeo, 1968).

Marvin C. Alkin, "Evaluation Theory Development," UCLA CSE Evaluation Comment, No. 2 (1969), 2-7.

National Study of Secondary School Evaluation. Evaluative Criteria, 1960 Edition (Washington, D.C.: National Study of Secondary School Evaluation, 1960).

Ralph W. Tyler, "General Statement on Evaluation," Journal of Educational Research, 35 (1942), 492-501.

Table 3

Comparisons of Contemporary Evaluation Models on Selected Characteristics
(Table appears on pages 210-215)

STUFFLEBEAM	ALKIN	PERSONAL JUDGEMENT (e.g. Accreditation)	TYLER[a]
(1) Provides a service function by supplying data to administrators & decision-makers charged with conduct of the program. (2) Is sensitive to feedback. (3) Allows for evaluation to take place at any stage of the program. (4) Wholistic.	(1) Provides a service function to administrators & decision-makers. (2) Allows for evaluation to take place at any stage of the program. (3) Wholistic.	(1) Is easy to implement; team can observe & make judgment. (2) Has little lag time between observations made, data collected, & feedback. (3) Breadth of variables noted is large. (4) Leads to self-study habit & self-improvement.	(1) Is easy to assess whether behavioral objectives are being achieved. (2) Is easy for practitioners to design evaluative studies. (3) Checks degree of congruency between performance & objectives; focus on clear definition of objectives.
(1) Little emphasis on value concerns. (2) Decision-making process is unclear; methodology undefined. (3) May be costly & complex if used entirely. (4) Not all activities are clearly evaluative.	(1) Role of values in evaluation unclear. (2) Description of decision-making process incomplete. (3) May be costly & complex. (4) Not all activities are clearly evaluative.	(1) Objectivity & empirical basis are questionable. (2) Attention to process of education not balanced by attention to consequences. (3) Replicability is questionable.	(1) Tendency to oversimplify program & focus on terminal rather than on-going & pre-program information. (2) Tendency to focus directly & narrowly on objectives, with little attention to worth of the objectives.

[a]A variation of the Tylerian model developed by N.S. Metfessel and W.B. Michael is included in Chapter 4. The Metfessel-Michael paradigm is not included in this compilation of evaluation frameworks because of the substantial overlap with the Tylerian model which is included here.

evaluator's role differs across evaluation approaches and has come to be a controversial issue in evaluation. This topic is treated in more depth in the next chapter.

5. *Relationship to objectives.* Listed here is the type of information about the objectives of a program required by each evaluation approach. If there is any one thing upon which all evaluators agree, it is that objectives are a central part of evaluation. However, the relationship of objectives to the evaluation process is somewhat different from one model to another. The preparation and use of objectives in evaluation is discussed in the next chapter.

6. *Relationship to decision making.* Each author has a theory of how the information produced by an evaluation study is related to the decision-making process. Several writers suggest that the evaluation study should service the decision-making process; others do not describe the relationship of the evaluation study to decision making at all.

7. *Types of evaluation.* Certain distinctions, unique to each evaluation approach, are made by the contributors. It is often the case that terms used by one writer are equivalent in meaning to other terms used by other authors. It would be a valuable exercise for the reader to list the types of evaluation and constructs presented in Table 3 and to describe differences and similarities among these terms.

8. *Constructs proposed.* Unique theoretical contributions or logical relationships among known terms are presented in all approaches. Again, equivalent constructs are often assigned different labels by different authors. One major task for the student of evaluation is to sort out the terminology to form a good gestalt of the overall field of evaluation theory.

9. *Criteria for judging evaluation studies.* Michael Scriven (1969) coined the term "meta-evaluation" to refer to the evaluation of evaluation studies. Each evaluation approach has a set of criteria, often only implicitly defined, which may be used for meta-evaluation purposes.

10. *Implications for evaluation design.* Certain structures, procedures, or content are suggested by each author. It is essential that these suggestions be studied by the evaluator since they have definite implications for the plan of any evaluation study.

11. *Contributions.* Each author has made an important contribution to the design of evaluation studies. This part of Table 3 is used to note the important points made by each approach that

may have been overlooked in other parts of the comparative figure.

12. *Limitations.* There are a few admonitions which should be made concerning each approach. This part of the figure is used primarily to note possible misuses of each approach that may compromise the effectiveness of a design based on any one evaluation strategy.

4 Considerations in Planning Evaluation Studies

There are a number of critical problems still facing the evaluation specialist. The previous chapters contain theoretical discussions of evaluation as an emerging inquiry process. Practical questions about the role or roles of the evaluator, criteria for judging excellence in evaluation design, and appropriate methods for producing exemplary evaluation proposals and reports have not been directly addressed. This chapter contains discussions of selected considerations in evaluation planning which are of great importance to the specialist in evaluation. The topics addressed in this chapter include (a) criteria for judging evaluation studies; (b) the role of experimental design methods in evaluation studies; (c) the use of behavioral objectives and specifications in evaluation studies; (d) measurement problems and techniques in evaluation studies; (e) guidelines for writing evaluation proposals and reports; and (f) the role of the evaluator.

Criteria for Judging Evaluation Studies

Quality control is as important in disciplined inquiry as it is in engineering or product development. We, as inquirers, need guidelines for evaluating research and evaluation reports. The question of criteria for evaluating research studies has been addressed elsewhere (see, for example, Gephart, Ingle and Remstad [1967] and Suydam, M.N. [1968]). We will concern ourselves here with criteria for judging evaluation studies.

Sets of standards for judging evaluation studies have been discussed by several writers. The set of criteria described by Guba and Stufflebeam (1968) and Stufflebeam, et al. (1971) is the most inclusive of any set of criteria suggested. Although the criteria which they described were essentially intuitive, they are useful as guidelines for evaluating evaluation studies. There are no other compelling reasons for using these criteria, however, and the evaluator might well choose only those criteria which he agrees are important. The criteria are as follows:

1. *Internal validity.* Does the evaluation design provide the information it is intended to provide? The results of the evaluation study should present an accurate and unequivocal representation of the phenomena under scrutiny.

2. *External validity.*[1] To what extent are the results of the study generalizable across time, geography and environment, and human involvement? In many small evaluation studies, the concept of external validity will be irrelevant since the evaluator will be interested in collecting and interpreting information about one specific program at one point in time. However, the concept may be quite important in large-scale evaluation studies where sampling is used and findings must be generalized back to the total population.

3. *Reliability.* How accurate and consistent is the information that is collected? The evaluator should be quite concerned about the adequacy of his measures since his results can only be as good as the information on which they are based.

4. *Objectivity.* How public is the information collected by the evaluator? The evaluator should strive to collect information and make judgments in such a way that the same interpretations and judgments would be made by any intelligent, rational person evaluating the program.

5. *Relevance.* How closely do the data relate to the objectives of the evaluation study? Defining objectives for an evaluation study enables the evaluator to check himself on the relevance of his activities.

6. *Importance.* Given a set of constraints on the design of an evaluation study, what priorities are placed on the information to be collected or program components to be evaluated? It is often tempting to study one relevant aspect of a program in depth and to collect much information which may subsequently prove to be less important at the conclusion of the study than less detailed information about another aspect might have been. It is the responsibility of the evaluator to set priorities on the data to be collected.

---

1. The reader is directed to an excellent discussion of the concept of external validity by Bracht and Glass (1968).

7. *Scope.* How comprehensive is the design of the evaluation study? There are a wide variety of considerations to explore, as emphasized in several papers presented in the previous chapter. The evaluator must consciously avoid the possibility of developing "tunnel vision" by taking a wholistic approach to program evaluation.

8. *Credibility.* Is the evaluator believed by his audiences? Are his audiences predisposed to act on his recommendations? The evaluator-client relationship is an important one if the evaluator wants his efforts to have some impact on the program he is evaluating.

9. *Timeliness.* Will evaluation reports be available when they are needed? It has often been the case that evaluators missed the chance to influence action because they reported too much, too late. When decisions affecting a program are being made, any reliable information is better than none. The provision of interim, often informal, reports will help to avoid this problem of being too late to influence the decision.

10. *Pervasiveness.* How widely are the results of the evaluation study disseminated? It is true that, in many cases, only one audience needs to be addressed. However, the evaluator is responsible to provide the results of his study to all individuals or groups who should know about the results.

11. *Efficiency.* What are the cost/benefits of the study? Have resources been wasted when the waste could have been avoided? Operating under the constraints imposed on most evaluation studies, the evaluator is responsbile to make the most out of the material and human resources available to him.

The first four criteria listed above are categorized by Stufflebeam, et al., (1971) as *scientific* criteria, since they are appropriate for any rigorous, scientific study. The next six criteria are labeled as *practical* criteria that are most applicable to evaluation studies. By the very nature of the evaluation process, these practical criteria are extremely important standards to consider when planning any evaluation study. The last criterion is referred to by the authors as a *prudential* criterion.

The Role of Experimental Design in Evaluation Studies

Some of the meta-evaluation criteria discussed in the preceding section were labeled as scientific criteria—criteria which would apply in some degree to any scientific inquiry. If controlled experimental research can be construed to be scientific inquiry, and if the criteria of internal validity, external validity, objectivity, and reliability apply to both controlled experimental studies and evaluation studies, then some overlap, in terms of the methods used, between these inquiry processes is implied. Such an overlap points out that the methods used in controlled experimental research may also serve the evaluator well in many instances.

Some evaluators, however, have denied the utility of the controlled experiment in evaluating educational programs. The arguments stem primarily from a conservative conception of the nature of experimental design in the social sciences. For example, Guba and Stufflebeam wrote: "On the surface, the application of experimental design to evaluation problems seems reasonable, since traditionally both experimental research and evaluation have been used to test hypotheses about the effects of treatments. However, there are ... distinct problems with this reasoning" (1968, p. 14). Most of the alleged problems, however, stem from the conception of the comparative experiment held by most persons who oppose the use of experimental design in evaluation. Of all such writers, Guba and Stufflebeam (1968) have articulated the position most clearly. Several of their concerns about using experimental designs in evaluation are listed below along with attempts to examine their points and to argue for experimental design as one legitimate evaluation tool.[2]

Guba and Stufflebeam asserted that for comparative designs to yield valid results "the treatment and control conditions must be applied and held constant throughout the period of the experiment, i.e., they must conform to the initial definitions of these conditions. The new or traditional program conditions could not be modified in process, since in that event one could not tell what was being evaluated" (1968, p. 13). This concern is valid only if "treatments" are so narrowly and strictly defined that they permit decision-makers no freedom to adapt and modify treatments as they are being applied. Surely such confining treatments are not required for valid experimental comparisons. An educational treatment may simply create an identifiable context within which decision-makers are free to adapt *the* program to the exigencies of the moment. A medical researcher evaluating a drug against a placebo is free to administer other substances to control side effects or to vary the amount of dosage in accord with his observations of the progress of remission of the disease. Minor modifications during the course of an experiment do not destroy the validity of the drug vs. placebo comparison since they are often a necessary part of the *context* which is being evaluated, namely the

---

2. Portions of the following five paragraphs are excerpted from a paper by Glass and Worthen (1972).

"treatment of Disease X by Drug A." The decision-maker could, of course, so alter the context of the application of a treatment that the originally defined treatment is no longer being evaluated, as for example when a medical researcher stops administering the experimental drug because serious side effects show up in the patients. In such instances, the opportunity to evaluate comparatively has simply been lost. However, that some comparisons may not be feasible does not make all comparisons impossible.

Guba and Stufflebeam maintained that "all students in the experiment must receive the same amount of the treatment to which they are assigned . . ." (1968, p. 13). Comparative experimental designs require no such thing. A "treatment" is not a fixed entity in nature like a quart of milk or an aspirin. A "treatment" in a comparative experiment is usually an abstraction—a construct—with defining characteristics which create a context; the context created is all that one can evaluate. The context seldom demands that all experimental subjects receive the same *amount* of something. If the experimental procedures are used to define all that happened to each individual in the experimental group as the experimental treatment and all that happened to each individual in the comparative group as the comparative treatment, then valid inferences are quite possible. Economists ran experiments on the "negative income tax" in New Jersey in the late 1960s; persons on a negative income tax plan were compared with persons on the conventional IRS plan on variables such as unemployment rate, work incentive, and spending and saving habits. The very essence of the negative income tax is that its amount varies from person to person, yet no one claims that the comparison is thereby invalidated. Indeed, not all subjects need even receive the same *thing*. For example, the evaluation of individualized instruction could make use, in part, of a controlled experimental design having different students receiving different measureable treatments or different amounts of one treatment in an educational setting.

Guba and Stufflebeam (1968, pp. 14, 15) claimed that the application of comparative experimental design to evaluation problems "conflicts with the principle that evaluation should facilitate the continual improvement of a program" and that "it is useful for making decisions after a project has run full cycle but almost useless as a device for making decisions during the planning and implementation of a project." As Scriven (1967) pointed out in answer to Cronbach (1963), this criticism is not valid. A program does not have to run full cycle before an experimental design will prove useful. Many small interim experimental studies may be run, to provide formative information to the decision-maker. The question, "Which of two alternative patterns of routing school buses is most efficient in terms of time and fuel consumption?" can be answered quickly with a short-term, small-scale comparative experiment. Similarly, small comparative experiments on specified curriculum outcomes can be run to provide formative evaluation data (interim product evaluation data) about two competing curricula.

Guba and Stufflebeam faulted comparative experimental design because of the "near impossibility" of controlling or eliminating "confounding variables" through randomization or otherwise. Cronbach raised the same point: "Any failure to equate the classes taking the competing courses will jeopardize the interpretation of an experiment and such failures are almost inevitable" (1963, p. 676). That "equation" of groups is impossible was recognized early in the history of experimental design. In comparative experimental design, groups are made "randomly equivalent"—which is not strictly equivalent at all—and post-experimental differences are inspected to reveal whether they are small enough to be attributed to the original random assignment or whether a treatment effect must be postulated to account for a large difference. Thus, valid experimental comparisons are not impossible just because experimenters cannot perfectly equate groups. Valid, probabilistic comparisons are possible, as the growing number of well-designed comparative experiments in education demonstrates. It is true that valid experimental designs are difficult and expensive to implement, but we feel that such designs are usually well worth the cost.

Finally, Guba and Stufflebeam (1968, p. 16) wrote that "A fourth problem inherent in the application of conventional experimental design is the possibility that *while internal validity may be gained through the control of extraneous variables, such an achievement is accomplished at the expense of external validity.*" Internal and external validity are *not* incompatible; neither need be compromised in field studies of the type used in most evaluation studies. As noted by Bracht and Glass (1968), designing experiments which evidence both types of validity to a high degree is simply a technological problem in instrumentation, data collection, and statistical analysis.

To this point, we have argued that experimental designs can be used in evaluation studies. An excellent example of this use is provided by Anderson (1969). Given that experimental designs can be used, questions are raised about the types of experimental design that are most appropriate and when their use is justified. Addressing the last question first will help us to answer the first question. As we look at the purposes of any inquiry, we should be able to identify (a) a set of questions which are to be answered by the study, and (b) the information we need to answer these questions. If the needed information is comparative, then an experimental design seems entirely appropriate to produce an answer to the evaluator's question. This is especially true if the programs to be evaluated have stabilized to a degree where they are clearly definable. ... If, as is often the case, no comparative evaluation questions are asked, then the evaluator should in no way feel obliged to make use of comparative experimental designs. Often critics of evaluation studies have noted the lack of explanation of why observed phenomena are happening in a program as a weakness in a particular study. As was argued in Chapter 2, explanation is not a necessary aspect of evaluation. Determining that curriculum A yields better results than curriculum B is an important and sufficient evaluation finding, even in the complete absence of an understanding of the "whys of the outcomes." Many excellent evaluation studies have been conducted without any explanatory attempts.

Having identified some appropriate uses of experimental design as part of evaluation studies, the question of what designs are most useful in school settings becomes important. Campbell and Stanley (1966) have discussed in detail several experimental and quasi-experimental designs which might be used in certain evaluation studies. As no attempt will be made to duplicate the presentation of Campbell and Stanley here, the reader would be well-advised to master the content of their monograph. Popham (1967) has also discussed the application of several of the Campbell and Stanley designs for school research.

Practical constraints (such as inability to randomly assign students or teachers to classrooms and treatments, lack of a usable comparison group, insufficient resources) often force the evaluator to compromise the ideal experimental design. Glass (1969) suggested several designs as useful alternatives when more ideal experimental designs are impossible.[3] Excerpts from Glass's paper are presented below.

---

3. Glass (1969) pointed out that "control" groups in educational evaluation studies are normally not the same things referred to in psychological research as control groups. Rather, in education, we are comparing a treatment of interest to "something else"—usually a complex package of many variables called a program or program component. For this reason, it is better to speak of "comparison" groups rather than "control" groups when using experimental designs as part of any evaluation study.

Excerpts from

Design of Evaluation Studies

Gene V Glass

Laboratory of Educational Research
University of Colorado

1. Intact-Group Design

The first compromise design is a submission to the "experimental unit problem." One simply throws up his hands and accepts the dire consequences of treating one intact experimental and one intact comparison group as though each gave thirty, say, independent replications of an experiment instead of just one—that "one" being the group mean. To strengthen this mildly defective design, care should be taken to assign pupils randomly to the two conditions. Though all confounding variables associated with pupils will be controlled (i.e., randomly equated between the two groups) by random assignment of pupils, possible confounding variables associated with such elements of the experiment as the teacher, her staff, time of day, and classroom will not be randomly equated. It is true that one could assign teachers, meeting times, meeting places, etc., to the two groups, but essentially no control is gained since with respect to these influences (and not the influences of pupils' characteristics which have been "equated by randomization") the experiment must surely remain an unreplicated design with an n of 1. Hence, I would advocate random assignment of pupils and careful and explicit *matching* of all other sources of variation present in the experiment if I were attempting an unreplicated comparative experiment with intact groups. The design is given diagramatically in figure 25.

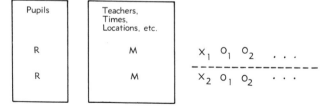

Figure 25

Quasi-experimental Design for Comparative Experiments
with Two Intact Groups

A paper presented at the Council for Exceptional Children Special Conference on Early Childhood Education, New Orleans, La., December 10-13, 1969, pp. 22-29. Reprinted with permission of the author.

In a large, amply replicated experiment employing many groups randomly assigned to conditions, there is no need to worry about unknown influences collecting on the side of one experimental condition and confounding the experiment. The improbability of such an unfortunate happening can be controlled by the manipulation of significance levels of inferential statistical techniques. However, in the unreplicated, intact groups design depicted in figure 25, the experimenter must guard against an uncontrolled force tipping the scales in favor of one of the conditions being compared. Thus, in this sort of quasi-experimentation the experimenter must be a perceptive observer of the daily conduct of the experiment; he must juggle the inevitable extraneous influences which threaten to give illicit advantage to an undeserving treatment group. If teacher A gets sick and misses a week of school, the experimenter must seriously consider dismissing

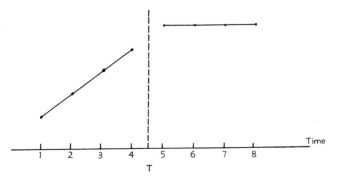

A Time-Series Showing a Change of Direction of Drift but No Change in Level at T.

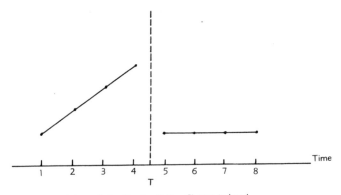

A Time-Series Showing Both a Change in Level and a Change of Direction of Drift at T.

Figure 26

Illustration of Treatment Effects and Time Series Experiments teacher B and replacing her with a substitute for the duration. If school assemblies take up six days of experimental period 1, then perhaps comparison period 2 should be dismissed or distracted for six days. And so it must go down a huge list of confounding influences. By comparison, the more costly, fully replicated, multi-group experiment is a researcher's holiday.

2. Time-Series Experiment

A second compromise with the ideal comparative experiment is distinctly different from the intact-group design. The time-series quasi-experimental design involves studying the progression of the behavior of an individual or group over time. Several observations of the group are taken prior to experimental intervention to establish a baseline performance level for the group. After a sufficient number of pre-treatment observations have been taken, the experimental treatment is applied to the individual or the group. The post-intervention behavior of the time-series is observed and analyzed statistically (see Glass and Maguire, 1968) to determine whether the experimental intervention has had an effect. Hypothetical results from two time-series experiments showing effects of experimental intervention are presented in figure 26. In figure 27 the results of a time-series experiment on a single child are illustrated.

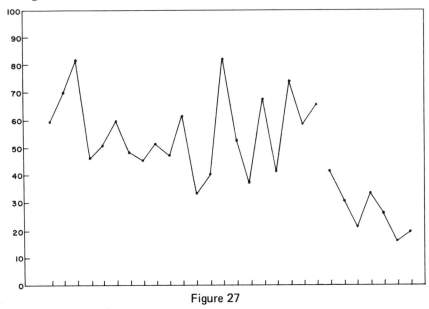

Figure 27

Number of Activity Changes in a 50-Minute Period by *S* over 28 Days.
Social Reinforcement Given for Attending
Behavior Exceeding One Minute over the Last Seven Days. (Allen, et al., 1967).

The child was hyperactive and showed a short attention span. After twenty-eight days of recording the child's inattentive behavior, the teacher began rewarding the child each time he attended to one task for more than one minute. The resulting increase in attention span is apparent in figure 27 and was confirmed as nonchance by appropriate statistical techniques.

The time-series experimental design is actually an extension and strengthening of the simple pretest-posttest design. Time-series experimental designs applied to the social sciences were first examined in detail by Campbell and Stanley (1963). The possible applications of such designs in social science research appear to be numerous. They are somewhat less useful for summative curriculum evaluation. Before anything about the behavior of most time-series can be concluded, several points in time must be observed. Four or five observations prior to the introduction of the experimental treatment and a couple afterwards are not enough. A total of forty or fifty points in time is a reasonable requirement for most time-series experiments. The logical unit of time for evaluating a preschool education program is generally a semester or a year instead of a day or an hour. A design extended over forty semesters or forty years is beyond the patience of all but the most prudent decision-makers. However, when the experimental intervention can be expected to show nearly immediate effects (if any at all), the time-series design may be quite useful. An experimental group could be given some irrelevant activity for a period of twenty-five days, say, then the treatment would be applied and the behavior of the group assessed for the fifteen subsequent days.

An interesting variation on the prototype of the time-series design is one in which the members of the pre-treatment "group" change from one point in time to the next. For example, the unit of observation might be Grade One for the past fifteen years. Even though the pupils in Grade One change from year to year, the grade has an identity of its own and can be said to be repeatedly observed for a fifteen year span. This design has greater possibilities for time-series experiments in educational evaluation than the design which requires that the same group of pupils be observed repeatedly. If retrospective data can be obtained from school records on the performance of the past first grades, the base-line data of evaluating the effects of this year's experimental program will exist. Unfortunately school record keeping seldom permits observing the same behavior over a period of years sufficient for the time-series design. Moreover, the only measures for which much retrospective data are available are usually ability on standardized achievement tests, which are often irrelevant to the objectives of the curriculum being evaluated. Attendance data, drop-out rates, reports of discipline problems, etc. are occasionally available for extended time periods, but such behaviors are seldom the primary goals of a program.

Where subjects are scarce and time to work with them is plentiful, the time-series design may be worth trying. It has the advantage of not requiring a separate comparison group. The "advantage" referred to is a matter of the sociology of experimentation involving human subjects and not a matter of the logic of experimental design. It is a fact that most people prejudge the results of educational innovations that are widely publicized and served up with proper sentiment and unction. In their eyes, it is a heinous crime for the evaluator to deny any child the "obvious" benefits of exposure to the innovation. Sermons on the courage of the experimenters who tested the Salk vaccine or short courses on the history of educational fiascos are wasted on such detractors from the ultimate morality of controlled, comparative experimentation. If the conditions are favorable (i.e., many time periods observable, a quick-acting treatment, etc.), the evaluator is well-advised to resort to the time-series quasi-experiment.

3. *Ex Post Facto* Experiment

The least acceptable compromise with the ideal experimental design is probably the *ex post facto* experiment. The name indicates that the experimenter first intervenes in the process *after* the *fact* of the assignment—by nonrandom means—of subjects to experimental conditions and the complete exposure of the subjects to the treatments. The experimenter's first exposure to the experiment is usually after it has run its course and the data await analysis. No statistician enjoys reconstructing an "experiment" after the fact. At best he can produce convincing results on the comparative effects of treatments only at great cost. The Surgeon General's report on smoking and lung cancer is *ex post facto* experimentation at its best. At its worst, the *ex post facto* experiment merely convinces one of the necessity of designing *pre facto* experiments.

Despite the inadvisability of investigating important evaluative questions with *ex post facto* designs, a word or two are in order concerning their analysis when they are unavoidable. The best analysis of an *ex post facto* experiment is simple to describe but difficult to accomplish. Data on outcome variables are tested for significant treatment differences after every conceivable covariate one can measure is used to adjust posttest differences by means of analysis of covariance. (Matching on pre-experimental variables or

partial correlational techniques of path analysis are nearly equivalent to the analysis of covariance for this purpose.) "Every
conceivable covariate" includes variables descriptive of pupils
(their abilities, interests, past academic records, etc.), their parents
(e.g., educational attainment, social status), the teachers (e.g., age,
experience), and so forth. One must be careful not to measure
covariates *after* the experiment which may show the effects of the
experimental treatments. To covary on these variables will adjust
out of the differences on the outcome variable the very treatment
effects one wishes to discover.

Frequently the covariance adjustment in an *ex post facto*
analysis will remove all posttest differences among the treatment
groups. After an investigation of the particular circumstances of
such an analysis, I would probably be inclined to accept such
results as showing no treatment differences. I would remain critical of any but the most ambitiously done *ex post facto* analysis
which showed significant differences among treatment groups.
Some methodologists would not accept the results of an *ex post
facto* experiment regardless of how thorough the investigator had
been in identifying and adjusting for antecedent differences among
treatment groups (see Lord, 1963; Meehl, 1969). Rare successes
like the smoking and lung cancer study make me more sanguine.
At the same time the successful *ex post facto* experiment reveals
the tremendous expense and effort which are required to establish
causal relationships with nonexperimental data. A few conspicuous successes can not justify claiming success in dozens of lesser
efforts.

The Evaluation Program of
the Single Project or School

The experimental design considerations raised here, together
with other concerns not mentioned, have an important bearing on
the question of the role evaluation can play in the program of a
single project or school. The ideal comparative experiment in the
evaluation of an educational program generally requires far more
resources than a single school can command. Comparative,
summative curriculum evaluation can most profitably be pursued
as a cooperative effort involving dozens of schools or projects. The
recent "first grade reading studies" sponsored by the USOE may
be typical of the scope required of definitive summative curriculum evaluation. One may also point to the School Mathematics
Study Group (SMSG) evaluation of a few years ago which was
designed and analyzed by R. Darrell Bock of the University of
Chicago, as another example of the massive scale required of

definitive summative curriculum evaluation. Perhaps investigators engaged in research and evaluation of preschool education should unite in a consortium of projects through which, at the proper time, comparative experiments could be designed and conducted cooperatively to evaluate promising programs.

The single school or project is a unit organized to provide instruction. It is not organized appropriately for conducting all types of research and evaluation. Educationists must consider new ways of organizing personnel and resources to accomplish summative curriculum evaluation.

The individual school or project would be best advised to invest its evaluation dollars for a few years in formative, developmental evaluation of the type discussed by Dan Stufflebeam in the symposium on Process Evaluation. A poorly executed, premature, and inconclusive comparative summative evaluation will only drain precious resources which could be spent more wisely on formative evaluation during the developmental stages of the program. A rigorous program of formative evaluation should replace the undisciplined tinkering and impressionistic fiddling with a program which too often pass for "developmental research." Cronbach's (1963) classic paper on "Evaluation for Course Improvement" remains the best guide for the formative evaluator.

While I encourage educationists to defer summative evaluation until it is appropriate and can be accomplished as a cooperative effort of many projects, I hasten to remind them that the ultimate summative evaluation cannot be postponed indefinitely. Eventually a hardheaded summative evaluation based largely upon a comparative experiment must be performed.

The Use of Behavioral Objectives and Specifications in Evaluation Studies

Having considered organizational frameworks, criteria, and the use of experimental designs in planning evaluation studies, we are faced with the task of determining the focus of the evaluation study. As we stated in the previous chapter, if evaluators agree on anything, it is that program objectives written in unambiguous terms are useful information for any evaluation study. Thus, program objectives and specifications become an extremely important consideration when an evaluation study is constructed.

Recently there have been a number of papers written by educators who have discussed the uses of behavioral objectives and the advantages and limitations of this use in curriculum development, instruction, and evaluation. Some writers have argued for the use of behavioral objectives as a prerequisite to *any* educational endeavor. This is an extreme case. Others have argued for the complete abolishment of the practice of writing behavioral objectives. This is also an extreme case. In practice we find that the use of behavioral objectives for educational activities, including evaluation, is an important activity *when* this use does not obstruct progress. The first two papers in the following section represent conflicting views about the topic. Atkin discusses limitations of behavioral objectives and argues for caution in their use. Popham's paper contains a refutation of arguments against the use of behavioral objectives. Juxtaposition of these conflicting views here is an attempt only to highlight the debate surrounding the issue, not to resolve it. The third paper in this section, written by Krathwohl, provides a useful overview of the use of taxonomies of human behavior developed by Bloom, et al. (1956) and Krathwohl, et al. (1964).

Behavioral Objectives in Curriculum Design:

A Cautionary Note

J. Myron Atkin

Dean and Professor of Science Education
College of Education
University of Illinois, Urbana

In certain influential circles, anyone who confesses to reservations about the use of behaviorally stated objectives for curriculum planning runs the risk of being labeled as the type of individual who would attack the virtues of motherhood. Bumper stickers have appeared at my own institution, and probably at yours, reading, STAMP OUT NON-BEHAVIORAL OBJECTIVES. I trust that the person who prepared the stickers had humor as his primary aim; nevertheless the crusade for specificity of educational outcome has become intense and evangelical. The worthiness of this particular approach has come to be accepted as self-evident by ardent proponents, proponents who sometimes sound like the true believers who cluster about a new social or religious movement.

From *The Science Teacher*, Volume 35, Number 5, May 1968. Copyright 1968 by the National Science Teachers Association, 1201 Sixteenth Street, N.W., Washington, D.C. Reprinted with permission of the author and publisher.

Behavioral objectives enthusiasts are warmly endorsed and embraced by the systems and operations analysis advocates, most educational technologists, the cost-benefit economists, the planning-programming budgeting system stylists, and many others. In fact, the behavioral objectives people are now near the center of curriculum decision making. Make no mistake; they have replaced the academicians and the general curriculum theorists—especially in the new electronically based education industries and in governmental planning agencies. The engineering model for educational research and development represents·a forceful tide today. Those who have a few doubts about the effects of the tide had better be prepared to be considered uninitiated and naive, if not slightly addlepated and antiquarian.

To utilize the techniques for long-term planning and rational decision making that have been developed with such apparent success in the Department of Defense, and that are now being applied to a range of domestic and civilian problems, it is essential that hard data be secured. Otherwise these modes for developmental work and planning are severely limited. Fuzzy and tentative statements of possible achievement and questions of conflict with respect to underlying values are not compatible with the new instructional systems management approaches—at least not with the present state of the art. In fact, delineating instructional objectives in terms of identifiable pupil behaviors or performances seems essential in 1968 for assessing the output of the educational system. Currently accepted wisdom does not seem to admit an alternative.

There are overwhelmingly useful purposes served by attempting to identify educational goals in nonambiguous terms. To plan rationally for a growing educational system, and to continue to justify relatively high public expenditures for education, it seems that we do need a firmer basis for making assessments and decisions than now exists. Current attention to specification of curriculum objectives in terms of pupil performance represents an attempt to provide direction for collection of data that will result in more informed choice among competing alternatives.

Efforts to identify educational outcomes in behavioral terms also provide a fertile ground for coping with interesting research problems and challenging technical puzzles. A world of educational research opens to the investigator when he has reliable measures of educational output (even when their validity for educational purposes is low). Pressures from researchers are difficult to resist since they do carry influence in the educational community, particularly in academic settings and in educational development laboratories.

Hence I am not unmindful of some of the possible benefits to be derived from attempts to rationalize our decision-making processes through the use of behaviorally stated objectives. Schools need a basis for informed choice. And the care and feeding of educational researchers is a central part of my job at Illinois. However, many of the enthusiasts have given insufficient attention to underlying assumptions and broad questions of educational policy. I intend in this brief paper to highlight a few of these issues in the hope that the exercise might be productive of further and deeper discussion.

Several reservations about the use of behaviorally stated objectives for curriculum design will be catalogued here. But perhaps the fundamental problem, as I see it, lies in the easy assumption that we either know or can readily identify the educational objectives for which we strive, and thereafter the educational outcomes that result from our programs. One contention basic to my argument is that we presently are making progress toward thousands of goals in any existing educational program, progress of which we are perhaps dimly aware, can articulate only with great difficulty, and that contribute toward goals which are incompletely stated (or unrecognized), but which are often worthy.

For example, a child who is learning about mealworm behavior by blowing against the animal through a straw is probably learning much more than how this insect responds to a gentle stream of warm air. Let's assume for the moment that we can specify "behaviorally" all that he might learn about mealworm *behavior* (an arduous and never-ending task). In addition, in this "simple" activity, he is probably finding out something about interaction of objects, forces, humane treatment of animals, his own ability to manipulate the environment, structural characteristics of the larval form of certain insects, equilibrium, the results of doing an experiment at the suggestion of the teacher, the rewards of independent experimentation, the judgment of the curriculum developers in suggesting that children engage in such an exercise, possible uses of a plastic straw, and the length of time for which one individual might be engaged in a learning activity and still display a high degree of interest. I am sure there are many additional learnings, literally too numerous to mention in fewer than eight or ten pages. When any piece of curriculum is used with real people, there are important learning outcomes that cannot have been anticipated when the objectives were formulated. And of the relatively few outcomes that can be identified at all, a smaller number still are translatable readily in terms of student behavior. There is a possibility the cumulative side effects are at least as important as the intended main effects.

Multiply learning outcomes from the mealworm activity by all the various curriculum elements we attempt to build into a school day. Then multiply this by the number of days in a school year, and you have some indication of the oversimplification that *always* occurs when curriculum intents or outcomes are articulated in any form that is considered manageable.

If my argument has validity to this point, the possible implications are potentially dangerous. If identification of all worthwhile outcomes in behavioral terms comes to be commonly accepted and expected, then it is inevitable that, over time, the curriculum will tend to emphasize those elements which have been thus identified. Important outcomes which are detected only with great difficulty and which are translated only rarely into behavioral terms tend to atrophy. They disappear from the curriculum because we spend all the time allotted to us in teaching explicitly for the more readily specifiable learnings to which we have been directed.

We have a rough analogy in the use of tests. Prestigious examinations that are widely accepted and broadly used, such as the New York State Regents examinations, tend over time to determine the curriculum. Whether or not these examinations indeed measure all outcomes that are worth achieving, the curriculum regresses toward the objectives reflected by the test items. Delineation of lists of behavioral objectives, like broadly used testing programs, may admirably serve the educational researcher because it gives him indices of gross achievement as well as details of particular achievement; it may also provide input for cost-benefit analysts and governmental planners at all levels because it gives them hard data with which to work; but the program in the schools may be affected detrimentally by the gradual disappearance of worthwhile learning activities for which we have not succeeded in establishing a one-to-one correspondence between curriculum elements and rather difficult-to-measure educational results.

Among the learning activities most readily lost are those that are long term and private in effect and those for which a single course provides only a small increment. If even that increment cannot be identified, it tends to lose out in the teacher's priority scheme, because it is competing with other objectives which have been elaborately stated and to which he has been alerted. But I will get to the question of priority of objectives a bit later.

The second point I would like to develop relates to the effect of demands for behavioral specification on innovation. My claim here is that certain types of innovation, highly desirable ones, are hampered and frustrated by early demands for behavioral statements of objectives.

Let's focus on the curriculum reform movement of the past 15 years, the movement initiated by Max Beberman in 1952 when he began to design a mathematics program in order that the high school curriculum would reflect concepts central to modern mathematics. We have now seen curriculum development efforts, with this basic flavor, in many science fields, the social sciences, English, esthetics, etc. When one talks with the initiators of such projects, particularly at the beginning of their efforts, one finds that they do not begin by talking about the manner in which they would like to change pupils' behavior. Rather they are dissatisfied with existing curricula in their respective subject fields, and they want to build something new. If pressed, they might indicate that existing programs stress concepts considered trivial by those who practice the discipline. They might also say that the curriculum poorly reflects styles of intellectual inquiry in the various fields. Press them further, and they might say that they want to build a new program that more accurately displays the "essence" of history, or physics, or economics, or whatever. Or a program that better transmits a comprehension of the elaborate and elegant interconnections among various concepts within the discipline.

If they are asked at an early stage just how they want pupils to behave differently, they are likely to look quite blank. Academicians in the various cognate fields do not speak the language of short-term or long-term behavioral change, as do many psychologists. In fact, if a hard-driving behaviorist attempts to force the issue and succeeds, one finds that the disciplinarians can come up with a list of behavioral goals that looks like a caricature of the subject field in question. (Witness the AAAS elementary-school science program directed toward teaching "process.")

Further, early articulation of behavioral objectives by the curriculum developer inevitably tends to limit the range of his exploration. He becomes committed to designing programs that achieve these goals. Thus if specific objectives in behavioral terms are identified early, there tends to be a limiting element built into the new curriculum. The innovator is less alert to potentially productive tangents.

The effective curriculum developer typically begins with *general* objectives. He then refines the program through a series of successive approximations. He doesn't start with a blueprint, and he isn't in much of a hurry to get his ideas represented by a blueprint.

A situation is created in the newer curriculum design procedures based on behaviorally stated objectives in which scholars who do not talk a behavioral-change language are expected to describe their goals at a time when the intricate intellectual subtleties of their work may not be clear, even in the disciplinary language with which they are familiar. At the other end, the educational evaluator, the behavioral specifier, typically has very little understanding of the curriculum that is being designed—understanding with respect to the new view of the subject field that it affords. It is too much to expect that the behavioral analyst, or anyone else, recognize the shadings of meaning in various evolving economic theories, the complex applications of the intricacies of wave motion, or the richness of nuance reflected in a Stravinsky composition.

Yet despite this two-culture problem—finding a match between the behavioral analysts and the disciplinary scholars—we still find that an expectation is being created for early behavioral identification of essential outcomes.

(Individuals who are concerned with producing hard data reflecting educational outputs would run less risk of dampening innovation if they were to enter the curriculum development scene in a more unobtrusive fashion—and later—than is sometimes the case. The curriculum developer goes into the classroom with only a poorly articulated view of the changes he wants to make. Then he begins working with children to see what he can do. He revises. He develops new ideas. He continually modifies as he develops. *After* he has produced a program that seems pleasing, it might then be a productive exercise for the behavioral analyst to attempt with the curriculum developer to identify *some* of the ways in which children seem to be behaving differently. If this approach is taken, I would caution, however, that observers be alert for long-term as well as short-term effects, subtle as well as obvious inputs.)

A third basic point to be emphasized relates to the question of instructional priorities, mentioned earlier. I think I have indicated that there is a vast library of goals that represent possible outcomes for any instructional program. A key educational task, and a task that is well handled by the effective teacher, is that of relating educational goals to the situation at hand—as well as relating the situation at hand to educational goals. It is impractical to pursue all goals thoroughly. And it does make a difference *when* you try to teach something. Considerable educational potential is lost when certain concepts are taught didactically. Let's assume that some third-grade teacher considers it important to develop concepts related to sportsmanship. It would be a rather naive teacher who decided that she would undertake this task at 1:40 P.M. on Friday of next week. The experienced teacher has always realized that learnings related to such an area must be stressed in an appropriate context, and the context often cannot be planned.

Perhaps there is no problem in accepting this view with respect to a concept like sportsmanship, but I submit that a similar case can be made for a range of crucial cognitive outcomes that are basic to various subject-matter fields. I use science for my examples because I know more about this field than about others. But equilibrium, successive approximation, symmetry, entropy, and conservation are pervasive ideas with a broad range of application. These ideas are taught with the richest meaning only when they are emphasized repeatedly in appropriate and varied contexts. Many of these contexts arise in classroom situations that are unplanned, but that have powerful potential. It is detrimental to learning not to capitalize on the opportune moments for effectively teaching one idea or another. Riveting the teacher's attention to a few behavioral goals provides him with blinders that may limit his range. Directing him to hundreds of goals leads to confusing, mechanical pedagogic style and loss of spontaneity.

A final point to be made in this paper relates to values, and it deals with a primary flaw in the consumption of much educational research. It is difficult to resist the assumption that those attributes which we can measure are the elements which we consider most important. This point relates to my first, but I feel that it is essential to emphasize the problem. The behavioral analyst seems to assume that for an objective to be worthwhile, we must have methods of observing progress. But worthwhile goals come first, not our methods for assessing progress toward these goals. Goals are derived from our needs and from our philosophies. They are not and should not be derived primarily from our measures. It borders on the irresponsible for those who exhort us to state objectives in behavioral terms to avoid the issue of determining worth. Inevitably there is an implication of worth behind any act of measurement. What the educational community poorly realizes at the moment is that behavioral goals may or may not be worthwhile. They are articulated from among the vast library of goals because they are stated relatively easily. Again, let's not assume that what we can presently measure necessarily represents our most important activity.

I hope that in this paper I have increased rather than decreased the possibilities for constructive discourse about the use of behavioral objectives for curriculum design. The issues here represent a few of the basic questions that seem crucial enough to be examined in an open forum that admits the possibility of fresh perspectives. Too much of the debate related to the use of behavioral objectives has been conducted in an argumentative style that characterizes discussions of fundamental religious views among adherents who are poorly informed. A constructive effort might be centered on identification of those issues which seem to be amenable to resolution by empirical means and those which do not. At any rate, I feel confident that efforts of the next few years will better inform us about the positive as well as negative potential inherent in a view of curriculum design that places the identification of behavioral objectives at the core.

Excerpts from

Objectives and Instruction

W. James Popham

University of California, Los Angeles
Southwest Regional Laboratory for
Educational Research and Development

. . . .

The Threat Potential of Precision [4]

Notwithstanding apparently cogent arguments in favor of precise objectives, most educators have been inordinately successful in avoiding them. In the remaining paragraphs ten reasons will be examined which educators employ to escape the practice of stating their objectives behaviorally. Each of the reasons has been advocated in print or in public meetings during recent months.

From *Intructional Objectives* (AERA Monograph 3) by W. James Popham et al., ©1969 by Rand McNally and Company, Chicago, pp. 46-52. Reprinted with permission of the author and publisher.

4. The remaining paragraphs are based on symposium presentations at the 19th Annual Conference on Educational Research, California Advisory Council on Educational Research, San Diego, California, November 16, 1967 and the annual meeting of the American Educational Research Association, Chicago, Illinois, February 8-10, 1968.

Each reason has its own degree or reasonableness or emotionality. Each reason carries its own peculiar appeal to different sorts of educators. Each reason is essentially invalid. Following each, an attempt will be made to refute the objection contained in or implied by that reason.

Reason one: Trivial learner behaviors are the easiest to operationalize, hence the really important outcomes of education will be under-emphasized.

This particular objection to the use of precise goals is frequently voiced by educators who have recently become acquainted with the procedures for stating explicit, behavioral objectives. Since even behavioral objectives enthusiasts admit that the easiest kinds of pupil behaviors to operationalize are usually the most pedestrian, it is not surprising to find so many examples of behavioral objectives which deal with the picayune. In spite of its overall beneficial influence, the programmed booklet by Robert Mager (1962) dealing with the preparation of instructional objectives has probably suggested to many that precise objectives are usually trivial. Almost all of Mager's examples deal with cognitive behaviors which, according to Bloom's *Taxonomy*, would be identified at the very lowest level.

Contrary to the objection raised in reason one, however, the truth is that explicit objectives make it far *easier* for educators to attend to *important* instructional outcomes. To illustrate, if you were to ask a social science teacher what his objectives were for his government class, and he responded as follows, "I want to make my students better citizens so that they can function effectively in our nation's dynamic democracy," you would probably find little reason to fault him. His objective sounds so profound and eminently worthwhile that few could criticize it. Yet, beneath such facades of profundity, many teachers really are aiming at extremely trivial kinds of pupil behavior changes. How often, for example, do we find "good citizenship" measured by a trifling true-false test? Now if we'd asked for the teacher's objectives in operational terms and had discovered that, indeed, all the teacher was really attempting to do was promote the learner's achievement on a true-false test, we might have rejected the aim as being unimportant. But this is possible *only* with the precision of explicitly stated goals.

In other words, there is the danger that because of their ready translation to operational statements, teachers will tend to identify too many trivial behaviors as goals. But the very fact that we can make these behaviors explicit permits the teacher and his colleagues to scrutinize them carefully and thus eliminate them as unworthy of our educational efforts. Instead of encouraging unimportant outcomes in education, the use of explicit instructional objectives makes it possible to identify and reject those objectives which are unimportant.

Reason two: Prespecification of explicit goals prevents the teacher from taking advantage of instructional opportunities unexpectedly occurring in the classroom.

When one specifies explicit *ends* for an instructional program there is no necessary implication that the *means* to achieve those ends are also specified. Serendipity in the classroom is always welcome, but, and here is the important point, *it should always be justified in terms of its contribution to the learner's attainment of worthwhile objectives.* Too often teachers may believe they are capitalizing on unexpected instructional opportunities in the classroom, whereas measurement of pupil growth toward any defensible criterion would demonstrate that what has happened is merely ephemeral entertainment for the pupils, temporary diversion, or some other irrelevant classroom event.

Prespecification of explicit goals does not prevent the teacher from taking advantage of unexpectedly occurring instructional opportunities in the classroom, it only tends to make the teacher justify these spontaneous learning activities in terms of worthwhile instructional ends. There are undoubtedly gifted teachers who can capitalize magnificently on the most unexpected classroom events. These teachers should not be restricted from doing so. But the teacher who prefers to probe instructional periphery, just for the sake of its spontaneity, should be deterred by the prespecification of explicit goals.

Reason three: Besides pupil behavior changes there are other types of educational outcomes which are important, such as changes in parental attitudes, the professional staff, community values, etc.

There are undoubtedly some fairly strong philosophic considerations associated with this particular reason. It seems reasonable that there are desirable changes to be made in our society which might be undertaken by the schools. Certainly, we would like to bring about desirable modifications in such realms as the attitudes of parents. But as a number of educational philosophers have reminded us, the schools cannot be all things to all segments of society. It seems that the primary responsibility of the schools should be to educate effectively the youth of the society. To the extent that this is so, all modifications of parental attitudes, professional staff attitudes, etc., should be weighted in terms of a later measureable impact on the learner himself. For example, the school administrator who tells us he wishes to bring about new kinds of attitudes on the part of his teachers should ultimately have to demonstrate that these modified attitudes result in some kind of desirable learner changes. To stop at merely modifying the behavior of teachers, without demonstrating further effects upon the learner, would be insufficient.

So while we can see that there are other types of important social outcomes to bring about, it seems that the school's primary responsibility is to its pupils. Hence, all modifications in personnel or external agencies should be justified in terms of their contribution toward the promotion of desired pupil behavior changes.

Reason four: Measurability implies behavior which can be objectively, mechanistically measured, hence there must be something dehumanizing about the approach.

The fourth reason is drawn from a long history of resistance to measurement on the grounds that it must, of necessity, reduce human learners to quantifiable bits of data. This resistance probably is most strong regarding earlier forms of measurement which were almost exclusively examination-based, and were frequently multiple-choice test measures at that. But a broadened conception of evaluation suggests that there are diverse and extremely sophisticated ways of securing qualitative as well as quantitative indices of learner performance.

One is constantly amazed to note the incredible agreement among a group of judges assigned to evaluate the complicated gyrations of skilled springboard divers in the televised reports of national aquatic championships. One of these athletes will perform an exotic, twisting dive and a few seconds after he has hit the water five or more judges raise cards reflecting their independent evaluations which can range from 0 to 10. The five ratings very frequently run as follows: 7.8, 7.6, 7.7, 7.8, and 7.5. The possibility of reliably judging something as qualitatively complicated as a springboard dive does suggest that our measurement procedures do not have to be based on a theory of reductionism. It is currently possible to assess many complicated human behaviors in a refined fashion. Developmental work is under way in those areas where we now must rely on primitive measures.

Reason five: It is somehow undemocratic to plan in advance precisely how the learner should behave after instruction.

This particular reason was raised a few years ago in a professional journal (Arnstine, 1964) suggesting that the programmed instruction movement was basically undemocratic because it spelled out in advance how the learner was supposed to behave after instruction. A brilliant refutation (Komisar and McClellan,

1965) appeared several months later in which the rebutting authors responded that instruction is by its very nature undemocratic and to imply that freewheeling democracy is always present in the classroom would be untruthful. Teachers generally have an idea of how they wish learners to behave, and they promote these goals with more or less efficiency. Society knows what it wants its young to become, perhaps not with the precision we would desire, but certainly in general. And if the schools were allowing students to "democratically" deviate from societally mandated goals, one can be sure that the institutions would cease to receive society's approbation and support.

Reason six: That isn't really the way teaching is; teachers rarely specify their goals in terms of measurable learner behaviors; so let's set realistic expectations of teachers.

Jackson (1966) recently offered this argument. He observed that teachers just don't specify their objectives in terms of measurable learner behavior and implied that, since this is the way the real world is, we ought to recognize it and live with it. Perhaps.

There is obviously a difference between identifying the status quo and applauding it. Most of us would readily concede that few teachers specify their instructional aims in terms of measurable learner behaviors: *but they should.* What we have to do is to mount a widespread campaign to modify this aspect of teacher behavior. Instructors must begin to identify their instructional intentions in terms of measurable learner behaviors. The way teaching really is at the moment just isn't good enough.

Reason seven: In certain subject areas, e.g., fine arts and the humanities, it is more difficult to identify measurable pupil behaviors.

Sure it's tough. Yet, because it is difficult in certain subject fields to identify measurable pupil behaviors, those subject specialists should not be allowed to escape this responsibility. Teachers in the fields of art and music often claim that it is next to impossible to identify acceptable works of art in precise terms, but they do it all the time. In instance after instance the art teacher does make a judgment regarding the acceptability of pupil-produced artwork. What the art teacher is reluctant to do is put his evaluative criteria on the line. He has such criteria. He must have to make his judgments. But he is loath to describe them in terms that anyone can see.

Any English teacher, for example, will tell you how difficult it is to make a valid judgment of a pupil's essay response. Yet criteria must be made explicit. No one who really understands education has ever argued that instruction is a simple task. It is even more difficult in such areas as the arts and humanities. As a noted art educator observed several years ago, art educators must quickly get to the business of specifying "tentative, but clearly defined criteria" by which they can judge their learners' artistic efforts (Munro, 1960).

Reason eight: While loose general statements of objectives may appear worthwhile to an outsider, if most educational goals were stated precisely, they would be revealed as generally innocuous.

This eighth reason contains a great deal of potential threat for school people. The unfortunate truth is that much of what is going on in the schools today is indefensible. Merely to reveal the nature of some of the behavior changes we are bringing about in our schools would be embarrassing. As long as general objectives are the rule, our goals may appear worthwhile to external observers. But once we start to describe precisely what kinds of changes we are bringing about in the learner, there is the danger that the public will reject our intentions as unworthy. Yet, if what we are doing is trivial, educators should know it, and those who support the educational institution should also know it. To the extent that we are achieving innocuous behavior changes in learners, we are guilty. We must abandon the ploy of "obfuscation by generality" and make clear exactly what we are doing. Then we are obliged to defend our choices.

Reason nine: Measurability implies accountability; teachers might be judged on their ability to produce results in learners rather than on the many bases now used as indices of competence.

This is a particularly threatening reason and serves to produce much teacher resistance to precisely stated objectives. It doesn't take too much insight on the part of the teacher to realize that if objectives are specified in terms of measurable learner behavior, there exists the possibility that the instructor will have to become *accountable* for securing such behavior changes. Teachers might actually be judged on their ability to bring about desirable changes in learners. They should be.

But a teacher should not be judged on the particular instructional *means* he uses to bring about desirable *ends*. At present many teachers are judged adversely simply because the instructional procedures they use do not coincide with those once used by an evaluator when "he was a teacher." In other words, if I'm a supervisor who has had considerable success with open-ended discussion, I may tend to view with disfavor any teachers who cleave to more directive methods. Yet, if the teacher using the more direct methods can secure learner behavior changes which are desirable, I have no right to judge that teacher as inadequate. The possibility of assessing instructional competence in terms of the teacher's ability to bring about specified behavior changes in learners brings with it far more assets than liabilities to the teacher. He will no longer be judged on the idiosyncratic whims of a visiting supervisor. Rather, he can amass evidence that, in terms of his pupils' actual attainments, he is able to teach efficiently.

Even though this is a striking departure from the current state of affairs, and a departure that may be threatening to the less competent, the educator must promote this kind of accountability rather than the maze of folklore and mysticism which exists at the moment regarding teacher evaluation.

Reason ten: It is far more difficult to generate such precise objectives than to talk about objectives in our customarily vague terms.

Here is a very significant objection to the development of precise goals. Teachers are, for the most part, far too busy to spend the necessary hours in stating their objectives and measurement procedures with the kind of precision implied by this discussion. It is said that we are soon nearing a time when we will have more teachers than jobs. This is the time to reduce the teacher's load to the point where he can become a professional decision-maker rather than a custodian. We must reduce public school teaching loads to those of college professors. This is the time when we must give the teacher immense help in specifying his objectives. Perhaps we should *give* him objectives from which to choose, rather than force him to generate his own. Many of the federal dollars currently being used to support education would be better spent on agencies which would produce alternative behavioral objectives for all fields at all grade levels. At any rate, the difficulty of the task should not preclude its accomplishment. We can recognize how hard the job is and still allocate the necessary resources to do it.

While these ten excuses are not exhaustive, they should suggest the nature of the reasons used to resist the implementation of precise instructional objectives. In spite of the very favorable overall reaction to explicit objectives during the past five to ten years, a small collection of dissident educators has arisen to oppose the quest for goal specificity. The trouble with criticisms of precise objectives isn't that they are completely without foundation. In fact, there are probably elements of truth in all of them. Yet, when we are attempting to promote the wide-scale adoption of precision in the classroom, there is the danger that many teachers will use the comments and objections of these few critics as an excuse for not thinking clearly about their goals. Any risks we run by moving to behavioral goals are miniscule in contrast with our current state of confusion regarding instructional intentions. Threatening or not, instructors must abandon their customary practices of goal-stating and turn to a framework of precision.

The Taxonomy of Educational Objectives— Use of Cognitive and Affective Domains

David R. Krathwohl

Dean, School of Education
Syracuse University

When was the last time you sat through a staff meeting devoted to curriculum revision? Was much time at that meeting, or the previous one, consumed by discussing the meanings of the terms involved? The phrases in our curriculum statements and objectives often have a political platform style in order to sound convincing and appropriate, but as a result their value for guiding us in the selection of learning experiences is markedly reduced. When we try to exchange ideas about them, we spend too much time trying to find out what is "really meant" by even such a universally desirable goal as critical thinking. On examination it turns out to mean many different things to many people. If you need further convincing no example is perhaps more obvious than the common use of such a term as "understand."

When teachers say they want their students to "really understand" the principle of acceleration, what do they mean? Is it that the student recalls a formula about acceleration? Should he be able to understand an article written about it? Should he be able to apply the formula to a new situation? Should he be able to think up new situations to which the formula is relevant? Any or all of these are possible interpretations of the term "really understand." Do you think two teachers, both of whom agreed that they wanted their students to "really understand this principle," would independently select the same aspects from among those just mentioned? It seems unlikely. Yet, rarely do our curriculum meetings get this specific. But only as one becomes this specific

Reprinted from *Defining Educational Objectives*, edited by C.M. Lindvall, by permission of the author and the University of Pittsburgh Press. © 1964 by the University of Pittsburgh Press.

Selections from the books *Taxonomy of Educational Objectives, Handbook I: Cognitive Domain* edited by Benjamin S. Bloom, copyright 1956 by David can one decide which among the possible learning experiences to use in the classroom. Usually it is not until the curriculum is translated into learning experiences that this becomes apparent.

The state of communication with respect to a term like "really understand" is nothing compared to the confusion that surrounds objectives dealing with attitudes, interests and appreciation. When we say that we want a child to "appreciate" art, do we mean that he should be aware of artwork? Should he be willing to give it some attention when it is around? Do we mean that he should seek it out—go to the museum on his own, for instance? Do we mean that he should regard artwork as having positive values? Should he experience an emotional kick or thrill when he sees artwork? Should he be able to evaluate it and to know why and how it is effective? Should he be able to compare its esthetic impact with that of other art forms?

We could extend this list, but it is enough to suggest that the term "appreciation" covers a wide variety of meanings. And worse—not all of these are distinct from the terms "attitude" and "interest." Thus, if appreciation has the meaning that we want him to like artwork well enough to seek it out, how would we distinguish such behavior from an interest in art—or are interests and appreciations, as we use these words, the same thing?

If the student *values* art, does he have a favorable *attitude* toward it? Are our appreciation objectives the same as, overlapping with, or in some respects distinct from our attitude objectives? Most of us would argue that there are distinctions in the way we use the terms "appreciation," "attitude" and "interest." It is, however, much less certain that when we use these terms in our discussions of curriculum that we are using them in ways that do not differ from one person to another person. When we delve deep enough to determine which meaning we are using, we get into lengthy discussions—and many of our meetings turn out to be just that.

These kinds of problems which exist for curriculum builders are equally serious for those who have the responsibility of evaluating the success of the teacher in meeting the curriculum's objectives. For them there is the problem of very specific communication between curriculum builder and evaluator. In addition, if there are any similarities among different curriculums, similarities that can be meaningfully and precisely communicated, one could compare the effectiveness of learning devices, materials and curricular organizations. It was with this in mind that a group of college and university examiners, under the leadership of Dr. Benjamin S. Bloom, attempted to devise some means which would permit greater precision of communication with respect to educational objectives. The taxonomy is this means.

What is a taxonomy? You've undoubtedly heard of the biological taxonomies which permit classification into the categories of phylum, class, order, family, genus, species and variety. Ours is also a classification scheme, but the objectives being classified are not plants or animals but educational objectives, and the categories are terms descriptive of the kinds of behavior that we seek from students in educational institutions.

The taxonomy is based on the assumption that the educational program can be conceived as an attempt to change the behavior of students which respect to some subject matter. When we describe the behavior and the subject matter, we construct an educational objective. For instance: the student should be able to recall the major features of Chinese culture; he should be able to recognize form and pattern in literary and art works. The two parts of the objective, the subject matter by the student, are both categorizable. It is, however, the latter, what is to be *done* with the subject matter, which constitutes the categories of the taxonomy. The categorization of subject matter we leave to the librarian.

The taxonomy is divided into three domains: cognitive, affective, and psychomotor. The cognitive includes those objectives having to do with thinking, knowing, and problem solving. The affective includes those objectives dealing with attitudes, values, interests and appreciation. The psychomotor covers objectives having to do with manual and motor skills and has yet to be developed. Our *Handbook* (Bloom, et al., 1956) on the cognitive domain has been published for some time, and has been developed in the most detail. The affective domain, on the other hand, is going through its second and, we hope, final draft. Let us look at the cognitive study first.

The Cognitive Domain

Similar to the distinctions most teachers make, this domain is divided into the acquisition of knowledge, and the development of those skills and abilities necessary to use knowledge. Under the heading "Knowledge" which is the first major category of the cognitive domain, one finds a series of sub-categories, each describing the recall of a different category of knowledge. Each of the subheadings is accompanied by a definition of the behavior classified there and by illustrative objectives taken from the educational literature. In addition, there is a summary of the kinds of test items that may be used to test for each category, a discussion of the problems which beset the individual attempting to evaluate behavior in the category, and a large number of examples of test items—mainly multiple choice, but some essay type. These illustrate how items may be built to measure each of the categories.

The classification scheme is hierarchical in nature, that is, each category is assumed to involve behavior which is more complex and abstract than the previous category. Thus the categories are arranged from simple to more complex behavior, and from concrete to more abstract behavior.

Perhaps the idea of the continuum is most easily gained from looking at the major headings of the cognitive domain, which include knowledge, comprehension (ability to restate knowledge in new words), application (understanding it well enough to apply it), analysis (understanding it well enough to break it apart into its parts and make the relations among ideas explicit), synthesis (the ability to produce wholes from parts, to produce a plan of operation, to derive a set of abstract relations) and evaluation (be able to judge the value of material for given purposes). An objective may include many elementary behaviors, but it is properly classified at the highest level of behavior involved.

There are a number of subheads which lend a specificity and precision to the main headings and help to further define them.

Basically the taxonomy is an educational-logical-psychological classification system. The terms in this order reflect the emphasis given to the organizing principles upon which it is built. It makes educational distinctions in the sense that the boundaries between categories reflect the decisions that teachers make among student behaviors in their development of curriculums, and in choosing learning situations. It is a logical system in the sense that its terms are defined precisely and are used consistently. In addition, each category permits logical subdivisions which can be clearly defined and further subdivided as necessary and useful. Finally the taxonomy seems to be consistent with our present understanding of psychological phenomena, though it does not rest on any single theory.

The scheme is intended to be purely descriptive so that every type of educational goal can be represented. It does not indicate the value or quality of one class as compared to another. It is impartial with respect to views of education. One of the tests of the taxonomy has been that of inclusiveness—could one classify all kinds of educational objectives (if stated as student behaviors) in the framework. In general we have been satisfied that it has met this test.

The categories of the cognitive domain and some illustrative objectives follow (Bloom, et al., 1956, p. 201).

A. Knowledge

1.00 Knowledge

Knowledge, as defined here, involves the recall of specifics and universals, the recall of methods and processes, or the recall of a pattern, structure or setting. For measurement purposes, the recall situation involves little more than bringing to mind the appropriate material. Although some alteration of the material may be required, this is a relatively minor part of the task. The knowledge objectives emphasize most the psychological processes of remembering. The process of relating is also involved in that a knowledge test situation requires the organization and reorganization of a problem such that it will furnish the appropriate signals and cues for the information and knowledge the individual possesses. To use an analogy, if one thinks of the mind as a file, the problem in a knowledge test situation is that of finding in the problem or task the appropriate signals, cues and clues which will most effectively bring out whatever knowledge is filed or stored.

1.10 Knowledge of Specifics

The recall of specific and isolable bits of information. The emphasis is on symbols with concrete referents. This material which is at a very low level of abstraction, may be thought of as the elements from which more complex and abstract forms of knowledge are built.

1.11 Knowledge of Terminology

Knowledge of the referents for specific symbols (verbal and nonverbal). This may include knowledge of the most generally accepted symbol referent, knowledge of the variety of symbols which may be used for a single referent, or knowledge of the referent most appropriate to a given use of a symbol.

• To define technical terms by giving their attributes, properties or relations.[5]
• Familiarity with a large number of words in their common range of meanings.

1.12 Knowledge of Specific Facts

Knowledge of dates, events, persons, places, etc. This may include very precise and specific information such

---

5. Illustrative educational objectives selected from the literature are indicated by black dots.

as the specific date or exact magnitude of a phenomenon. It may also include approximate or relative information such as an approximate time period or the general order of magnitude of a phenomenon.

- The recall of major facts about particular cultures.
- The possession of a minimum knowledge about the organisms studied in the laboratory.

1.20 Knowledge of Ways and Means of Dealing with Specifics

Knowledge of the ways of organizing, studying, judging and criticizing. This includes the methods of inquiry, the chronological sequences and the standards of judgment within a field as well as the patterns of organization through which the areas of the fields themselves are determined and internally organized. This knowledge is at an intermediate level of abstraction between specific knowledge on the one hand and knowledge of universals on the other. It does not so much demand the activity of the student in using the materials as it does a more passive awareness of their nature.

1.21 Knowledge of Conventions

Knowledge of characteristic ways of treating and presenting ideas and phenomena. For purposes of communication and consistency, workers in a field employ usages, styles, practices and forms which best suit their purposes and/or which appear to suit best the phenomena with which they deal. It should be recognized that although these forms and conventions are likely to be set up on arbitrary, accidental, or authoritative bases, they are retained because of the general agreement or concurrence of individuals concerned with the subject, phenomena or problem.

- Familiarity with the forms and conventions of the major types of works, e.g., verse, plays, scientific papers, etc.
- To make pupils conscious of correct form and usage in speech and writing.

1.22 Knowledge of Trends and Sequences

Knowledge of the processes, directions and movement of phenomena with respect to time.

- Understanding of the continuity and development of American culture as exemplified in American life.

- Knowledge of the basic trends underlying the development of public assistance programs.

1.23 Knowledge of Classifications and Categories

Knowledge of the classes, sets, divisions and arrangements which are regarded as fundamental for a given subject field, purpose, argument or problem.

- To recognize the area encompassed by various kinds of problems or materials.
- Becoming familiar with a range of types of literature.

1.24 Knowledge of Criteria

Knowledge of the criteria by which facts, principles, opinions and conduct are tested or judged.

- Familiarity with criteria for judgment appropriate to the type of work and the purpose for which it is read.
- Knowledge of criteria for the evaluation of recreational activities.

1.25 Knowledge of Methodology

Knowledge of the methods of inquiry, techniques and procedures employed in a particular subject field as well as those employed in investigating particular problems and phenomena. The emphasis here is on the individual's knowledge of the method rather than his ability to use the method.

- Knowledge of scientific methods for evaluating health concepts.
- The student shall know the methods of attack relevant to the kinds of problems of concern to the social sciences.

1.30 Knowledge of the Universals and Abstractions in a Field

Knowledge of the major schemes and patterns by which phenomena and ideas are organized. These are the large structures, theories and generalizations which dominate a subject field or which are quite generally used in studying phenomena or solving problems. These are at the highest levels of abstraction and complexity.

1.31 Knowledge of Principles and Generalizations

Knowledge of particular abstractions which summarize observations of phenomena. These are the abstractions which are of value in explaining, describing, predicting or in determining the most appropriate and relevant action or direction to be taken.

- Knowledge of the important principles by which our experience with biological phenomena is summarized.
- The recall of major generalizations about particular cultures.

1.32 Knowledge of Theories and Structures

Knowledge of the *body* of principles and generalizations together with their interrelations which present a clear, rounded and systematic view of a complex phenomenon, problem or field. These are the most abstract formulations, and they can be used to show the interrelation and organization of a great range of specifics.

- The recall of major theories about particular cultures.
- Knowledge of a relatively complete formulation of the theory of evolution.

B. Intellectual Skills and Abilities

Abilities and skills refer to organized modes of operation and generalized techniques for dealing with materials and problems. The materials and problems may be of such a nature that little or no specialized and technical information is required. Such information as is required can be assumed to be part of the individual's general fund of knowledge. Other problems may require specialized and technical information at a rather high level such that specific knowledge and skill in dealing with the problem and the materials are required. The ability and skill objectives emphasize the mental processes of organizing and reorganizing material to achieve a particular purpose. The materials may be given or remembered.

2.00 Comprehension

This represents the lowest level of understanding. It refers to a type of understanding or apprehension such that the individual knows what is being communicated and can make use of the material or idea being communicated without necessarily relating it to other material or seeing its fullest implications.

2.10 Translation

Comprehension as evidenced by the care and accuracy with which the communication is paraphrased or rendered from one language or form of communication to another. Translation is judged on the basis of faithfulness and accuracy, that is, on the extent to which the material in the original communication is preserved although the form of the communication has been altered.

- The ability to understand non-literal statements (metaphor, symbolism, irony, exaggeration).
- Skill in translating mathematical verbal material into symbolic statements and vice versa.

2.20 Interpretation

The explanation or summarization of a communication. Whereas translation involves an objective part-for-part rendering of a communication, interpretation involves a reordering, rearrangement or a new view of the material.

- The ability to grasp the thought of the work as a whole at any desired level of generality.
- The ability to interpret various types of social data.

2.30 Extrapolation

The extension of trends or tendencies beyond the given data to determine implications, consequences, corollaries, effects, etc., which are in accordance with the condition described in the original communication.

- The ability to deal with the conclusions of a work in terms of the immediate inference made from the explicit statements.
- Skill in predicting continuation of trends.

3.00 Application

The use of abstractions in particular and concrete situations. The abstractions may be in the form of general ideas, rules of procedures or generalized methods. The abstractions may also be technical principles, ideas and theories which must be remembered and applied.

- Application to the phenomena discussed in one part of the scientific terms or concepts used in other papers.
- The ability to predict the probable effect of a change in a factor on a biological situation previously at equilibrium.

4.00 Analysis

The breakdown of a communication into its constituent elements or parts such that the relative hierarchy of ideas is made clear and/or the relations between the ideas expressed are made explicit. Such analyses are intended to clarify the communication, to indicate how the communication is organized, and the way in which it manages to convey its effects, as well as its basis and arrangement.

4.10 Analysis of Elements

Identification of the elements included in a communication.

- The ability to recognize unstated assumptions.
- Skill in distinguishing facts from hypotheses.

4.20 Analyses of Relationships

The connections and interactions between elements and parts of a communication.

- The ability to check the consistency of hypotheses with given information and assumptions.
- Skill in comprehending the interrelationships among the ideas in a passage.

4.30 Analysis of Organizational Principles

The organization, systematic arrangement and structure which holds the communication together. This includes the "explicit" as well as "implicit" structure. It includes the bases, necessary arrangement and the mechanics which made the communication a unit.

- The ability to recognize form and pattern in literary or artistic works as a means of understanding their meaning.
- Ability to recognize the general techniques used in persuasive materials, such as advertising, propaganda, etc.

5.00 Synthesis

The putting together of elements and parts so as to form a whole. This involves the process of working with pieces, parts, elements, etc., and arranging and combining them in such a way as to constitute a pattern or structure not clearly there before.

5.10 Production of a Unique Communication

The development of a communication in which the writer or speaker attempts to convey ideas, feelings and/ or experiences to others.

- Skill in writing, using an excellent organization of ideas and statements.
- Ability to tell a personal experience effectively.

5.20 Production of a Plan, or Proposed Set of Operations

The development of a plan of work or the proposal of a plan of operations. The plan should satisfy requirements of the task which may be given to the student or which he may develop for himself.

- Ability to propose ways of testing hypotheses.
- Ability to plan a unit of instruction for a particular teaching situation.

5.30 Derivation of a Set of Abstract Relations

The development of a set of abstract relations either to classify or explain particular data or phenomena, or the deduction of propositions and relations from a set of basic propositions or symbolic representations.

- Ability to formulate appropriate hypotheses based upon an analysis of factors involved, and to modify such hypotheses in the light of new factors and considerations.
- Ability to make mathematical discoveries and generalizations.

6.00 Evaluation

Judgments about the value of material and methods for given purposes. Quantitative and qualitative judgments about the extent to which material and methods satisfy criteria. Use of a standard of appraisal. The criteria may be those determined by the student or those which are given to him.

6.10 Judgments in Terms of Internal Evidence

Evaluation of the accuracy of a communication from such evidence as logical accuracy, consistency and other internal criteria.

- Judging by internal standards, the ability to assess general probability of accuracy in reporting facts from the care given to exactness of statement, documentation, proof, etc.
- The ability to indicate logical fallacies in arguments.

6.20 Judgments in Terms of External Criteria

Evaluation of material with reference to selected or remembered criteria.

- The comparison of major theories, generalizations and facts about particular cultures.
- Judging by external standards, the ability to compare a work with the highest known standards in its field—especially with other works of recognized excellence.

The Affective Domain

The cognitive domain was developed first since it was expected to be the most useful of the three domains. Work on the affective domain was begun immediately but has proceeded much more slowly (Krathwohl, et al., 1964). It presented some special problems. For example, the hierarchical structure has been most difficult to find in the affective part of the taxonomy. We found the principles of simple to complex and concrete to abstract were not sufficient for developing the affective domain. Something additional was needed.

We hoped that in seeking the unique characteristics of the affective domain we would discover the additional principles needed to structure an affective continuum. Analysis of affective objectives showed the following characteristics which the continuum should embody: the emotional quality which is an important distinguishing feature of an affective response at certain levels of the continuum, the increasing automaticity as one progresses up the continuum, the increasing willingness to attend to a specified stimulus or stimulus type as one ascends the continuum, and the developing integration of a value pattern at the upper levels of the continuum.

We had at first hoped that somehow we could derive a structure by attaching certain meanings to the terms "attitude," "value," appreciation" and "interest." But the multitude of meanings which these terms encompassed, as we observed their use in educational objectives, showed that this was impossible. After trying a number of schemes and organizing principles, the one which appeared best to account for the affective phenomena and which best described the process of learning and growth in the affective field was the process of internalization.

The term internalization is perhaps best defined by the descriptions of the categories of the affective domain. Generally speaking, however, it refers to the inner growth that occurs as the individual becomes aware of and then adopts the attitudes, principles, codes and sanctions that become a part of him in forming value judgments and in guiding his conduct. It has many elements in common with the term socialization. At its lowest level we have:

1.0 Receiving (Attending)

At this level we are concerned that the learner be sensitized to the existence of certain phenomena and stimuli—that is, that he be willing to receive or to attend to them. To the uninitiated, Bach is repetitive and boring. To those who know what to listen for, his music is intricate and complex; but even the unsophisticated can understand that in some of his works he has written "rounds" if they are made aware of it. The teacher who makes the student aware of such a characteristic in Bach's work is accomplishing the lowest level of behavior in this category.

1.1 Awareness

Though it is the bottom rung of the affective domain, "Awareness" is almost a cognitive behavior. But unlike "Knowledge," the lowest level of the cognitive domain, we are not so much concerned with a memory of, or ability to recall, an item or fact as we are that, given an appropriate opportunity, the learner will merely be conscious of something; that he takes into account a situation, phenomenon, object or state of affairs.

- Develops awareness of esthetic factors in dress, furnishings, architecture, city design and the like.
- Observes with increasing differentiation the sights and sounds of the city.

1.2 Willingness to Receives,

In this category we have come a step up the ladder, but are still dealing with apparently cognitive behavior. At a minimum level, we are describing the behavior of being willing to tolerate a given stimulus, not to avoid it. Like "awareness" it involves neutrality or suspended judgment toward the stimulus. This is a frequently used category of teachers of the arts since we are prone to reject and avoid some of the newer art forms.

- Develops a tolerance for a variety of types of music.
- Accepts differences of race and culture, among one's acquaintances.

1.3 Controlled or Selected Attention

At a somewhat higher level we are concerned with a new phenomenon, the differentiation of a given stimulus into figure and ground at a conscious or perhaps semi-conscious level, the differentiation of aspects of a stimulus which are perceived as clearly marked off from adjacent impressions. The perception is still without tension or assessment, and the student may not know the technical terms or symbols with which to correctly or precisely describe it to others.

- Listens to music with some discrimination as to its mood and meaning and with some recognition of the contributions of various musical elements and instruments to the total effect.
- Listens for rhythm in poetry or prose read aloud.

2.0 Responding

At this level we are concerned with responses which go beyond merely attending to the phenomenon. The student is sufficiently motivated that he is not just "willing to attend" but perhaps it is correct to say that he is actively attending. As a first stage in a "learning by doing" process, the student is committing himself in some small measure to the phenomena involved. This is a very low level of commitment, and we would not at this level say that this was "a value of his" or that he had "such and such an attitude." These terms belong to the next higher level that we will describe. But we could say that he is doing something with or about the phenomena beside merely perceiving it as was true at the

level previously described—of "selected or controlled attention. An example of such "responding" would be the
compliance with rules of good health or safety, or obedience
to rules of conduct.

The categoy of "responding" has been subdivided into three
subcategories to describe the continuum of responding as the
learner becomes more fully committed to the practice and
phenomena of the objective. The lowest stage is illustrated in
the preceding paragraph and is named "acquiescence in
responding." As the name implies, there is the element of
compliance or obedience at this level which distinguishes it
from the next level, that of "willingness to respond." Finally,
at a still higher level of internalization, there is found a
"satisfaction in response" not reached at the previous level of
willingness or assent to respond. When there is an emotional
response of pleasure, zest, or enjoyment, we have reached
this third level.

2.1   Acquiescence in Responding
· Willingness to comply with health regulations.
· Observes traffic rules on foot and on a bicycle at
intersections and elsewhere.

2.2   Willingness to Respond
· Engages, on his own, in a variety of constructive
hobbies and recreational activities.
· Keeps still when the occasion or the situation
calls for silence. (Situation must be clearly defined.)
· Contributes to group discussion by asking
thought-provoking questions.

2.3   Satisfaction in Response
· Finds pleasure in reading for recreation.
· Enjoys listening to a variety of human voices,
with wide variations in pitch, voice quality and
regional accents.

3.0   Valuing

This is the only category headed by a term which is in
common use among the expressions of objectives by teachers.
Further, it is employed in its usual sense—namely, that a
thing, phenomenon or behavior has worth. This abstract
concept of worth is not so much the result of the individual's

own valuing or assessment as it is a social product that has been slowly internalized or accepted and come to be used by the student as his own criterion of worth.

Behavior categorized at this level is sufficiently consistent and stable that it has come to have the characteristics of a belief or an attitude. The learner displays this behavior with sufficient consistency in appropriate situations that he comes to be perceived as holding a value. At the lowest level of valuing, he is at least willing to permit himself to be so perceived, and at the higher level, he may behave so as to actively further this impression.

3.1 Acceptance of a Value

- A sense of responsibility for listening to and participating in a discussion.

3.2 Preference for a Value

- Draws reticent members of a group into conversation.
- Interest in enabling other persons to attain satisfaction of basic common needs.
- Willingness to work for improvement of health regulations.

3.3 Commitment

- Firm loyalty to the various groups in which one holds membership.
- Practices religion actively in his personal and family living.
- Faith in the power of reason and in the methods of experiment and discussion.

4.0 Organization

As the learner successfully internalizes values, he encounters situations for which more than one value is relevant. Thus necessity arises for (a) organizing the values into a system, (b) determining the interrelationships among them, (c) finding which will be the dominant and pervasive ones.

4.1 Conceptualization of a Value

- Desire to evaluate the thing appreciated.
- Finding and crystallizing the basic assumptions which underlie codes of ethics and are the basis of faith.

4.2 Organization of a Value System

• Weigh alternative social policies and practices against the standards of the public welfare rather than the advantage of specialized and narrow interest groups.

5.0 Characterization by a Value or Value Concept

At this level of internalization the values already have a place in the individual's value hierarchy, are organized into some kind of internally consistent system, have controlled the behavior of the individual for a sufficient time so that he has adapted to behaving this way, and an evocation of the behavior is no longer regularly accompanied by emotion or affect.

The individual consistently acts in accord with the values he has internalized at this level, and our concern is to indicate two things—(a) the generalization of this control to so much of the individual's behavior that he is described and characterized as a person by these pervasive controlling tendencies, (b) the integration of these beliefs, ideas and attitudes into a total philosophy or world view. These two aspects constitute the subcategories.

5.1 Generalized Set

• Readiness to revise judgments and to change behavior in the light of evidence.

• Acceptance of objectivity and systematic planning as basic methods in arriving at satisfying choices.

5.2 Characterization

• Develop for regulation of one's personal and civic life a code of behavior based on ethical principles consistent with democratic ideals.

• Develop a consistent philosophy of life.

• Develop a conscience.

Use of the Taxonomy

You now know what the taxonomy is. Of what value is it? Earlier in discussing some of the problems of curriculum construction we hinted at some of its potential uses.

As you now realize, it focuses on the student's behavior as it is expressed in educational objectives. While objectives are by no means foreign to the elementary and secondary school, not all objectives specify these goals in terms of student behavior. Often they are in terms of teacher behavior—on the assumption that student behavior changes follow certain teacher actions—surely not an airtight assumption! We have found that stating objectives as student behavior puts the focus where it belongs, on the change to be made in the student. It leaves the way open to experimentation with different teacher behaviors to attain most effectively and efficiently the desired goal. Stated this way, the taxonomy provides a basis for working with objectives with a specificity and a precision that is not generally typical of such statements. Further, this specificity and precision in the description of a student behavior makes it much easier to choose the kinds of learning experiences that are appropriate to developing the desired behavior and to building evaluation instruments.

No longer is a teacher faced with an objective like this: "The student should understand the taxonomy of educational objectives." Rather the teacher now specifies whether this would be at the lowest level of Comprehension where he would at least expect the student to be able to translate the term "taxonomy" into something like "a classification system of educational goals," or perhaps at a deeper level of understanding, classified as Interpretation, where the student could restate the ideas of the taxonomy in his own words. In short, you should find the taxonomy a relatively concise model for the analysis of education objectives.

In building a curriculum you have undoubtedly paused to consider, "Are there things left out—behaviors I'd have included if I'd thought of them?" The taxonomy, like the period table of elements or a "check-off" shopping list, provides the panorama of objectives. Comparing the range of the present curriculum with the range of possible outcomes may suggest additional goals that might be included. Further, the illustrative objectives may suggest wordings that might be adapted to the area you are exploring.

Frequently when we are searching for ideas in building a curriculum we turn to the work of others who have preceded us. Where both your work and that of others are built in terms of the taxonomy categories, comparison is markedly facilitated. Translation of objectives into the taxonomy framework can provide a basis for precise comparison. Further, where similarities exist, it becomes possible to trade experiences regarding the values of certain learning experiences with confidence that there is a firm basis for comparison and that the other person's experience will be truly relevant.

It is perhaps also important to note the implication of the hierarchical nature of the taxonomy for curriculum building. If our analysis of the cognitive and affective areas is correct, then a hierarchy of objectives dealing with the same subject matter concepts suggests a readiness relationship that exists between those objectives lower in the hierarchy and those higher in it. While we regularly give some attention to this kind of sequential relation for objectives in the cognitive domain, it is less a prominent feature of the affective—a point to which we shall return.

How might the taxonomy be useful in better evaluating teaching? For one thing, teachers rarely analyze standardized tests. They have the feeling that these were put together by experts who know more than they do and, though they may feel a vague discontent with the test, too often they do not analyze the content of these tests against their objectives to determine how well they match. Here again, by using the taxonomy as a translating framework one can compare the test with the teacher's goals. In its simplest form this may be a determination of the proportion of items in each of the major taxonomy categories. This alone is often enough information to help a teacher determine a test's relevance. Such an analysis is particularly useful where one test must be selected from several considered for adoption. For instance, the taxonomy could be used as a common framework for comparing the Iowa Tests of Basic Skills with the revised Stanford Achievement Test.

A similar analysis of the items of the tests the teacher constructs himself checked against his own objectives may be revealing of over- or under-emphasis on particular objectives.

As has already been indicated, the *Handbook's* sample items and discussions of how to build test items at each of the taxonomy levels may be quite helpful to a teacher. But above and beyond this, the teacher will find the taxonomy is a key to increasing numbers of item collections. Dressel and Nelson (1956) have published an 805-page folio of test items in science keyed to the taxonomy and subject matter. A teacher can use such a folio to select the items needed for a test, modifying them to fit the class level.

A related use of the taxonomy is its role in facilitating evaluation of a school's educational experiments. The most frequent type of school experimentation is the comparison of teaching methods, devices or curricula. In all of these comparisons, use of the taxonomy facilitates better communications and comparisons between experiments and between experimenters and adds to the precision of the operational definitions of the variables involved. Thus some television experimentation has resorted to taxonomic classifications to determine the instructor's competence in teaching abilities and skills as well as in conveying knowledge via this medium.

The emphasis in programmed learning on a complete and detailed analysis of the behaviors to be taught immediately suggests a possible role for the taxonomy. Recent literature on programming (Fry, 1963; Mager, 1962) has recognized the taxonomy as a tool for the analysis of curriculums as the first step in programming. Because of its hierarchical structure, analysis by means of the taxonomy assists programming in still another way. The level of categorization aids in placing the material in the program sequence and in planning the over-all sequential development of the skill or ability.

So far, we have been discussing largely those uses of the taxonomy which stem from the cognitive domain. Curricula trends seem to show a move away from emphasis in the affective area. Indeed, schools have been attacked because of their concern with these kinds of objectives. But even though teachers continue to think affective goals are important, in comparison with the emphasis on cognitive objectives, there is little direct attack on these goals. There are occasional sociometric tests, group work, and some class elections, but the bulk of learning in this area is incidental learning. Partly this is a matter of not knowing how best to seek the goals even if the confusion were resolved.

The analytic framework which the taxonomy brings to the affective area should aid in the clarification of what goals are being sought. Guidance and counseling personnel using instruments dealing with the affective domain may find it useful to categorize the measures yielded by their instruments and, to the extent possible, compare this information with that needed by the teachers to reach their goals. The qualification "to the extent possible" is necessary because the taxonomy does not provide categories for all behavior, but only that which is desirable behavior, such as would be sought in a school curriculum. Psychological tests frequently include measures of undesirable behavior. In general, however, it is hoped that the affective domain categories will prove a useful framework for clarification of terminology and relating counselor data to teacher goals.

Along these same lines, an analysis of existing instruments demonstrates that the bulk of our measurement is concentrated at the very top levels—at the most complex behavior. Use of this framework to analyze the Edwards Personnel Preference Schedule or the California Test of Personality, for instance, shows no measures of the lower levels of the affective area. This suggests that increased concentration on measurement instruments for the lower levels of the affective area might be helpful.

If our analysis of the affective domain is correct, we have a developmental picture of the way in which these goals are reached, from simple receiving and responding through characterization. It makes clear the beginnings of complex objectives such as appreciations, interests and attitudes. It focuses the teacher's attention on the development of these simple behaviors which are the building blocks out of which the more complex objectives grow—simple behaviors which rarely are now deliberately taught.

You can, no doubt, now think of additional implications of the taxonomy for your school situation. This material may be enough to help you "understand" the taxonomy a little better. By "understand" we mean that you have some knowledge of the taxonomy, that you have been able to comprehend what it is about—that is, be able to describe it in your own words. Hopefully, you are at least at the level of application and can see some possible uses. Perhaps in the discussion of this material at the Conference it will be time for some evaluation to see how well my objectives were achieved.

The Evaluator's Use of Objectives

The evaluator should not expect to find precisely stated behavioral objectives in many educational programs. Frequently, school personnel feel most comfortable working with broadly stated aims that are open to many interpretations (which often depend on the political atmosphere of the day). Some lack the skill to write unambiguous behavioral objectives. Thus, it becomes highly important in most evaluation studies for the evaluator to have the necessary objectives-writing skills; he must be able to communicate effectively with his clients to produce a list of operational, precisely stated objectives. Both Stake and Scriven have emphasized that it is the responsibility of the evaluator to see that objectives are well stated. If a client comes to the evaluator with broad, ambiguous goals, he should not be turned away with instructions to be more specific. It is the evaluator's job to sit down with this client and help him to write clearly stated objectives. The best way to accomplish the task is to try writing examples of behavioral objectives for each goal and to ask, "Is this what you mean?" Thus, a list of precisely stated objectives may be developed. This process requires considerable skill on the part of the evaluator in writing behavioral objectives and in communicating effectively with his clients.

Once a list of behavioral objectives and specifications has been developed, the evaluator will have a clear idea about what goals his client wants to achieve. This list of objectives is actually a set of priorities or value statements provided by the client. Stake (1970) called information about objectives one type of "judgmental" data. Since the objectives stated are, in fact, a set of value statements, it is important that the evaluator describe as clear a picture of these priorities as possible. There are basically two sources of information about the objectives from which he can draw. *Explicit* sources are those which contain statements of objectives written or stated in some public document. A list of behavioral objectives written by a client would be an explicit statement of program priorities. Often, however, many high priority objectives are never written down. They are *implicit* objectives which the client would like to see happen, but which he didn't include on any public list of goals. Stake (1971) pointed out that since any public display of educational objectives will evoke political and social reaction (Lortie, 1967), educators, as anyone else, are likely to be less than candid in writing out objectives.

The goal of the evaluator at this point is to describe the priorities of the educational program in as much detail as possible. Once a full description of the program objectives is written, Scriven has suggested that the objectives themselves be evaluated to determine their worth. Either relative standards (for example, objectives of another program) or absolute standards (for example, meeting the empirically determined needs of the school) could be used to evaluate the program objectives.

Two broad types of evaluation procedures may be used for evaluating objectives. The *logical analysis* of the objectives would concentrate on the cogency of arguments for setting the goals, the consequences of achieving the objectives, and the congruency of the objectives with existing, higher order values. All of this analysis can and should be done as an armchair exercise before program objectives are accepted as valuable goals. A second type of analysis, *empirical analysis* of objectives, has been discussed elsewhere by Stake (1970). He has suggested that empirical studies can, and should, be designed to determine how widespread a certain value position (statement of objectives) really is. The types of study most appropriate for the evaluation of objectives include the collection of information from groups (by such means as surveys, interviews, Q-sorts, observations of group behavior), from specialists in the program area (such as critical appraisal by curriculum specialists), and from public documents (such as newspaper accounts, school records, employer interview schedules). The information gained from the logical and empirical analysis of program objectives, compared against specified standards, will verify the worth or lack of worth for the fully described set of objectives.

Having a set of precisely stated, worthwhile objectives in hand, the evaluator should be able to identify much of the information required to evaluate the educational program. It is worth noting that the final list of objectives does not provide a complete list of information needed to conduct an evaluation study,[6] but it does give the evaluator much direction in the collection of information.

Measurement Problems and
Techniques in Evaluation Studies

Once the evaluator has listed all of the information that he needs in order to answer evaluative questions about an educational program, he is faced with the problems of how to identify the sources of the information and how to collect the information. Stake (1971) noted that most measurement specialists subscribe to the view that it is possible to measure most specific educational outcomes and to use the measurements in improving educational decisions. This view is implicit in the following paper which contains both an evaluation paradigm similar to Tyler's approach to evaluation and an appendix of criterion measures which can be used in program evaluation studies. Although the list of measures is not exhaustive and does concentrate largely on program outcomes, it is presented here because of its utility in broadening the evaluator's view of measures that may provide useful evaluative information. The paper also provides a starting point for a discussion of measurement techniques. Following the Metfessel-Michael paper, we will discuss some limitations to standardized testing in evaluation and then consider the development of measures other than those which are taken using outcome, or already available, instruments.

---

6. This point is clearly made by several writers in chapter 3.

A Paradigm Involving Multiple Criterion Measures for the Evaluation of the Effectiveness of School Programs

Newton S. Metfessel

and

William B. Michael

University of Southern California

Although much of what is to be presented has been said before, the writers believe that in the light of the recent emphasis upon evaluation of exemplary and innovative school programs receiving federal support it may be helpful to set forth a rationale to facilitate their evaluation. Despite the risk of redundancy with the previous efforts of Tyler (1942, 1964) Bloom et al. (1956), Krathwohl (1964), Krathwohl et al. (1964), Lindvall et al. (1964), and Michael and Metfessel (1967), both the paradigm to be presented and the list of suggested criterion measures that may be used in evaluation of the attainment of objectives in school programs may be of some help to teachers, administrators, counselors, consultants to public schools, and certain other professional personnel whose experience in evaluation may be somewhat limited.

Purpose

Thus, the twofold purpose of this paper is (1) to present an eight-step procedural outline of the evaluation process in the form of a paradigm (or flow chart) that maps out in a step-by-step sequence the key features of the evaluation process and (2) to furnish a detailed listing of multiple criterion measures that may be used in the evaluation of specific behavioral objectives. (For maximum clarity and usability these objectives are preferably stated as operational definitions involving measurable and observable changes in behaviors that have been judged to be significant and relevant to the broad goals and the philosophy of the educational institution under study.) The experience of the writers in working with school personnel has pointed to the need not only for a model which can be followed in evaluation of school programs but also for a listing of multiple criterion measures of

Based on a paper given at the 1967 annual meeting of AERA, February 16, 1967, held in New York City. Reprinted from *Educational and Psychological Measurement*, 1967, 27, 931-943. Reprinted with permission of the authors and publisher.

potential utility in the instrumentation phase of the evaluation process.

The Paradigm

Since the purposes and assumptions underlying the evaluation process as well as ways in which specific objectives in both the cognitive and affective domains can be stated have been explicitly formulated in the sources already indicated as well as in many textbooks in college courses in educational measurement and evaluation, no attention will be given at this point to these specific concerns. Instead, emphasis will be placed on a brief statement of the key steps of the evaluation process, the details of which are outlined in the paradigm portrayed in Figure 28. The multiple criterion measures that correspond to the fourth segment of the evaluation process as shown in Figure 28 are included in the self-explanatory appendix. The eight major steps in the evaluation process may be enumerated as follows:

I. Involve both directly and indirectly members of the total school community as participants, or facilitators, in the evaluation of programs—lay individuals and lay groups, professional personnel of the schools and their organizations, and students and student-body groups.

2. Construct a cohesive paradigm of broad goals and specific objectives (desired behavioral changes) arranged in a hierarchical order from general to specific outcomes (both cognitive and noncognitive) in a form, for example, that might resemble one or both of the taxonomies set forth by Bloom et al. (1956) and Krathwohl et al. (1964). Substeps involved in this second phase include (a) setting broad goals that embrace the philosophical, societal, and institutional expectations of the culture; (b) stating specific objectives in operational terms permitting relatively objective measurement whenever possible and/or empirical determination of current status or of changes in behaviors associated with these objectives; and (c) developing judgmental criteria that permit the definition of relevant and significant outcomes as well as the establishment of realistic priorities in terms of societal needs, of pupil readiness, of opportunities for pupil-teacher feedback necessary in motivating and directing learning, and of the availability of staff and material resources.

3. Translate the specific behavioral objectives into a form that is both communicable and applicable to facilitating learning in the school's environment.

4. Develop the instrumentation necessary for furnishing criterion measures from which inferences can be formulated concerning program effectiveness in terms of the objectives set forth.

5. Carry out periodic observations through use of the tests, scales, and other indices of behavioral change that are considered valid with respect to the objectives sampled.

6. Analyze data furnished by the status and change measures through use of appropriate statistical methods.

7. Interpret the data in terms of certain judgmental standards and values concerning what are considered desirable levels of performance on the totality of collated measures—the drawing of conclusions which furnish information about the direction of growth, the progress of students, and the effectiveness of the total program.

8. Formulate recommendations that furnish a basis for further implementation, for modifications, and for revisions in the broad goals and specific objectives so that improvements can be realized—recommendations which for their effectiveness depend upon adequate feedback of information to all individuals involved in the school program and upon repeated cycles of the evaluation process.

In addition the paradigm points to the individuals having primary responsibility for evaluation at each of the successive stages of the process. These responsibilities in the form of facilitating roles are indicated by the insertion of the letter L for lay individuals and lay groups, the letter P for professional staff members and their professional groups, and the letter S for students and student-body groups. These letters are placed in the lower right-hand corner of each of the principal blocks of the paradigm. Each block corresponds to a given phase of the evaluation process. Whenever the individuals designated by P, L, or S serve as primary or major agents (facilitators or inhibitors) at a given stage of the evaluation process, the letter is *not* placed within a parenthesis; whenever the individuals serve as secondary or indirect agents, a parenthesis is placed around the corresponding letter. The arrows from one block to the next indicate the approximate temporal sequence in which the steps occur, although in practice the order may be quite varied.

A Few Cautions

It should also be emphasized that judgmental decisions are involved throughout all phases of the evaluation process, as the

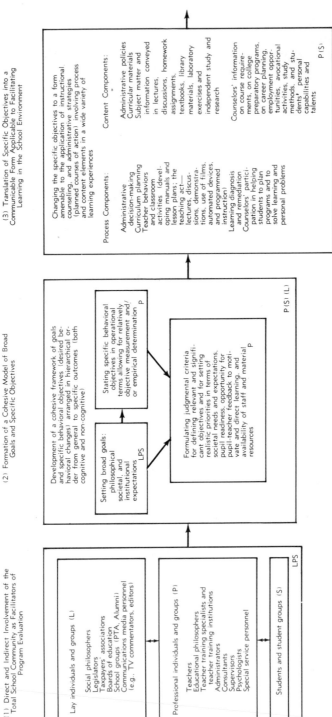

(1) Direct and Indirect Involvement of the Total School Community as Facilitators of Program Evaluation

(2) Formation of a Cohesive Model of Broad Goals and Specific Objectives

(3) Translation of Specific Objectives into a Communicable Form Applicable to Facilitating Learning in the School Environment

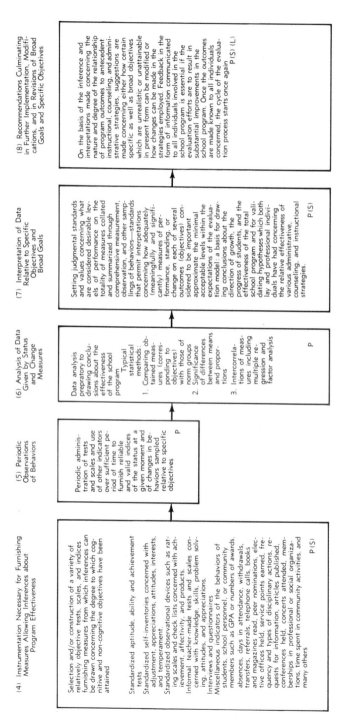

Figure 28

Paradigm showing eight major phases of process of evaluating school programs in approximate temporal sequence numbered (1) through (8). The facilitating role of lay individuals (L), professional personnel (P), and students (S) is indicated in lower right hand corner of boxes. The parentheses around L, P, and S in lower right corner of boxes indicate a secondary or indirect role and the absence of parentheses a primary role.

participants of each stage may be expected to make adjustments in their activities in terms of the amount and kinds of feedback received. The alert evaluator needs also to be aware that measures may yield indications of false gains or false losses that are correlated with (1) experiences in the school environment as well as outside the school environment that go beyond the intent of the specific behavioral objectives, (2) uncontrolled differences in the facilitating effects of teachers and other school personnel (usually motivational in origin), (3) inaccuracies in collecting, reading, analyzing, collating, and reporting of data, and (4) errors in research design and statistical methodology. In such situations, the wisdom and seasoned judgment of the trained evaluator are particularly helpful and necessary if meaningful, honest, and realistic conclusions are to be derived from the data obtained in the evaluation process

Appendix

Multiple Criterion Measures for Evaluation of School Programs

I. Indicators of Status or Change in Cognitive and Affective Behaviors of Students in Terms of Standardized Measures and Scales

Standardized achievement and ability tests, the scores on which allow inferences to be made regarding the extent to which cognitive objectives concerned with knowledge, comprehension, understanding, skills, and applications have been attained.

Standardized self inventories designed to yield measures of adjustment, appreciations, attitudes, interests, and temperament from which inferences can be formulated concerning the possession of psychological traits (such as defensiveness, rigidity, aggressiveness, cooperativeness, hostility, and anxiety).

Standardized rating scales and check lists for judging the quality of products in visual arts, crafts, shop activities, penmanship, creative writing, exhibits for competitive events, cooking, typing, letter writing, fashion design, and other activities.

Standardized tests of psychomotor skills and physical fitness.

II. Indicators of Status or Change in Cognitive and Affective Behaviors of Students by Informal or Semiformal Teacher-made Instruments or Devices

Incomplete sentence technique: categorization of types of responses, enumeration of their frequencies, or rating of their psychological appropriateness relative to specific criteria.

Interviews: frequencies and measurable levels of responses to formal and informal questions raised in a face-to-face interrogation.

Peer nominations: frequencies of selection or of assignment to leadership roles for which the sociogram technique may be particularly suitable.

Questionnaires: frequencies of responses to items in an objective format and numbers of responses to categorized dimensions developed from the content analysis of responses to open-ended questions.

Self-concept perceptions: measures of current status and indices of congruences between real self and ideal self—often determined from use of the semantic differential or Q-sort techniques.

Self-evaluation measures: student's own reports on his perceived or desired level of achievement, on his perceptions of his personal and social adjustment, and on his future academic and vocational plans.

Teacher-devised projective devices such as casting characters in the class play, role playing, and picture interpretation based on an informal scoring model that usually embodies the determination of frequencies of the occurrence of specific behaviors, or ratings of their intensity or quality.

Teacher-made achievement tests (objective and essay), the scores on which allow inferences regarding the extent to which specific instructional objectives have been attained.

Teacher-made rating scales and check lists for observation of classroom behaviors: performance levels of speech, music and art; manifestation of creative endeavors, personal and social adjustment, physical well being.

Teacher-modified forms (preferably with consultant aid) of the semantic differential scale.

III. Indicators of Status or Change in Student Behavior Other than Those Measured by Tests, Inventories, and Observation Scales in Relation to the Task of Evaluating Objectives of School Programs.

Absences: full-day, half-day, part-day and other selective indices pertaining to frequency and duration of lack of attendance.

Anecdotal records: critical incidents noted including frequencies of behaviors judged to be highly undesirable or highly deserving of commendation.

Appointments: frequencies with which they are kept or broken.

Articles and stories: numbers and types published in school newspapers, magazines, journals or proceedings of student organizations.

Assignments: numbers and types completed with some sort of quality rating or mark attached.

Attendance: frequency and duration when attendance is required or considered optional (as in club meetings, special events, or off-campus activities).

Autobiographical data: behaviors reported that could be classified and subsequently assigned judgmental values concerning their appropriateness relative to specific objectives concerned with human development.

Awards, citations, honors, and related indicators of distinctive or creative performance: frequency of occurrence or judgments of merit in terms of scaled values.

Books: numbers checked out of library, numbers renewed, numbers reported read when reading is required or when voluntary.

Case histories: critical incidents and other passages reflecting quantifiable categories of behavior.

Changes in program or in teacher as requested by student: frequency of occurrence.

Choices expressed or carried out: vocational, avocational, and educational (especially in relation to their judged appropriateness to known physical, intellectual, emotional, social, aesthetic, interest, and other factors).

Citations: commendatory in both formal and informal media of communication such as in the newspaper, television, school assembly, classroom bulletin board, or elsewhere (see Awards).

"Contacts": frequency or duration of direct or indirect communications between persons observed and one or more significant others with specific reference to increase or decrease in frequency or to duration relative to selected time intervals.

Disciplinary actions taken: frequency and type.

Dropouts: numbers of students leaving school before completion of program of studies.

Elected positions: numbers and types held in class, student body, or out-of-school social groups.

Extracurricular activities: frequency or duration of participation in observable behaviors amenable to classification such as taking part in athletic events, charity drives, cultural activities, and numerous service-related avocational endeavors.

Grade placement: the success or lack of success in being promoted or retained; number of times accelerated or skipped.

Grade point average: including numbers of recommended units of course work in academic as well as in non-college preparatory programs.

Grouping: frequency and/or duration of moves from one instructional group to another within a given class grade.

Homework assignments: punctuality of completions, quantifiable judgments of quality such as class marks.

Leisure activities: numbers and types of; times spent in; awards and prizes received in participation.

Library card: possessed or not possessed; renewed or not renewed.

Load: numbers of units or courses carried by students.

Peer group participation: frequency and duration of activity in what are judged to be socially acceptable and socially undesirable behaviors.

Performance: awards, citations received; extra credit assignments and associated points earned; numbers of books or other learning materials taken out of the library; products exhibited at competitive events.

Recommendations: numbers of and judged levels of favorableness.

Recidivism by students: incidents (presence or absence or frequency of occurrence) of a given student's returning to a probationary status, to a detention facility, or to observable behavior patterns judged to be socially undesirable (intoxicated state, dope addiction, hostile acts including arrests, sexual deviation).

Referrals: by teacher to counselor, psychologist, or administrator for disciplinary action, for special aid in overcoming learning difficulties, for behavior disorders, for health defects or for part-time employment activities.

Referrals: by student himself (presence, absence, or frequency).

Service points: numbers earned.

Skills: demonstration of new or increased competencies such as those found in physical education, crafts, homemaking, and the arts that are not measured in a highly valid fashion by available tests and scales.

Social mobility: numbers of times student has moved from one neighborhood to another and/or frequency with which parents have changed jobs.

Tape recordings: critical incidents contained and other analyzable events amenable to classification and enumeration.

Tardiness: frequency of.

Transiency: incidents of.

Transfers: numbers of students entering school from another school (horizontal move).

Withdrawal: numbers of students withdrawing from school or from a special program (see Dropouts).

IV. Indicators of Status or Change in Cognitive and Affective Behaviors of Teachers and Other School Personnel in Relation to the Evaluation of School Programs

Articles: frequency and types of articles and written documents prepared by teachers for publication or distribution.

Attendance: frequency of, at professional meetings or at in-service training programs, institutes, summer schools, colleges and universities (for advanced training) from which inferences can be drawn regarding the professional person's desire to improve his competence.

Elective offices: numbers and types of appointments held in professional and social organizations.

Grade point average: earned in postgraduate courses.

Load carried by teacher: teacher-pupil or counselor-pupil ratio.

Mail: frequency of positive and negative statements in written correspondence about teachers, counselors, administrators, and other personnel.

Memberships including elective positions held in professional and community organizations: frequency and duration of association.

Model congruence index: determination of how well the actions of professional personnel in a program approximate certain operationally-stated judgmental criteria concerning the qualities of a meritorious program.

Moonlighting: frequency of outside jobs and time spent in these activities by teachers or other school personnel.

Nominations by papers, students, administrators' or parents for outstanding service and/or professional competencies: frequency of.

Rating scales and check lists (e.g., graphic rating scales or the semantic differential) of operationally-stated dimensions of teachers' behaviors in the classroom or of administrators' behaviors in the school setting from which observers may formulate inferences regarding changes of behavior that reflect what are judged to be desirable gains in professional competence, skills, attitudes, adjustment, interests, and work efficiency; the perceptions of various members of the total school community (parents, teachers, administrators, counselors, students, and classified employees) of the behaviors of other members may also be obtained and compared.

Records and reporting procedures practiced by administrators, counselors and teachers: judgments of adequacy by outside consultants.

Termination: frequency of voluntary or involuntary resignation or dismissals of school personnel.

Transfers: frequency of requests of teachers to move from one school to another.

V. Indicators of Community Behaviors in Relation to the Evaluation of School Programs

Alumni participation: numbers of visitations, extent of involvement in PTA activities, amount of support of a tangible (financial) or a service nature to a continuing school program or activity.

Attendance at special school events, at meetings of the board of education, or at other group activities by parents: frequency of.

Conferences of parent-teacher, parent-counselor, parent-administrator sought by parents: frequency of request.

Conferences of the same type sought and initiated by school personnel: frequency of requests and record of appointments kept by parents.

Interview responses amenable to classification and quantification.

Letters (mail): frequency of requests for information, materials, and servicing.

Letters: frequency of praiseworthy or critical comments about school programs and services and about personnel participating in them.

Participant analysis of alumni: determination of locale of graduates, occupation, affiliation with particular institutions, or outside agencies.

Parental response to letters and report cards upon written or oral request by school personnel: frequency of compliance by parents.

Telephone calls from parents, alumni, and from personnel in communications media (e.g., newspaper reporters): frequency, duration, and quantifiable judgments about statements monitored from telephone conversations.

Transportation requests: frequency of.

Standardized Instruments
and Their Limitations

It is evident from a review of the history of testing (DuBois, 1970) that the technology of testing has far surpassed the psychological theory underlying the development of tests. Indeed, testing is replete with examples of instruments that are highly sophisticated in a technical sense (for example, that have high reliability, objectivity, and useful norms) but purport to measure constructs about which there is little agreement among psychologists as to meaning or practical utility. Indiscriminate use of such instruments gives rise to serious validity questions. Even when standardized instruments seem valid for the purposes for which they are used, additional problems arise. Stake (1971) has pointed out that errors in testing (measurement error) are most dangerous when attempting to measure higher cognitive processes (for example, synthesizing information).[7] In addition, even when standardized instruments are valid and reliable, the scores they produce are often woefully misinterpreted or misused by many practitioners and would-be evaluators unacquainted with the technical aspects of instrument construction and use.

Such difficulties have resulted in several recent warnings about the limitations of standardized instruments for program evaluation studies (such as by Glaser, 1963; Lennon, 1971; Stake, 1971). Although other authors such as Metfessel and Michael include a number of standardized instruments in their lists of suggested evaluation measures, it is apparent they would urge discrimination in their use. So that standardized instruments can be used more discriminately in evaluation studies to produce valid and reliable information, solutions must be found for a variety of problems which face anyone attempting to use these instruments for evaluation purposes. Eight of the most serious problems associated with the use of standardized measures are discussed briefly below.

1. *Selection of Inappropriate or Technically Inadequate Instruments.* The inane practice of using a traditional subject matter test to assess pupil progress with innovative curriculum materials (for example, testing students in a modern mathematics program with a traditional arithmetic test) is too well known to need much comment. Apparent failures of many programs may be traced to foolish selection of irrelevant instruments. Whether the decision to use the test is based on prior familiarity with the instrument, a persuasive salesman, or apparent lack of an alternative measure, the use of an inappropriate instrument—simply because it exists—is

---

7. Bloom's (1956) handbook provides the reader with examples of higher order processes in the taxonomy of mental processes.

indefensible. A second type of selection error is that of choosing a test which fails to meet minimal acceptable standards of validity, reliability, or interpretability. Use of such inadequate instruments will result in evaluation data which are an embarrassment to the evaluator.

2. *Content Validity of the Tests.* Standardized tests used for evaluation purposes must be content valid at the very minimum. What is measured by the test should reflect the objectives of the program. In other words, the test items should be objectives- or criterion-referenced. Most standardized achievement tests (the most frequently used standardized tests for evaluation purposes) have been developed to measure a wide range of generally accepted objectives. The objectives of any specific program may not overlap one hundred percent with the content covered by any one standard achievement test, and the objectives covered by any one test will not overlap with the objectives covered by any other standardized achievement test.

3. *Temptation of Teaching for the Test.* Measurement instruments can easily influence the direction of an educational program or what is taught in the classroom. The knowledge of what a test measures can cause that content to supplant the original set of specified objectives and become the goal of instruction or the program.

4. *Levels of Cognitive Behavior Measured.* It is very easy to construct good items to measure lower-level cognitive skills. It is much more difficult to design items that measure higher-order mental processes. Because of this difficulty and because of the format (mostly multiple-choice) used in standardized achievement tests, higher-order cognitive behavior, and savings for future learning are often not measured.

5. *Unreliability of Gain Scores.* If we measure individual gains by the difference between a pre-program and post-program score, the accuracy of the gain score will be a function of the accuracy of the pre- and post-tests. In essence, if the accuracy of standardized instruments is not perfect, then gain scores will be even more inaccurate than the separate pre- and post-tests. Stake and Wardrop (1970) demonstrated that if one hundred students were tested four times over a year using a standardized achievement test of average reliability, there would be better than a fifty-fifty chance that two-thirds of the group would show a one year "gain" from the first to the fourth testing, *even though no instruction occurred.* This "gain" would be strictly due to the unreliability of the gain scores.

6. *Errors of Measurement.* This problem is the underlying problem contributing to the unreliability of gain scores. Every
psychological measure has some error involved in producing a
score on a given attribute. The less reliability a measure has, the
larger the measurement errors will be and the less sure one can be
of making a wise decision based on those scores.

7. *Use of Norms.* Many standardized achievement tests have
norm reporting scales based on unequal interval grade equivalent
of age equivalent scales. These scales were originally developed by
test publishers to aid practitioners in interpreting test scores and in
mapping longitudinal change for individuals. By close inspection of
several standardized achievement tests, however, it can be noted
that an increase of one grade equivalent for an individual may
mean that he answered only four or five more items correctly on
the second testing. If the test is not completely reliable to begin
with, this change in score could quite readily be due to measurement error rather than to any change in the individual's behavior.
Furthermore, it is easy for the layman to misinterpret grade or age
equivalence scores by inferring that because an individual has a
grade score of 4.0 he is equal in all respects to a child ready to
begin the fourth grade. This is simply not true.

8. *Exclusive Use of Cognitive Measures.* A quick scanning of
Buros's *Mental Measurement Yearbooks,* the best source of information on standardized measures, reveals a wide selection of
standardized tests of cognitive processes. Unfortunately, there are
relatively few standardized affective and psychomotor measures
available, despite the fact that affective information (for example,
motivation, attitudes, values of parents, faculty, children, and
community) and psychomotor information are obviously important in many program evaluation studies.

Each of the problems listed above is potentially serious; however, each can be avoided or solved to some extent. Several strategies for alleviating these problems are discussed here. These suggestions are by no means exhaustive and the reader may well be able
to provide additional solutions.

1. *Selection of Inappropriate or Technically Inadequate Instruments.* The obvious solution here is to select appropriate, technically adequate instruments. However, such selection requires as a
basis for judgment, accurate, unbiased information about each
standardized measure. Several good sources of information about
standardized instruments do exist, including the following:

(a) *Tests in Print* (Buros, 1961). A bibliography of available tests, listing the following information about each
test: test title, grade levels for each test booklet, pub-

lication dates, special comments on the test, number and type of scores provided, authors, publishers and reference to reviews of the test in Buros's *Mental Measurements Yearbooks.*

(b) *Mental Measurements Yearbooks* (Buros, 1938, 1940, 1949, 1953, 1959, 1965, 1972). The yearbooks are designed to assist test consumers in locating, choosing, and using standardized tests. The later yearbooks are divided into three sections: the test section (test reviews by measurement specialists), the book section (a list of measurement books with selected book reviews), and the index section for all tests.

(c) Test review sections of professional journals. Several journals contain regular review sections where measurement specialists critique standardized tests. Such journals include the *Journal of Educational Measurement, Educational and Psychological Measurement,* the *Journal of Counseling Psychology,* and the *Personnel and Guidance Journal.*

(d) Catalogs of test publishers. Many test publishers provide useful information about the tests they market. Such publishers include the California Test Bureau; Harcourt, Brace, and Javonovich; Houghton Mifflin; the Psychological Corporation; and Science Research Associates.

Despite heroic efforts by Buros and journal review editors, the number of standardized instruments is proliferating much more rapidly than present review services are able to handle. As a result, evaluators who lack sufficient expertise to critique the measures themselves should either seek help from measurement experts or avoid the use of standardized measures that have not been critiqued by unbiased judges.

2. *Content Validity of the Tests.* One solution to the problem of the low content validity of standardized achievement tests might be to avoid their use entirely. Instead, locally content-valid unit tests (often referred to as criterion-references tests) could be developed. Short-term tests of this type present many problems themselves, however. One primary problem is the time and resources needed to develop such tests. Local schools and evaluation projects almost never have the resources required to generate content-valid, reliable tests to measure all important variables. Forsaking standardized tests completely would also be throwing away a great amount of useful information in the form of norms. When used properly, norms do give us evaluative information. A second, more realistic, strategy to solve the problem would be to

select locally content-valid items after standardized tests are administered and to use subsets of the items for the program evaluation. Evaluators can be selective, too, about which test they choose to use so that they can choose the one which covers their objectives best. Data from the entire test can be used also for large program decisions (such as "Should we be teaching this content?" or "How good is our instruction in this area?") Criterion-referenced tests (and item pools) may be developed, as time and resources permit, to supplement the information provided by the standardized achievement test.

   3. *Temptation of Teaching for the Test.* Not allowing instructors or program directors to see the test or other standardized instrument is the best solution to this problem. Perhaps it would be wise to have an outside evaluator, who has helped the developer or instructor refine his objectives, administer the instrument. If the developer or instructor is going to collect the data himself, it is recommended that he specify his objectives in detail *before* an instrument for data collection is developed or selected. He should then make a conscious effort to adhere to those objectives, regardless of specific content on the instrument. Knowing that the problem may exist and consciously trying to avoid this problem is important.

   4. *Levels of Cognitive Behavior Measured.* Since most standardized achievement tests do not cover complex mental processes, it is up to the evaluator to find ways to measure, or in some way quantify, these behaviors. Again, it is not realistic to suggest that the evaluator develop and administer measures of complex mental processes when his time and resources (including training) may not permit it. Rather, the evaluator should look for or develop items or sets of items that correlate highly with complex cognitive performance, and use these items to measure complex behaviors indirectly. To supplement this indirect measurement, measures other than paper and pencil tests should be considered. For example, one could use observation techniques for observing complex mental processes (such as reading comprehension or problem solving behaviors).

   5. *Unreliability of Gain Scores.* Although there are no good solutions to the problem, there are several ways to avoid it. One way would be to analyze pre- and post-program information using some other means than gain scores. Cronbach and Furby (1969) have provided an excellent discussion of the analysis of gains. Another way to avoid the problem is to develop parallel forms of the test designed to minimize the unreliability of the difference

scores. Psychometricians are currently working on this approach. A third way to avoid the problem is to design the evaluation study so that only post-program scores need be used to make inferences about the effectiveness of the program; Campbell and Stanley (1966) have suggested appropriate methods to accomplish this. Finally, the evaluator could analyze gain score information by *group* rather than by individual. This would decrease the seriousness of the problem greatly, but would also eliminate the chance to look at individual gains which are oftentimes of great concern in school programs.

6. *Errors of Measurement.* The best solution to the problem, of course, would be to choose or develop the most reliable instrument available. Even when this is possible, psychological measures will not be perfectly reliable. The best way to avoid problems with measurement errors, then, is to be able to interpret test scores using confidence intervals on an individual's true score. That is, since standardized test data is fallible, we must make probabilistic statements (how confident we are) about a person's true score on a test. Such statements should keep us out of trouble. Finally, up to a point (the fatigue point), a test's reliability can be enhanced by increasing the number of items (by adding more items measuring the same factors as do existing items) on the test. There is, of course, a point of diminishing returns when using this technique.

7. *Use of Norms.* Normative scales such as grade or age equivalence scales are not the best scales to use. They are not interval scales and scores cannot be meaningfully compared across tests. It is recommended that the evaluator always use standard scores (that is, z scores or stanines) or, at least, percentile ranks when working with test data and norms. Such scores are easily interpretable, indicate a person's relative position within a norm group, and do give us comparable scales. The evaluator should also always be critical of the norm groups by asking himself, "Are these norms representative (or relevant) for this specific program?"

8. *Exclusive Use of Cognitive Measures.* Evaluators need a great deal of important noncognitive information to conduct an adequate appraisal of most educational programs. Standardized instruments are not readily available to collect that information. Thus, evaluators are often left up to their own devices in attempting to collect such data. The Metfessel-Michael appendix suggested measures other than standardized tests that should be considered. In the next section, both noncognitive and nonstandardized instruments are discussed. Much of that section is relevant to the solution of this problem.

I. DATA COLLECTED BY A MECHANICAL DEVICE (E.G., AUDIO OR VIDEO TAPE, GALVANIC SKIN RESPONSES).

STRENGTHS	WEAKNESSES
Avoid human errors.	Cost.
Stay on job — avoid fatigue.	Cannot make independent judgment.
May capture content missed by written records (e.g., voice inflection).	Complexity can cause problems in operating devices.

II. DATA COLLECTED BY AN INDEPENDENT OBSERVER.

STRENGTHS	WEAKNESSES
Can be used in natural or experimental settings. Most direct measure of behavior.	Observer's presence often causes an artificial situation.
Most direct measure of behavior.	Hostility to being observed.
Experienced, trained, or perceptive observers can pick up subtle occurrences or interactions sometimes not available by other techniques.	Inadequate sampling of observed events.
	Ambiguities in recording.
	Frequent observer unreliability.

A. Written accounts.

STRENGTHS	WEAKNESSES
Can use critical incident technique, eliminating much "chaff."	Hard to be complete.
	Hard to avoid writing interpretation as factual data (e.g., "Mary kicked John because she was angry with him.").

B. Observation forms (e.g., observation schedules).

STRENGTHS	WEAKNESSES
Easy to complete; saves time.	Not as flexible as written accounts — may lump unlike acts together.
Can be objectively scored.	Criteria for ratings are often unspecified.
Standardizes observations.	May overlook meaningful behavior that is not reflected in instrument.

III. DATA PRODUCED BY THE SUBJECT HIMSELF.

   A. Self reports.

STRENGTHS	WEAKNESSES
Can collect data too costly otherwise (e.g., eliminates the endless observation necessary to really get to know a person's philosophy, attitudes, etc.).	Depends on respondent's real awareness of self.
Can collect data not accessible by any other means (private thoughts, feelings, actions; emotion-laden material).	Depends on respondent's honesty and/or security.
	Depends on respondent's "accurate memory" when dealing with past events (selective recall).
	May necessitate anonymous responses where threat is perceived.

   1. Diary — may be difficult to analyze, but can be comprehensive.
   2. Check lists — sometimes force choices between unacceptable responses.
   3. Rating scales (covered earlier) — often tell more about the respondent than about the topic under consideration.
   4. Semantic differential.[a]

STRENGTHS	WEAKNESSES
Adaptable to varying research demands.	Often tells more about the respondent than about the topic under consideration.
Quick and economical to administer and score.	

   5. Questionnaires.

STRENGTHS	WEAKNESSES
Self-administered.	Frequent low percentage of returns.
Anonymity can bring about more honest responses.	No assurance that the intended respondent understands the questions.
Economical.	No assurance that the intended respondent actually completed the form himself.

Table 4

Some Methods of Collecting Evaluation Data
(continued on facing page)

[a]See Osgood, Suci, and Tannenbaum (1957)

6. Interviews

STRENGTHS	WEAKNESSES
Allow depth and free response.	Costly in time and personnel.
Flexible and adaptable to individual situations.	Require skilled interviewers.
	Often difficult to summarize.
Allow glimpse of respondent's gestures, tone of voice, etc., that reveal his feelings.	Many biases possible (e.g., interviewer's, respondent's, or situational biases).

7. Sociometry.

STRENGTHS	WEAKNESSES
Easy to analyze.	Criteria used in making choices are often vague.
Naturalistic method.	
Clinically insightful.	

8. Projective techniques.

STRENGTHS	WEAKNESSES
Clinically insightful.	Lack of objectivity in interpretation.
Allow measurement of variables typically unavailable through other techniques.	Uncertain reliability and validity.

B. Personal products.

1. Tests

STRENGTHS	WEAKNESSES
Practicality — do away with need for observer to gather similar data.	Validity is always a problem in work sample sense — i.e., is test representative of criterion?
Most reliable measures we have at present.	
Can record products or thought or thought processes themselves.	Lend themselves to "law of the instrument" — we often exclude other techniques.

a. Supplied answer.

i. Essay.

STRENGTHS	WEAKNESSES
Allow students to synthesize their knowledge about a topic.	Difficult to score objectively.
	Sampling of topics is relatively limited.

ii. Completion.

STRENGTHS	WEAKNESSES
Can be quite objective.	May lend themselves to testing trivia (factual recall only).

iii. Short response

STRENGTHS	WEAKNESSES
Can be quite objective.	May lend themselves to testing trivia (factual recall only).

iv. Problem-solving.

STRENGTHS	WEAKNESSES
Can look at actual processes (diagnostic).	Lend themselves to mechanical drill.
Can look at actual mastery.	

b. Selected answer tests (multiple-choice, true-false, matching, rank order).

STRENGTHS	WEAKNESSES
Greater objectivity in scoring.	Problem of validity is always present.
Speed of scoring.	Standardized tests sometimes used in situations requiring specially constructed tests.
Potentially higher reliability.	
Can be item analyzed for improvement.	
Quantity of available standardized tests.	Apparent precision often masks very bad items.

2. Samples of work.

STRENGTHS	WEAKNESSES
Best measure of ability, mastery, etc.	May be difficult or costly to administer.

IV. DATA COLLECTED BY USE OF UNOBTRUSIVE MEASURES.

STRENGTHS	WEAKNESSES
Nonreactive.	Hidden measures are considered unethical by some.
Nonconsciously biased.	
Often readily available and easily measurable.	Doubtful validity when used alone.

Table 4

Some Methods of Collecting Evaluation Data
(continued from facing page)

Nonstandardized Instruments

The evaluator will frequently use nonstandardized instruments and techniques to collect data on many evaluation studies. This section is intended to introduce the potential evaluator to the variety of nonstandardized instruments which he may wish to consider in collecting descriptive or evaluative data. The section comprises three major parts: (a) a classification scheme for alternative methods of collecting data, including a listing of important strengths and weaknesses of each method, (b) a paper by Sechrest on the use of unobtrusive measures, and (c) summaries of several suggested data-collection techniques which are potentially useful for collecting evaluation data.

The classification of methods of collecting data presented in Table 4 is intended as a suggestive, rather than an exhaustive, listing of ways one might go about collecting evaluative data.[8] Only the most salient advantages and disadvantages of each method are discussed. Some of the classes of instruments listed include standardized measures; however, the emphasis in this listing is on nonstandardized techniques of data collection.

Rosner (1966) advocated the use of professional test construction personnel for the development of special (perhaps criterion-referenced) measures in evaluating educational programs. When such resource people are available, this recommendation is appropriate. When the evaluator is forced to develop his own measures, however, there are several ways to proceed. Rosner suggested:

> . . .if I were interested in developing a measure of pupil interest in reading or an index of parental attitudes towards the school, I would ask myself, "What concrete student or parent behavior can I observe which would lead to the reasonable inference of a change in interest or a change in attitude?" I would, moreover, qualify the nature of the observation so that it was not only easily observed but also routinely recorded [Rosner, 1966, pp. 65-66].

Rosner gave some examples using student interest in reading as the measure. He suggested that appropriate data might be the number of books borrowed from the school library, the number of different kinds of books borrowed, or the number of children in a class who would rather read than paint or engage in some other activity. Such measures are easily collected and can be used in most educational programs. These special measures could all fit under the category of unobtrusive or nonreactive measures. That

8. In developing this classification system, the authors have been influenced by the thinking of Furst (1958) and have adapted some of his categories for use in our system.

is, subjects don't know their behavior is being observed, so they don't have a chance to react in a way that would change their typical behavior. The following paper contains a more detailed overview of this measurement technique.

Use of Innocuous and Noninterventional Measures in Evaluation

Lee Sechrest

Northwestern University

Whenever any action is taken with a view to producing change, it is essential that some provision be made for determining whether change has, in fact, occurred. That is true whether we propose to rectify an individual child's spelling deficiencies, improve discipline in a classroom, or ameliorate a serious social inequity. We must have some way of evaluating the results of our efforts. In a very influential book, especially considering its size, Mager (1962) has quite correctly pointed out that the first step in planning for change is to state in explicit terms what objectives are to be accomplished. Only when we can state some definite and observable outcome are we in a position to evaluate any effort. However, the problem is by no means simple, and it may well be far more than Mager implies.

In his presentation Mager concentrates on the problem of translating vague, general objectives into terms which provide for direct and reasonably reliable observations, e.g., can the problem be solved, does the essay convince, is the motor repaired? That problem is, of course, an important one, and it is often difficult to get people to state their objectives in such clear ways. However, a serious deficiency will exist if we do not get beyond Mager's prescriptions, for they obscure what is an exceedingly important matter, namely that what he refers to as "terminal" objectives are by no means easy to specify in many cases, and for different areas of action so-called terminal objectives are at very different behavioral and conceptual levels. For example, we may take it as reasonable that the terminal objective in a shop course on repair of electric motors is the ability to repair a variety of motors. But what is the terminal objective of a social studies course at the fourth grade level? Is it really sufficient to say that a child should be able to answer correctly at least seventy percent of the questions on a

Reprinted with permission of the author.

multiple choice examination? In fact, don't we really have in mind some more ultimate objectives in teaching social studies than the ability of a child to answer a few factual questions or even questions of interpretation? Then if that is the case, we should busy ourselves with specifying our real terminal objectives. After all, the terminal objective in a course on motor repair is the ability to repair an actual motor and not merely to answer some test questions about motor repair.

There is much too great an inclination to specify objectives in terms of performance on tests or other "proximate" criteria, e.g., essay writing, of more ultimate goals. There are several serious problems in the sole reliance on such measures, problems which are discussed in Webb, et al. (1966). First, we may observe a certain degree of "slippage" whereby a proximate objective such as test performance becomes a truly terminal objective. Emphasis on formal tests in evaluation may bias pedagogy toward test performance. The writer knows well of one school in which the principal was very aware and remindful of the fact that classes taught by her more experienced teachers showed higher achievement as measured by standardized tests when compared with classes taught by new and presumably inexperienced teachers. However, in her school new teachers gradually became aware of the degree to which more experienced teachers were teaching explicitly for performance on the tests. Test performance had become the terminal objective.

A most unfortunate limitation of most tests is that they are highly reactive in the sense that taking the test on one occasion alters the performance of subjects in such a way that the test is no longer useful. One cannot use the same test, and probably not even similar tests, for repeated observation. Practice effects, opportunity to look up answers, etc., make repeated use of tests untrustworthy. We need measures which can be applied in such a way that they do not change, in and of themselves, the phenomenon being measured.

There is also a danger in excessive reliance on tests that too much variance in performance scores will come to be determined by individual differences in test taking skills. Moreover, not only will there be differences between children in the same classroom, there will be far greater differences between children in one class and those in another if tests are used with different frequency. Thus, as prior experience with taking of tests comes to differentiate groups, the utility of the tests will decrease. It would be nice to suppose that some fairly simple equation adding a constant could compensate for test naiveté, but that seems unlikely. It should also be clear that the more often tests are used, the greater will become the importance of test-specific abilities. One highly consistent principle of human performance is that experience and training increase rather than decrease individual differences.

Another facet of objective setting that is neglected in Mager's work and very likely in many other places is that in most important areas of instruction we have plural rather than singular objectives. Some of the objectives are obvious, some are subtle, some are simple, some are complex, some are immediate, and some are in the future. By and large formal tests are directed to narrow and singular objectives, usually the acquisition of fairly specific items of information. Moreover, there are objectives which, however laudable and however easily assessed in a paper and pencil format, are in such sensitive areas from the standpoint of the general public that it would be risky to attempt their direct assessment. For example, certain units in social science or certain arrangements in schools may have the implicit objective of improving attitudes of minority and majority group members toward each other. However, few persons in the public schools would dare to administer an attitude test in the classroom in order to determine the effectiveness of their efforts. The problem of reactivity again arises here, for in many areas of attitude and personality measurement responses will be biased by the measurement process, e.g., some subjects may try to perform as they think the examiner wishes them to perform. It may also be that in some areas the use of a very obvious measure will bias responses of subjects to subsequent programs of change. If we are to know how we are progressing in such sensitive areas, it will have to be through application of indirect or unobtrusive measures.

In any evaluation program it is dangerous to rely exclusively upon one measure. All measures are fallible, both because of their inherent limitations and because they are often susceptible to serious misinterpretation. Unhappily the employment of several measures does not guarantee success and satisfaction in an evaluation effort, often because diverse measures may yield conflicting results. Nonetheless, evaluations are likely to be much more satisfactory if there are several measures which either converge upon the same conclusion or which point toward differential effects of a program planned to produce change.

One final point about current evaluations in education should be made before proceeding to some specific instances of evaluation through unobtrusive and nonreactive measures. There is a great deal of emphasis in current evaluation efforts on the use of standard achievement tests. For example, in the Hartford and

Philadelphia programs of bussing inner city children to suburban or otherwise better schools, the investigators are relying heavily on achievement test results to evaluate the success of the program. Other investigators who are studying the effects of special teaching materials or special approaches to classroom instruction such as team teaching are also relying heavily on standardized achievement tests. Great caution should be exercised in drawing conclusions from such research. First, I would like to point out that in all the history of evaluation in education it has proven exceedingly difficult to demonstrate the superiority of *any* procedure in terms of test performance. Democratic versus authoritarian teaching, phonics versus look-and-say reading methods, ability grouping, enrichment, etc., have all proven recalcitrant to evaluation in terms of achievement. I would suggest, then, that it is unreasonable to evaluate other programs solely in terms of achievement. Why school integration should produce improved achievement test performance when nothing else does is problematic. A second reason for caution in use of standardized achievement tests in evaluation is that such tests may just be *too* standardized for some evaluation problems. Achievement tests for nationwide or even areawide evalution have of necessity something like a lowest common denominator built into them. In order to be standard they tap only the barest core of each subject, and in so doing they neglect the very things in which individual programs or schools may excel. A given program might not produce any better performance on a standard arithemetic test than any other program, but if it, in addition, introduces children to matrix algebra and probability theory, areas not included in the test, its value as a program will be grossly underestimated.

Some Suggestions for Noninterventional and Nonreactive Assessment

At the outset of this section it should be noted that the degree to which any given method of assessment will represent an intrusion and will produce a reaction to itself will depend in large part on the circumstances of its use. Classroom observers, for example, whose use has been so well described by Medley and Mitzel (1963), might be intruders in a small class, unnoticed in a large one, and perhaps absolutely unknown if there are possibilities for concealed observation. They might be intruders if they needed cameras or other bulky instruments and pass unnoticed if they need only use tally sheets. Even certain kinds of standardized tests might become unobtrusive by being incorporated into usual school routines. For example, it might be possible and desirable to reproduce by a school's usual means, ditto, mineo, or whatever, portions of standardized tests which could be given as part of the school's ordinary testing program without much of the "to do" that goes along with formal testing. On the other hand, any other measure may become a positive intervention if care is not taken in its employment.

To turn to a few specific examples of other measures, it may first be recommended that in relation to the more salient educational goals, i.e., acquisition of information, changes in habits, etc., it might be very helpful to state the implications of those goals in the form of terminal behaviors. An excellent instance is one of the earliest in the literature. Urban (1943) was interested in the effects of a course on health and hygiene and could have compared test scores of students in the course with those not so enrolled. However, he chose instead to look for the occurrence of critical behaviors in the classroom which should have been affected if the course was successful. He did, in fact, find that students in the hygiene course showed a lower incidence over a period of twelve weeks in such behaviors as chewing on pencils, sneezing without covering their noses, etc. Similar direct behavioral observations were, of course, made in the famous studies of Character Education by Hartshorne and May (1928). Presumably art courses should result in better pictures, science courses in better experiments, woodworking courses in better products, etc. It is often, perhaps usually, possible to make assessments of the quality and quantity of such products without students being especially aware of the evaluation. In the classic studies on group leadership conducted by Lewin, Lippitt, and White (1939) the boys in democratically-led clubs apparently did produce higher quality products than those in authoritarian-led clubs although their quantity was lower. In one school known to the writer the cafeteria utilizes student cashiers, and the errors they make are recorded. The magnitude of error seems to be inversely related to ability in math, and the errors decrease in size during the school year. Often it will take only a little ingenuity and a little extra research effort to obtain highly interesting information which can be obtained as often as one wishes without affecting the source.

It may also be of great value to make assessments relative to direction and duration of interest. For example, when students have free time, it is definitely of interest and relevant to note upon what projects they choose to work or how they otherwise use their time. Topics of conversation in spontaneous interactions may also be noted in relation to interests. Moreover, it has been found interesting in other investigations to make use of duration of interest as a measure, e.g., how long a child will persist in some activity. We would hope that many programs would affect both direction and duration of interest. Use of library facilities is also a highly relevant and potentially useful measure by which many programs might be evaluated. Certainly children cannot read if they don't take books. In many situations it should be possible to note not only number of books, but type of books taken for use.

The study of use of library facilities raises the important point that for some evaluations it is not absolutely necessary to have data on individual children. Thus, even though we may not be able to tell just how each individual child uses a book, we may, from the condition of a book, be able to tell something about how it was used by a class, e.g., which sections are smudged or dirty, which appear unused. In reporting on the effects on reading habits of the advent of television in a small town, Parker (1963) did not have the capability of assessing each individual child, but he was able to show that library use did not decline, and perhaps what is more important, that interest in nonfiction increased relative to fiction.

A second area of inquiry in which much more effort should be directed toward unobtrusive measures of outcome is in pupil and teacher morale. There may be no very persuasive demonstration of a relationship between morale and objectively measured performance, but morale may be important for other reasons. For one thing, while morale may not be important in determining level of performance for those persons who remain in a program, it may be an important determinant of the decision to remain in or to drop out of a program. Attendance, for example, would seem an obvious datum for consideration since it is clear that whatever it is that a school does specifically cannot be done while the student is absent. However, the writer believes that most schools know very little about the attendance of pupils other than that some miss a good bit more than others. What we should look for is pattern in attendance and absences. For example, the writer is examining the attendance records of a school system in order to try to identify children with different patterns of nonattendance which might help reflect problems both within and outside the school. As one specific instance, there is one group of children with a high frequency of absence, most of which is on days when many children are absent. A second group has an equally high frequency of absence, but more nearly random with respect to background level. It appears that the first group misses on bad weather days and on days when many children are sick. The second group, which tends to miss many single days rather than several days at a time, seems to be kept out of school to suit parental convenience or whim. Moreover, in a high school we are finding some evidence that the absences of some pupils definitely coincide with curriculum. When subject matter gets too abstract or tough, absences increase.

Disciplinary infractions should also provide a useful tool for study, particularly, again, if we look for patterning in the infractions. Overall level may be useful, too, and we may check to see whether changes in program are associated with increasing or decreasing pupil discipline problems. Not that panic or elation should reign in either case, but if a program results in increasing discipline problems, and we are sure of it, then either the program should be compensatorily good in other ways, or it should be altered. Morale in schools might also be reflected in destructive or careless use of school property. The quantity of trash collected by janitors, or even observed, in corridors, the number of broken windows, damaged shop tools, and the like, might all reflect important attitudinal and morale variables in pupils. Even the amount of smiling by pupils as they sit in classes or pass through hallways might be worth recording, e.g., by closed circuit TV or automatic cameras. If a group of children or young people is grim when gaiety would be more ordinary, the reason should be known. Nervous mannerisms and gestures may also index important aspects of a child's school experience.

We might also mention that morale of teachers is worth investigating by both direct and indirect means. Problems in recruitment and training of teachers being what they are, it is costly to lose a teacher. Therefore, even if a special program does not produce demonstrable effect on pupil performance, it may be worth retaining if teachers like it and if it gives some indication of decreasing staff turnover. Thus, one important outcome measure in evaluating any program may be changes in annual turnover of teachers and other staff. Another similar measure may be absenteeism among staff. Still others might be teacher attendance at voluntary workshop sessions, care taken by teachers in the decor of their rooms, and even the number of cigarette butts remaining in the faculty lounge at the end of a day.

The third area of inquiry in which additional and nonreactive measures are much needed is in the study of the effects of various programs on social behaviors and interactions. There now exist a diverse lot of programs for improving overall level of education by integrating schools along social class, ethnic, and racial lines. Those programs very much need evaluation, but the evaluation should be careful and multidimensional so that we know as nearly as possible

the exact effects which are being produced. It will not be sufficient to say either that the programs do or do not improve performance on standardized tests. The area is often extremely
sensitive and fraught with danger, but it cannot be ignored because
of its importance.

To begin with, we might well expend some effort in determining the progress of actual integration once the opportunity for it
has been made. One potentially useful measure has to do with
spatial integration in school situations. In classrooms where seating
patterns are determined by student preferences, then at least
conceivably it ought to be possible to determine whether segrega-
tion takes place along racial, sexual, social class, or any other lines.
Campbell, Kruskel, and Wallace (1966) have shown that in two
Chicago institutions of higher learning classroom seating patterns
give evidence of increasing integration, but seating integration
obviously lags behind verbally expressed attitudes in reflecting
improving race relations. We might study spatial integration in a
variety of situations, e.g., classrooms, libraries, hallways, locker
rooms, buses, etc., varying in intimacy and in formality in order to
discern the influences which operate on integration at the micro
level.

Beyond spatial integration we are probably interested in cultural interchange and integration, and there should be a variety of
measures employed there too. For example, manner of dress is
highly salient and easily observed, and at the high school level
where the student's own preference plays some part in his dress, it
would be interesting to note whether, when two different
populations are mixed, there is any evidence of increasing homo-
geneity in dress and appearance and, if so, in what direction it
occurs. Moreover, in some circumstances it may be possible to
determine whether changes in reading patterns, radio programs,
TV programs, and the like are taking place in a manner suggestive
of cultural integration, or at least of cultural interchange. We need
not believe or even imply that to look for evidence of cultural
integration means that it "ought" to occur, that one group should
alter its manner of dress or music preferences to conform to
another group's standards. To study the occurrence of cultural
integration may be valuable from the standpoint of protecting a
minority culture rather than transforming it. We should be aware of
changes when they occur, whether they are valued or not. Moreover, we would point out that at least *some* degree of cultural
integration is explicitly called for in the complaints of inner city
residents that their children are not exposed to the right kinds of
educational influences, the kinds that presumably abound in

suburban schools. Thus, if the reading patterns of an inner city student change from comic books and show business magazines to more serious fare, it cannot be maintained that an alien culture is being unfairly imposed. If integration has socially desirable effects, then it ought to be manifested in social behaviors; and if speech, manners, dress, and interests change in ways which make an individual student a better employment or educational risk, then such changes should be known.

Conclusion

In conclusion, the writer would note that the key point in this presentation is not that tests have no value. They certainly have an important place in any evaluation of a program. Nor would the writer wish to be understood as suggesting that any of the other measures proposed might stand alone in indexing effects of a special program. Rather, what is important is that all of our measures are fallible. They all have their weaknesses. For example, one cannot escape the psychometric problems of reliability, etc., by resorting to measures other than tests. Therefore, we should try as much as possible to index in a *variety* of ways the things in which we are interested, and it will be more instructive and more convincing if our measures have compensatory strengths and unshared weaknesses. Obtrusive and unobtrusive measures are complementary to each other and not inter-substitutable.

The book written by Webb, et al. (1966) contains additional suggestions for using unobtrusive measures to collect the following types of information.

1. *Physical traces*: physical evidence left from some past behavior. Such information would include natural erosion measures (such as worn carpeting in front of a picture in an art museum), natural accretion measures (of natural deposits of information such as creative work done by past civilizations), controlled erosion measures (such as pre- and post-measures of shoe wear on children), and controlled accretion measures (such as glue sealing pages of a book to detect how many and which pages are read).

2. *Archival records:* the ongoing, continuing records of society. Such sources of information would include actuarial records, political and judicial records, government records, and mass media files.

3. *Private records:* records that are not ordinarily left open to the public. Such sources would include sales records, institutional records, and written documents such as diaries and homework.

4. *Simple observations:* the observer has no control over the behavior in question. Such methods would include the use of visible observers, participant observers, exterior physical signs (e.g., mode of dress), expressive movements, physical locations (e.g., minority group clustering in a classroom), and conversation sampling.

5. *Contrived observation:* the use of hardware devices for observation (e.g., videotapes, audiotapes).

It is important to note that the use of just one unobtrusive method for collecting information will often not yield reliable data. It is essential that the evaluator draw from a variety of procedures to measure the same behavior. We recommend that the reader refer to the Webb, et al. (1966) text for a complete discussion, including many examples and their limitations, of unobtrusive or noninterventional measurement.

Ways to Evaluate
Curriculum Materials

Another information collection technique that is often overlooked in program evaluation studies is the systematic collection and use of information about curricula and curriculum materials. Three analysis procedures have been independently suggested by Morrisett and Stevens (1967), Tyler and Klein (1967), and Eash (1970).

Morrisett and Stevens (1967) developed a Curriculum Materials Analysis System to assist practitioners in asking important questions about curricula or sets of materials they are developing or considering for use. The main areas about which questions might be asked are listed as the following.

1. *Descriptive characteristics:* media available from producer, sources of materials, time needed to use materials, style, financial cost, availability, performance data availablility, subject area and content, dominant characteristics of curriculum forms.

2. *Rationale and objectives:* rationale, general objectives, specific objectives, behavioral objectives.

3. *Antecedent conditions:* pupil characteristics, teacher capabilities and requirements, community, school, articulation (vertical-horizontal fits in curriculum organization).

4. *Content:* cognitive structure, affective content, psychomotor skills.

5. *Instructional theory and teaching strategies:* author's orientation, elements of instructional theory and their uses in teaching strategies, teaching forms, modes, or transactions.

6. *Overall judgments:* sources of other descriptive data, effects reported or predicted by these sources, comparisons, recommended uses.

Tyler and Klein (1967) formulated a set of recommendations developed by the American Psychological Association for standardized tests and manuals. The recommendations have been categorized into seven groups: general recommendations, specifications, rationale, appropriateness, effectiveness, conditions, and practicality. The reader is referred to the original document for a detailed treatment of specific recommendations within each of these groups.

Eash (1970) suggested another instrument for the assessment of instructional materials. He proposed four main categories about which evaluative questions might be asked.

1. *Objectives:* stated objectives, implicit objectives, apparent source of objectives, quantitative rating of objectives.

2. *Organization of the material:* results of any task analysis, basis for the scope of the material, recommended sequence of materials, quantitative rating of organization.

3. *Methodology:* methodological approaches suggested, required preparation of the teacher, description of recommended methodology, quantitative rating of methodology.

4. *Evaluation:* recommended evaluation procedures contained in the package, results of previous use of evaluation instruments, description of evaluation procedure.

We recommend that the reader obtain the three papers mentioned above and become skilled in the application of each for program evaluation. These analysis procedures are valuable tools for any educational evaluation study.

Sjogren (1970) presented a review of measurement techniques that might be of use in evaluating educational programs. The outline of his review follows the framework suggested by Stake (1967). The following selected antecedent, transaction, and outcome measurement techniques are examples of valuable tools for any evaluation study.

1. *Antecedent measures:* pupil background files (such as mental ability scores, past achievement, sex, father's occupation, ethnic background), community records (such as city records, Chamber of Commerce files), questionnaire techniques, measurement of costs, teacher background files, curricular context descriptions.

2. *Transaction measures:* materials assessment techniques such as those discussed earlier (Morrisett and Stevens, 1967; Tyler and Klein, 1967; Eash, 1970), environmental assessment techniques

(for example, Astin and Holland, 1961), interaction analysis techniques (Medley and Mitzel, 1963).

3. *Outcome measures:* cost/benefit techniques, sampling techniques (item and person sampling), computer-assisted testing techniques, sequential testing techniques, empirical scoring techniques, scale construction techniques.

The foregoing discussion is only illustrative of the many instruments and techniques evaluators might use to collect evaluative information. Beyond this, evaluation specialists must continue to identify and consider a variety of possible ways that information can be collected. To meet the demands of describing and evaluating many different aspects of educational programs, evaluators will be forced to look beyond the common sources of measurement techniques—education and psychology—to identify useful techniques from disciplines such as management, quantitative business analysis, political science, economics, sociology, anthropology, and philosophy. Evaluation is one area where the advice to be interdisciplinary is completely sound.

Guidelines for Writing Evaluation
Proposals and Reports

Now that frameworks for designing evaluation studies have been presented and measurement problems and techniques discussed, the next consideration is how one organizes the overall evaluation plan, both at the proposal-writing stage and the report-writing stage of evaluation.

When an evaluator is first called in to evaluate a program, there are several things he must ascertain or decide at the outset. First, he needs to find out why the evaluation is taking place. Second, he needs to identify the various audiences for which he must provide evaluation information and determine their needs and backgrounds so that he can report his findings in the format most appropriate for the type of audience being addressed. (Parents will not likely be interested in the same information as the U.S. Office of Education.) Third, he will need to decide on an overall evaluation plan including the basic design, specification of what information will be collected, proposed collection and analysis techniques, and a description of how the information will be used.

These general steps are only examples of the many things which must be considered in planning an evaluation study. The following outline is recommended as a format for evaluation proposals. Although the outline need not be followed in sequence, consideration of each point by the evaluator is essential.

Suggested Format
for Evaluation Proposals

I. Rationale (Why is this evaluation being done?)

II. Objectives of the Evaluation Study

    A. What will be the product(s) of the evaluation study?

    B. What audiences will be served by the evaluation study?

III. Description of the Program Being Evaluated

    A. Philosophy behind the program

    B. Content of the program

    C. Objectives of the program, implicit and explicit

    D. Program procedures (strategies, media, etc.)

    E. Students

    F. Community (federal, state, local) and instructional context of program

IV. Evaluation Design

    A. Constraints on evaluation design

    B. General organizational plan (or model) for program evaluation

    C. Evaluative questions

    D. Information required to answer the questions

    E. Sources of information; methods for collecting information

    F. Data collection schedule

    G. Techniques for analysis of collected information

    H. Standards; bases for judging quality

    I. Reporting procedures

    J. Proposed budget

V. Description of Final Report

    A. Outline of report(s) to be produced by evaluator

    B. Usefulness of the products of the study

    C. Conscious biases of evaluator that may be inadvertently injected into the final report

The rationale should contain the charge to the evaluator (such as an administrative request or legislative requirement) and the general evaluation approach to which the evaluator is committed. The proposal should also contain precise statements of the objectives of the evaluation study and descriptions of its proposed products and benefits. Explicating the objectives of the study early should give direction to the rest of the plan. The products of the study should be considered in relation to the audience(s) which will be served.

In order to conduct a good evaluation study, the evaluator must describe in detail the program being evaluated. The proposal should include a description of the program philosophy, content, objectives—both explicit (public) and implicit (private)—procedures, students, and setting.

A detailed evaluation design is a must in any evaluation proposal. Since constraints such as time, money, or legal barriers will compromise the evaluation design, it is important to identify these constraints at this early stage. The evaluation design should be appropriate for the rationale of the study and the program being evaluated. The evaluator has a great amount of theoretical and technical information to draw from in building a good design, as evidenced by earlier portions of the text. It is up to him to use the frameworks, procedures, and techniques wisely and efficiently. Whether he uses one of the frameworks discussed in this text or develops one specifically for his study, it is important that he specify procedures for generating evaluative questions, identifying information required to answer the questions, identifying sources of information, collecting the information, analyzing the information, and reporting the results. The evaluator should also specify procedures for using standards to publicly arrive at a set of judgmental statements. Reporting procedures, including a discussion of when, what, to whom, and how reports will be delivered, and a budget are practical and important design considerations which should also be included in the proposal.

Finally, a description of the final report itself is essential information to include in the proposal. The reader of the proposal should know exactly what he is going to receive at the finish of the study. He should also be alerted to the uses that could or should be made of such information. A statement about the conscious biases of the evaluator should also be considered essential information in the proposal. If the evaluator has a mental set against the type of program he is about to evaluate, this information is important to note before the study is conducted. Evaluators are human and, therefore, not always completely objective. The evaluator should attempt to recognize this fact and note in the proposal any ways in which his objectivity may be questioned.

The outline for preparing an evaluation proposal would in many instances also serve very well in writing the final evaluation report. In addition to the content of the proposal, however, the final report must contain a considerable amount of information on the results and judgments produced by the study. Stake has suggested steps in writing a final evaluation report; his outline is presented in the following paper.

Evaluation Design, Instrumentation, Data Collection, and Analysis of Data

Robert E. Stake

Associate Director

Center for Instructional Research
and Curriculum Evaluation

University of Illinois

I am going to proceed in backward fashion. I am going to get at the things named in my title by looking first at a model Final Report. Let us see what we can infer about gathering data, analyzing data, and designing studies, by taking a look at the Evaluation Report.

In Table 5 you will find a Table of Contents for an evaluation report. I am going to go through that table step by step, and make a comment or two on each of those steps. I hope, by implication as well as explication, that you will see what I would include in an evaluation study, what data I would gather, and how I would analyze those data.

For each of the subtitles in *my* Table of Contents, *your* actual report might have only one sentence, or only one paragraph. It might have many, many pages. I have tried to devise a versatile Table of Contents, a very general one, which could be used in a small evaluation study as well as a very large evaluation study.

I am aware of the fact that there are many guidelines and models available for evaluation reports, especially those that are reports of projects funded with federal moneys. For example, just today the mail brought me a draft of guidelines for research studies, from the Bureau of Education of the Handicapped, U.S. Office of Education. It is a manual for evaluation specialists, with chapters on such things as reporting and dissemination. There are lots of guidelines, there are many forms to follow. They differ; but I have a general Table of Contents that will conform to most of

Reprinted with revisions from Joseph L. Davis (Ed.), *Educational Evaluation.* Columbus, Ohio: Ohio State Department of Public Instruction, 1969. Reprinted in this form with permission of the author and publisher.

the guidelines. There are, however, some unique emphases in my Table of Contents.

Table 5

Table of Contents, or Format, for a Final Evaluation Report

Section I — OBJECTIVES OF THE EVALUATION
    A. Audiences to be served by the evaluation
    B. Decisions about the program, anticipated
    C. Rationale, bias of evaluators

Section II — SPECIFICATION OF THE PROGRAM
    A. Educational philosophy behind the program
    B. Subject matter
    C. Learning objectives, staff aims
    D. Instructional procedures, tactics, media
    E. Students
    F. Instructional and community setting
    G. Standards, bases for judging quality

Section III— PROGRAM OUTCOMES
    A. Opportunities, experiences provided
    B. Student gains and losses
    C. Side effects and bonuses
    D. Costs of all kinds

Section IV — RELATIONSHIPS AND INDICATORS
    A. Congruences, real and intended
    B. Contingencies, causes and effects
    C. Trend lines, indicators, comparisons

Section V — JUDGMENTS OF WORTH
    A. Value of outcomes
    B. Relevance of objectives to needs
    C. Usefulness of evaluation information gathered

The first section in my evaluation report deals with the objectives *of evaluation*. There is a difference, of course, between program objectives and evaluation objectives. In this first section we are concerned with the specification of the purposes for the evaluation. Why are we doing the evaluation anyway?

I think it is important to distinguish among the possible audiences for the evaluation study. It is important because we gather different information for different audiences. Different people have different appetites for different information. One audience thinks that certain measurements are relevant and credible; another audience will ignore those measurements. I think we should be rather specific about whom we are writing the evaluation report for.

There is one audience that does not need much overall description of the project. The staff, the people who are closest to the project or program, the teachers, the administrators—they know what is going on, because they are there. They do not need to be told a lot of things that outsiders have to be told. They are there, they see them. Staff members can use other information, about things they cannot see for themselves.

Administrators or supervisors who are more remote do not know what is going on. And there are citizens, community leaders, patrons of various sorts, who need to be told what is going on. They are a second possible audience.

A third audience is the students and the parents of those students in the program. They desire, I think, still other information.

And then there is another possible audience. All too often in my opinion they turn out to be the primary audience of the evaluation study. They are the people called researchers. It is a very important fact that researchers make different demands upon the evaluation study. Not just in how technical it should be but in what it should focus on. Professors of education, specialists in measurement, etc. want information that may be of little use to the local people. The data you gather for one audience may not be appropriate for other audiences.

The second thing that I would advise a person who is writing an evaluation report is to discuss the decisions about the program which are anticipated as a result of the evaluation. That's a tough job. It is hard to know whether—a year from now, or three years from now—there are going to be any critical decisions with regard to goals, organization, student personnel, or staff. But the evaluator, I think, has a responsibility to snoop around and to guess at what decisions may be forthcoming. He should use these guesses to orient his evaluation plan. He should try to develop some of the objectives of the evaluation study so as to aid those future decisions. We evaluators should try to understand the local situation well enough so that we can suggest some of the decisions that may come up and so that we can gather data that are relevant to those decisions.

The second major section in my model final-evaluation report: the specification of the program. You can see by the long list of items in this section that in my evaluation report a lot of attention is going to be paid to the specification of the program. Compared to some evaluation specialists I personally emphasize program processes a lot. In my evaluation reports I want the reader to know what it was like, what happened in the classrooms, what was

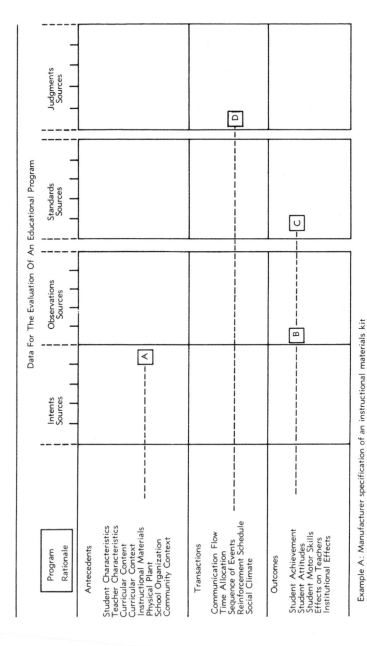

Example A: Manufacturer specification of an instructional materials kit
Example B: Teacher description of student understanding
Example C: Expert opinion on cognitive skill needed for a class of problems
Example D: Administrator judgment of feasibility of a field trip arrangement

Figure 29

Illustration of Data Possibly Representative of the Contents of Four Cells
of the Matrices for a Given Educational Program.

tried. Later I will tell what was gained, how much it cost, why it happened the way it did, how one can arrange it to happen like that again, etc. But first of all, I want to answer the question, "What was tried?" That may not be high priority information to the people *inside* the project, but if the audience is *outside* the project, then I want to spend a while in this section to spell out in detail what has happened; what the program is.

To do that, we need to have a structure, an outline, to organize the data-collection efforts. In my own work at CIRCE I have developed such an outline. It is in a paper entitled "The Countenance of Educational Evaluation." (See Figure 29) According to it we may collect data about the rationale or the philosophy of the program. We may collect data about antecedent conditions and about classroom processes that I call transactions. We may also collect data on the outcomes of the program. And I have a categorization in which I identify things that are intended, things that are observed, things that can be called educational standards, and things that serve as judgments. I will describe each of those as I go through these sections. These are just simple reminders of what sorts of data could be gathered in an evaluation study. These are mind-stretching devices, as I see them, reminding us of some things that our common sense impulses fail to remind us of.

Suppose that we were going to measure one thing, one outcome of a program. It could be a certain reading skill, an understanding of a chapter in a history book, or even as specific a knowledge as the concept of homeostasis. It could be any particular measure of achievement that you might think is important. We have various persons in the school that we are interested in getting scores from; persons 1, 2, 3, 4, 5, and so on. We might get scores on all persons; there are occasions when we would gather this pretest and posttest information every week, or every two weeks, or however often you need to get information. For person 1, 2, or 3, we can test once, twice, or three times, or four times, over the same concept and get ourselves a matrix of scores of achievement—persons by occasions—in order to get a measure of achievement, of gain in achievement over time, for one kind of objective, for one kind of achievement. This matrix of scores fits into our models as if it were Box B in Figure 29, covering only a small portion of the total field. But there is more to the expansion than that. Our measures are imprecise: I can say as a measurement specialist that we should seldom rely on one device, i.e., one way of looking at things. Besides using a standardized test, we should use some homemade tests, we should use some teachers' judgments, we should be redundant. For the measurement of understanding of *homeostasis* we should test for the same thing a second way and maybe a third way. Now I have stuffed even more data boxes inside Box B in Figure 29. This evaluation can get data-bank size if you want it to, or you can keep it very small—only measure two or three achievements. Each evaluator has to decide the amount of data needed in each of the twelve boxes in figure 29.

Back to Section 2 of the Table of Contents. I have tried, just now, to suggest some ways for organizing the data collection. Now we will proceed with program description.

First of all, I would say that the evaluation report needs to indicate the educational philosophy behind the program. It may be that the program philosophy is theoretical. It could be utilitarian. It could emphasize democracy or personal worth. There are lots of different philosophies behind our various school programs. Here we try to specify the philosophy of the particular program we are evaluating.

Secondly, I would have a section on the subject matter that is going to be included. Of course, certain programs emphasize subject matter very little. Others emphasize it a lot. We need more evaluation attention on what subject matter is being covered in the program. We can take the view that the most important subject matter is process. You can argue that certain content is essential. Either way, there is some subject matter that is part of the program; I want that information in the evaluation report.

Subsection C calls for a statement of the objectives of the program. We ought to know far more about the *different* objectives that are around—the students' objectives, parents' objectives, and of course what the staff has in mind. Behavioral statements? I personally do not care what form the statements of objectives take.

As a practicing evaluator I really do not expect much help in guiding my evaluation when I ask the question, "What are your objectives?" Personally I want to start with "what the program is," and not with what the objectives are. In laying out the evaluation study, I spend very little time and very little money in getting the educators to specify what it is they are up to. A little time, yes, but the fact that I have indicated this to be only one subsection of the evaluation report, I think indicates that I put it at a lower priority. I want to deal with objectives as we go along during the program and the evaluation, rather than as a first order of business. But we usually have to let our audiences know what the objectives are.

Section D says let us tell the people who are going to read this evaluation report something about the instructional procedures,

tactics and media that are used. I am not thinking about an evaluator sitting at a desk and writing about these things, but presenting
some data. He should have data gathered through interviews and
through observation techniques. It should be as objective and as
precise as he can make it (given the three dollars or whatever he
has in the budget for getting that particular information). One of
the things I like to see in an evaluation report is some indication of
what is happening between teachers and students in the classroom,
and for this purpose it seems useful to have a classroom observation schedule. Most of you are familiar with the Flanders'
procedure. Somebody sits in the classroom and maps the flow of
information, noting the amount of instructor talking, how much
time the instructor is spending responding to the questions of the
students, how much time he is giving to supportive comments of
various kinds, and so forth.

As I see it the research on these interaction analyses gives us
little encouragement in our search for better ways to deal with
students. The correlations between how a teacher behaves in the
classroom, and student achievement are rather discouraging, I
would say. If our purpose is to nail down the causes of achievement, I do not think we are going to get it by studying classroom
interaction. I am saying today that we should gather observational
data not because it leads to information about why the kids are
learning but because some audience needs to know what is going
on in the classroom. Audiences have ideas about what is good and
bad classroom activity. These are data that are fairly inexpensive
to get. It takes a few hours to train a data-gatherer. How representative are the data gathered in a brief visit to the classroom? That
is something to worry about, of course, but the worry should not
prevent initial efforts to get such information. The evaluator
studies the data and decides what more is needed. If the data turn
out to be questionable the evaluator tells the audience what he
found and why he does not find the finding credible.

Subsection E says let us describe the students. For one thing we
need to describe the previous level of student competence. But
there are things in addition to the scholastic characteristics that we
might measure. We might want to know something about the
social situation we are dealing with. We may choose in the evaluation report to offer a sociogram, or perhaps to show change in a
sociogram over time to indicate what kind of social contacts occur
with the students in the project.

Subsection F suggests that we should have a description of the
instructional setting, i.e., the school, the campus, the community
setting. I think this is particularly important because if the study is

going to be useful in some other community, in some other locality, the readers are going to have to make a guess as to whether or not the conditions under which this occurred are similar to the ones he would have in his system. By reporting the instructional setting, we make the guess less hazardous. The purpose of our research designs—using sampling and control procedures—is to give us some guarantee as to the generality of the conclusions we get. We do not have the same controls and the same guarantees in evaluation settings, and so the best thing we can do is to describe as fully as possible "under what conditions which things occurred." A wise and experienced administrator can say, "I think those are like the ones that we have. I may want to pay more attention to a program like that." Or he may say, "I think those conditions are really wild, I do not think we could ever get those, I am not going to pay too much attention to the results of this study. It is just not like it would be in our situation." But in order for him to make that kind of judgment, he is going to have some information about the classroom, school grounds, community setting in the project being evaluated.

Subsection G calls for a report of some of the standards, some of the bases for judging quality. I hesitate every time I put this down as one of the kinds of data we need to collect. It is important but so difficult to do. We need to examine the whole basketful of general standards, the beliefs, the demands, that exist in our society for various learnings, for various school situations. We demand a certain amount of training for teachers, we demand a certain sort of control in the classroom. We need to relate these demands to the local situation. I do not know how many of these things we need to record for an evaluation study, but I think we should record some. Some day we may be able to obtain these standards from the ERIC centers and from R & D centers such as the one at UCLA. Now we have to go through the literature and find, for example, what the Office of Education guidelines imply about mathematics or about citizenship. As I use the concept, standards exist *outside* the project. They are standards that are relevant to educational programs broadly. They are tough to find. Maybe you cannot, in your modest evaluation study, report anything in Subsection G, but it is something to scratch your head about. Do we really want to ignore what the American Library Association says about staffing the library? Do we want to report what the biologists say about BSCS? These are standards that our readers may want to know about in deciding whether or not this program has any value.

Section III calls for program outcomes, the impact of the teaching. Impact not of the evaluation study but impact of the program of the school. Much more than other consultants, perhaps, I want to emphasize in my report that certain experiences were provided. I want to gather data about what sort of opportunities occurred in this project. I have noticed that in present legislation there is almost no talk about what impact the legislation is going to have, or that change in student behavior will occur. Interpreters of that legislation translate it according to their own perspectives. The guidelines and most consultants talk about the emphasis in that legislation on providing social change. Well, as an evaluator I want to find out about social change but I also want to find out about what opportunities exist. I want to find what impact a program is having, but I also want to find out if we provided some opportunity for things to happen. Were there unique experiences for the students, did they have an opportunity to see things they had not seen before, did they have an opportunity to study arithmetic with a mathematics lover, literature with a poet? I want to know what some of the opportunities were as well as what some of the student gains were. So I indicate a separate subsection here in the part on Outcomes to indicate the opportunities attributable to the project.

Section III B would indicate the student gains we can identify. Hopefully, we will be able to identify many gains—unfortunately, we will be able to identify very few. We just do not have devices for measuring many educational impacts. In forty years we have developed precise testing instruments for finding differences among aptitudes and achievements in our children. We have not concentrated on testing instruments to find differences in the curricula. Most present tests do not tell us what impact our programs have. I would submit that there are many technical differences between those two purposes, and until our testing industry and psychometricians—like myself—get at the problem of identifying what a particular teacher is accomplishing in algebra or in geography, the evaluator and the administrator are going to have difficulty in reporting a true picture of what the school is doing. We are trying to make some changes and I have indicated how our thinking has been going and what our new design is in Table 6. The testing program would become oriented to finding out whether or not kids as a class are learning anything important about biology. The specifics of a certain curriculum are washed out by conventional tests—those tests are intended to be "curriculum-general." Biology tests are usually built so they do not penalize a student for having a special kind of biology. Well, we want a test that *does* discriminate between the kinds of biology a student has studied. We want to *know* that he does not know "BSCS green" biology, that he does know "BSCS blue" biology. We want a test that will tell us what he has learned in "BSCS blue" biology. We want to know the difference in impact between one curriculum and another.

Section III C says, "Let us look at the side effects and bonuses." What do I mean by that? Well, one way of looking at it is that things are happening besides those things that are indicated by the objectives and the expectations of the staff. Who is going to identify them? The evaluator has to be ingenious. He may wonder, "What are the critics of the particular program worried about?" He should get some measurements to ascertain whether or not they are right, whether or not those things they are afraid of are happening. The evaluator has to look at other research studies to find possibly useful variables. Not very many of our projects say anything about the concern for parental support of education in general. In his study of educational opportunities James Coleman learned that it was important to find out whether or not parents are generally supportive of education as a basis for achievement in life. Some parents are very supportive, some parents are very much disinterested in schools. This may be a useful indicator as to what is going on in the project. We look at evaluation studies such as Coleman's and find pregnant variables, ones that may really tell us a lot about the situation, the program, and lead us to the bonuses and unwanted side effects in the project.

Section III D calls for us to report on the costs of the program; costs in terms of money, costs in terms of staff, costs in terms of anguish, costs in terms of student involvement. What did we have to give up in order to undertake this particular program? It embarrasses me to admit that I do not know anything about the measurement of costs. I will have to leave that to somebody else.

Section IV deals with relationships and indicators. In the model I have developed, you are urged to look at the congruence between what was intended and what actually was observed. It is extremely important, I think, to have a report of the discrepancy between intents and observations. Some discrepancies indicate better-than-expected performance. We need to get judgments as to whether or not the discrepancies are desirable or undesirable. The idea of congruence and the idea of discrepancy, I believe, are closely related.

The second category in the last section of my outline has to do with contingencies, that is, what is causing what. You do certain

Table 6

A Testing Program for Assessing the Collective Academic Growth of the Student Body of a School District, Using Trend-Lines over Time

The school district curriculum specialists decide what subject-matter they want the assessment to cover. From a catalogue of subject-matter divisions and subdivisions they select several (perhaps 12) scales on which all students collectively will be assessed. The full catalogue includes all or a large pool of items to be used with each scale to help the specialists make their decisions. A partial listing of subject-matter is shown below.

SUBJECT-MATTER DIVISIONS (AN EXAMPLE)

Mathematics
1. Numerical operations
2. Word problems
3. Algebra
4. Geometry
5. New Mathematics
6. Trigonometry

Communication
1. Learning resources
2. Grammar
3. Spelling
4. Composition
5. Reading Comprehension
6. Listening Comprehension

American Culture
1. Traditional History
2. Contemporary Socio-Political
3. Economics
4. Literature
5. Visual & Performing Arts
6. Philosophy and Values

Physical Science
1. Earth Science
2. Physics
3. Chemistry
4. Biology (Green)
5. Biology (Yellow)
6. Biology (Blue)

Each month (or as otherwise regularly scheduled) each student is tested for perhaps ten minutes with a different sample of items. On some subjects he gets one or two items, on others none.

With such tests (unmatched tests, item sampling) no two students in the same classroom are likely to get the same test item for any subject. Thus, no basis for comparing, grading, or counseling individual students results from the testing program.

For assessment of the program of a specific classroom, specialists and teachers may identify additional subject-matter subdivisions. During the day when those classes are in session, an additional, brief, periodic test is administered. The items are randomly assigned to students, as before, but only for the specific subject-matter of their class.

For both district-wide and classroom assessment, test results are processed and translated into performance scale scores. A trend-line over time is kept for each subject-matter subdivision.

things in the classroom and you get certain results. But it is very risky to talk about attribution. What *causes* what? Very seldom do things covary in such a way in our evaluation studies so that we can say, "Yes, the more we have of that, the more we have of this, and when that dropped off, this dropped off too; therefore, we can conclude that that causes this." We seldom have the opportunity; but some covariation *does* occur, and we take some pride in reporting those contingencies. Because the relationship may be unique to the particular conditions in the project we need to invite the reader's attention to the conditions under which the contingency occurred.

I did want to make an extra fuss about this last section because there has been talk about whether the evaluator gets into the question of the worth of the program and whether you get into the worth of the information that you have gathered and whether you get into the relevance of the objectives. As Mike Scriven has emphasized in the first AERA Monograph on Curriculum Evaluation, much of the business of evaluation is finding out about the specific merits and shortcomings of the program, i.e. its values. If there is diversity of perceptions as to the worth of things, the evaluator finds out and reports that diversity. He does not necessarily look for consensus. He reports the diversity that he finds as to what students and townspeople and scientists and others see as good and bad in the program. The people making judgments may be the teachers, may be the parents, may be the Chamber of Commerce, may be almost anyone. The evaluator has to decide what sources of information to use, but he goes to many different ones. There *are* many, many sources of judgment data for an evaluation report.

In Section V–B, we would examine the relevance of objectives to needs. Most of the designs we have for evaluation start with objectives given. I say, let us go beyond that responsibility and see whether or not we can find a match-up between needs of the community, or the nation, and this particular project. Let us find out from the people involved whether or not they see the project's objectives as highly appropriate.

Lastly, I want a section on the relevance of evaluation study itself. That is to say, our efforts should have their own quality control mechanism. Is this evaluation relevant? Did we use good sense in gathering information? Did it communicate effectively to its audience?

Now, having said all that about a final report, let me question the value of final reports. Let me be the skeptic for a moment. Maybe the Table of Contents which I have offered you deserves a place in the circular file. If the evaluation is formative evaluation, i.e. developmental evaluation; if the purpose of the evaluation is to provide quality control, to keep the program running; if the purpose of evaluation is to serve the "insiders," the people running the program; then we do not, I think, need much in the way of formal evaluation reports. But when the audience is outside, we need to worry much more about the form of our formal report.

Let me be more skeptical still. Maybe the whole idea of evaluation should go in the circular file. School districts in Ohio, Illinois, and everywhere have problems. Many of the problems are aggravated by people who come in to evaluate. We do not know whether or not evaluation is going to contribute more to the problems of education or more to the solutions. There is reason for skepticism. As I look at evaluation and education, I say to myself, there is not any going back to those good old days when education was everybody's idea of what makes America great. TV, travel, and newspapers have changed all of that. People know some of what is going on in the schools and a lot of it they do not like. We are on the defensive. We have to make a case for education. How should we appeal to our audience? Should we use the emotional arguments emphasizing the rights of each child for a decent education? Should we emphasize the fact that our football team has a great chance to capture the Conference title this year? Of course we should. So also should we use the rational arguments. We should ally ourselves with the social sciences and behavioral sciences to learn about ourselves and to report about what is going on in our schools. Our schools are working, I think. They are doing their job, they are doing their job as they define that job. They could be doing a better job in many ways. Still they are doing many jobs that we can take pride in. But I believe we should find out more about what is going on.

There is a risk in disclosure. There is a big risk. The public is not a single public. It is a pluralistic public. Values are in conflict; from one neighborhood to the next people expect different things. They are at odds about what the schools ought to be. Maybe they all expect too much from education, but we cannot go back. People are going to demand more information about what is going on. They have a right to know what is going on. And I think they are going to demand that we are more technically competent in reporting what is going on. For our own protection, to save our own skins, if for no other reason, I think we are going to evaluate.

In our work at CIRCE we occasionally interview assistant superintendents, principals, and heads of department. Following one procedure, midway through the interview we take a written copy of a recent evaluation conducted with that institution. We open it to what seems to be a major table of graphs, examine it for a few minutes, then ask the person we are talking to, "Would you interpret this for me?" And the response all too often is:

"Well, I am really not a specialist in curriculum, not a specialist in research at all. My specialty is public relations. The people at the lab did it for us, and I have not had time to look at it."

Now, that is terrible! Not the fact that the man has not read the report, but the fact that whoever did the evaluation study did not make the study valuable to him.

Evaluation responsibility is communication responsibility. It is a responsibility to gather information that will be useful to specific audiences. In many ways it would be nice if the U.S. Office of Education could be that audience and could read our reports and learn from them. It would be nice if the State Department of Education could read our report and learn more about what is

going on in our state. But they cannot read our reports for a
variety of reasons. Therefore, it is the opportunity and the obligation of each program evaluator to translate the evaluation requirements, given by the State or Federal government, into a plan that
will gather useful information for the people who will read the
report, particularly the local people. I think that the topics which
I have emphasized in my idealized Table of Contents will serve
that purpose.

The Role of the Evaluator

The final consideration which we will address in this chapter is
related to an identity problem felt by many evaluators. Evaluation
is an emerging field, and the present state of the art leaves much to
be desired. One result is that the evaluator's role in educational
improvement is not well-entrenched in schoolmens' minds. Public
institutions are just beginning to become aware of the many roles
evaluators can play within their organizational structures. The
following paper contains a detailed suggestion of one type of
role—in curriculum development—that evaluators can play in
education.

Process Accountability in Curriculum Development

Dennis D. Gooler and Arden Grotelueschen

Center for Instructional Research
and Curriculum Evaluation
University of Illinois, Urbana-Champaign

The Case for Accountability

The politician studies problems, consults his constituents, notes
his constraints, weighs his alternatives, and anticipates consequences. He seeks to understand both cause and effect. So also
does the educator.

The politician, however, has learned the intricacies of accountability to a greater extent than has the educator. The politician
knows the pressures and consequences of being held accountable
by a wide variety of groups and individuals for his decisions.
Experience has taught him to be sensitive to the needs, goals, and
expectations of his constituency, his colleagues, indeed of his

From F.M. Connelly, J. Herbert, and J. Weiss (Eds.), *Curriculum Theory
Network*, Special Issue, No. 1, Fall. Toronto: OISE, 1970. Reprinted with
permission of the authors.

society. The politician's search for answers, guided primarily by his experience, his beliefs, and his insight, is realistically influenced by those to whom he is, fairly or unfairly, held accountable.

Accountability applies not only to the politician, but to the doctor, the office manager, the plumber, the newsboy. The degree to which each is held accountable is a function of the kind of service he provides, and of the people who receive it.

And the curriculum developer? He too seeks answers, but his service requires more: He must convey those answers to a large number of other people. Can he be held accountable? It is our contention that the curriculum developer *can* be held accountable for a number of decisions, by a number of groups (audiences), for a number of reasons. Further, we contend that the curriculum developer has an obligation to attend to the needs, goals, and expectations of the myriad of special interest groups as they relate to the decisions he makes.

The genesis of our remarks must be attributed to our involvement in the world of evaluation. We thus begin with some bias toward the belief that evaluation, as we conceive the term and the process, can be of use to the curriculum developer, not only in his evaluation of student outcomes resulting from the implementation of a curriculum, but also in the developmental process itself. Our observations about curriculum, evaluation, and accountability are not offered as a grandiose analysis of curricular problems, but rather as a statement of our perception of one purpose evaluation can play in curriculum development. We raise more questions than answers. The examples we include are illustrative, not definitive.

Traditionally curriculum developers have focused their attention solely on the intents, contents, and methodologies of an instructional package, to the exclusion of the audiences who will react to decisions they make. Usually if attention is paid to an audience, it is given to teachers and students, in terms of "what's best for them," not "what are they thinking, feeling, demanding." To be sure, some audiences suggest only generalities: "The school should teach my child how to prepare for adult life." Other audiences suggest specifics: "Teach my child how to read." In both instances, it remains for the curriculum developer to develop the details of a curriculum. Nonetheless, even the generalities espoused by the various audiences provide meaningful cues for the curriculum developer concerned about building and implementing his curriculum.

Any curriculum tends to touch a variety of people, in a variety of ways, at a variety of times. These various groups can be viewed as audiences who come with various biases and demands, public and private concerns, and motives of assorted legitimacies: Each of these "pockets of persuasion" may serve its notice of accountability to the curriculum developer. The amount of "clout" they possess in serving that notice is not at question here; the reality of their existence is. The manner in which the developer must account for (report, explain, or justify) the curriculum will differ according to who is raising the questions, what those questions are about, and when they are raised.

Curriculum Development

Curriculum development *may* be seen as a series of decision points at each of which an alternative, or combination of alternatives, is selected by some process. The alternative selected at each decision point determines subsequent developmental procedures.

Noticeably absent from this view of curriculum development is any mention of goals, content, or methodology. Each of these factors is involved in the development of a curriculum, of course. But the *process* of curriculum development, as we see it, can be best described in terms of: a) decisions to be made; and b) people who make and influence the decisions.

In the development of a curriculum of national scope, a vast number of decisions must be made by a wide variety of decision-makers. Many of these decisions are made on a daily basis; many are implicit, a few explicit. There exist, however, some decisions that must be made explicitly. These decisions determine the ultimate nature of the curriculum package. The *major moments* are the focal points in the decision-making process, and, as such, are the points at which various interest groups may direct their claims of accountability.

Figure 30 illustrates a very general conception of the curriculum development process. We have identified five major moments in the development of the curriculum package. Field testing is a major moment also, as "Go or No-Go" decisions related to the curriculum package as a whole or parts of it thereof are sought prior to consumer purchase of the package.

A continual process of interaction, over time, occurs among ideas brought into play by the curriculum developers. Thus ideas about content interact with ideas about goals, as well as ideas about methodology and ideas about the format of the package. As the development process unfolds, widely divergent ideas may be expressed. Daily decisions will be made about some of these ideas; some will be eliminated, some kept, and some revised. However, a number of "ultimate" decisions must be made: debate about which goals to pursue cannot continue indefinitely; some content must be selected, a methodology suggested, a format chosen. These "ultimate" decisions we have called major moments.

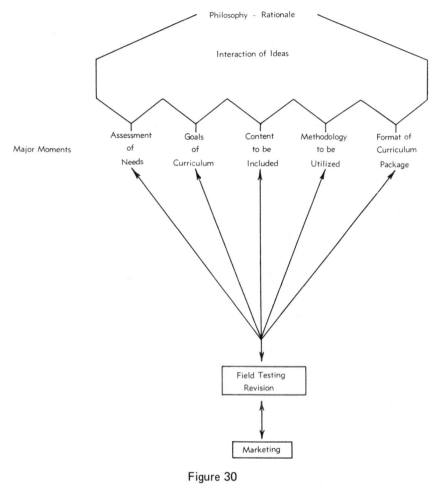

Figure 30

The Process of Curriculum Development

In some instances, the decision made at a major moment may actually have been made early in the development of the curriculum package. The needs to which the developers address themselves may have, for example, been determined early by a few prominent individuals (subject matter scholars), or by an influential group (professional society), or by the curriculum development team itself. The developmental process may not have included a great deal of debate about needs. The decision made about needs, however, will greatly influence decisions made about other elements of the development project. Over time, ideas will undergo constant scrutiny and change, as each element affects thinking about the others.

We have chosen to "cap" our model with the philosophy or rationale for the developmental process. The rationale for the curriculum being developed defines, in some sense, the parameters of the project. The interaction of ideas about content, methodology and all other relevant (and irrelevant) variables is bounded by the developer's rationale. To be sure, this rationale may not always be clearly discernible, thus presenting problems for the evaluator, those working on the curriculum, as well as those who finally *use* the curriculum. The evaluator may see as a part of his responsibility an attempt to have the rationale clearly stated by the curriculum developer.

Curriculum development, viewed as a series of decisions about the curriculum package and its testing, usually involves a host of people, only some of whom are directly connected with the curriculum project. Each person who is directly involved brings his beliefs, attitudes, values, and assumptions to the decision points. Each represents a perspective influence on the final shape of the package. It may be difficult to separate the decision from the man who most influenced it.

Our treatment of curriculum development has been brief, but we hope these statements provide a frame of reference for subsequent remarks. The major moments we have identified may be too many, too few, or too vague. Nonetheless, the idea of major moments suggests a rather unique role for evaluation in the curriculum process.

One Role for Evaluation

Those involved in the work of developing a curriculum package make the decision suggested by each major moment. We contend that the curriculum developers' decisions should not be made without a careful analysis of the "hopes, fears, and aspirations," (not to mention the *demands*) of the several audiences who are but indirectly connected with the curriculum project, yet who might reasonably lay claim to providing input into each major moment.

This is the problem—parties interested in the curriculum development and outcome are often not at the decision-making scene. They appear later, to directly voice their protest against a decision made earlier, or to displace their protest toward an object (e.g., school tax issue) which they themselves can influence directly. They question the alternatives from which a choice was selected; they hold the distributor (the school) accountable for what the developer did, or failed to do. Educators repeatedly find themselves backpedaling to rationalize a decision already made, rather than anticipating the nature of the demand and inquiry *prior* to making decisions.

Exit for now the mode of evaluation concerned with outcomes, statistics, and compare-this-program-to-another, and enter evaluation operating in a who's-asking-what, who's-doing-what, how-do-the-groups-with-an-interest-stack-up-in-terms-of-potential-influence mode. In this mode, evaluation raises many questions (few answers), alerts the curriculum developer (sensitizes?), and causes a lot of concern about justifying, explaining, relating. It's not a comfortable mode. But neither is it comfortable to be holding a beautifully structured, logically sequenced curriculum that no one can or will let into his schools!

Consider, if you will, the major moment; "What are the objectives of our proposed social studies curriculum package?" Suppose we decide our curriculum ought to enable students to think critically about our social system—a reasonable objective. Some of the "best" minds tell us this is the essence of social studies; students must learn critical thinking. With that decided, move on to deciding content and methodology and format.

But why was that one objective chosen to the exclusion of others? Members of a discipline-oriented audience may not see it as an appropriate objective. A culturally different audience is likely to say "Forget critical thinking; let's tell it (the social system) as it is." A parent audience wants to know the relationship between a curriculum centered around this objective and the skills college entrance exams measure. And so it goes. These groups may be verbal and are likely to exert their influence on the curriculum distributor (the school): The telephone rings, the principal and the superintendent incur pressure, the school board reacts. And that curriculum, with that objective, must go. The curriculum package can be defended by any group of experts who *know*—but it is gone.

Does the curriculum developer have a responsibility to support the curriculum distributor (the school) as the curriculum consumer (the student) and consumer-related people raise questions? Look at this decision again. What audience may react? What groups may protest, support, resist, affirm? What do they want to know? What are they demanding? What group can you antagonize and still see your curriculum implemented? What are the trade-offs? Where are you likely to be held accountable for failure, and where are you likely to be given credit for accomplishment?

You need not call it evaluation, but we suggest that the curriculum developer spend part of his time identifying audiences, "pockets of potential persuasion." Furthermore, it is not enough merely to acknowledge the existence of different audiences. Judgments made by these audiences about the focus of the major moments and the reasons given for decisions made at these moments must be ascertained and considered by the developer in his decision-making. The developer, or the evaluator, may be able to uncover (not by second guessing but by direct inquiry) the questions these groups will be asking, the claims they will be making, the axes they seem to want to grind. Armed with that information, the developer, or evaluator, can determine what kinds of data should be ready for use in response to potential questions. Perhaps more important, the data can be used as developmental input; it can exert an influence on what is developed. The curriculum developer cannot follow suggestions made by all audiences, nor should he. Suggestions may be in direct opposition to each other, for example. However, by considering possible suggestions and possible demands the developer has determined, before the fact, what the consequences of not attending to a particular suggestion or group might be. He need not yield only to those who speak the loudest; he may not follow the demands of audiences. He *does* need to know what people want and think, if only to know better how he is to report, explain, or justify what has been done, and why.

Selling your expert's soul? Yielding principle to pressure? Not as we see it. Evaluation, by identifying questions, groups, and data available, enables the curriculum developer to confront reality nose-to-nose. The expert skills of the curriculum developer include the ability to successfully combine the substance and methodology of a certain discipline, with the expectations of audiences who come in contact with the developmental process and the curriculum package. To operate effectively in a democratic, pluralistic society such as ours, a few knowledgeable professionals can no longer decide without serious consultation for so many other publics. The question is how to best provide an educational commodity responsive to all who will be affected by it, and how to best explain that commodity in a manner that is understandable to the consumer.

Evaluation in the Scheme of Things

Evaluation is not usually seen as an explicit and systematic part of the process of curriculum development. To be sure, the process is not without the informal, daily evaluation that occurs in any endeavor which brings talent and effort together for some common end. What we are suggesting is that by using a more formal system of evaluation, the curriculum developer can promote action, rather than mere reaction: He may anticipate audience reaction *before* it happens, thus reducing the necessity for the curriculum developer and distributor to react rather than constructively act.

If the reader will buy, if only for the moment, the validity of what we have suggested, he must ask, "Who is to do all that has been suggested?" The curriculum developer recognizes the need for other kinds of evaluation, such as student outcomes measurement and product evaluation. From the very practical standpoint of time and expertise, the developer cannot perform all the evaluative tasks needed. Thus, the curriculum development *team* may well include an evaluator.

There are a number of roles the evaluator can play in the performance of this task. He may be a raiser of questions; he may collect and interpret data; he may serve as judge. In our scheme, the evaluator collects, throughout the developmental process, data about what the audiences are thinking, feeling, and wanting with respect to various developmental foci. He may, after appropriate study of the data, interpret what he has found for or with the curriculum developer, thus continually reminding the curriculum developer of his accountability. The evaluator can be the amplifier of consumer demands, as well as the communicator of curriculum distributor needs.

Perhaps the most difficult task facing the curriculum development team is the integration of accountabilities to create a curriculum that is most responsive to the audiences that are affected by it. The evaluator is not unlike the symphony conductor who must blend individual sounds into a pleasing composite for his audience. The evaluator must amplify some audience demands, increase the fidelity of others, filter others, and eliminate still others in his attempt to help the curriculum development team determine the best combination of accountabilities.

Implicit (and unfortunately, usually *too* implicit) in all of this are the value systems of everyone concerned with curriculum development and usage. The developers value some things more than others; their product reflects their value orientations. But what of the values of other audiences, particularly the consumer-related people? Potential conflict is only too apparent. The developers of curriculum err when they do not consider the values of those who will use the curriculum package. The introduction of sex education courses is a case in point. Valuable though such courses may be, their impact will not be felt if the value orientations of the potential consumer-related persons block implementation of the program.

Again, the evaluator serves the function of providing information about consumer values to the curriculum developer. The object of this information is not to rule out all things contrary to the expressed values of the consumer, but rather to utilize knowledge about consumer values in the most appropriate means for organizing, explaining, and justifying the curriculum package. It just may be that "a curriculum in operation is worth two on the shelf," assuming that the curriculum in operation has been carefully and thoughtfully evaluated throughout the developmental process.

Curriculum development involves a lot of decisions. Some of these decision, which we have called *major moments*, determine the ultimate format of the curriculum. The curriculum developer can be held accountable for the decision he makes at each of these major moments. There exists a wide variety of audiences to whom, fairly or unfairly, the developer is accountable. The success of the curriculum package that is developed will depend greatly on the extent to which the developer has recognized and acted upon his accountabilities.

Evaluation can play many roles in curriculum development and implementation. One role for evaluation emphasized here concerns what has traditionally been denied by curriculum developers, not what they have affirmed. This role involves the identification of "pockets of potential persuasion": evaluation can seek to provide information about demands, assumptions, values, and beliefs held by these pockets, and to present this information in a manner useful to the curriculum developer in his attempt to build an interesting, useful curriculum. The evaluator, as part of the curriculum development team, provides throughout the developmental process the incentive and capability to act, rather than only react.

Bob Ogle put it nicely: The evaluator can help bridge the *accountability gap*.

The Relationship Between the
Evaluator and the Decision-Maker

There have been many arguments for the evaluator to take on specific roles. Guba and Stufflebeam (1968), for instance, while noting several different activities in which evaluators are engaged, argued that the primary role of the evaluator should be to provide information to decision-makers. The evaluator, thus, should be a specialist who identifies, collects, analyzes, and reports information. The role of making summary judgments is left to program administrators.

Stake (1967) implicitly suggested that the evaluator is the one who actually should make the judgments. Following his model, a set of conditional (that is, "If these conditions exist, then this is best") statements should be offered by the evaluation specialist. Ideally, from this viewpoint, the output from an evaluation study would include (a) a complete description of all important variables operating in and on the program and (b) a set of judgmental statements. If this is done completely, then any rational person should be able to reach the same conclusions about which course of action is best.

Other writers, influenced by the political nature or nonrationality of much administrative decision-making, have argued that an evaluator should be given the responsibility of making decisions based on the results of his evaluation study. The rationale for this argument is that the evaluator is the one person who has become knowledgeable about all the important aspects of the program. He has literally "gotten his hands dirty" with the relevant data. Thus, he is viewed as being in the best position to judge all aspects of the program, while the nominal decision-maker may be only superficially informed. Moreover, administrators' perceptions may be biased by the fact that they have been associated with the program from its outset and have a vested interest. Since the evaluator can produce a complete mosaic of the program and is less apt to be politically influenced, adherents of this position would argue that the evaluator should make the final judgments.

Each of the positions outlined above has its supporters and can be argued on logical grounds. Each position also has its weaknesses. The argument presented immediately above, for example, has considerable appeal. However, in reality, the administrator is the person who holds both the legal responsibility and the authority for making decisions. He is the one person who is accountable for actions which are taken. Thus, he must be a party in making the final judgments. In addition, it is not likely, given the constraints of most evaluation studies, that the evaluator can produce a sufficiently complete description of all aspects of an educational program to provide the evaluator with a view of the program necessarily superior to that of the administration.

What does seem to be feasible and logically justifiable is that the making of final decisions about a program be a two-man team effort. The evaluator and administrator should work together, revising all aspects of the program and bringing in any new information that isn't contained in the evaluation report, to produce a set of rational judgments. The evaluator should bring his final report, including judgments and recommendations, to the administrator. The administrator should in turn review this report and agree or disagree with the judgments which he feels are not supported by the data. If there is disagreement, then more information should be collected before a final set of judgments is produced. The manner in which the final judgments are made (for example, any political influences exerted on the decisions, compromises reached, or disagreements unresolved) should be explicitly reported as a supplement to the evaluation report; at times a minority report may be in order if the evaluator and administrator cannot agree or if the evaluator feels that the final decision ignores the evaluation data. In this way the public will be informed about how and why a judgment was made and the persons who were accountable for the judgment will have fulfilled their responsibilities.

5

The Future of Evaluation

The first four chapters of this volume contain numerous suggestions for improving the planning and conduct of evaluation studies. Each of the suggestions should prove useful in strengthening the practice of evaluation. However, some needs remain which must be satisfied if evaluation is to improve educational programs and practices to the levels demanded by society. This final part of the volume will outline those needs to which evaluation theorists and practitioners must attend if the future of evaluation is to be a potent force in the improvement of American education.

This section is divided into two parts. First, an excellent paper by Stake and Denny (1969) is presented; the paper includes both a comprehensive look at future evaluation needs and suggestions as to how these needs might best be satisfied. Following the Stake and Denny paper, we discuss several additional needs which are important to the future development of educational evaluation.

Needed Concepts and Techniques for Utilizing More Fully the Potential of Evaluation

Robert E. Stake and Terry Denny

University of Illinois, Urbana

From the *NSSE 68th Yearbook, Part II*, 1969, 370-390. Copyrighted 1969 by the National Society for the Study of Education. Reprinted with permission of the authors and the Society.

Considered broadly, evaluation is the discovery of the nature and worth of something. In relation to education, we may evaluate students, teachers, curriculums, administrators, systems, programs, and nations. The purposes for our evaluation may be many, but always, evaluation attempts to describe something and to indicate its perceived merits and shortcomings.

Evaluation is not a search for cause and effect, an inventory of present status, or a prediction of future success. It is something of all of these but only as they contribute to understanding substance, function, and worth.

Evaluation in education occasionally features normative distributions of student achievement, self-study of curriculums by members of a local school faculty, and experimental comparisons of new and old instructional treatments. But the preponderance of evaluation features informal, intuitive monitoring by teachers, students, and administrators. Evaluation reports, unfortunately, usually tell little more than that the work proposed was completed, that the complaints of the staff were justified, and that there were greater differences within groups of students (or schools or curriculums) than there were between the groups. Most evaluation reports give only the participants some notion of what occurred; the outsider gains little insight. Most formal reports avoid explicit subjective judgments by insiders and outsiders as if they were evil.

Educators and laymen alike cannot now visualize and explain what is happening in our classrooms. Part of the reason for this failing is our inability to share perceptions and measurements. Part is our lack of motivation to share them. What *should* be told? What should be shared? Our needs are not only procedural; we need also a commitment to full and accurate reporting.

Regarding the Recruitment and Training of Evaluators

Before considering the needs for new evaluation methodology, we wish to acknowledge that the successful use of methods depends on the people who use them. We will point out that the specific technical skills suited to educational testing and to educational research are not (to the surprise of some readers) perfectly suited to educational evaluation. Mobilization of the appropriate skills will require recruitment of already skilled persons from other fields in addition to the training of persons from our own ranks.

As is indicated in the sections that follow, the concepts and techniques that will serve evaluation have roots in philosophy, sociology, anthropology, linguistics, history, and economics as well as in psychology. Men from these disciplines have contributed often to educational practice. Whether the school needs just a consultant or the director of evaluation, these several fields should be regarded as sources of personnel. The responsibility of evaluation usually involves creating a better frame of reference for understanding educational programs. The contributions of men from allied fields are not the answers they have generated but the perspectives they bring. New viewpoints do not automatically solve problems, improve decision-making, and increase satisfactions—but they do enable a teacher, an administrator, or a curriculum-director to see the situation in a new way and lead him to try a remedy that otherwise may not have seemed reasonable.

Few graduate programs aim at training evaluation (as we have defined the term "evaluation") specialists. In contrast, many programs are devoted to the training of testing-and-measurement specialists and of research-design-and-analysis specialists. The demand for research specialists continues to grow. A recent head of the U.S. Office of Education Bureau of Research cited the need for training researchers as one of two outstanding national needs. (Welsh, 1968)

The plea for training evaluators is much less frequently heard. In spite of the fact that evaluation is a desirable and often mandatory responsibility within funded programs, few schools of education provide explicitly relevant course work and supervised experience.

Evaluation specialists are and will be increasingly needed—but more of the same will not suffice. From what source should they be recruited? How should they be trained and what should they know as a result of their training?

Consideration of the core content of a program to train educational evaluators reveals a variety of needs. Doctoral-level programs must be designed to produce evaluation theorists and consultants with competences to cope with evaluation problems of great intellectual import and administrative size. In addition, less-extensive evaluation training programs are needed to provide a large number of persons who are able to gather useful evaluation information at the local level. Training programs at all levels will have to be created which will provide task-oriented experiences for teams of researchers drawn from a variety of disciplines and specialities, having heterogeneous backgrounds and different future roles. Experiences would be designed to broaden the base from which educational evaluation problems are viewed. A variety of methodological and evaluation strategies might be employed in prototypic evaluation exercises. Training might include experience in working with a social demographer, a mechanical engineer, a philosopher of science, and others in designing strategies to attack school evaluation problems. Such training exercises should include confrontation experiences and work problems drawn from the workaday world of educational evaluators. Prototypic instruments will have to be constructed for use with work problems and for use in simulation exercises.

Some research-oriented professors ignore some important distinctions between educational research and educational evaluation. The researcher is concerned foremost with the discovery and building of principles—lawful relationships with a high degree of generalizability over several instances of a class of problems. He seeks to develop rules (explanatory statements) about processes which govern common educational activities. He seeks to understand the basic forces that interact whenever there is teaching and learning. He seeks the causes of maturity and sophistication, of retardation and alienation. The evaluator shares some of these concerns. He is particularly concerned with deriving principles on which to make decisions about instructional practice. Gagné (in press) has observed that the evaluator's and the survey researcher's assessment tasks coalesce when the evaluator centers his attention on the accomplishment of certain performance objectives as the crucial part of a set of comprehensive educational goals. These concerns are important for educational evaluation.

But educational evaluation is more than assessing student performance. It includes the task of gathering information about the nature and worth of educational *programs* in order to improve decisions about the management of those programs. The evaluator must attend to the effects of the program on teacher performance, administrative arrangements, and community attitudes, and to how the program complements and obtrudes upon other parts of the total curriculum. The evaluator has his own collection of concepts and issues. Scriven (1967) has spelled out many of them—the distinction between formative and summative evaluation, the distinction between evaluation and process studies, and the distinction between intrinsic and payoff evaluation, for example. All these are central to the training of the evaluation specialist.

Evaluation can be seen as a form of applied research, but one which places special demands on the methods of inquiry. The evaluator is concerned with finding immediately relevant answers for decision making. He has an obligation to deal directly with personal standards and subjective judgments. The focal point of his work—unlike that of the researcher—is that one curriculum, or that one program, or that one lesson, or that one textbook he is evaluating.

The distinction between research and evaluation can be overstated as well as understated. The principal difference is the degree to which the findings are generalizable beyond their application to a given product, program, or locale. Almost always the steps taken by the researcher to attain generalizability tend to make his inquiries artificial or irrelevant in the eyes of the practitioner. The evaluator sacrifices the opportunity to manipulate and control but gains relevance to the immediate situation. Researcher and evaluator work within the same inquiry paradigm but play different management roles and appeal to different audiences.

Some work has been done on field-testing training programs for the preparation of local educational evaluators. Filep (1967) reported on the development of a prototypic training program developed for the Educational Products Information Exchange Institute (EPIE) which utilized videotaped feedback procedures, sensitivity training, simulation exercises, and the exploration of nonreactive measures of teachers' views of educational materials. Many similar programs can be identified in centers and laboratories across the nation. They have yet to draw effectively upon the experience and training materials of each other.

Both the evaluation-theory and local-evaluation training programs, like educational-research training programs, must include skill development in general educational research methodology. Educational evaluators should have some familiarity with alternative social-science research strategies—those found in sociology, anthropology, and ethnology, for example. Their skills in devising techniques and constructing instruments idiosyncratic to the evaluation tasks at hand and in training other professionals and paraprofessionals in the use of such instruments and techniques should be considerable.

Whatever the level of training, we need evaluators who are facile in using unobtrusive measures for data collection as well as in indexing programs through more traditional measures (Webb, et al., 1966). Educational evaluators must understand the fallibility of tests and of less traditional avenues of assessment and be able to conceptualize assessment problems related to process and outcome in a variety of ways. The argument for the use of unobtrusive measurements in educational evaluation rests on the presumption that it is possible to select a group of measures which have compensatory strengths and unshared weaknesses (Sechrest, 1968). Traditional educational research measures and unobtrusive measures are complementary to one another and not intersubstitutable in the training of educational researchers.

It seems apparent that the tasks subsumed under the heading of "curriculum evaluation" are sufficiently complex to discourage any expectation of producing a significant number of seasoned curriculum specialists to meet existing and anticipated evaluative needs. A broad recruiting base insofar as undergraduate and previous graduate training are concerned seems well advised for both doctoral and subdoctoral training programs. Which feeder groups will prove to be most helpful, most productive of theory advancement, and most appropriate for local evaluator roles, we have no way of knowing. Each specialist viewing the scene discovers a crying need for more of his particular *expertise*.

One final observation: In the selection and training of educational evaluation trainees, regardless of the depth and breadth of the training program and the academic qualifications of the candidates, consideration should be given to their tolerance for ambiguity and to their ability to persevere in working on unpleasant tasks.

Regarding the Representation
of Goals and Priorities

At the present time, evaluation specialists have little ability for reporting what persons and programs and institutions are trying to do. They can, of course, ask them, and report what they say. But there is some distinction between what educators propose to pursue, what they see themselves pursuing, and what they in fact do pursue. It is not a matter of deception. Evaluators, educators, all human beings, have enormous difficulties in reporting the sum and sweep of their objectives. We all have goals, and we consciously give priority to some goals over others. But we have few reliable ways to report them to others, or even to reveal them to ourselves.

An evaluator's technical skill should help the educator convey his purposes, both those that quickly come to mind and those implicit in what he does. What are the present methods for getting him to formulate a statement of philosophy or a rationale; to detail the encounters he wants students to attain; or to sketch the way the ideal individual, team, or system works? Our methods now are crude, unstandardized, and unvalidated. They should be more evocative, more sensitive than indicated by the bald request, "Please state your objectives in the following space."

To supplement the offered statement of goals, our evaluation methods must tease out the additional concerns and purposes of the educator. Some of our goal-listing methods must rely on something other than the educator's ability to originate goal dimensions. The evaluator must offer choices: "Which is more your hope—outcome A or outcome B?" and as practicable. "Which of these two video-taped sequences most closely represents what you are trying to accomplish?" The evaluator must develop a battery of standard routines for seeking out unique and subtle purposes.

Scriven (1967) has proposed representing objectives through test items. Krathwohl (1965) helped clarify the problem by discussing the levels of specificity of objectives. Gagne (1965) has shown how student achievements can be analyzed to indicate intermediate objectives. Taylor and Maguire (1966) offered a model for the transformation of objectives from societal needs to student behaviors. Atkin (1963, 1968) and Eisner, (1967) in a different vein, protested against the constraining effects of specified objectives on educators. These writings are a part of a foundation for new methods of representing educational objectives.

Not only must the evaluator report the goals but also he must indicate the relative importance of the goals. Goals are not equally desirable; some have priority over others. Different educators will set different priorities, and the same educator will change his priorities over time. Priorities are complex and elusive, but the evaluation responsiblity includes the job of representing them. New conceptualizations and new scaling techniques are needed to take a first step toward discharging this responsibility.

The great weakness in our present representation of goals is that it does not guide the allocation of resources. Goals compete for our support, for our efforts. Relying on some explicit or implicit priority system, those who administer education decide among alternate investments, operational expenditures, and insurances. Evaluation requires an acknowledgement of priorities. But to say only "Goal H ranks higher than Goal D" is trivial, perhaps misleading. It is necessary to show what that priority means operationally. A conceptualization and symbolic language that will permit at least gross representation of what priorities mean (i.e., how hard do we work on what) is needed. Ultimately, an outside evaluator should be able to examine our goal specifications, priority lists, and progress reports and identify objectively the areas of under- and over-allocation of resources.

Later in the life of a program, its impact, as seen and as judged, will serve as a basis for reallocating resources. Until then, the logic of the connections between what is intended and what is provided is a principal focus of evaluation.

Regarding Techniques for Assessing
Instructional Materials
and Classroom Instruction

Publishers of instructional materials usually provide the purchaser with information on the nature of the content, on the sort of technological and instructional *expertise* involved in the writing of the materials and on the results of whatever field-testing took place prior to publication. They also indicate the cautionary measures that were employed during the developmental stages. Such information tends to add a measure of credibility to the products, and this is good. But the evaluator's needs range wide— from the structure of the materials to the extent of their coverage. The evaluator needs to know the intentions of the materials' authors or developers insofar as they are known, the reasons which underlie the particular ordering or sequencing of the materials, the instructional settings for which the materials are primarily designed, the assumptions made about the entry behavior of the learner, the kind and extent of teacher control required for effective instructional use, and the outcomes likely to be achieved under acceptable conditions of use.

Presently we have little information about such matters. Only a few of the techniques and instruments needed to get it are available, and there is too little interest in their development. However, some beginnings can be seen in the recent work of the Eastern Regional Institute for Education (ERIE), the Educational Products Information Exchange Institute (EPIE), the Social Science Education Consortium (SSEC), and the UCLA Center for the Study of Evaluation of Instructional Programs (CSEIP).

Louise Tyler's (1968) recent report presents workable guidelines for the development of a list of specifications termed "essential," "necessary," and "needed" for published materials of instruction. The organization, format, and spirit of this report are comparable to those of the APA (1966) *Standards for Educational and Psychological Tests and Manuals,* and Lumsdaine's (1963) guidelines for programmed instruction. Hopefully research institutes, consortia, laboratories, professional groups, and individual researchers will attempt to produce needed analytical techniques to assess the structure and coverage of the content of instructional materials as well as to produce performance criteria for evaluating the behavior of the users of such materials under a variety of specifiable conditions of use. Preliminary work which holds promise of applicability to the tasks of curriculum-material evaluation includes content analysis, content-coverage assessment by subject experts, semantic-differential-technique applications, and structured interviews of users. Hopefully, the impetus provided by Tyler and others for specifications of standards will be sustained and a coherent set of systematic techniques for scrutiny of existing materials will emerge. Given useful specifications and workable analyses, it seems imperative that we integrate information about the use and misuse of the same materials in the context of the formal curriculum—in the transactions of the classroom.

Traditional observation schedules and techniques have not markedly advanced understanding of what happens in a classroom in the name of teaching. The reviews of Medley and Mitzel (1963) and more recently those of Meux (1967) and Simon and Boyer (1968) reveal the strengths and weaknesses of verbal-interaction analysis, observation scales, sign systems, and the like.

Shortcomings of these techniques lie more with our lack of understanding of how widely they may validly be used than with their inherent weaknesses. Micro teaching and other techniques utilizing video-tape playback are potential evaluation tools, particularly when teacher and student judgments are sought.

Needed but not available are reliable classroom-observation techniques and instruments oriented to a variety of subject-matter contents as well as to the verbal interaction of the teacher and learners. For example, evaluators interested in assessing the teaching of elementary reading, science, social studies, foreign languages, and English find few field-tested techniques and instruments for assessing classroom instruction in these instructional areas. There are promising signs of help in the making. Social-studies-curriculum-evaluators should note the classroom-analysis scheme of Oliver and Shaver (1966). Smith, et al. (1967) has pointed the way for those interested in charting theological development of ideas in the classroom. Content specialists need to be involved in the production of schedules and techniques for assaying transactions in content areas.

Still another lack is evident in that the affective component of instruction is almost neglected in the current instructional-assessment schedules. Techniques and controls to check on the reliability of the classroom observer's perceptions of such important transactions as surprise, interest, hostility, eagerness, and boredom are needed. Also needed are indicators of the shifts and consistencies in the climate and general goal orientations of a class as it goes about its tasks. McKeachie (1959) studied the effects of classroom organizational structure on an individual's "personalogical" variables; and Lindvall (1968) has developed a schedule for use for IPI programs. All of this called-for research and development will have to pay attention to the widely reported phenomenon of experimenter bias and the obtrusiveness of the classroom observer. These represent important research problems for the evaluator who seeks distortion free assessments of classroom transactions. Should the problem of reactivity be resolved satisfactorily, the perceptual inputs of the observer would remain to be minimized or checked. Some progress has been made in controlling these contaminators of objective assessment (Simon and Boyer, 1968)

Regarding the Measurement
of Student Performance

There is a great need for simple ways of meaningfully describing to "outsiders" what the students are doing in and after training.

There are those who claim that all evaluation should be centered on what the students have learned—"for if no learning is apparent, what education has there been?" There are those who claim that evaluation should concentrate on providing opportunity for experience rather than on standardized performance—"for only self-directed and individually meaningful learning escapes the limits of indoctrination." People differ in the extent to which they find knowledge of student performances useful. But few contend that knowledge of what students can do before and after training is not a part of the evaluation picture. Yet we have a marked inability to show how students perform.

Some educators are less handicapped than others. Many elementary school teachers, for example, escort parents around the classroom, showing samples of work done by the sons or daughters of other children. Teacher marks, comments, and other judgments are usually available. The parent has an opportunity to contemplate the sophistication and the uniqueness of his child's work.

The school administrator has no corresponding medium for showing a visitor what students as a whole are doing. Obviously the diversity of tasks and undertakings in his many classrooms is great. Conventional test scores are available but total test scores represent a confusing collage of student knowledge and are rendered obscure by technical denotation (e.g., reference-group norms, predictive validity). Outstanding work by a few students cannot satisfy the inquiry about what the students are accomplishing. Work samples, performance, or mastery-test results, drawn from large numbers of students, can be carefully chosen to represent both the school's typically intellective and the school's typically non-intellective pursuits.

For effective use in evaluation, these tasks must be meaningful; each must have content validity. Can students of this group write a check a bank would accept? Can students of that group solve a certain type of quadratic equation? Can students of still another group propose and analyze arguments for and against the continuation of the Peace Corps? Obviously, information as to the performance of a specified percent of the students and randomly chosen examples of the compositions would not indicate the balance of breadth of the curriculum; but they would give evaluators and audiences opportunity to share an important conceptualization of what is happening in the schools.

These mastery items or work samples are what Tyler sought:

> Because current achievement tests seek to measure individual differences among pupils taking the tests, the items are concentrated on those which differentiate among the children. Exercises which all or nearly all can do, as well as those which only a very few can do, are eliminated because these do not give much discrimination. But, for the purposes of assessing the progress of education, we need to know what all, or almost all, of the children are learning and what the most advanced are learning as well as what is being learned by the middle or "average" children. To obtain exercises of this sort is a new venture for most test constructors. [Tyler, 1966].

The descriptors he sought are the little-recognized main contribution of the National Assessment Program. The uniqueness and merit of those self-contained descriptors have been obscured by attention to the program's sampling plan and the possible misuse of its findings. Throughout education today, whether evaluation is national or local, new descriptors, new indices, new concepts are needed.

The choice of content is a difficult problem. Many items will not be high-priority tasks for many curriculums. Many tasks will be branded as "irrelevant" and "trivial." But a trial period must not be prevented by these objections. Educators are sometimes unreasonably opposed to having their students measured on tasks not taught in the school—perhaps on items they do not even consider important. (Certainly they have an obligation to plead for more relevant tasks.) The value of performance indicators cannot be known until they have had a chance to enrich the communicability of educators and evaluators.

A second major concern regarding the measurement of performances is the need for better techniques for generating test items.

Whether they are to be used to evaluate programs or individual pupils, ways of defining the universe of anticipated outcomes are needed. This need might have been discussed in the section relating to goals. It is not important whether we think of performance as objectives for teaching or as outcomes of learning—the need is for rational, step-by-step procedures for deriving specifications of student behavior from the more general objectives that have been established.

The need for these procedures is not based on a claim that test items or performance tasks are better devised by engineers and artists. As Bormuth (1968) pointed out, present practice is intuitive and artistic rather than deliberate and rational. Content-process grids, taxonomies of objectives, item analyses, and other devices of the contemporary psychometrician provide little assurance that the content of education will be suitably represented in any collection of items. It is only a possibility, not a certainty, that a more systematic engineering of items will yield representativeness, that automatically generated items will yield better generalizations about student competence. But it is a possibility to which more attention should be given.

The theoretical foundations for rational item generation rest in several disciplines. From psychology, Gleser, Cronbach, and Rajaratnam (1965) have conceptualized the complex of sampling errors that make some items more generalizable for some purposes than others. Decision theory, from mathematics and economics, as conceived by von Neumann and Morgenstern (1947) or Wald (1950), has promise. Gagné's (1962) analyses of subject matter and the skills involved in mastering subject matter—though more pragmatic than theoretical—imply a certain philosophy of subject matter. Other epistemological writings deal more explicitly with the problem of *what* is to be learned (Scriven, 1966; Elam, 1964). Bormuth (1968) has found a theoretical paper by Menzel (1967) helpful in developing a transformational grammar of test questions. Others who are working on the item-generation problem include Lord (1965), Hively (1968), and Osburn (1967).

In calling for task-descriptor language and rational item-generation procedures, we have not intended to imply that conventional achievements tests are without value. They are well conceived. Their reliabilities are high. For their primary purpose (i.e., describing individual student standing) they have merit, and their authors should be encouraged to continue their work. For comparing programs, unfortunately, they are of little value.

Regarding Diagnosis for
Purposes of Selecting from
Alternative Instructional Treatments

Diagnostic tests and techniques currently enable us to establish the status or condition of the learner, the teacher, the classroom operation, or, as in the case of large-scale accreditation studies, the institutional milieu. Diagnostic instruments are commonly validated on their ability to predict, from the results of tests of a skill or content area, the future performance level of an individual or group. For example, if current performance on tests of reading or school readiness correlates highly with future performance, these instruments are regarded as having strong diagnostic power. Such tests can yield descriptive statements of the current strengths and weaknesses of individuals or groups and serve well as future performance indicators. For the evaluator who wishes to go beyond status assessment and is less concerned with predictive validity in the usual psychometric sense, such diagnoses are inadequate.

Current diagnostic tools generally do not prescribe which treatments are most appropriate among those available to us. We need a large catalogue of performance indicators which underlie learning strengths and weaknesses within and across subject-matter domains. The important characteristic of such indicators is neither that they correlate highly with terminal performance nor that they are logically integral to the process. Rather, it is critical that they provide bases for selecting from among competing instructional treatments. As things now stand, we are sometimes able to diagnose ills quite well and to make predictions about subsequent learner performance, only to find that we cannot then prescribe treatments likely to deter undesirable behavior or to facilitate change in desirable directions.

The activity of the Pittsburgh Research and Development Center in diagnosing pupil achievement in the Individually Prescribed Instruction project impresses us (Cox, 1967). Student-performance outcomes and attitudes are compared with teacher attitudes in the context of the teacher's perceived and observed pedagogical adequacy to ferret out prescriptions for self- or in-service training that are suggested by the results of such analyses. An outcome of Gagné's (1962) instructional task-analysis work may be to advance the art of diagnosis. Glaser (1963) distinguished between tests which assess student performance and tests which reveal the relative standings of students. Gagné, also, distinguished between tests designed for the purpose of predicting performance and those that measure learning outcomes.

The lack of clear conceptions of the structure and dynamics of the construct being diagnosed makes diagnostic-test development and sampling procedures very difficult. This problem is a persistent one in assaying the instructional needs of a student, class, or full-range curriculum program, and in choosing between alternatives to employ as remedial procedures. Moving diagnosis from an assessment to a prescription will increase the need for specificity in statements of instructional intents. We need a catalogue of statements of curricuum aims which have common meaning to the evaluator and to the practitioner. The question of the optimal degree of specificity of intents is currently *de rigueur* and is most visible in the behavioral objectives "controversy" (Popham, et al., 1969). Unfortunately, the current discussions have not led to the solution of problems involved in developing diagnostic instruments of the sort advocated for educational evaluation.

Instruments are needed to identify deterrents to learning; to reveal the misunderstandings, the poor habits, the debilitative attitudes, the prepotent needs of individuals and of groups which interfere with the achievement of the sought-after goals. Clinicians have amassed considerable diagnostic evidence that suggests that current, undesirable behavior can be as important as are personal inadequacies or shortcomings. It is one thing to assess what is lacking for the achievement of an intended educational goal and quite another matter to identify present factors which may militate against the accomplishment of that goal.

Reconceptualization of diagnosis as a heuristic or as a preventative procedure (as well as a procedure in remediation) is a necessary first step toward assessing the strengths and weaknesses of an instructional program designed to enable optimal selection from among possible subsequent tactics. We need, then, to develop an array of diagnostic strategies which will make more rational the choice of tactics based on instructional intents, on the pool of available tactics, on the contingencies between intents and tactics and between tactics and outcomes, and on the personnel and material resources available. The availability of such diagnostic-decision strategies and techniques could facilitate the needed change of role of the curriculum-evaluation specialist from describer to prescriber, from passive assessor to active interventionist.

Regarding Standards and
Judgments of Merit

In preparation for claiming the worth of any component of education, it is necessary to know what is expected of it, both locally and afar. Immediate expectations are likely to be called objectives. More enduring expectations are likely to be called standards. We especially look for standards among the statements of leaders in and outside the field of education.

Different spokesmen and authorities expect different things—their several standards should be known to the evaluator and ultimately by his audience. A complete evaluation report should contain a statement of what experts contend should be provided by every school in the way of instructional materials, classroom settings, and laboratory facilities. The reader should know what these leaders say about what students should be able to do.

Minimum standards are not the only useful ones. It is also useful to know what specialists and authorities consider to be exemplary, commendable, satisfactory; unsatisfactory, and intolerable.

At the present time, an evaluator is faced with a discouraging search for standards. Some are available in check lists and accreditation schedules but most are to be found in the literature, buried in problem-oriented appeals for improvement. With today's automated information storage and retrieval systems, the evaluator can be saved much of the search for them. He should have access to as complete an array of standards as he would like merely by specifying the referent, the context of use, and the authorities he recognizes. The ERIC system should acknowledge an obligation to provide information about standards and should have its entries coded accordingly. The evaluator should get answers to such inquiries as "I want to know what specialists in school libraries say is the minimum librarian-student ratio," or "As far as college admissions officers are concerned, how important is it for students to have at least two years of high-school credit in a foreign language? or "On what grounds do reading specialists object to teaching reading in preschool programs?" Since these same requests would occur repeatedly, the retrieval system could develop sophisticated inquiry procedures for them.

As to judgments, we need (*a*) to be willing to admit them into our studies and (*b*) to devise instruments for collecting them. Polling is a respectable aspect of social science research, but it has yet to be accepted in educational evaluation. When plans for evaluating one of the federal-aid-to-education programs were being developed, a suggestion that a subcontract be let to an opinion-survey organization was rejected on the grounds that paying for such a survey would not represent a proper use of evaluation funds. Such irrational objection to survey data is likely to continue.

Survey data do need cautious interpretation. *Some* questions are misleading; *some* opinions are "phony". We do not know which ones. Still we must examine opinions. They are an important background to education and part of the foreground in education planning. We cannot ignore the informal traffic in evaluative opinions. Technically competent pollsters provide a flow of much more valid information.

The principal obstacle to using public-opinion (and professional-opinion) data seems to be that a single viewpoint is likely to be given too much credence. The evaluator's obligation is not so much to examine the credibility of opinions. Nor will it often be his obligation to get a precise representation of community feeling (as the Gallup poll people do). It should be his responsibility to assure that the scope and diversity of opinions of the community are known. Values and decisions are not expected to derive directly from popularity—the audience of the evaluation will make up its mind as to how to weight the opinions offered.

We need simple instruments and protocols for gathering opinions. Usually the questions or sortings should be tailored to deal with the local or institutional situation. The specialist in evaluation should be more reluctant than many of them are to use a device built for some other community. Those imports do have value as models, of course. No matter how brief or simple, the polling device should be subjected to professional review and trial runs before being used in the evaluation study (Stephan and McCarthy, 1958).

And Synthesis

But what is to be done after all the information is collected? Have we techniques to fit together the separate pieces? Can we tease out the logical inconsistency, the departure from precedent, the emerging trend, the consensus of opinion? Can we relate the immediate situation to abstract standards? Can we portray the whole as a whole, ignoring the insignificant elements without sacrificing its complexity? Can we use the aggregate as a foundation for planning, for decision-making, for correcting errors, for rewarding the greater successes, for understanding the impact of what we do? Full access to information does not guarantee wise use of it. What can be done to increase wise usage?

One school of thought holds that we should invest in the development of formal procedures for processing evaluation information and drawing inferences. Accordingly, the evaluator needs something akin to the experimentalist's factorial design and analysis of variance. Accordingly, he needs some device for accounting for a multiplicity of variations, for drawing inferences, and for registering his confidence in them. This is the way of operations analysis, the systematic organization and processing of data to improve the operation (Cook, 1967).

Another point of view is that we should invest in the development of model evaluation projects. Reports from (more than personal observation of) such projects provide examples for other projects, guiding the collection and analysis of information as well as the reporting of it. This approach would rely more on the intuitive powers of the evaluator to organize and less on his ability to formulate a language to convey his conclusions to others. Both approaches appear to be worth pursuing. There may be no replacement for the evaluator's personal powers of synthesis and composition, but we should try to bring a more objective technology into this critical endeavor.

What resources are needed to produce the necessary concepts and techniques for utilizing more fully the potential of evaluation in education? What agencies will produce the needed theory, the needed measuring scales, the needed representations, and the needed training activities? How should we allocate our resources to overcome these needs? We have many questions, but few answers.

In discussing ways to strengthen evaluation methods, we have alluded to different strategies, different viewpoints and different research findings. Some needs we have merely noted, identifying them as candidates for future attention. We are aware that other authors would have emphasized other needs. How similar has been our assignment here to an evaluation assignment—in the necessity to highlight some dimensions and treat others lightly! We suppose that there is no one right way, no one value, no one Truth. Successful evaluation depends on recognition of many purposes, many outcomes, and many values—and it depends on a methodology that portrays these complexities throughout education.

Critical Needs in Educational
Evaluation

Beyond those discussed by Stake and Denny, there are additional steps which must be taken if the potential utility of evaluation is to be realized. These further essential steps fall into three major areas of need, each of which is discussed below.

Evaluation Must Be Researched

Perhaps the greatest impediment to progress in evaluation is lack of unequivocal knowledge about many of its critical components. For example, there is little or no data-based information about the relative efficacy of alternative evaluation plans or techniques. Virtually no empirical information exists about the most effective way to conduct a needs assessment or to weight criteria in reaching a summative judgment. Little is known about the amount of interference with ongoing educational phenomena introduced by various data collection techniques. Goal setting and establishing priorities among goals still proceed anew with every evaluation, since there is no evidence available to suggest any one way of conducting these activities that might be more effective than any other. Elaborate systems are developed for providing evaluative feedback, but there is no real knowledge base about the relative effectiveness of feedback under differing conditions and scheduling. One could go on with an exhaustive list of phenomena and procedures in evaluation which badly need to be systematically studied, but these should make the point.

One type of research essential to the development of evaluation methodology is that of examining the methods and techniques used in other professions and disciplines in order to identify those which might have utility in educational evaluation. Psychology has already provided most of the evaluative techniques used in education, and educational evaluation will profit if this close relationship to psychology is continued. However, psychological phenomena represent only a subset of the areas of concern in educational evaluation. Educationists must make systematic efforts to identify potentially relevant methods and techniques from other disciplines and then submit them to careful study before considering their widespread adoption. For example, Barro (1970), from the perspective of an economist, has proposed an intriguing multi-step multiple-regression procedure as an accountability measure for public schools.[1] However, he wisely suggested

---

1. Dyer (1970) has also suggested use of regression analysis in measuring accountability, but his suggestions relate to its use to compute school-effectiveness indices of a somewhat different nature from those proposed by Barro.

that the proposed methodology is in need of experimental verification to determine empirically (from field testing in actual school systems) the validity and usefulness of the results. Similarly, techniques from political science, sociology, law, and other areas should be studied for possible applications. Guba (1965) has suggested that educational evaluation might well adapt the legal paradigm, resulting in a system of evaluative evidence wherein information about any product or program being evaluated might consist of testimony about the program from persons involved. The testimony of expert witnesses might be considered almost as fact, whereas circumstantial evidence would be considered less valuable than eyewitness reports. Although the data are admittedly soft, Guba suggests that rules of admissability of evidence might be applied as in all legal proceedings. It is an intriguing notion for some evaluation situations; and one can hardly quarrel that such data are insufficient, since matters of life and death are often dependent on them. However, tests of the feasibility and cost-effectiveness of this proposal must be conducted before final judgments about its utility can be made.

Evaluation Practices
Must Be Improved

There are many aspects of evaluation which are inadequately attended to in most current evaluations. Four of them are discussed briefly below.

1. There is *a need to have evaluation included from the very beginning of any program*, including the planning stages. Lessinger (1970) incorporates this notion in his suggestions relating to performance contracting and auditing systems for education. Gooler and Grotelueschen (see their paper in chapter 4 of this volume) view the evaluator as an important member of any curriculum development team; they argue that the early use of evaluation to identify the concerns of interest groups with political influence is as important as its use to make summative judgments about the curriculum. However, in most educational practices, evaluation is something which is inserted after the program has been implemented. Evaluators are by now accustomed to being contacted for the first time at the point where (a) the program or project objectives have been (at least implicitly) decided upon, and (b) the program or project plan for achieving those objectives has been set. In the terminology of the CIPP evaluation model, this means that process and product evaluation are all that is left to the evaluator and, while these are obviously very important, evaluation will never reach its full potential until educationists begin to see its

value for providing evaluative data about alternate objectives and plans as well as about final judgments.

2. There is *a need to tolerate delay of some final judgments until evaluative studies of long-term outcomes can be conducted.* Timeliness is indeed an important criterion in evaluation, but it would be folly to submit so entirely to a sense of immediacy as to cause premature judgments or decisions. Education cannot tolerate interminable longitudinal studies before some key decisions must be made, but neither can it afford to be hurried pell-mell into making decisions based on patently inadequate information—especially where the study of short-term outcomes could prove to be misleading. For example, future learnings and savings such as delayed student internalization of values or attitudes may well not show up until significantly later; similarly, long-term retention may be much more important than immediate learning. The dysfunction of making final judgment on the basis of short-term outcomes must be avoided wherever there is reason to suppose that long-term and short-term outcomes might be significantly different.

3. There is *a need for evaluators to understand that there are often multiple audiences for any evaluation effort.* For example, evaluators should not be satisfied with objectives or criteria defined only by educators. The would-be evaluator must be made cognizant of the necessity of identifying (or at least ratifying) the objectives, priorities, and criteria of all groups or individuals who are legitimately concerned with what the schools should produce (for example, teachers, students, parents, or taxpayers). Stake (1970) has made an excellent case for such procedures and has reviewed methods for collecting judgmental data from all appropriate audiences. Identifying all relevant audiences is essential to an evaluation, and each step in its conduct should be made with complete awareness of possible differences in the information required by (or understandable to) the different audiences. Considerable work remains to be done in this area before evaluation studies will be as effective as they must be to produce information which reflects broad societal values and which can be understood by all significant persons involved in the program.

4. There is *a need for evaluators to be sensitized to the importance of the context* in which the evaluation is conducted in determining how (or whether) the evaluation data will be used. It is a frequent practice to conduct evaluation studies that are technically unimpeachable but are ignored by their audiences because they fail to take into account political realities. Such a practice is unhelpful at best; at worst it represents an enormous waste of

human and material resources. Political pressures and other constraints on rational decision-making do exist, however much their existence is ignored. Evaluators can ill afford to adopt an ostrichlike stance, refusing to consider such factors. One position often taken by evaluators goes something like: "My job is to provide information that is accurate and portrays a 'true picture' of the program. I have to assume the decision processes in using these results are rational. It simply is not my job to interfere or try to impose anything on the decision-maker since ultimately he must be responsible." This position is in part correct and in part naive. Of course the decision-maker is legally responsible for decisions and the evaluator (if different from the decision-maker) has no rights in such matters. However, evaluation should also serve to help rationalize the decision-making process. Evaluators should work with program directors to identify objectives; they should provide program directors with information about the worth of alternatives to help them make intelligent planning decisions; feedback about program operation should serve to influence operational decisions; and summative evaluation of the program should be easily translated by program directors into defensible decisions relating to continuation, modification, or termination of programs.

If, in the final analysis, the evaluator is aware that outside influences enter into the decision process in his situation, he has at least two options. First, he can build political considerations into each step of the evaluation by identifying differing political positions or values, collecting data on their relative frequency among legitimate influence groups, and conducting the evaluation to take into account prevailing political views. Secondly, the evaluator might well evaluate the decision process itself and point out to its participants such things as those decisions which are unsupportable by any available evaluation data, and how the decision process is viewed by others involved in the program. Regardless of how he chooses to approach them, the evaluator can ill afford to ignore political considerations. The fact that we know so little about how he should go about taking such considerations into account suggests that considerable effort still needs to be devoted to delineating the roles of the evaluator versus the role of the decision-maker.

Training of Evaluators
Must Be Improved

An overwhelming majority of those persons now conducting educational evaluation studies can be placed in two categories. The first one comprises "retreaded" personnel with academic training in educational research, testing, and statistics. That these persons normally have good quantitative and design skills is unquestioned, but the orientation of such persons is dysfunctional. The cautions about confusing research and evaluation (see Chapter 2) are relevant here. The second category includes able practitioners who have been moved into evaluation positions. Such persons also lack specific training in evaluation; in addition, they frequently lack adequate quantitative skills. Persons in both categories are in serious need of retraining before they can function effectively as evaluators. Programs for retraining are almost nonexistent; every effort should be made to establish such programs through in-service training conducted by the collaborative efforts of local education agencies, universities, and professional associations.

The present situation points to a serious need to train persons directly for evaluation roles. Yet, although many universities have an introductory course on evaluation, only a handful have programs designed to train evaluators as such. University education colleges and departments should give serious attention to establishing full-fledged training programs for specialists in educational evaluation, at both the graduate and undergraduate levels. There are many factors which will contribute to the success of such training programs. These factors and other considerations in how to train evaluation personnel are discussed in detail in the section on training in chapter 2.[2]

Evaluation and Educational Improvement

Educational systems have most of the earmarks of classical bureaucracies and, historically, have been reasonably successful in resisting change in practices and policies. Recently, strong social forces have coalesced to push many educational systems out from behind their barriers; change in education has become a much more frequent reality. However, without a tradition of planned change or systematic inquiry into the effectiveness of potential new programs, the changes which are occurring in education can be often little more than random adoption of faddish innovations. Perhaps the most important deficiency which fosters such a situation is the lack of dependable information in the performance of educational products, practices, and programs. Without such infor-

2.   Stake and Denny have discussed in their paper in this chapter some concerns related to training. Several considerations relating to training are also discussed in chapter 2 of this volume. The points raised here are additional ones to which future attention must be given.

mation, educators cannot readily correct deficiencies or malfunctions in present practices or intelligently select new products or practices for adoption.

Evaluation, as described in this volume, holds great promise in providing educators with badly needed information which can be used to improve the process of education. While obviously not a panacea, evaluation can have a profound impact on the field of education. Francis Caro said it well when speaking of the importance of evaluation ("evaluation research," as he calls it) in solving general social problems:

> Evaluation research, not a new but nevertheless an increasingly robust enterprise, can have a major impact on social problems. While it would be foolish to argue that all the deficiencies of current programs or all the political and conceptual problems can be swept away by evaluation studies, the adequate assessment of existing and innovative programs can be a vital force in directing social change and improving the lives and the environments of community members [Caro, 1971, p. 1].

References

Alkin, M. C. Evaluation theory development. *Evaluation Comment*, 1969, 2,(1), 2-7.

Allen, K. E., Henke, L. B., Harris, F. R., Baer, D. M., & Reynolds, N. J. Control of hyperactivity by social reinforcement of attending behavior. *Journal of Educational Psychology*, 1967, 58, 231-237.

American Council on Education. *Educational measurement*. Washington, D.C.: American Council on Education, 1951.

American Psychological Association. *Standards for educational and psychological tests and manuals*. Washington, D. C.: American Psychological Association, 1966.

Anderson, R. C. The comparative field experiment: An illustration from high school biology. In *Proceedings of the 1969 Invitational Conference on Testing Problems*. Princeton, N. J.: Educational Testing Service, 1969.

Armstrong, R. J., Cornell, T., Kramer, R. E., & Roberson, E. W. *The development and evaluation of behavioral objectives*. Worthington, Ohio: Charles A. Jones, 1970.

Arnstine, D. G. The language and values of programmed instruction: Part 2. The Educational Forum, 1964, 28, 337-345.

Astin, A. W., & Holland, J. L. The environmental assessment technique: A way to measure college environments. *Journal of Educational Psychology*, 1961, 52, 308-316.

Atkin, J. M. Some evaluation problems in a course content improvement project. *Journal of Research in Science Teaching*, 1963, 1, 129-132.

Atkin, J. M. Behavioral objectives in curriculum design: A cautionary note. *The Science Teacher*, 1968, 35, 27-30.

Baker, E. L. *The differential effect of behavioral and nonbehavioral objectives given to teachers on the achievements of their students*. Interim report to the U. S. Department of Health, Education, and Welfare, 1967.

Barro, S. M. An approach to developing accountability measures for the public schools. *Phi Delta Kappan*, 1970, 52, 196-205.

Bassham, H. Teacher understanding and pupil efficiency in mathematics: A study of relationship. *Arithmetic Teacher*, 1962, 9, 383-387.

Berlak, H. Comments recorded in I. Morrissett (Ed.), *Concepts and structure in the new social science curricula*. Lafayette, Ind.: Social Science Education Consortium, Purdue University, 1966, 88-89.

Bloom, B. S. Quality control in education. *Tomorrow's teaching*. Oklahoma City, Okla.: Frontiers of Science Foundation, 1961.

Bloom, B. S. Peak learning experiences. *Innovation for time to teach*. Washington, D. C.: Department of Classroom Teachers, National Education Association, 1966.

Bloom, B. S. Learning for mastery. *Evaluation Comment*, 1968, 1(2), 1-12.

Bloom, B. S., Engelhart, M. D., Furst, E. J., Hill, W. H., & Krathwohl, D. R. *Taxonomy of educational objectives: Handbook I: Cognitive domain*. New York: David McKay, 1956.

Bormuth, J. R. On the theory of achievement test items. Chicago: University of Chicago, 1968. (mimeo)

Bracht, G. H., & Glass, G. V. The external validity of experiments. *American Educational Research Journal*, 1968, 5, 437-474.

Buros, O. K. *Mental measurements yearbooks*. Highland Park, N. J.: Gryphon Press, 1938, 1940, 1949, 1953, 1959, 1965, 1972.

Buros, O. K. (Ed.) *Tests in print*. Highland Park, N. J.: Gryphon Press, 1961.

Campbell, D. T., Kruskal, W. H., & Wallace, W. P. Seating aggregation as an index of attitude. *Sociometry*, 1966, 29, 1-15.

Campbell, D. T., & Stanley, J. C. Experimental and quasi-experimental designs for research of teaching. In N. L. Gage (Ed.), *Handbook of research on teaching*. Chicago: Rand McNally, 1963.

Campbell, D. T., & Stanley, J. C. *Experimental and quasi-experimental designs for research*. Chicago: Rand McNally, 1966.

Caro, F. G. (Ed.) *Readings in evaluation research*. New York: Russell Sage Foundation, 1971.

Carroll, J. B. School learning over the long haul. In I. D. Krumboltz (Ed.), *Learning and the educational process*. Chicago: Rand McNally, 1965.

Clark, D. L., & Guba, E. G. An examination of potential change roles in education. Paper presented at the Seminar on Innovation in Planning School Curricula, Airliehouse, Virginia, October 1965.

Coleman, J. S. *Equality of educational opportunity*. Washington, D. C.: U. S. Department of Health, Education, and Welfare, Office of Education, 1966.

Combs, A. W. Foreward in F. T. Wilhelms (Eds.), *Evaluation as feedback and guide*. Washington, D. C.: National Educational Association, Association for Supervision and Curriculum Development, 1967.

Cook, D. L. *Program evaluation and review techniques, applications in education*. U. S. Office of Education Cooperative Research Monograph, No. 17, OE-12024. Washington, D.C.: USOE, 1966.

Corey, S. M. *Action research to improve school practices*. New York: Bureau of Publications, Teachers College, Columbia University, 1953.

Cox, R. C. Achievement testing in a program of individualized instruction: Some considerations. *Learning Research and Development Center Newsletter*, University of Pittsburgh, 1967, 4.

Cronbach, L. J. Course improvement through evaluation. *Teachers College Record*, 1963, 64, 672-683.

Cronbach, L. J., & Furby, L. How we should measure "change"—or should we? Palo Alto, Calif.: Stanford University, 1969. (mimeo)

Cronbach, L. J., & Suppes, P. *Research for tomorrow's schools: Disciplined inquiry for education.* New York: Macmillan, 1969.

Dressel, P., & Nelson, C. *Questions and problems in science—Test folio no. 1.* Princeton, N. J.: Cooperative Test Service, Educational Testing Service, 1956.

DuBois, P. H. *A history of psychological testing.* Boston: Allyn and Bacon, 1970.

DuBois, P. H., & Mayo, G. D. (Eds.) *Research strategies for evaluating training.* Chicago: Rand McNally, 1970.

Duda, M. J., & McBroom, J. Unpublished paper, Pittsburgh, 1968.

Dyer, H. S. The discovery of development of educational goals. Paper presented at the 1966 Invitational Conference on Testing Problems, Educational Testing Service, Princeton, New Jersey, 1967.

Dyer, H. S. Toward objective criteria of professional accountability in the schools of New York City. *Phi Delta Kappan,* 1970, 52, 206-211.

Eash, M. J. Developing an instrument for the assessment of instructional materials (Form IV). Paper presented at the annual meeting of the American Educational Research Association, Minneapolis, March 1970.

Ebel, R. L. *Measuring educational achievement.* Englewood Cliffs, N. J.: Prentice-Hall, 1965.

Educational Testing Service. A long, hot summer of committee work on national assessment of education. *ETS Developments,* 1965, 13.

Eisner, E. W. Educational objectives: Help or hindrance? *The School Review,* 1967, 75, 250-260.

Elam, S. E. (Ed.) *Education and the structure of knowledge.* Fifth annual Phi Delta Kappa symposium on educational research. Chicago: Rand McNally, 1964.

Elashoff, J. D., & Snow, R. E. *Pygmalion reconsidered.* Worthington, Ohio: Charles A. Jones, 1971.

Faunce, R. C., & Munshaw, C. L. *Teaching and learning in secondary schools.* Belmont, Calif.: Wadsworth, 1964.

Ferguson, G. A. On learning and human ability. *Canadian Journal of Psychology,* 1954,8, 95-112.

Ferris, F. L. Testing in the new curriculums: Numerology, "tyranny," or common sense? *School Review,* 1962, 70, 112-131.

Filep, R. T. IRA training program has successful dress rehearsal. *EPIE FORUM,* 1967, 1(3), 10-15.

Flanagan, J. C., Davis, F. B., Dailey, J. T., Shaycroft, M. F., Orr, D. B., Goldberg, I., & Neyman, C. A., Jr. *Project TALENT. The identification, development, and utilization of human talents: The American high school student.* Pittsburgh: University of Pittsburgh Press, 1964.

Flanders, N. A. *Teacher influence, pupil attitudes, and achievement.* Cooperative Research Monograph No. 12, U. S. Department of Health, Education, and Welfare, Office of Education. Washington, D.C.: U. S. Government Printing Office, 1965.

French, W., and Associates. *Behavioral goals of general education in the high schools.* New York: Russell Sage Foundations, 1957.

Fry, E. *Teaching machines and programmed instruction.* New York: McGraw-Hill, 1963.

Furst, E. J. *Constructing evaluation instruction.* New York: David McKay, 1958.

Gagné, R. M. The acquisition of knowledge. *Psychological Review,* 1962, 69, 355-365.

Gagné, R. M. *Factors in acquiring knowledge of a mathematical task.* Washington, D.C.: American Psychological Association, 1962.

Gagné, R. M. *The conditions of learning.* New York: Holt, Rinehart and Winston, 1965.

Gagné, R. M. The analysis of instructional objectives for the design for instruction. In R. M. Glaser (Ed.), *Teaching machines and programmed learning, II: Data and directions.* Washington, D. C.: National Education Association, 1965.

Gagné, R. M. Elementary science: A new scheme of instruction. *Science,* 1966, 151,49-53.

Gagné, R.M. Instructional variables and learning outcomes. Paper presented at the UCLA Symposium on Problems in the Evaluation of Instruction, Los Angeles, December 1967. (Also will appear in *Proceedings,* Holt, Rinehart and Winston, in press.)

Galfo, A. J., & Miller, E. *Interpreting educational research.* (2nd ed.) Dubuque, Iowa: Wm. C. Brown, 1970.

Gephart, W. J., Ingle, R. B., and Remstad, R. C. *A framework for evaluating comparative studies.* In Henry Cody (Ed.), *Conference on Research in Music Education.* U.S. Office of Education Cooperative Research Report No. 6—1388. May, 1967.

Glaser, R. Instructional technology and the measurement of learning outcomes: Some questions. *American Psychologist,* 1963, 18, 519-521.

Glaser, R. (Ed.) *Teaching machines and programmed learning, II: Data and directions.* Washington, D.C.: Department of Audio-Visual Instruction, National Education Association, 1965.

Glass, G. V. Reflections on Bloom's "Toward a theory of testing which includes measurement-evaluation-assessment." Research paper no. 8. Boulder, Colo.: Laboratory of Educational Research, University of Colorado, 1967. (mimeo)

Glass, G. V. Some observations on training educational researchers. Research paper no. 22, Boulder, Colo.: Laboratory of Educational Research, University of Colorado, 1968. (mimeo) (Also to appear in *The Record,* in press.)

Glass, G. V. The growth of evaluation methodology. Research paper no. 27. Boulder, Colo.: Laboratory of Educational Research, University of Colorado, 1969 (mimeo) (Also to appear in the American Educational Research Association monograph series on curriculum evaluation, no. 7, in press.)

Glass, G. V. Design of evaluation studies. Paper presented at the Council for Exceptional Children Special Conference on Early Childhood Education, New Orleans, December 1969.

Glass, G. V., & Maguire, T. O. *Analysis of time-series quasi-experiments.* U. S. Office of Education Report No. 6-8329. Boulder, Colo.: Laboratory of Educational Research, University of Colorado, 1968.

Glass, G. V., & Worthen, B. R. Educational evaluation and research: Similarities and differences. *Curriculum Theory Network,* Fall 1971.

Glass, G. V, & Worthen, B. R. Educational inquiry and the practice of education. In H. D. Schalock & G. R. Sell (Eds.), *The Oregon studies in educational research, development, diffusion and evaluation: Vol. III, conceptual frameworks for viewing educational RDD&E.* U. S. Office of Education Grant No. OEG-0-70-4977. Project No. 0-0701, Monmouth, Oreg.: Teaching Research, Oregon College of Education, 1972.

Gleser, G. C., Cronbach, L. J., & Rajaratnam, N. Generalizability of scores influenced by multiple sources of variance. *Psychometrika*, 1965, **30**, 395-418.

Goodlad, J. I. Final report contract No. F8E-8024, Project No. 254. Los Angeles: Institute of Development of Educational Activities, University of California, Los Angeles, 1966.

Goodlad, J. I., Klein, M. F., & Associates. *Behind the classroom door.* (2nd ed.) Worthington, Ohio: Charles A. Jones, 1973.

Gooler, D. D., & Grotelueschen, A. Process accountability in curriculum development. *Curriculum Theory Network*, Fall 1970, special issue no. 1.

Grobman, H. *Evaluation activities of curriculum projects: A starting point.* Chicago: Rand McNally, 1968.

Guba, E. G. Evaluation and the new media. Paper presented to the Ohio State University Annual Conference on Modern Media, Columbus, Ohio, July 1962.

Guba, E. G. Evaluation in field studies. Paper presented at the evaluation conference sponsored by the Ohio State Department of Education, Columbus, Ohio, June 1965.

Guba, E. G. Methodological strategies for educational change. Paper presented to the Conference on Strategies for Educational Change, Washington, D. C., November 1965.

Guba, E. G. Evaluation and the process of change. In *Notes and working papers concerning the administration of programs.* Title III ESEA. Washington, D. C.: U. S. Senate, Committee on Labor and Public Welfare, Subcommittee on Education, 1967.

Guba, E. G., & Clark, D. L. Types of educational research. Columbus, Ohio: Ohio State University. (undated mimeo)

Guba, E. G., & Stufflebeam, D. L. Evaluation: The process of stimulating, aiding, and abetting insightful action. Paper presented at the 2nd Phi Delta Kappa National Symposium for Professors of Educational Research, Boulder, Colorado, November 1968.

Hammond, R. L. Evaluation at the local level. Tucson, Ariz.: *EPIC* Evaluation Center. (undated mimeo)

Hammond, R. Context evaluation of instruction in local school districts. *Educational Technology*, 1969, 9(1), 13-18.

Hand, H. C. National assessment viewed as the camel's nose. *Phi Delta Kappan*, 1965, 47, 8-12.

Harrison, G. V. *The instructional value of presenting explicit versus vague objectives.* Santa Barbara, Calif.: California Educational Research Studies, University of California, Santa Barbara, 1967.

Hartshorne, H., & May, M. A. *Studies in the nature of character.* Vol. 1. New York: Macmillan, 1928.

Hastings, J. T. The kith and kin of educational measures. *Journal of Educational Measurement*, 1969, 6, 127-130.

Hauenstein, A. D. *Curriculum planning for behavioral development.* Worthington, Ohio: Charles A. Jones, 1972.

Hemphill, J. K. The relationship between research and evaluation studies. In R. W. Tyler (Ed.), *Educational evaluation: New roles, new means.* The 68th Yearbook of the National Society for the Study of Education, Part II. Chicago: National Society for the Study of Education, 1969.

Herrick, V. E., & Tyler, R. W. (Eds.) *Toward improved curriculum theory.* Supplementary Education Monograph No. 71. Chicago: University of Chicago Press, 1950.

Hillway, T. *Introduction to research.* (2nd ed.) Boston: Houghton Mifflin, 1964.

Hively, W. Generalizability of performance by job corps trainees on a universe-defined system of achievement tests in elementary mathematical calculation. Paper presented at the annual meeting of the American Educational Research Association, Chicago, 1968.

Hook, J. N. *The teaching of high school English.* New York: Ronald Press, 1965.

Hook, S. The experimental investigation of psychoanalysis. In S. Hook (Ed.), *Psychoanalysis, scientific method and philosophy.* New York: New York University Press, 1959.

Hughes, M. M. *A research report: Assessment of the quality of teaching in elementary schools.* Salt Lake City, Utah: University of Utah, 1959.

Jackson, P. W. *The way teaching is.* Washington, D. C.: Association for Supervision and Curriculum Development, National Education Association, 1966.

Kaplan, A. *The conduct of inquiry.* San Francisco: Chandler, 1964.

Kerlinger, F. N. *Foundations of behavioral research.* New York: Holt, Rinehart and Winston, 1964.

Kershaw, J. A., & McKean, R. N. *Systems analysis and education.* Santa Monica, Calif.: Rand Corp., 1959.

Komisar, P. B., & McClellan, J. E. Professor Arnstine and programmed instruction. Reprinted from *Educational Forum*, 1965.

Krathwohl, D. R. The taxonomy of educational objectives—Use of the cognitive and affective domains. In C. M. Lindvall (Ed.), *Defining educational objectives.* Pittsburgh: University of Pittsburgh Press, 1964.

Krathwohl, D. R., Bloom, B. S., & Masia, B. B. *Taxonomy of educational objectives: Handbook II: Affective domain.* New York: David McKay, 1964.

Krathwohl, D. R. Stating objectives appropriately for program, for curriculum, and for instructional materials development. *Journal of Teacher Education,* 1965, 12, 83-92.

Kresh, E. Team teaching program 1967 report. Unpublished paper, 1968.

Lazarus, A., & Knudson, R. *Selected objectives for the English language arts, grades 7-12.* Boston: Houghton Mifflin, 1967.

Lennon, R. T. Accountability and performance contracting. Paper presented at the annual meeting of the American Educational Research Association, New York, February 1971.

Lessinger, L. M. Engineering accountability for results in public education. *Phi Delta Kappan,* 1970, 52, 217-225.

Lessinger, L. M., & Tyler, R. W. (Eds.) *Accountability in education.* Worthington, Ohio: Charles A. Jones, 1971.

Lewin, K. Principles of re-education. In K. D. Benne (Ed.), *Human relations in curriculum change.* New York: Dryden Press, 1951.

Lewin, K., Lippitt, R., & White, R. K. Patterns of aggressive behavior in experimentally created social climates. *Journal of Social Psychology,* 1939, **10**, 271-299.

Lindquist, E. F. *Design and analysis of experiments in psychology and education.* Boston: Houghton Mifflin, 1953.

Lindvall, C. M. IPI instrument. In A. Simon & E. G. Boyer (Eds.), *Mirrors for behavior: An anthology of classroom observation instruments.* Philadelphia: Research for Better Schools, 1968.

Lindvall, C. M., Nardozza, S., & Felton, M. The importance of specific objectives in curriculum development. In C. M Lindvall (Ed.), *Defining educational objectives.* Pittsburgh: University of Pittsburgh Press, 1964.

Lippitt, R., Watson, J., & Westley, B. *The dynamics of planned change.* New York: Harcourt, Brace, 1958.

Lord, F. M. Estimating norms by item-sampling. *Educational and psychological measurement,* 1962, **22**, 259-268.

Lord, F. M. Elementary models for measuring change. In C. W. Harris (Ed.), *Problems in measuring change.* Madison, Wisc.: University of Wisconsin Press, 1963.

Lord, F. M. Item sampling in test theory and in research design. *Research bulletin no. 65-22.* Princeton, N. J.: Educational Testing Service, 1965.

Lortie, D. C. National decision-making: Is it possible today? *EPIE Forum,* 1967, 1(3), 6-9.

Lueck, W. R., Campbell, E. G., Eastman, L. E., Edwards, C. W., Thomas, C. R., & Zeller, W. D. *Effective secondary education.* Minneapolis, Minn.: Burgess, 1966.

Lumsdaine, A. A. Criteria for assessing programmed instructional materials. *Audiovisual Instruction,* 1963, 8, 84-89.

Lumsdaine, A. A. Assessing the effectiveness of instructional programs. In R. Glaser (Ed.), *Teaching machines and programmed learning, Vol. II: Data and direction.* Washington, D. C.: National Education Association, 1965.

Mager, R. F. *Preparing instructional objectives.* Palo Alto, Calif.: Fearon Press, 1962.

Mager, R. F. *Preparing objectives for programmed instruction.* San Francisco: Fearon Press, 1962.

Mager, R. F., & McCann, J. *Learner-controlled instruction.* Palo Alto, Calif.: Varian Assoc., 1961.

McKeachie, W. J. *The appraisal of teaching in large universities.* Ann Arbor, Mich.: University of Michigan, 1959.

Mecklenburger, J. *Performance contracting.* Worthington, Ohio: Charles A. Jones, 1972.

Medley, D. M., & Mitzel, H. E. Measuring classroom behavior by systematic observation. In N. L. Gage (Ed.), *Handbook of research on teaching.* Chicago: Rand McNally, 1963.

Meehl, P. E. Nuisance variables and the ex post facto design. *Reports from the research laboratories of the Department of Psychiatry.* Report No. PR-69-4. Minneapolis, Minn.: University of Minnesota, 1969.

Menzel, P. The transformation count. Technical report. Inglewood, Calif.: Southwest Regional Laboratory, 1967.

Metfessel, N. S., & Michael, W. B. A paradigm involving multiple criterion measures for the evaluation of the effectiveness of school programs. *Educational and Psychological Measurement*, 1967, **27**, 931-943.

Meux, M. O. Studies of learning in the school setting. *Review of Educational Research*, 1967, **37**, 539-562.

Meux, M. O., & Smith, B. O. Logical dimensions of teaching behavior. Urbana, Ill.: Bureau of Educational Research, University of Illinois, 1961. (mimeo)

Michael, D. N., & Maccoby, N. Factors influencing verbal learning from films under varying conditions of audience participation. *Journal of Experimental Psychology*, 1953, **46**, 411-418.

Michael, D. N., & Maccoby, N. Factors influencing the effects of student participation on verbal learning from films: Motivating versus practice effects, "feedback," and overt versus covert responding. In A. A. Lumsdaine (Ed.), *Student response in programmed instruction: A symposium*. Washington, D. C.: National Academy of Sciences, National Research Council, 1961.

Michael, W. B., & Metfessel, N. S. A paradigm for developing valid measurable objectives in the evaluation of educational programs in colleges and universities. *Educational and Psychological Measurement*, 1967, **27**, 373-383.

Miles, M. B. *Innovation in education*. New York: Bureau of Publications, Teachers College, Columbia University, 1964.

Miles, M. B. *Change processes in the public schools*. Eugene, Oreg.: University of Oregon, 1965.

Miller, R. I. *Catalyst for change: A national study of ESEA Title III (PACE).* Notes and working papers concerning the administration of programs authorized under Title II of Public Law 89-10, the Elementary and Secondary Education Act of 1965 as amended by Public Law 89-750, prepared for the Sub-committee on Education of the Committee on Labor and Public Welfare, U. S. Senate. Washington, D. C.: U. S. Government Printing Office, 1967.

Modell, W. Hazards of new drugs. *Science*, 1963, **139**, 1180-1185.

Morrisett, I., & Stevens, W. W. Steps in curriculum analysis outline, Boulder, Colo.: Social Science Education Consortium, University of Colorado, 1967. (mimeo)

Morsh, J. E., & Wilder, E. Identifying the effective instructor: A review of the quantitative studies, 1900-1952. *USAF Personnel Training Research Center, Research Bulletin No. AFPTRC-TR-54-44*, 1954.

Munro, T. The interrelation of the arts in secondary education. In *The creative arts in American education*. Cambridge, Mass.: Harvard University Press, 1960.

National Science Foundation. *Reviews of data on research and development*. No. 17, NSF-60-10. Washington, D. C.: National Science Foundation, 1960.

National Study of Secondary School Evaluation. *Evaluative criteria, 1960 edition*. Washington, D. C.: National Study of Secondary School Evaluation, 1960.

Nerbovig, M. *Unit planning: A model for curriculum development*. Worthington, Ohio: Charles A. Jones, 1970.

von Neumann, J., & Morgenstern, O. *Theory of games and economic behavior.* Princeton, N. J.: Princeton University Press, 1947.

Oliver, D. W., & Shaver, J. P. *Teaching public issues in the high school.* Boston: Houghton Mifflin, 1966.

Osburn, H. G. Item sampling for achievement testing. Houston: Psychology Department, University of Houston, 1967. (mimeo)

Osgood, C.E., Suci, G. J., & Tannenbaum, P. H. *The measurement of meaning.* Urbana, Ill.: University of Illinois, 1957.

Parker, E. B. The effects of television on public library circulation. *Public Opinion Quarterly,* 1963, **23**, 578-589.

Popham, W. J. *The teacher empiricist.* Los Angeles: Aegeus Press, 1964.

Popham, W. J. *Educational criterion measures.* Inglewood, Calif.: Southwest Regional Laboratory for Educational Research and Development, 1967.

Popham, W. J. *Development of a performance test of teaching proficiency.* Final report. Washington, D. C.: U. S. Department of Health, Education, and Welfare, 1967.

Popham, W. J. Simplified designs for school research. Inglewood, Calif.: Southwest Regional Laboratory for Educational Research and Development, 1967. (mimeo)

Popham. W. J. Objectives and instruction. In *Instructional objectives.* American Education Research Association monograph series on curriculum evaluation, no. 3. Chicago: Rand McNally, 1969.

Popham, W. J., & Baker, E. L. Development of performance test of teaching proficiency. Paper presented at the annual meeting of the American Educational Research Association, New York, February 1966.

Popham, W. J., Eisner, E. W., Sullivan, H. J., & Tyler, L. L. *Instructional objectives.* American Educational Research Association monograph series on curriculum evaluation, no. 3. Chicago: Rand McNally, 1969.

Provus, M. M. *Teaching for relevance, an in service training program.* Chicago: Whitehall, 1969.

Provus, M. M. Evaluation of ongoing programs in the public school system. In R. W. Tyler (Ed.), *Educational evaluation: New roles, new means.* The 68th Yearbook of the National Society for the Study of Education, Part II. Chicago: National Society for the Study of Education, 1969.

Rogers, C. R. Persons or science? A philosophical question. *The American Psychologist,* 1955, **10**, 267-278.

Rosner, B. The development of special measures. In *On evaluating Title I programs.* Princeton, N. J.: Educational Testing Service, 1966;

Scriven, M. Definitions, explanations, and theories. In H. Feigl, M. Scriven, & G. Maxwell (Eds.), *Minnesota studies in the philosophy of science, Vol. II.* Minneapolis, Minn.: University of Minnesota Press, 1958.

Scriven, M. Student values as educational objectives. Publication No. 124. Boulder, Colo.: Social Science Education Consortium, University of Colorado, 1966.

Scriven, M. The methodology of evaluation. In R. E. Stake (Ed.), *Curriculum evaluation.* American Educational Research Association monograph series on evaluation, no. 1, Chicago: Rand McNally, 1967.

Scriven, M. An introduction to meta-evaluation. *Educational Product Report,* 1969, 2(5), 36-38.

Sechrest, L. The use of innocuous and non-intervening variables as evaluative criteria. Paper presented at the annual meeting of the American Educational Research Association, Chicago, 1968. (mimeo)

Silvern, L. C. *Administrative factors guide to basic analysis.* Los Angeles: Education and Training Consultants, 1965.

Simon, A., & Boyer, E. G. (Eds.) *Mirrors for behavior: An anthology of classroom observation instruments.* Philadelphia: Research for Better Schools, 1968.

Simpson, E. J. *The classification of educational objectives, psychomotor domain.* Urbana, Ill.: University of Illinois, July 1, 1965—May 31, 1966.

Sjogren, D. D. Measurement techniques in evaluation. *Review of Educational Research,* 1970, **40**, 301-320.

Smith, B. O., & Meux, M. O. *A study of the logic of teaching.* Urbana, Ill.: Bureau of Educational Research, University of Illinois, undated.

Smith, B. O., Stanley, W. O., & Shores, J. H. *Fundamentals of curriculum development.* (2nd ed.) New York: World Book, 1957.

Smith, B. O., et al. *A study of the strategies of teaching.* Project No. 1640, U. S. Department of Health, Education, and Welfare, Office of Education. Urbana, Ill.: College of Education, University of Illinois, 1967.

Smith, E. R., & Tyler, R.W. *Appraising and recording student progress.* New York: Harper and Row, 1942.

Stake, R. E. The countenance of educational evaluation. *Teachers College Record,* 1967, **68**, 523-540.

Stake, R. E. Evaluation design, instrumentation, data collection, and analysis of data. *Educational evaluation.* Columbus, Ohio: State Superintendent of Public Instruction, 1969.

Stake, R. E. Objectives, priorities, and other judgment data. *Review of Educational Research,* 1970, **40**, 181-212.

Stake, R. E. Measuring what learners learn (with a special look at performance contracting). Urbana, Ill.: Center for Instructional Research and Curriculum Evaluation, University of Illinois, 1971. (mimeo) (Also published in part in *Phi Delta Kappan,* 1971, **52**, 583-589.)

Stake, R. E., & Denny, T. Needed concepts and techniques for utilizing more fully the potential of evaluation. In R. W. Tyler (Ed.), *Educational evaluation: New roles, new means.* The 68th Yearbook of the National Society for the Study of Education, Part II. Chicago: National Society for the Study of Education, 1969.

Stake, R. E., & Wardrop, J. L. Gain score errors in performance contracting. Urbana, Ill.: Center for Instructional Research and Curriculum Evaluation, University of Illinois, 1971. (mimeo)

Stephan, F. F., & McCarthy, P. J. *Sampling opinions: An analysis of survey procedures.* New York: John Wiley and Sons, 1958.

Stufflebeam, D. L. A depth study of the evaluation requirement. *Theory into Practice,* 1966, **5**, 121-133.

Stufflebeam, D. L. Evaluation as enlightenment for decision-making. Columbus, Ohio: Evaluation Center, Ohio State University, 1968.

Stufflebeam, D. L., Foley, W. J., Gephart, W. J., Guba, E. G., Hammond, R. L., Merriman, H. O., & Provus, M. M. *Educational evaluation and decision-making in education.* Itasca, Ill.: Peacock, 1971.

Suydam, M. N. Procedures for the evaluative analysis of research. Paper presented at the annual meeting of the American Educational Research Association, Chicago, 1968. (mimeo)

Taylor, P. A., & Maguire, T. O. A theoretical evaluation model. *Manitoba Journal of Educational Research*, 1966, 1, 12-17.

Thorndike, R. L., & Hagen, E. *Measurement and evaluation in psychology and education.* New York: Wiley, 1969.

Tukey, J. W. Conclusions vs. decisions. *Technometrics*, 1960, 2, 423-433.

Tyler, L. L. Technical standards for curriculum evaluation. Paper presented at the annual meeting of the American Educational Research Association, Chicago, 1968. (mimeo)

Tyler, L. L., & Klein, M. F. Recommendations for curriculum and instructional materials. Los Angeles: University of California, Los Angeles, 1967. (mimeo)

Tyler, R. W. General statement on evaluation. *Journal of Educational Research*, 1942, 35, 492-501.

Tyler, R. W. *Basic principles of curriculum and instruction.* Chicago: University of Chicago Press, 1950.

Tyler, R. W. The functions of measurement in improving instruction. In E. F. Lingquist (Ed.), *Educational measurement.* Washington, D. C.: American Council on Education, 1951.

Tyler, R. W. The evaluation of teaching. In R. M. Cooper (Ed.), *The two ends of the log.* Minneapolis, Minn.: University of Minnesota Press, 1958.

Tyler, R. W. Some persistent questions on the defining of objectives. In C. M. Lindvall (Ed.), *Defining educational objectives.* Pittsburgh: University of Pittsburgh Press, 1964.

Tyler, R. W. Assessing the progress of education. *Phi Delta Kappan*, 1965, 47, 13-16.

Tyler, R. W. The objectives and plans for a national assessment of educational progress. *Journal of Educational Measurement*, 1966, 3, 1-10.

Tyler, R., Gagne, R., & Scriven, M. *Perspectives of curriculum evaluation.* Chicago: Rand McNally, 1967.

Urban, J. *Behavior changes resulting from a study of communicable diseases.* New York: Bureau of Publications, Teachers College, Columbia University, 1943.

Verhaegen, R. M. The effect of learner-controlled instruction in a tenth grade biology curriculum. Master's thesis, University of California, Los Angeles, 1964.

Von Haden, H. I., & King, J. M. *Educational innovator's guide.* Worthington, Ohio: Charles A. Jones, 1973.

Wald, A. *Statistical decision functions.* New York: John Wiley and Sons, 1950.

Webb, E., Campbell, D. T., Schwartz, R. D., & Sechrest, L. *Unobtrusive measures: Nonreactive research in the social sciences.* Chicago: Rand McNally, 1966.

Welsh, J. Bright seeks "basic" educational research. *Educational Researcher*, official newsletter of the American Educational Research Association, 1968, 2.

Wiener, N. *Cybernetics.* New York: John Wiley and Sons, 1948.

Wiles, D. K. *Changing perspectives in educational research.* Worthington, Ohio: Charles A. Jones, 1972.

Womer, F. B. *What is national assessment?* Ann Arbor, Mich.: National Assessment of Educational Progress, 1970.

Worthen, B. R., & Gagne, R. M. The development of a classification system for functions and skills required of research and research-related personnel in education. Technical paper no. 1. Boulder, Colo.: AERA Task Force on Research Training, Laboratory of Educational Research, University of Colorado, 1969.

Worthen, B. R., & Roaden, A. L. *The impact of research assistantship experience.* Final report of Phase I of special Phi Delta Kappa study. Columbus, Ohio: Evaluation Center, Ohio State University, 1968.

Worthen, B. R., & Roaden, A. L. *Relationships between research productivity and specific antecedent experiences as a research assistant.* Final report of Phase II of special Phi Delta Kappa study. Columbus, Ohio: Evaluation Center, Ohio State University, 1970.

Name Index

Subject Index